Landscapes

of the

New West

Landscapes of

CULTURAL STUDIES
OF THE UNITED STATES

ALAN TRACHTENBERG,
EDITOR

the New West

Gender and
Geography in
Contemporary
Women's
Writing

Krista Comer

The
University
of North
Carolina
Press
Chapel Hill
and London

© 1999 The University of North Carolina Press
All rights reserved
Manufactured in the United States of America
This book was set in Aldus by Keystone Typesetting, Inc.
Book design by April Leidig-Higgins

The paper in this book meets the guidelines for permanence
and durability of the Committee on Production Guidelines
for Book Longevity of the Council on Library Resources.

Library of Congress Cataloging-in-Publication Data
Comer, Krista. Landscapes of the New West: gender and
geography in contemporary women's writing / by Krista
Comer. p. cm.—(Cultural studies of the United States)
Includes bibliographical references (p.   ) and index.
ISBN 0-8078-2485-2 (cloth: alk. paper)
ISBN 0-8078-4813-1 (pbk.: alk. paper)
1. American literature—West (U.S.)—History and
criticism. 2. Women and literature—West (U.S.)—
History—20th century. 3. American literature—Women
authors—History and criticism. 4. West (U.S.)—In
literature. 5. Landscape in literature. 6. Geography in
literature. I. Title. II. Series.
PS 271.C66 1999   810.9'3278'082—DC21   98-47516 CIP

Chapter 3 originally appeared in a substantially abbreviated
form as "Sidestepping Environmental Justice: 'Natural'
Landscapes and the Wilderness Plot" in *Breaking Boundaries:
New Perspectives on Women's Regional Writing*, edited by
Sherrie A. Inness and Diana Royer (Iowa City: University of
Iowa Press, 1997), 216–36.

03 02 01 00 99   5 4 3 2 1

*In recognition of
Wellesley College's
Davis Scholar
Program, for helping
me put the pieces
together anew*

Contents

Acknowledgments
ix

Introduction:
Postmodernism,
Literary Nationalism,
and Western
Cultural Production
1

**Part One.
Toward a Spatial
History of the New
Feminist Regionalism**

1. Landscapes of
Westernness: Gender,
Race, and the Politics
of American Spaces
19

2. Urbanscapes in the
Golden Land: California
as Western Continuum
61

**Part Two.
Gender and the "Master"
Landscapes of Western
Narrative**

3. Sidestepping
Environmental Justice:
"Natural" Landscapes
and the Wilderness Plot
123

4. Queering
Heterosexual Love:
Trailer Parks,
Telenovelas, and
Other Landscapes of
Feminist Desire
155

5. A Good Country
Is Hard to Find:
Journeys toward
Postnational
Landscapes
199

Epilogue 235

Notes 241

Bibliography 267

Index 291

Acknowledgments

Even if it was western literary discourse of the 1940s–60s that set the historical and political stage for the emergence of the new western history, it will be the new western history, I think, that opens the door for a new western criticism. Hence, lead thanks go to the various intellectual and political projects contained within the rubric of the "new western history." Whatever its blind spots, the new western history remains the single most enabling context for this book. For the edgy, inelegant shake-up it has incited in western studies, I, for one, am grateful.

Particular thanks go to Laura Santigian, a friend of great generosity, who introduced me both to the field of western women's history and to many historians, including Peggy Pascoe and Susan Johnson. And heartfelt thanks to environmental historian Dorothee Kocks, who held fast to the conviction that this project would make a difference in western studies. All of these people have nurtured my hope that an audience for materials on culture might be found in western history.

Formative acknowledgments are due also to the American Civilization Department at Brown University, where this project was originally conceived. There, immersed in discussions about women's history and the role of cultural history in American political life, I initially realized that no one else was talking about my own stumbled-upon interest: western literary studies. As far as I could tell, no one was talking about me, that is, about western intellectual or literary women whose political commitments and intellectual characters were trained upon what I call in this book *competing geographical and historical imaginations*. I had an inkling, then, that in order to work between western criticism, women's history, race and American studies, and cultural studies, in order to enact in western criticism the intellectual and political values embodied by the new western history as well as Brown's American Civilization program, I would have to make new connections, forge new alliances, try to generate some new kinds of conversations.

The Western Literature Association (WLA) was the first and, until quite recently, the only academic organization that wanted my conference papers; it provided nearly all of my early publishing opportunities and thus holds a special place in my heart and in the evolution of this project. I want most especially to thank Melody Graulich, whose groundbreaking work facilitated my own and who read this manuscript at many stages and encouraged me all the way. Forrest Robinson responded to my often urgent letters, while tolerating my many attempts to come to terms with the Stegnerian legacy. Tom Lyon accepted one of my essays on the new female regionalism for *Updating the Literary West,* and his gentle editorial intelligence deepened my sense of WLA as a benevolent institution. In Steve Tatum I have found rich intellectual company. I am grateful for the intellectual challenges he brings to the field.

In closing, many thanks go to Mari Jo Buhle, a mentor whose exacting standards encourage her graduate students to shoot for the best. I have internalized her historian's demands for clear argumentative narrative, and to the extent that this book succeeds therein, readers have Mari Jo to thank. Thanks, too, to Thadious Davis, who commented extensively on the dissertation form of this book and from whom I first learned of the complicated intermixing of discourses about region, race, and gender. Melani McAlister acted as theoretical sounding board as well as dedicated reader and supportive friend. Vera Norwood gave much care to her review of the manuscript for University of North Carolina Press. I also gladly acknowledge my mother, Jean H. Comer, a provider both of financial and moral support, a woman who was my first intellectual mentor, a kind of "pure" intellectual, uncompetitive and honest.

The person deserving of the deepest thanks is José F. Aranda, whom I had the good fortune to meet in 1991 and to marry. It was José who first suggested that I organize the project as a landscape study, which aided me in reframing a vast amount of material far more effectively than I had until then. The influence of his work in Chicano/a Studies can be seen throughout this book, too. My mother once remarked with annoyance that my ideas about marriage, such as they are, were "rarefied," because they were based on a relationship with a feminist man. It's true. José is deeply kind to me, and it's a good thing! With our two (all be they beautiful) boys and the career challenges of writing in a field not yet fully recognized by the academy, I'd have written a lesser book without his generous love.

The range of topics I cover in this book is likely to open me to criticism, for with range comes error. I have hoped to initiate some different and, in my estimation, better conversations in western studies, and it is to those future conversations that this book is dedicated.

Landscapes
of the
New West

Introduction: Postmodernism, Literary Nationalism, and Western Cultural Production

In the early 1970s, when our study begins, regionalism is pretty much dead and buried. It has enjoyed a considerable following at the turn of the century and in the 1920s–1940s,[1] counting among its participants American social scientists and political policy makers as well as historians, writers, artists, photographers, and literary critics.[2] But by midcentury, the alleged "age of consensus" reigns. Television, World War II, the Cold War, and economic prosperity have created, at least on the surface, a relatively homogeneous national culture out of formerly disparate parts. In midcentury literary studies, the aesthetic philosophies of a group like the Southern Agrarians give way to the more centrist cultural politics of the Myth and Symbol School and the New Criticism.[3] Despite their important dissimilarities, both of the new schools share a belief in something like "the American mind." Then, of course, comes the 1960s and the shattering of surface calm. The wave of intellectual movements set in motion by this sea change in American political and cultural life—the new social history, feminism, ethnic studies, poststructural theory, and various types of canon busting in literary criticism—devastates the belief in a unified American mind, without, however, returning to regionalism as a register of noteworthy national, or other, defining differences. In the onslaught of the 1960s, regionalism of the 1920s–40s variety, like the idea of the national mind, is rendered intellectually obsolete, considered inevitably productive of conservative literary nationalisms. To speak of regionalism is to speak of small matters, and smallness, in the midst of "deep water" or oceanic revolution, never seemed more beside the point.

So, how then are we to understand the fact that in this same period a new regionalist movement is taking shape in American political culture, among writers and artists and on college and university campuses? How are we to read, moreover, the important shift in its leadership? For this time the regional movement is headed not by the South or southerners, but by the West and westerners.[4] When it comes to the literary component of the new regionalist movement—and literary discourse paves the way for the splashy emergence of the new western history—this change in leadership is all the more interesting.[5] For at no time in American cultural history prior to the 1970s has western literature garnered anything like a national (critical) reputation.[6] Before the 1970s, western literature *has* no reputation.

One argument I advance throughout this book is that the new regionalism is born out of, and responds to, the emerging culture of postmodernism. By advancing this claim, I hope to open up what is otherwise a tendency among scholars to view the movement primarily in demographic or domestic economic terms. I hope also to shift the location of the debate so that it makes sense of culture, and particularly of cultural production, in more sophisticated and central ways. But to say that one can track firm trends in the ways the new regionalism is represented or evaluated begins to overstate the case, for less than a handful of western historians and literary critics have yet taken up the subject.[7] Part of the reason this movement is not well investigated, I believe, has to do with the problems that both modernism and postmodernism pose for western studies scholars. It would be difficult to understand the new regionalist phenomenon without some gesture toward postmodern culture, economics, or art. And yet it is difficult to initiate the postmodern gesture because the prior historical and political relationships between modernism and western regionalism are themselves not broadly established.

Though a few scholars have explored the tensions between modernism and western literary traditions,[8] the bulk of critical opinion holds that if one can point to any general genre identity to characterize western literature, it would probably be realism. The reasons for this are many and complex, having to do with the nineteenth-century narratives of exploration like those of Lewis and Clark, which are believed to undergird the formal structure of (white male) literary westerns,[9] and also with the fact that western critics and literary writers always work against that nemesis of high culture: formula fiction. Critics thus write about and teach literary westerns that attempt historicist or realist portraits of the West in order to distinguish the High West from more mythic or formulaic popular narratives. Though anyone familiar with the literary West can readily think of texts that complicate the realist rule (i.e., even a classic like Wallace Stegner's 1943 *Big Rock Candy Mountain* often feels manifestly modernist in pathos), an antimodernist feel nonetheless dominates the western critical enterprise.

This complex alliance between realism, regionalism, and antimodernism articulates not only the dominant western aesthetic but also a strategic rebuttal of, and counterattack upon, the dominant *national* aesthetic, which regards regionalism as a second-rate literary and critical undertaking. If, as western critic William Bevis puts it, the antiregionalism of contemporary criticism "issues from modernist tradition and expresses it,"[10] why wouldn't regionally inclined critics cut literary paradigms from some intellectual cloth other than the modernist? Antimodernism is but a first line of defense. And if modernist values, narrative styles, or philosophy threaten the regionalist endeavor as it has been conventionally configured, *post*modernist values push critics to the very limit. If western studies has not yet come to terms with the modernist, the *post*modernist has, well, nearly caught critics in a Rip Van Winkle–like cultural slumber. Postmodernism is thought to have little to do with that which is "really western."

I mean to make a decidedly different case in this book, one that shows both modernism and postmodernism, but especially the latter, exercising crucial enabling roles in the evolution of the new regionalism. I believe it no accident that the new regionalism appears at roughly the same historical moment as does postmodernist American culture.[11] In the early 1970s, writers such as Wallace Stegner, Edward Abbey, Ivan Doig, John Nichols, and Norman Maclean are very much in conversation with postmodernism—often furiously, even if unconsciously or indirectly so. At the outset, that is, new regionalist narratives come into discursive play most often as *antidote* to the postmodern.[12] If one of the defining dilemmas postmodern culture represents is that of the subject's inability to locate itself, regionalist discourse seemingly would rescue the subject's ability to find and claim some "real place," some permanent and trustworthy identity. In this view, western regionalism maps what it sees as an otherwise unmappable world.

But the above claim for the new regionalism as antidote to postmodernism must be fundamentally qualified, and the bulk of this book is, in fact, the qualification. For by no means will I suggest that new regionalists never make use of postmodern narrative strategies. Many do. Nor do all writers see "the postmodern condition" as somehow foreign, disabling, or even new.[13] Quite the contrary. Of those writers who relate to the postmodern, evidence suggests most are women writers and/or writers of color. Many are urbanites. Which is to say that there exists a racialized and gendered pattern as well as a subregionalist pattern as to who rejects postmodern narrative strategies and who indeed *needs* those strategies in order to tell their own versions of western stories. Postmodernism as both economic and cultural context as well as narrative practice must be part of our study, then, part of the founding explanation for the rise of the new regionalism, for through writers' engagements with the postmodern we observe some of the major competing tensions within the regionalist movement itself.

Of course "postmodernism" enters this discussion as an enormously freighted term, a supersensitive conductor of all kinds of cultural politics, which, particularly in western studies, often causes confusion and ill will. By making some beginning attempt here to define postmodernism[14]—even if the constellation of meanings surrounding it are so contentious that any effort invariably disappoints—I hope to clear out some critical space from which to proceed. At the broadest, by postmodernism I mean Frederic Jameson's sense of "the cultural dominant," of postmodernism as that broad, contemporary, cultural "force field in which very different kinds of cultural impulses . . . must make their way."[15] I concur with many of the male Marxists, like Jameson or David Harvey or Edward Soja, that postmodernism reflects "the cultural logic of late capitalism," that postmodernism dialogues with (among other things) First World consumerism, the recent culture of cyberspace technologies, and economic globalization.[16] Thus, in the pages that follow, "postmodernism" operates implicitly as a period label for a culture that reflects and supports, as well as resists and continually reformulates, what Harvey calls advanced capital's new, decentralized, and more flexible regimes of accumulation.

At the same time, postmodernism will operate here as critique of and intervention into that same radical masculinist tradition.[17] Postmodernism, I am saying, dialogues explicitly with the very crisis in the production of knowledge, and production of the subject, that global feminist and antiracist/anticolonial political movements and scholarship have occasioned. Seen through this genealogy, the historical roots of postmodernism lie not just in the waning of high modernism or in global capital restructuring but simultaneously and indivisibly (however contradictorily) in new, internationalist, anticolonial and postcolonial discourses on human rights, of which *female* civil rights are one major, if largely overlooked, component.[18] Postmodernism is therefore produced by, as well as produces, new female and racial subjectivities that take as normative their own (relatively) more fragmented, nonuniversalist, evolving ontologies and their own complex and usually disempowered relationships to language(s) and political subjectivity. This "bias," if one wants to view it as such, fundamentally destabilizes the more hallowed principles of modernist as well as radical thought and puts forward new epistemologies upon which alternative knowledges can be formulated.

Certainly postmodernism will denote formal literary characteristics too. Whether it is a tendency toward reflexivity or positionality or the investment in irony that accompanies split or multiple subjectivity, postmodernist textuality departs from modernist faiths in universalist "man" and distrusts progressive notions of Enlightenment-style history. It regards with pervasive suspicion any claim for objective or omniscient "master" narratives. In contrast to high modernism most particularly, postmodernism plays with pastiche, embraces popular cultural forms, legitimates the experiential and ontological, often revels in the commercial, and takes place upon the site of the un-grand, particular locale. Its ultimate expression might be found in the figure of the hybrid and in notions of hybridity and hybridized subjectivity. It is this last proposition that, at bottom, is so often at issue in western contexts. For if the default subjectivity in postmodernist culture is always multiple, bastard, miscegenistic, gender-bent, hybridized, or—à la Donna Haraway—"cyborg," there can be no such thing as western authenticity. There can be no defensible, insider, regional discourse, no ethnic or racial purity, no sure opposition between masculinity and femininity, no "natural" nature, no final claim on what counts as "westernness."[19]

Likewise, there can be no final claim on the one "true" nation—which introduces the second relevant and very broad arena of cultural contention of interest to my project in this same historic moment: the symbolic site known as "the nation." Critic Roberto Dainotto, not a western studies scholar, has insightfully argued that though regionalism and nationalism would seem to be mutually exclusive discourses, they are in fact, mutually sustaining.[20] Both implicitly claim a center or "genuine" membership, and in so doing, practice exclusions and police the borders of community belonging. This claim will come as little surprise to western intellectuals, who have long observed that the West operates in nationalist discourse as symbol not only for region but also for nation. It is a commonplace of both western history and literary studies to note that the story of western settlement serves as the nation's founding myth. The West *is* America, as the Smithsonian's 1991 exhibition of western art proclaimed.[21] Or as Wallace Stegner once remarked, western landscape is the landscape upon which (dominant) national identity was forged.[22]

What I want to argue, however, is that western regionalist dialogue with U.S. hegemonic nationalism *changes* in the post-1970s period. No longer will popular symbols of westernness lend themselves so handily to the maintenance of nationalist empire. Courtesy of the antiwar, gay, feminist, and civil rights movements, the assault on the notion of a unified nation and its national subject—what critic Lauren Berlant calls the "official National Symbolic"[23]—is well underway by the early 1970s. But the new regionalism has a special role to play in its demise. What is different, this time around, is *not* that western regionalism comes into discursive play at the same moment when traditional national ideals need to be shored up—in the wake of a failed war effort, the Arab oil embargo, and domestic social revolution. The difference is that the new regionalists are so uncommitted to performing that traditional cultural task.[24] Certainly the new regionalism dialogues with the crisis of the National Symbolic, but from its earliest examples it dialogues by way of critique (again I would cite Doig, Abbey, or Maclean and would add James Welch, N. Scott Momaday, Frank Chin, Richard Rodriguez, and Rudolfo Anaya). It will not symbolically clean up the mess of Watergate, of Cambodia, of a new globalizing economy that restructures and disempowers the workplace at home. Further, early regionalist discourse is generally open and searching about questions of racial and gendered identity, and this openness has important implications for the movement's evolution and its production of a new, emergent National Symbolic.

Yet throughout the 1970s—and here is the point of immediate departure for this study—the new regionalism languishes. It bursts onto the cultural scene fully and powerfully only some ten years later, in the late 1980s, when the new western history takes "the new West" (including the literary West) positively and provocatively public.[25] What has changed in the geopolitical scene? First of all, the Reagan era has officially ended.[26] During most of the 1980s, Reagan's own crafted, western, public persona—invoking, as it does, supposed attributes of the Old West like self-reliance and individualism even as Reagan's policies resemble more the realpolitik of cowboy diplomacy—competes with new regionalist sensibility for dominance of the movement.[27] Judging by the lull the movement experiences in these years, the Reagan regime and the "remasculinized America" that his persona consolidates retain the upper hand.[28] Reaganism effectively mobilizes western discourses about national subjectivity for federalist policy appeals, including increased state powers, deregulation, the dismantling of the welfare state, and a hyperculture of free enterprise. Further, the "western experience," as Reagan deploys it, underwrites his administration's backlash against feminist and civil rights challenges to white patriarchal authority.[29] The new regionalists' alternative political and cultural agendas wait in the wings during these years, wondering how far Reaganism can go before something checks it.[30]

By the late 1980s, the geopolitical scene shifts in unforeseen, shocking ways. The Soviet Bloc falls, the Soviet Union implodes, the Cold War has been won, and new nationalist revolutions break out all over the globe in what was supposed to be a postnationalist era. America needs a new program of national self-definition more than it has since the American century began—and now with Reaganism out of the way, *this* political vacuum pulls the new western history into immediate cultural orbit. It is this opening, that is, that makes the new western history's project of national mythbusting hit such a receptive popular chord. According to the sign-in books that traveled with *The West as America*, the very controversial and media-watched art exhibit sponsored by the Smithsonian in 1991, museum visitors approved the left/liberal political slant of the exhibit by a margin of 2:1.[31] Apparently, the changed political climate of the post-Vietnam, post-Reagan, and post–Cold War era prompted museum visitors to approve interventions into the official National Symbolic such that a far more sober myth of national origins was deemed not only appropriate but overdue. Visitors did not shy away from the word "conquest" to characterize western history.

What else changes? Interestingly, on the history side of the new regionalist movement, women of all races come to the fore as historical subjects, and gender emerges as a pivotal category of historical analysis. Western women's history grows into a legitimate, reviewed, recognized field—one of the most promising fields in American women's history, with measurable institutional presence in national universities. On the literary side of the movement, women's writing in the 1980s charts new literary territory. Writers' festivals in sexy western towns such as Steamboat Springs, Colorado, headline sudden female stars like Pam Houston.[32] And Leslie Marmon Silko, Sandra Cisneros, Louise Erdrich, and Maxine Hong Kingston earn collectively two MacArthurs and two National Book Critics Circle Awards.[33] In typical postmodern fashion, the center of the literary side of the movement (the Doigs and Abbeys) relocates to its former borders, if in fact one might still speak of borders. By the late 1980s and into the 1990s, women's writing makes up the literary movement's heart, soul, intellectual vitality, and, not at all incidentally, its commercial visibility and viability. It is the feminist component of the new movement, even, that dominates its "new story." As we approach the year 2000, "the western experience" circulates today in American cultural life with considerably more circumspection than at any time in recent memory. The feminist West has jockeyed for imaginative control of Reagan's remasculinized America and, for the time being, enjoys a surprisingly sympathetic audience.

Why then—and here is the second motivating question for this study— have scholars not yet substantively addressed this feminist movement or its writers? The new western history has created a profoundly enabling environment in which such work might be undertaken. Still, however, critical silence prevails. Certainly one reads plenty about Silko, Kingston, Erdrich, and Cisneros, but analyses generally are framed through the categories of race or ethnicity rather than through western regionality in any geographic, historic, or imaginative sense. And, as of mid-1998, hardly a single critical piece has been published about the most popular of white women writers: Barbara Kingsolver, Terry Tempest Williams, Mary Clearman Blew, Kim Barnes, Gretel Ehrlich, or Pam Houston. Why?

This book explores—in its broadest implications—the "why" question. To do so, it offers an initial survey of the new female regionalism, considers various writers' major claims, concerns, differences, and shared critiques of the West's enduring masculinist identity. On the way to offering this survey, I necessarily address the cultural politics that surround regionalism in twentieth-century American intellectual circles.

One point to make from the start is that practically no institutional presence of western literary criticism exists in American universities—feminist or otherwise. Though western historians have secured for themselves a place (and tenure lines) in American history departments, the same cannot be said for western literary critics. Most western critics came into their work on the literary west through fairly traditional job lines in nineteenth-century or twentieth-century American literature. So, although western literary criticism is indeed a field, it makes its way on the margins of institutional visibility, security, legitimacy, opportunity, and currency. This fact fundamentally shadows any discussion of the new regionalism.

It is also worth noting here, in a discussion about cultural politics, that some may challenge my decision to label several of these writers—such as Kingston, Silko, and Cisneros (who comes from Chicago)—as "western" writers. Many, probably most, critics in the fields of Asian American or Native American or Chicano/a Studies would not do so. It is a fair and related challenge, moreover, to ask whether the process of so labeling these writers constitutes a kind of colonizing act. I should say in response to this legitimate concern that one goal of this study is to engage critics whose attitude may be, quite understandably, that western regionalism is a "white thing," a critical category that, like the Wild West or conquest stories it is assumed to mimic, offers little relevance to the literature and concerns of contemporary people of color. To be sure, the discourse of western regionalism is indeed racialized white, including, perhaps even especially (though not always), when it talks about Native Americans. But to continue to concede the category of region altogether, to consent to its remaining a "white thing," is in my view an error of progressive political strategy, not to mention a misreading of the cultural phenomenon. Region, like any category in American critical thought, depends upon figurations of people of color and/or women for its coherence and intelligibility *as* a "white man's discourse." Exposing the racial and gendered assumptions that comprise the discourse and make it politically meaningful and oppressive may be relevant not least, but rather most of all, to women and/or peoples of color.

Of the many, many writers who could have been featured, I settled on those I did for several reasons. The first is because sometimes—as is true of Joan Didion, Leslie Marmon Silko, and Wanda Coleman—their critical *reception* suggests the unstated biases of dominant literary paradigms. I spend much time both revealing and exploring those biases and the obstacles they pose for theorizing a "new western literature." The second reason for my choices is that, taken together, this collection of writers seems to suggest the various political moods of the new movement, its own desire to "remap" or "respatialize" the West, this time with a feminist, antiracist, and often postnationalist logic. In no way are these the only writers I could have chosen to make the case. Third, I settled on what might be received as a "multicultural" representation of the movement *not* from a pluralist desire to celebrate diversity in American culture—a desire that lends itself to underestimating racial hatreds and injustice—but as a representational methodology that might heed the various new tellings of western *history* that issue from this body of literature.[34]

Reading Gloria Anzaldúa, for example, enacts several kinds of engagements with Mexican American history, including the destabilization of the geopolitical space we take for granted today as Texas. In the process of respatializing that borderlands area—reconnecting it to the nexus of the Mexican, colonial Spanish, and indigenous histories from which it arises— an alternative geographic imaginary as well as history and sensibility come into being. Occupation of that new sensibility, as it were, constitutes occupation of a different "West," if indeed that territory can be called "western" in any meaningful sense. Anzaldúa is not unique. Many of the new regionalists are as invested in rewriting history, and in reimagining the spatial terrain on which particular histories play out their various power struggles, as they are in producing something like Art or a Great American Novel. The emphasis here is less on multiple histories, however, than on multiple geographic knowledges. These new knowledges demonstrate that minority discourse cannot be shunted to the fringe of western studies or culture, for minority historical experience is always at the center of majority or dominant geographical history, even when repressed.

Although I have chosen the particular writers I have because, in one way or another, they deal with women's issues or female subjectivity from a variety of feminist perspectives, the attempt here is *not* to make a claim for a cohesive or distinctly female literary tradition. I concede freely that these women's texts belong as much to women's as to racial, subregional, heterosexual or lesbian, or specific genre traditions. I should note, further, some slippage throughout this book between the terms "female" regionalism and "feminist" regionalism. To be sure, not every new female regionalist writes feminist stories, or stories with feminist sensibilities. Nonetheless, the literature by women, in the main, unquestionably expresses feminist politics of one or another type. It is not too much to say that the new female regionalism produces a consistent (though entirely internally contentious) feminist cultural politic. Hence, the slippage. By the same token, if women are not necessarily feminists, men are not necessarily antifeminists. Indeed, as I implied earlier, many of the male writers of the new regionalism narrate their own stories through "women's values" of community, relationships, social interdependence, and family, and in so doing, they reorient the geocultural imaginary away from masculinist and toward feminist social emplotments. (As examples, I offer Ivan Doig, William Kittredge, James Welch, Richard Rodriguez, Luis Rodriguez, and Norman Maclean.)

With such fundamental qualifications, why then put out a study centered on female writers? The category of "women" organizes this project for the simple reason that, as historian Susan Johnson has ably argued, despite the accomplishments of western women's history, gender analysis continues to be the most invisible category in western studies.[35] The West as a geo-cultural imaginary remains so deeply associated with masculinism that, in my view, any study that reckons with the male-gendered character of the regionalist enterprise and manages to get a few feminist words in edgewise does the field of western studies a service.

Because landscape is the single most telling signature of western identity, I organize this survey of the new female regionalism through a series of landscape studies. To claim landscape as a principal signature of western identity means several things. First, it means that one cannot escape, in discussions of the American West, some kind of dialogue with what I loosely call a "landscape perspective." Countless western narratives—whether literary, historical, popular, visual, or theoretical, and including counternarratives like Anzaldúa's—take up landscape and/or nature (not the same thing, to be sure) as defining parts of western, and counterwestern, experience.[36] Critics do so too.[37] Big country, big sky, majestic mountains, mystical desert-scapes, rough ranchlands, clean rivers, and fresh, rejuvenative air, symbolize that which is deeply, truly western, including, again, counterwestern.

Landscape is not only one of the most telling features of western region-alism, it is also the most analytically slippery—what I call the "wild card" of western discourse. Herein is landscape's usefulness to cultural critics: it is one of the most defended, but also most vulnerable and revealing, signs in western studies. Though landscape would appear to be a stable entity or category, tied to something "really there" like earthly topography, it is deployed all the time, in many different political guises, to make all kinds of extratopographic meanings.

The meta-argument holding my series of landscape studies together is that the new female regionalists deploy representations of western lands and nature to talk about and, more, to challenge and change myriad *social and political* topics: the qualities and compromises of women's lives, racial history (especially white racial history), the pain of racism, feminist political dreams and utopic societies, feminist erotics, postmodern economics, the relationships between human and nonhuman nature, the relationship of non-Europeans to nonhuman nature, female-imagined nationalisms, Anglo female stoicism, a female-imagined ecology, a feminist State—and the list goes on.

I approach landscape studies from the conviction that landscape represen-tation, in the words of British art critic Stephen Daniels, is a "powerful mode of knowledge and social discourse."[38] Certainly this way of thinking, if not the language or theoretical disposition, is behind western critics' sense that landscape means something fundamental to westerners and western discourse. Critics would implicitly agree that landscape is not "real" but is rather a particular type of social discourse around which various cultural questions get discussed—especially, as I suggested earlier, questions of national identity. But if western critics are generally attuned to the nationalist narratives written through western landscape representation, the many, many other social plots that landscape articulates and maintains are far less often a topic. Particularly in comparison to the highly developed and sophisticated field of landscape studies in British studies,[39] America's western landscapes continue to masquerade as "the natural."

To some extent, feminist critics have "denaturalized" western landscapes and made inroads into the gendered plots written upon western nature. Many of the themes that surface in my own work—a focus on landscape, on links between narratives of nature and nation, between nature and female sexuality, between nature and racial formation, and between nature and "women's culture"—were initially formulated by scholars whose work showed the way for my own. But feminists too have stopped short of a wholesale retheorization of landscape. One of the most conspicuous indicators of this half-commitment to landscape as discourse is the pervasive association of landscape with the sacred and transcendental. Claims for landscape *as* nature and nature as the realm of the sacred suggest not simply that an extrarepresentational, nonhuman world exists in nature (a claim I support), but that that world can redeem the ills that plague human society (a claim I question).[40] Nature as social savior? Surely this is one of the most heavy-handed signs of human projection available in western discourse. It is also one of the most complex, for it underlies many racist political projects at the same time that it underlies all kinds of antiracist, nonwhite ethnicity–affirming, region-affirming, female-affirming, and pro-environmental political projects.

Part of the scholarly problem arises from the theoretical base (perceptual geography) from which the best of critics work. Perceptual geography holds that landscape perception and representation is a function of "landscape tastes"—a reasonable beginning, to be sure, but one that is finally inadequate.[41] For natural spaces themselves, when mapped by human minds, not only reflect human social organization but, as representational systems, participate in both the construction and maintenance of every kind of racial, gender, class, sexual, regional, and nationalist relationship imaginable. One group of landscape representations might further, for example, heroic white history or even ironic or tragic but nonetheless white-centered history, whereas another group of representations might question that dominant history, reveal its internal contradictions, and put forward a new past that tells the story of days gone by through relatively new narrative forms and tropes and, importantly, through a very different conceptualization of "landscape" and human relationships to one another and to nonhuman nature. This latter kind of history is often associated, for example, with Native American literary traditions.[42] Critic W. J. T. Mitchell's sense of the *activity* of landscape discourse speaks to my own notions of the ways landscape representations operate. Mitchell's idea is to make landscape less a noun, as he puts it, than a verb, for, he argues, "landscape doesn't merely signify or symbolize power relations; it is an instrument of cultural power, perhaps even an agent of power that is (or frequently represents itself as) independent of human intentions."[43] Landscape is not just mystified text; rather, it *makes* history.

If we were to begin from the above premise—that landscape is not an empty field of vision (the premise of perceptual geography) but rather a brimming-full *social* topography that creates and enacts the various cultural assumptions and power struggles of the age—we might approach western landscape studies, and all of the social relations that landscape represents and negotiates, from a more nuanced and proactive vantage point. To treat southwestern desertscapes or the mountainscapes of the Rockies or Sierra Nevada as historically evolving representations of western and American social relations, as symbolic projections of those social relations, and, finally, to consider them as actors on the western stage enables us not only to evaluate the ways that landscape embodies social conflicts over time but to be alerted to landscape itself as a social player, a protagonist, a dynamic form of cultural practice.[44] Such a perspective also enables critics to approach environmental issues (often quite dear to western narratives about landscape and nature) from a less mystified perspective, for it encourages us to assume less and question more what it is we think we know about nature and society and, in the end, to intervene in environmental problems, including the definition of those problems, with more political savvy.

I hope I have thus far intimated that the very invocation of "landscape" in western discourse predetermines the ways we talk about the environments in which people find themselves.[45] Mitchell, in fact, calls the "landscape perspective" a "particular historical formation associated with European imperialism."[46] Given that the female subjects of this study are, to differing degrees, nondominant subjects and that dominant landscape discourse makes objects out of both women and that which is gendered female (most obviously, nature), I am, as are feminists all the time, faced with the initial task of proposing paradigms, mappings, structures, conceptual systems, and theories that permit the entry of women into discourses that have been formed explicitly and foundationally by excluding women or marginalizing that which is female.

In an effort to think through different parameters, then, I make use of the notion of landscape in strategic and unconventional ways. Although I consider, often straightforwardly, how different writers inhabit various landscapes as well as represent nature, I also "bend" conventional methods of landscape study in order to represent what seems to me a different collective sensibility about space and the different way in which women imaginatively relate to it, construct it, and thus construct and inhabit the West. To illustrate or map this difference, which constitutes really a remapping of what counts as "western," each of the book's chapters is organized around a different kind of landscape—urban, wild, erotic, national. This organization allows me to pursue, on terms disallowed by traditional landscape discourse, those subjects, themes, spaces, and places that are valued or examined by the women of this study.

Thus, my primary interest here is to understand the dynamism of spatial relations and the ways that other kinds of relations (i.e., between nonhuman and human nature, between races, between men and women) are represented and contested *in space*. One of my theoretical goals is to import into western studies some of the founding assumptions of theoretical geography, chief among them, in the words of Doreen Massey, the idea that "the spatial organization of a society . . . is integral to the production of the social, and not merely its result."[47] This landscape study is a kind of "spatial history," then, a history that takes the changing status of spaces—as represented in and representative of contemporary feminist issues—as part of its subject and method. Though I begin here with the earliest of the new female regionalists, which predisposes the reader to think historically, my broader goal is to negotiate this territory as one might negotiate an unfamiliar map. Though my commitments to historicist narrative trajectories will become clear, my arguments work together in terms of spatial rather than temporal logics.[48]

The claim for landscape as discursive "wild card" suggests, finally, this study's most ambitious theoretical desires. Though some of postmodern geography sees the gesture toward place as inescapably reactionary, it will become clear that I do not.[49] Certainly, as my chapter on "natural" landscapes illustrates, some place-identified writers participate in and profit from a culture that hypercommodifies and fetishizes the local and primitive, even if participation is unwitting and politically poignant. At the same time, I have deliberately conceptualized this project in such a way that the regionalist impulse might offer postmodern theory some clues as to how a resistant politics can in fact be tied to particularized place without capitulating to nostalgia or antimodernism (which are generally counterproductive for western women) or to violent, exclusivist claims to place-belonging (such as those dooming Bosnia or Rwanda)—without, in short, turning one's back on the world.

It may be worth remembering, as critics of nineteenth-century southern and New England regionalism have recently argued, that in American cultural history, the regional impulse has often authorized the less powerful of society to speak.[50] As a genre that historically permitted—indeed, made a virtue of—observing and recording that which was unknown or marginal to dominant cultural trends, regional writing, according to Richard Brodhead, "enfranchised a new set of social knowledges as a source of literary expertise"; and this enfranchisement in turn sanctioned the assertion of female knowledge and public authority.[51] If nineteenth-century regionalism enabled early republican women writers to dialogue with evolving meanings of the state and the state's place in the broader global (or, in their terms, spiritual) order, *contemporary* regionalism permits a similar entry point, enfranchises a whole new set of social knowledges, and, from the vantage point of the local, comments now on the postmodern, which always includes the global.

In this study, the vehicle for commentary on the link between the local and the global is the landscape "wild card." Through landscape discourse, writers enact the connectedness between "place" and "space," if critics will only read it as such. In some of the most beloved strands of western studies, western landscape comes into representation by and large as symbol of a fixed and specific place—whether that place is the cold river country of high Montana, the windscaped otherworldliness of Utah's canyonlands, or the sandy beaches of Southern California. By attending not to the specificity of particular landscapes but rather to the flexibility and malleability of landscape as a broader discursive and cultural practice, by bending what counts as legitimate landscape, I aim to show that the concepts of place and space always permeate one another, that, in fact, place cannot be said to constitute "the local" whereas space constitutes "the global." This intervention is of first importance to any kind of gender- or race-sensitive paradigm shift in western criticism. Particularized place offers no shelter from the global storm, whether it is the storm of global capital restructuring, domestic immigration, postmodern culture, female civil rights (and loss of male supremacy), or whatever ails.

Part One

Toward a

Spatial History

of the New

Feminist

Regionalism

Landscapes of Westernness: Gender, Race, and the Politics of American Spaces

As a writer from the West, I ... discovered how it felt to be misinterpreted. Even well-intentioned people who wanted to praise me often saw in me, or expected from me, things that I was not prepared to deliver, and misread things that I was prepared to deliver. ... We rode under the shadow of the big hat. ... We were big hat, no cows. Nothing could convince them in New York or Massachusetts that there was anything of literary interest in the West except cowboys.
—Wallace Stegner, 1990, accepting PEN's Lifetime Achievement Award

When I was starting to write —in the late fifties, early sixties—there was a kind of social tradition in which men novelists could operate. Hard drinkers, bad livers. Wives, wars, big fish, Africa, Paris, no second acts. A man who wrote novels had a role in the world, and he could play that role and do whatever he wanted behind it. A woman who wrote novels had no particular role. Women who wrote novels were quite often perceived as invalids. I didn't much like it.
—Joan Didion, 1977 interview

East versus West:
Competing for the Territory of the Nation

In 1962, when news reached the Northern California campus of Stanford University that John Steinbeck had been awarded the Nobel Prize for literature, a half dozen graduate students, all from New York, were not just surprised, as was Mr. Steinbeck himself, but indignant, even outraged. As Wallace Stegner, director of Stanford's creative writing program, told the story: "They thought it was the greatest insult to intelligence that ever happened."[1]

The up-and-coming intellectual elite at Stanford were not alone in decrying the Academy's choice. The international press and the northeastern domestic press received the news with dismay. The Swedish press called the award "one of the academy's biggest mistakes."[2] The *New York Times* wondered on its editorial page why the award had gone to a writer whose work had not "made a more profound impression on the literature of our age."[3] In a thorough *New York Times* rebuke entitled "Does a Moral Vision of the Thirties Deserve a Nobel Prize?" Cornell professor Arthur Mizener called Steinbeck an "incurable amateur philosopher," a writer who cared so much for the morals of his stories that the moral, finally, mangled the story.[4] Was European literary judgment behind the times, Mizener wondered, influenced by a socialist democratic political culture inclined toward "sentimental humanitarianism"?[5] Or was Europe still under the spell of America as a "natural," even "primitive," place, and Steinbeck popularly embodied that ideal?[6]

Steinbeck, of course, had his defenders—notably among West Coast intellectuals. One of the most visible was novelist John Haase, who reviewed the award in the *Los Angeles Times*.[7] In a heated answer to Professor Mizener, one that echoes the Stegner epigraph that opens this chapter, Haase frames the controversy over Steinbeck as a regional contest between the cultural values of the eastern establishment and those of western literary men. How can humanitarianism be out of fashion, Haase wants to know. Is there no place in serious fiction for the warmth or compassion found in Steinbeck's work?

For his part, Haase despises the writers he assumes Mizener would promote as substitute Nobel contenders. In his view, the Beats are "merchants of hopelessness." The elite, like F. Scott Fitzgerald, speak for "a rotten, fruitless society, a people whose problems were inconsequential, where

Steinbeck spoke of good, simple people in serious trouble." Haase dismisses writers of "the Ivy League Cotillion," as nothing more than "young men in . . . tight little pants . . . who write endlessly about their private schools." They are not real men, who write about real world experience, Haase suggests, but pale, privileged parochials "whose only contact with the outdoors is standing in line for a foreign movie, whose knowledge of the Common Man comes from hearing a folk singer at the Blue Angel." Nor is Haase impressed by "that little group of 'cool' writers of the last two decades . . . [who are] fascinated with homosexuality, with incest and cannibalism."[8]

"Look beyond Madison Avenue," Haase admonishes the eastern establishment. Heed the lessons of European experience,

> where age and apathy only served to produce monsters. Perhaps [the Europeans] are saying . . . 'Look West, look at the men against the mountains.' Perhaps they still look upon America as a promising child, 'natural, primitive,' if you will, but promising if it is allowed to continue the Noble Experiment.[9]

The American Experiment is noble still, Haase believes, and what better embodiment of it than Haase's western man, portrayed in dramatic relief against the backdrop of western mountains? "No, Mr. Mizener," Haase exhorts, "the Europeans are not behind the times. They are ahead of the times." And western men, Haase suggests—those who refute hopelessness, elitist excess, effete and/or cerebral masculinity, and perverse (including, for Haase, homo) sexuality—are also ahead of the times. They are the visionaries for an American cultural scene that, in 1962, no longer appeared quite so seamless, even to those in the supposedly seamless mainstream.

This dialogue between East and West introduces readers directly into the fray of a battle—the battle is for cultural authority, and it occurs because the Steinbeck award reveals the broader fact of instability, vulnerability, in northeastern cultural hegemony. Tantalizingly, the very terms by which cultural authority can be established and secured in the latter half of the twentieth century are up for grabs. If the Swedish Academy launches one attack, another will follow shortly in the name of region. For us, what is at issue in the controversy over Steinbeck's Nobel Prize is not whether he did or did not deserve the award, but rather the way in which "western" becomes a discursive space—*a sociocultural landscape*—in which competing worldviews and politics are laid out and fought over. The *New York Times* reviewer takes Steinbeck to task for what amounts to an underdeveloped modernist consciousness, the literary result of which is, in the easterner's view, "tenth-rate philosophizing."[10] In response, the *Los Angeles Times* reviewer takes the easterner to task because he unconsciously assumes that a modernist consciousness is the "truest" consciousness of the age. Given that the northeasterner speaks from the seat of American intellectual authority, he needn't defend the "truth" of his truth claims. This privilege, this ability to define "truth" without looking over one's shoulder, offends and enrages the westerner, who commands no comparable privilege in American intellectual history.

To compete with the established legitimacy of the northeastern intelligentsia and to resist the patronizing and dismissive label of "naïve" that accompanies rejection of the modernist project, the western reviewer invokes his own set of legitimating rationales—all of which revolve around meanings associated with the very gendered and racialized west. Haase implicitly calls upon western pioneer mythology, including, importantly for this study, images of western mountains, as a kind of "power discourse" that will rival the various power discourses that authorize eastern cultural dominance. Steinbeck as literary hero symbolizes first and foremost a "real man," a man whose unquestioned heterosexual masculinity is insulted by "tight little pants," a man whose worldliness comes from more than book learning. This man, Haase quickly points out, is no naïf, even if his intelligence is comparatively unschooled. He is just more optimistic, less jaded than his literary brothers back East. (This optimism marks him most certainly as white, for American Indian and Mexican American men hardly extract a hopeful mythology from western expansion.) Perhaps the "Ivy League Cotillion" ought to get out of the city, and citified habits too, Haase hints, take in some Rocky Mountain air. That would fix what ails them, remind them of what it's like to feel like men again. Then they would quit this defeatist modern thinking!

When Haase invokes "western men," he puts into play a system of meanings that signifies a good deal more than biological male humans living in the geographic terrain to the west of the 98th meridian. The West, in Haase's geographic imagination, *is* America. Western character as Haase forwards it—robustly masculine, natively hopeful, maverick, full of the promise of youth, suited intuitively to the rigors of the outdoors, representative of the "common man"—signifies both regional but also national character. Far more than a discussion of literary values, then, Haase and Mizener are fighting about national direction, national politics, national character and identity—in short, national manhood. At issue in this struggle is who—that is, which groups of white, intellectual men—will lead American culture into the second part of the American century.

By invoking the language of "the American century," I mean to locate this struggle for cultural authority in its most global contexts. Though the battle for dominant national masculinity that I've described above situates itself upon domestic territory, it nevertheless gestures simultaneously toward a broader international crisis over the direction of radical politics and the changing global status of white men. Socialism, before World War II the bedrock of leftist political vision in most of the world, after World War II must share the horizon of radical idealism with the antiracist and anti-colonial programs, as well as the political actors, of emergent postcolonial movements. As the American century unfolds, white working-class men no longer will dominate the internationalist narrative of The Struggle Against Oppression. The pressures to dislodge the working-class man from his standing as Principal Oppressed Person—or, if you prefer, Principal Radical Hope—and to dislodge class analysis (and the leaders who formulate it) as the singular logic underwriting cultural critique and political resistance, combine, by the late 1950s to mid-1960s, with the immediate and intense pressures generated by civil rights and women's movement agitation at home to force an emergency about masculinity and politics as they have been conventionally defined, up to that date. A mortal wound has been levied against America's body politic, the most powerful body politic in the world, ushering in an extended moment of truth and precipitating precisely the kinds of masculine contests for the National Symbolic underlying the critical row between Mizener and Haase at the start of this chapter.

If I have so far worked along fairly traditional definitions of "the political," let me hasten now to that less obvious site of political contestation—space itself—which is of primary interest to this study. I led into this chapter via the Steinbeck controversy because it illustrates my claim that authorizing, as well as marginalized, cultural projects are themselves linked to histories of particular spaces. Both of the spaces suggested above, the space of the "Ivy League Cotillion" and the space of "natural optimism," are associated loosely but nonetheless indelibly with, respectively, New England and Far Western regional history and identity. Each history, that is, forwards an alternative cartography of national and international space and men's places within it. I begin with the simpler fact of the westerner's anger at the easterner, a trespasser on the westerner's spatial turf. I point out that the easterner is empowered to trespass because he speaks from authorizing cultural space. The easterner says, in effect: We are the authorizing body, not you, and we refuse Steinbeck's and, by extension, western intellectuality; when it comes to the business of gatekeeping national literary treasures (and the imaginative terrain of the nation), your cultural cartography will not supersede our own.

But quite quickly the spatial politics fragment, for the westerner has at his disposal spatial prerogatives that, when aptly conjured, have the power to give the easterner pause. Namely, he summons the supremely confident, white masculinism that adheres to dominant western spaces, especially "natural" spaces like western mountains. Notice here that mountains operate as cultural signifiers (very masked) for the Common Man's dignified manhood. Also notice the particular kind of landscape perspective that operates here, that of panorama—the vast, unobstructed view from mountains and mountaintops. Such a panoramic visual frame preserves what is fundamentally under assault in modernity: a place of Archimedean overview, a place that enables an unambiguous survey of a presumably stable social world.[11] Revealing his desire to freeze, or at least still, a massively convulsing social order (it *is* 1963, after all), the westerner gestures toward stable points of origin, "fixed" or unmoving mountains. I suggest that this particular way of seeing, one very invested in forestalling modernity, is *the* dominant visual ideology emplotting the western imaginary, its ultimate landscape of westernness.[12]

The battle for cultural authority that I am mapping thus takes place over several spatial terrains. The most obvious is regionally conceived, that of East versus West. The East stands in for modernity's contradictions and anxieties, its profound and inescapable self-subversions, and its political liberalism too. The West protects some lingering hope of a world less complicated by "progress," which, in its own half-cocked way, is something of a critique of modernity, especially of the notion that humans are separate from or "above" nonhuman nature. But the East/West spatial divide also explicitly negotiates differing masculine approaches to, or responses to, the problems of modernity. In their embrace of modernist pathos, masculinities associated with the Northeast tolerate self-doubt, tolerate some bending of the heterosexual imperative, and lend themselves to elitism (even if elitist identity is liberal). As I have suggested above, one senses in the eastern reviewer's objections to the Steinbeck award the apprehension of a major political break, a watershed moment in contemporary history, and he labors, with a kind of manly moral integrity, toward understanding it, meeting it. By contrast, the spaces that surround and define western mountains maintain standards of "authentic," virile masculinity, derived, implicitly, from nineteenth-century male homosociality in the western wilds. No agonizing self-scrutiny or hyperintellectualism for the western outdoorsman; no "tight little pants" seen (supposedly) on western mountainsides; no Boston Brahmins seen there either. Western discourse answers modern problems by revisiting the past, invoking especially the masculine competence required to survive frontier days. But the response to modernity is finally less critique than refusal, one that pits a stubborn, individualist antimodernism against heavy odds.

In the end, when the western critic cannot map his intentions onto the national imaginary in literary terms—for the spatial politics of cultural production are stacked against him—he displaces the terms of his argument to the arena of gendered identity and fights more effectively there. "Natural" western landscapes (mountains) form the spatial basis that support the western critic's gendered prerogative, and when it comes to a fight over national manhood, spatial politics are now stacked in the *westerner's* favor. Bolstered by the no-nonsense masculinity associated with rugged western topography, the western critic can symbolically survey (from the mountaintops) international crises I laid out above. Unlike the northeastern reviewer, however, the westerner sees himself less as deposed world leader than as "authentic subject," working-class hero, who isn't about to give up privileges he's only just earned—especially not now, when Steinbeck's literary arrival would seem to suggest his own. Thus, if the northeasterner perceives the changes afoot at home and beyond and means, somehow, to greet them with a contemporary (versus 1930s-era), judicious response, the westerner says, in effect: You and I are coming at these global changes from differently empowered vantage points, and I am in no position to divest the little power I possess. Even if I could, I would not, for my vision of national good must be kept alive if we are to survive this new political environment. Cannibals, homosexuals—what is next?!

By now I hope to have introduced, at least in initial terms, the theoretical undertaking of this project: to demonstrate that spaces—particularly the various geocultural imaginaries that I have begun to elaborate and to which I will turn at length—play a determining (though not deterministic) role in the negotiation of this moment of American political crisis.[13] That is, the battle in the war for cultural authority occurs upon a discursive field that is flooded with highly spatialized representations of power. Certainly the new 1970s western regionalism, especially its female wing, will infiltrate national political terrain by way of deftly exploiting the larger, expanded role of space (including place signs) that accompanies postmodernity, including postmodern political crises about the status of the white male subject—but more on that later.

For now, in the interests of clarity, let me offer something of a theoretical genealogy. Generally, I take my lead from spatial theorists who are fond of noting that social relations unfold always in spatial contexts; human society cannot function and reproduce itself in anything other than spatialized terms.[14] Geographer Doreen Massey envisions the spatial as "social relations 'stretched out.'"[15] Emplotted by whatever narratives impart meaning in a specific historical context, space goes about its cultural work by calling relatively little attention to itself as power broker. For example, because he comes from the center of intellectual legitimacy, the northeastern reviewer justifies far less than does the westerner his right to name the truth that is real versus that which is second-rate or innocent. Given that so many spatial maneuvers happen quietly, the first task in a study of regionally conceived spaces is to render spatial power plays more audible, even clamorous. Toward that end, I attempt to denaturalize western spaces—that is, make less familiar what are assumed to be western spatial attributes—by exposing their various social contents and investigating the complex ways that social groups vie to hold or seize control of the spatial media under consideration.

Additionally, this book—itself a participant in the contest for cultural authority that it documents—hopes to address nagging theoretical problems that accompany more essentialist, geographically determinist, or "realist" definitions of regionalism.[16] Inspired by theoretical geography, I argue here that space is much more than a "social construction." To be sure, the particular shapes, contours, and feel of spaces do reflect or mirror society, in classic Marxist terms. But, more dynamically, spatial organization also *creates* particular social relations at the same time that it enforces and protects dominant groups in power. This last premise, of course, all but initiated postcolonial theory. As Edward Said put it some years ago, imperialism is at root an act of "geographical violence through which virtually every space in the world is explored, charted, and finally brought under control."[17] Or, to paraphrase postmodern geographer Edward Soja, geography is never innocent.

If dominant spaces arbitrate, discipline, and contrive difference, they nonetheless also remain contingent, and therefore open to challenge.[18] The notion of spatial resistance underlies and supports many recent theoretical rhetorics that deal—through spatial tropes—with issues of subjectivity, especially alterity. Consider the theoretical grammars of "borders," "boundaries," "alternative geographies," "deterritorialized" spaces, "locatedness" or "positionality," and notions of "situated knowledge."[19] Whatever their claims or disagreements, theoretical rubrics invested in interrogating space insist, as will I, upon the *materiality* of space.

Let us return, then, to the critical jousting that opens this chapter, to put a different spatial spin on the Steinbeck controversy. By now, some readers await acknowledgment that in the L.A. reviewer's representation of westernness no space exists for the fact of women's writing or, indeed, for women as social subjects. If "western mountains" are synonymous with the Common Man, what space can the women who make their practical or imaginative lives upon those mountains be said to occupy? And given that "wild" western mountains are a broader sign for that which is both "authentically" western as well as antimodern and white masculinist, what space can, say, urban women or, dare we say, modernist or postmodernist urban women be said to occupy in western discourse? Do they occupy, in fact, any recognized space at all?

The short answer is no. Traditional western space, gendered male from a myriad of directions, relegates women to a forever status of no-space. Because western space, throughout American history, usually has connoted outdoor or wild spaces rather than domestic or indoor spaces, it predominantly signals *public* space. Far less suggestive of "home on the range" than of the range itself and the expansive possibilities invoked thereby, the dominant spatial field—what I term the "dominant geocultural imaginary"—emplots normative western spaces in "open," "free," uncontained terms. These terms, we should be very clear, belong to the realm of the official and the public, which unmistakably are gendered male and racialized white. For who else, historically, exercises the spatial prerogatives implied by "openness"? To whom other belongs a visual ideology of the panoramic? As feminists across the disciplines have repeatedly demonstrated, public space is by definition male space, off-limits to women. Feminists consistently find that public space presents serious obstacles to female access, navigation, and safety. Feminist geographers, in particular, have pointed out that women's relationships to spatial structures most often revolve around female reproductive roles. Thus, home and hearth are the places most easily definable as "female space."[20] Geographers argue further that female spatial orientation is characterized generally by affinity for contained rather than expansive structures, by the home's four walls more so than by, say, the public marketplace—an implicit premise, geographers note, of the paradigm of separate spheres that dominated much of American women's historiography in the 1980s. Ultimately, as Gillian Rose observes, "When feminists talk about the experiences of space, very often they invoke a sense of difficulty. Being in space is not easy."[21]

However much one might complicate the above observation by inflecting (with racial, regional, or class differences) female relationships to "home" and the marketplace, it still speaks worlds to discussions of women and western space. Whether one is talking about "the great prairie fact," the "great basin deserts," "big skies," or "the forty-niners" (the forty-nine peaks above 14,000 feet in the Rockies), the most often celebrated feature of western space is its spatial *non*containment, its expansiveness, its vastness, its sheer, weighty limitlessness. And these kinds of characterizations—these broad, breath-taking, awesome, boundless, panoramic landscape perspectives—should register for us, loudly, the West's association with both public and male spatialities. The most "authentic" piece of the western epic, therefore, defines its authenticity through male-gendered spatial metaphors and logics, which means that in any beginning discussion of women in western space a multitude of exclusions work against locating female subjectivity at all.

Add to this the final and profound fact that the lands west of the 98th meridian acquire "western" identity only as a consequence of conquest and, of course, that the principal colonizer is the white man (we will return to the white woman colonizer), and we have a social space, a geographic social geometry, that is not only doggedly male and doggedly white but also fundamentally colonialist. Landscape representations operate at the center of colonialist discourse, deployable and deployed as strategies of colonial domination.[22]

Enter, here, both the obstacles and opportunities offered to women by landscape discourse. Female writers' engagements with landscape representations, as I see them, evidence female attempts to access public space, public discourse, public issues, public life, and public power. They serve to recast the spatial field in terms that do not render "openness" synonymous with male-gendered spatialities or "containment" necessarily synonymous with female-gendered ones. In the process, they alter the very contexts of political representativity *of* the public sphere. As I noted in the Introduction, landscape performs a kind of "wild card" function in western discourse. It serves as medium for the expression of every kind of nationalist and imperialist impulse. It permits articulation of Eurocentric and male-centered desire. In the guise of "natural" nature, landscape representation concocts primitivist attitudes about women and/or peoples of color. At the same time, landscape expresses anti-imperialist nationalisms, taboo desires. It often dispatches a vital critique of the Enlightenment mind/body split.

What I propose here is that female investment in landscape discourse is a strategy of "doing business with the boys," with the Teddy Roosevelts and Ronald Reagans of western history. And to do business in the official public realm—"at the office," or upon the mountaintops, as it were—in defiance of white male–only spatial and racial prohibitions. By figuring their own various projects through landscape discourse, women writers write themselves into dominant western history at the same time that they change the conditions and values that enable "official" history to be known and told. In many ways, therefore, I make a claim that coincides with claims often made by feminist critics about American female literary history: by finding, risking, and embracing public visibility, with all of its dangers and sanctions, women writers transform public spaces, make them more conducive to female subjectivity and political visions.[23]

But spatial politics, in western contexts, should also nuance feminist discussions about the realm of the public, for western examples show that the relationship of gender to public space shifts a good deal depending on which part of the national or (equally relevant in discussions about the West) the international imaginary a writer claims, or writes from. From its inception in the early 1970s, American feminist criticism showed a fairly large northeastern bias/blind spot in its own revisions of established male literary history. Studies explicitly devoted to explorations of female authority and its link to southern regionalism or New England–based local color writing are exceptions, of course, but notwithstanding this developed literature, the "major" trendsetting books did not interrogate the categories of regional or national, nor did they foreground issues of space in the production of national literary power.[24] As feminist literary studies dialogues with postcolonial and postmodern theory, certainly this is changing, and feminist criticism increasingly considers the ways that spatial classifications inflect every other significant category in feminist theory—including race, class, nation, empire, and sexual affinity, as well as, of course, gender.[25]

This trend is highly desirable, and I consider my own study of gender and western spaces to be an invested participant in it. To give just a quick example of the "spatial stakes" at issue for feminist and western studies, consider the epigraph by Joan Didion that opens this chapter. It alerts readers to the very narrow role permitted for the female writer, of any regional designation, in American culture. Feminists find no surprises here. But if, as Didion suggests, male novelists (major modernists, she means, like the Paris expatriates) occupy recognized and public social spaces—decidedly colonial, we might note, in their sense of unlimited global spatial freedom—women writers, if they are to *have* a cultural role during the 1950s and early 1960s, are consigned to "private" spaces, especially the space of the home, a space, as the epigraph suggests, that contains and expresses sickliness or invalidism. Operative in Didion's rendering of gendered literary politics is a region-implicated articulation of the public/private dichotomy as well as national/international dichotomies. To find big fish, romantic wars, and hard drinking, modernist men go to Africa. Or they run with the Spanish bulls. Or they drink and carouse on the French Riviera. But none of them, implicitly, locates his male identity or cultural role in the social spaces of Harvard Yard or Greenwich Village. Neither do "important" or "serious" literary men take aim upon the world from western mountaintops.

In telling contrast, the female western writer can indeed claim and occupy a national social space and, by extension, the high-cultural acceptance and prerogative that goes with such a status, if she joins herself to the northeastern cultural establishment. She can do so because the regional Northeast is already susceptible to an "effete" or cultivated signification. The trade-off, however, is that the female writer must submit to a "homely" identity, that of the Emily Dickinson–like, female shut-in. And she must eschew the designation "western." But faced with the alternative of being rendered spaceless, better to be a female, invalid writer heralded by northeastern intellectuals than to be no (western) writer at all.

What I want to highlight here are the spatial politics at work in *female* cultural production, for these politics become quite important, ultimately, to the reception of the new western female regionalism. As it turns out, northeasterners have maintained national gatekeeping authority in matters of high culture, even as the racial and gendered hierarchies among the gatekeepers have been relatively reorganized, even as California universities in particular exert more influence in national scholarly culture, even as an identifiable western literary infrastructure has emerged, even as growing western economic might has remapped the political landscape of the nation. It is indeed the continuing hegemony of northeastern aesthetic and cultural values, I will argue, especially in the conservative 1980s and early 90s, that has enabled the survival and, finally, the rise and current popularity of particularly the nonwhite writers among the new female regionalists. Northeastern social spaces—already emplotted by less aggressive masculinities, responsive to formal innovation, relatively sympathetic to racist suffering, and reflective about the fact that the world is changing and that the liberal thing to do is to invest in that change—are cultural spaces less prohibiting of the female and multiracial subjectivities of the new western literature. But I jump ahead here, for still there exists no category called "western woman writer."

What Is the New Female Regionalism?

The term "new female regionalism" is not widely used in discussions of western literature. I use it here, rather than "contemporary writing," to distinguish the post–1945 period of western cultural production from that of the mid-1970s to the present. One big stumbling block to conceptualizing any kind of recent female literary history of the West is that comparatively little synthetic work, or "sorting" of twentieth-century women's writing, has yet been done.[26] The need to do it is pressing, given that women writers, both major and minor, are very rarely mentioned when western critics at large put forward studies of twentieth-century literature.[27] Somewhat stalled at the cataloguing stage of recovery work, feminist criticism continues to compile the various writerly identities and literary cultures of women of different regions, at different historical moments, writing from different relationships to the dominant geocultural imaginary. But little analytic synthesis is yet complete.

Not surprisingly, then, the many women who produced western narratives from about 1945 to the early 1970s fall into something of a critical vacuum when it comes to their regionalist bent. And yet some of the most notable—Jean Stafford, Hisaye Yamamoto, Jessamyn West, Mildred Walker, Fabiola Cabeza de Baca, Nina Otero-Warren, Josephina Niggli, Dorothy Johnson, Edna Ferber, Katherine Anne Porter, Lois Phillips Hudson, Hope Sykes, Joanne Greenberg, Diane Wakoski, and Tillie Olsen—regularly wrote about the West, from within the West, and with some sense of themselves as "western women writers." Although a few recent biographies of individuals like Nina Otero-Warren and Fabiola Cabeza de Baca have appeared, and a fairly developed literature exists about Jean Stafford, all in all, the kinds of wests these writers collectively put forward during the first half of the American century remains something of a shadowy trace.

Shadowy as those wests might be, I would venture that in their writings one could outline a developed, alternative, geocultural imaginary, one that puts female-centered, and often nonwhite-centered, western space at the heart of the western drama. Female sexuality preoccupies these writers; race relations and the relationship of both sexuality and race to nationalism preoccupy them, too. As in most western narratives, representations of nature appear often and prominently. To call this group of writers an alternative tradition is not to imply, however, that they share a regional, political, gendered, or nationalist sensibility. They are quite at odds with each other on most important topics, and their differences prefigure many of the issues that divided the civil rights movement from early feminism and which continue to characterize some of the tensions within the new female regionalist movement today.

I mention this group of writers to highlight the immediate literary "foremothers" of the new western regionalists who emerge in the 1970s and thus to acknowledge, even if only briefly, midcentury female literary history. It is just as important, though, to distinguish between the two groups. They belong, finally, to different historical moments, and they are motivated by different social and aesthetic phenomena. In the final analysis, this earlier female literary tradition, in my view, does not establish the dynamic and enabling contexts that the civil rights movements, second-wave feminism, and postmodernism have provided for women regionalists of the last twenty-five years.

The new regionalists, like most 60s and 70s radicals, are their own breed. Theirs is a literary movement inspired by unprecedented social, demographic, and economic change in western states.[28] Many factors come together to produce this movement: the emergence of the alternative publishing industry headquartered in the West;[29] the consolidation of the cultural wings of the civil rights, women's, and environmental movements; the grassroots, anti-imperialist/anti-intervention activism of the 1970–80s; the new western history; and finally, criticism of western literature itself. Steinbeck's Nobel Prize marks a new beginning in western literary history, for he is the first to receive canonical recognition of this international stature. Moreover, Steinbeck's acclaim comes at precisely the historic moment when western criticism constitutes itself as an identifiable field of literary studies. The Western Literature Association (WLA) is founded in 1965, as is the association-sponsored journal *Western American Literature.* Thereafter, a formally incorporated body of critics takes it upon themselves to define, evaluate, and promote western literature. To them it seems a happy historical accident that a new regional movement is taking shape just as critics position themselves to participate in it.

Though the female side of the new regionalism is usually thought to have begun in the mid-1980s—with the appearance of many texts published by big, northeastern commercial houses and written by white women writers, in particular—it actually originates earlier, in the early 1970s. In these years a range of literary magazines regularly publish work by Chicano/as, Native Americans, and Asian Americans—*Revista Chicano-Riqueña, El Grito, Dacotah Territory,* the *Greenfield Review Press, Painted Bride Quarterly, Contact II.*[30] In these small and quirky publications, many of the now well-known works of poets like Lorna Dee Cervantes, Bernice Zamora, Leslie Marmon Silko, and Janet Campbell Hale initially surface. By the mid-1970s, disgruntled with the male bias of their brothers-in-the-cause and empowered by the "crossover" success of Maxine Hong Kingston and Leslie Marmon Silko—writers whose works are fabulously well received by the northeastern reviewing corps—western women of color increasingly establish literary ventures that feature their own works on their own terms and promote those of other feminist women. Cervantes publishes the first issue of her magazine *Mango* in 1976. Other magazines increasingly committed to feminist perspectives include *Maize* (1977–83), *Bamboo Ridge* (1978–present), *Sun Tracks* (1971–present). By 1981, *Third Woman* appears, devoted specifically to literatures of women of color, especially lesbians. The connection to the regional west is prominent throughout all of these magazines, though by no means do their writers produce conventional western narratives; many do not even accept the legitimacy of the geopolitical boundaries that define today's western states. The commercial boom that follows in the 1980s consolidates the careers of many other nonwhite writers, including Sandra Cisneros and Louise Erdrich. It is in these later years that white women writers such as Barbara Kingsolver, Teresa Jordan, Mary Clearman Blew, Gretel Ehrlich, Terry Tempest Williams, and Judith Freeman begin to be highly visible.

For the new female regionalists, the battle between modernist and realist pathos—an enormous underlying anxiety of many male literary westerns before the 1970s—will be less relevant than coming to terms with the postmodern. Raised in the years when most of the West's people live in urban spaces, this generation often grew up not in the western wild but in contemporary cities. Neither do they see the West as a culturally innocent symbolic landscape, one that guards against urban decay and degeneracy. Growing up in the heat and aftermath of the various social justice movements of the 1960s and 1970s, when the "military industrial complex" becomes a common target of derision for young liberals and the Vietnam War is viewed as another example of American imperial arrogance, these women feel less inclined than their western male predecessors to see any place in America— the West or otherwise—as the First World's last democratic stand.

The Geographical Imaginations of Civil Rights Literatures

Having begun this quick literary history of the new female regionalism in somewhat conventional conceptual terms, let me step back to meditate on the kinds of spatial histories at work in the narration of this cultural evolution. I want to focus on how spatialized cultural logics are implicated in what ultimately constitutes a "new West." We might begin from any number of directions, but for the sake of dramatic contrast, let's notice what or who is generally *not* present in the emerging alternative geocultural imaginary I've sketched above: African American writers. This nonpresence is conspicuous because the Black Arts Movement is the most visible and, initially, most productive of the alternative arts movements.[31] It authorizes writers/activists to write *not* for white audiences or highbrow cultural approval but for "their own." It sets the political stage, establishes the radical performative parameters that shape the Chicano/a cultural renaissance and, to a lesser but nonetheless appreciable degree, Native American and later Asian American cultural renaissances.

What I want to emphasize is that the various histories associated with different wings of the civil rights movements, are, again, histories of spaces, though they are not usually argued in self-consciously spatialist terms. As the Black Arts Movement moved into universities and became, in the 1970s, Black Studies, black literary history was, until recently (and then, unevenly) associated principally with New York City, Chicago, Philadelphia, and parts of the South.[32] Even if California universities are important sites for the establishment of Black Studies programs,[33] black geographic imaginaries—as scholars chart and represent them—are preoccupied primarily with North/ South historical conflicts, migration patterns, regional history, politics, and culture. This is not to say that, as the postmodern period develops, recognition is completely lacking for California writers like Ishmael Reed, Al Young, Ernest Gaines, Sherley Anne Williams, or, to a lesser extent, Wanda Coleman. But overall, African American geographical imaginaries tend to rehearse and be enabled by narratives tied to slavery and emancipation and to cultural forms like jazz and blues, all of which in spatial terms assume predominantly southern/northern shapes. The post–Civil War struggle for black recovery, education, community building, and racial respect continues to be facilitated by this same North/South guiding spatial design too. That spatial imaginary expresses most powerfully the suffering, injustice, and disabling legacy of slavery. Deploying it keeps the history of slavery always in sight, always narrativized, a real accomplishment in a culture that so often claims racism is a thing of the past.

By contrast, the spatial terrain most enabling of the emerging racial identities and histories of Chicano/as, Asian Americans, and Native Americans will be that of the West. In terms of its origins in the late 1960s to early 1970s, Chicano/a literature quite definitively associates its "racial soul," its principal cultural and political identity, with spaces that fall within today's American Southwest. In efforts to build racial solidarity among Mexican American workers, students, and citizens at large, early Chicano/a activists and artists nurtured Chicano/as' feeling for, and claim upon, southwestern spaces—spaces that directly corresponded to lands conquered by the United States in the Mexican-American War of 1846. In the Chicano/a geographic imaginary, this space was renamed "Aztlán," and it represented the mythic homeland of the Aztec peoples, through whom early Chicano/a cultural nationalists located a usable Mexican American past.[34] As a radical, anti-imperialist, civil rights ideology, the myth of Aztlán challenged U.S. political legitimacy in the Southwest. It symbolically "took back" lands wrongfully seized while imaginatively repopulating them with a new, working-class, mestizo/a citizenry. At the same time, the cultural nationalism of the Chicano/a spatial field enabled Mexican Americans to write themselves more visibly onto western American spaces, and through those, onto the terrain of the nation.

Quite alert to the fact that black/white racial—and *spatial*—paradigms did not adequately explain the particularities of their own racial histories, Chicano/as have grounded their own political visibility in distinctly *southwestern* spatial terms. In the late 1980s, even as Chicano/a cultural criticism and literary production have moved away from a founding reliance on the geographic imaginary of Aztlán and toward a broader, transnationalist spatial field, the dominant Chicano/a critical project has retained very spa-tialized conceptual strategies to define Chicano/a politics, critical practice, and a hybridized sense of racial identity and history. Nowhere today is the language of "borderlands"—or, to use Jose David Saldívar's more recent language of "topospatiality"—more central to the theoretical foundations and sense of racial particularity than in recent Chicano/a cultural studies texts.[35]

The cultural movements accompanying both American Indian and Asian American civil rights agitation also forwarded group political identity by tying histories of racial oppression to specifically western spaces. The major writers of the early civil rights period—whether N. Scott Momaday, Frank Chin, Leslie Marmon Silko, or Maxine Hong Kingston—wrote themselves and their respective racial communities into western history by re-emplotting western spaces from very nonwestern points of view. At the same time they put places like San Francisco's Chinatown or the tribal reservations of New Mexico on the cultural map of the nation in quite *western* terms too. Because of the perception that California, in particular, is a kind of clearinghouse for early Asian American immigration and because, until recently, Asian American cultural, political, social, and economic history has been told primarily in conjunction with the larger story of western settlement, a broad link exists between Asian American historical imagination or memory and western spatial fields.[36] Although Asian American historiography and criticism have moved to acknowledge and investigate Asian American presence all over the nation, and to make sense of the profound differences between Asian American ethnicities and immigration histories,[37] western geographic imaginaries nonetheless still "center" the field. The major institutional presence and resources of Asian American Studies remain overwhelmingly in California and, given the importance of the Pacific Rim to both California's and the nation's postmodern economic development, it is likely to remain so centered for years to come.[38]

The logic motivating the investment of African American literatures in north/south spatial fields can be extended, except with a western twist, to American Indian cultural production. Nowhere is the history of Indian racial genocide more effectively invoked than over western terrain. Nowhere, further, is the fact of an *un*vanished people more obvious. But if western spatiality lends itself to demonstrating racial decimation and dispossession, it nonetheless simultaneously works to appropriate that atrocity—to both shoot down the Indian, as it were, while crying over his (gendered language intended) tragic death. Therefore the relationship of American Indian cultural production to western spatiality is one of the most complex examples of spatial politics in western cultural history. As has been well established, European settlers lived out a long, ambivalent love affair with Indian peoples and their perceived premodern primitivism.[39] Consequently, to a far greater extent than other nonwhite peoples, American Indians have always figured largely in western literary traditions (both popular and high), in visual narratives (whether paintings, commercial sketches, or twentieth-century film, television, and advertising), in western history, politics, environmentalism, and so on. In fact, "Indian" spatialities—for instance, the allegedly more harmonious or democratic relationships between human and nonhuman nature—infuse much of what is most seductive and mystical about the dominant geographical imagination: in a word, its "authenticity."[40] Western spatiality is accordingly "written over," extremely laden with both an admission of and a silencing of the historical fact of *multicontinental* genocide. American Indian writers thus navigate an enormously toxic, even if at times licensing, spatial field.

The point herein is that the various literary traditions that come out of civil rights agitation are already conceived in spatial dimensions, by spatial logics. These logics map onto various emerging literary traditions a penchant for or rejection of certain spatial affinities. Moreover, these affinities "match up" with the nuts-and-bolts development of the alternative publishing industry in the late 1960s and early 1970s. Thus, for example, by 1972, a small press like *Quinto Sol*, out of Berkeley, has published the majority of major, early novels by male Chicano writers (i.e., what are now considered "classics" by Tomás Rivera, Oscar Hinojosa, Rudolfo Anaya, and José Montoya). Straight Arrow Press, out of San Francisco, publishes Oscar Zeta Acosta. Much of the early work by Chicanas, in the mid-1970s, comes out of *Revista Chicana-Riqueña*, initially founded in Indiana by scholar Nicolás Kanellos but later moved to Houston, Texas. By the early 1980s, Houston has become home to the major Chicano/a publishing house in the nation, Arte Público Press, also founded by Kanellos.[41] It will be Arte Público Press that first prints and then funnels Mexican American "crossover" books (like Sandra Cisneros's *House on Mango Street*) to big, northeastern commercial houses. Arte Público Press will also sponsor "Recovering the U.S. Hispanic Literary Past," a major cultural project that, when it is completed in 1999, promises to fundamentally remap the nineteenth-century American literary landscape.

No analogous "central press" exists for Asian American or Native American writing. Those literatures are published in a huge number of highly specialized, short-lived, literary magazines as well as in newly formed and established journals connected to western universities.[42] Asian American writing appears in venues like *Bamboo Ridge* (Honolulu), *Counterpoint* (Asian Studies Center, University of California, Los Angeles [UCLA]), and *Amerasia Journal* (UCLA) but also in multiracial forums like Lorna Dee Cervantes's *Mango* (San Jose, California).[43] Native American writing appears regularly in *Blue Cloud Quarterly* (Marvin, South Dakota), *Spawning the Medicine River* (Institute of Indian Arts, Santa Fe, New Mexico), *Wanbli Ho* (Sinte Gleska College in Mission, South Dakota), *Sun Tracks: An American Indian Literary Series* (University of Arizona, Tucson), *Native American Series* (American Indian Center, UCLA).[44] In addition, western presses that regularly publish all kinds of work by all kinds of writers include *New Mexico Quarterly* (Albuquerque), *Tooth of Time Books*, *Duck Down Press* (also known as *Scree*, Fallon, Nevada), *Frontiers* (Boulder, Colorado), *Bloodroot* (Grand Fork, North Dakota), *MELUS: Society for the Study of Multi-Ethnic Literatures* (Los Angeles), *Yardbird Reader*, published by Ishmael Reed (Berkeley), *Calyx: A Journal of Art and Literature by Women* (Corvallis, Oregon), *Rocky Mountain Review* (Durango, Colorado), *Maize* (San Diego), *Wassaja: The Indian Historian* (San Francisco), *Grito del Sol* (first called *El Grito*, Berkeley), *Sinister Wisdom* (Lincoln, Nebraska), *Western Black Studies* (Pullman, Washington), and *Western American Literature* (Logan, Utah). This list does not include university presses (especially Arizona, Nebraska, and New Mexico) that publish book-length manuscripts. And the above survey does not intend to erase the many important alternative publishing venues that come out of nonwestern states, like the *Greenfield Review Press* (New York) or *Painted Bride Quarterly* (Philadelphia). Rather, I have wished to advance the idea that for many civil rights–inspired, literary hopefuls of the late 1960s to mid-1970s, "western spaces" seemed, in more ways than one or two, a "natural," even heartening, place to carry on a literary life.

The Stegnerian Spatial Field and (New) Western Literary History

The various spatial fields I have outlined above are not the only fields that will ultimately collide and recombine to produce the new female regionalism. The geographic imaginations associated with western literary history as well as feminist spatialities—both of which are undergoing enormous change in the early 1970s—will have a crucial bearing on what becomes the new regionalism. It is to each of these influences that I turn now.

The first distinction to draw is between the geographic imagination charted by western literary history and that of the dominant geographic imaginary I outlined at this chapter's beginning. Western literary history—meaning major literary texts written mainly by white men but also the major works of literary criticism—positions itself most often as an interventionary discourse into what it terms the mythic west.[45] While I concur with this interventionist claim, I also take a more critical view. As the opening Steinbeck story illustrates, western literary spokesmen can, when they choose, invoke the enabling social logic of the dominant cultural imaginary. In other words, they can "pass." Although in later chapters I will speak to the ways that feminist and nonwhite spatialities manipulate dominant geocultural biases to their own political ends, I want to begin from a less complicated, argumentative starting point: that dominant western literary history exercises spatial privileges and that, given its relative implication in mythic geocultural imaginations, it often disables, even as it simultaneously enables, some of the very spatialities that figure most significantly in the new female regionalism.

To illustrate some of the complexities of the geographical imagination of western literary history, let us consult one of the most powerful cultural legacies in place in the early 1970s—that generated by Wallace Stegner. I wish here to consider Stegner less as a writer than as a critic and an overall advocate of western literature. In a field whose principal assumptions often go unarticulated, Stegner is one of the few comprehensive theorists of western regional culture and literature. His various critical writings from 1963 to 1993 mapped and remapped western literary culture to make sense of the various other spatial imaginations coming to the fore in the postmodern period.[46] Often called the "grandfather of western literature," Stegner, in his twenty-five-year tenure as the director of Stanford's creative writing program, oversaw the early careers of many now well-known writers, among them Larry McMurtry, Ken Kesey, Tillie Olsen, Robert Stone, Wendell Berry, Edward Abbey, Tom McGuane, Harriet Doerr, N. Scott Momaday, Max Brand, Ernest Gaines, and Philip Levine. He has also been acknowledged as paradigmatic by writers as diverse as Maxine Hong Kingston, Ivan Doig, and, in a very critical way, by Elizabeth Cook-Lynn.[47] On questions of the environment, western culture, gender relations, and, to a lesser extent, race issues, Stegner mapped the broader spatial field of "the West" more influentially than has any other single individual in contemporary times. So, for the sake of discussion, let us take Stegner's West as representative of western literary history's dominant spatial field at its most dynamic and sophisticated.

In "History, Myth and the Western Writer" (1967), Stegner set out his general thesis. Following in the footsteps of historian Walter Prescott Webb, Stegner mapped the West in topographic (as opposed to imaginative) terms: it started west of the 100th meridian, where consistently dry land was found, and ended at the Pacific Ocean. Also following Webb, Stegner argued that dryness, aridity, was the region's unifying characteristic, that all human cultural adaptations proceeded from this physical fact. Aside from its dryness, Stegner defined the West as dizzyingly heterogeneous. It was better conceived, he argued, as a region of subregions, whose different economies, development histories, topographies, climates, and particular ethnic mixes of peoples combined into a whole defined not by similarity but by diversity. That diversity made for a halting and varied regional literary development. Without the churches, schools, cultural institutions, and local governments in which and through which writers might define themselves, Stegner reasoned, western writing grew slowly, piecemeal. And without a single pathos or dialect that would characterize it, western subjectivity showed a more chaotic organization than did other regional literatures.

And yet Stegner nonetheless felt that similarities existed between literary westerns. Consulting a range of narratives written from 1880 to 1960 (by Vardis Fisher, Mary Austin, Conrad Richter, Willa Cather, O. E. Rolvaag, Walter Van Tilburg Clark, Frank Waters, Eugene Manlove Rhodes, and A. B. Guthrie), Stegner characterized them as displaying a tendency toward realist narrative, a nostalgic tone, a belief in heroic virtue, a focus on the romantic frontier past rather than the urban present, a marked attention to western landscape, and a recurrent concern for gendered conflict, represented via what Stegner calls the "roving man" and "civilizing woman." Above all, Stegner believed, western narratives were hopeful. In them lived the founding promise of westward expansion: the West was America's "geography of hope," the place where American dreams came true. The West represented the last stand of American liberal humanism.

In sum, the initial parameters through which Stegner thought about western literature were conscientiously historical in an era that valued New Critical, "text as all" practice. In a field in which no "totalizing theory" existed, Stegner's was a welcome metanarrative. Moreover, Stegner's observation that western narratives were more interested in the frontier past than in the present was not only astute but politically strategic, for it authorized him to revise and renarrativize what constituted "western" itself. By linking his definition of western regional culture to the arid lands west of the 98th meridian, Stegner brought a new historicism and, with it, a new dignity to western criticism. For Stegner's "real" West represented a quantum leap away from mythic constructions of the West that chronically connected western culture to a lost nineteenth-century frontier and to popular literary genres, especially formula fiction and Hollywood Westerns.[48] Critics could thereafter formulate a meaningful regional literary history through a realist-based aesthetic and make a convincing case for the inclusion of many serious western writers who were not finding their way into the American literary canon, writers like Vardis Fisher, Walter Van Tilburg Clark, A. B. Guthrie, Harvey Fergusson, and, implicitly, Stegner himself. These writers were not transplanted easterners, whose narratives were shaped for an eastern book-buying market—not the likes of Owen Wister, James Fenimore Cooper, Mark Twain, or Bret Harte. They were "real western writers," born and bred in the West, and what they had to say about the place, Stegner believed, deserved a hearing.

Moreover, as I argued at this chapter's beginning, because it was distinctly antimodern, Stegner's "real West" and "real western writer" contested the prevailing ethos of the nation's northeastern cultural vanguard. In Stegner's judgment, modernist aestheticism made American literature hypersexual, angst-ridden, nihilistic. He believed the modernist movement assaulted national identity in ways that were both unwestern and un-American.[49] Here, as the *Los Angeles Times* reviewer illustrates, Stegner found a wide audience among western male intellectuals, who resented the monopoly that northeastern opinion exerted over national aesthetics and whose regional identity and outdoorsy and rural upbringings made a modernist worldview distant.

Stegner's realist project could also contribute to an overall advocacy of ecological awareness. A lifelong environmentalist, Stegner took advantage of the fact that westerners, given their long history of dialoguing with the federal government about land disputes, were closer than most Americans to national debates about environmental issues. Stegner's usable western past protested the idea that the West was a land of inexhaustible abundance, where Captains of Industry or other profit-bent individuals could exploit natural resources without thinking of environmental impact. Stegner thus shaped the discourse of western public history so that its lessons encouraged environmental conservation over maximum use, stable and settled economies over boom-and-bust cycles, a sensitivity to subregional ecological variety, and an all-around policy direction that promoted conservation of western natural resources and wilderness. As a concerned and committed citizen, Stegner aimed to wrestle control of the West away from the mythmakers and profit takers. His deployment of a realist historical narrative in the service of a liberal political vision anticipated the new western history (especially its environmental wing) by at least twenty years.

To the extent that western literary history at large claimed the above political commitments and logics, it deployed "high" literary geographic imaginations to contest those of the dominant geocultural imaginary. Indeed it is precisely this sense that western literature performs *liberal* cultural works—a sense consolidated in the person and career of Wallace Stegner—that creates an interest in the West as a literary "home" for many of the young, white male regionalists writing from the early 1960s to the late 1970s. By adopting and adapting a Stegnerian map of western concerns, writers like Ken Kesey, Larry McMurtry, Gary Snyder, Richard Hugo, John Nichols, Gerald Haslam, Edward Abbey, and Ivan Doig soon produce novels, memoirs, poems, and stories that, notwithstanding profound differences, share some very basic political and regional commitments. Which is to say that the Stegnerian spatial field enables many of these writers to conceive of themselves *as* writers, enables them to write out their own relationships to western history, mythology, gender relations, the environment, and, significantly, to national literary culture at large.

If the spatial field claimed by western literary history, and now, by some of the young new regionalists, is environmentally sensitive, sometimes anticapitalist, and nearly always critical of the pioneer legacy, it is also a spatial field that fails to locate people of color anywhere at all in the western drama. It is obtuse, symptomatically so, to the issues that in the mid-1960s intensely preoccupied civil rights–inspired imaginaries. In spite of characterizing western history, in 1967, through a kind of "diversity model," Stegner nevertheless saw the nineteenth-century west as "an unrecorded, history-less, art-less new country."[50] In 1963, he would call the West "empty land" with an "imported population."[51] Throughout the 1960s it did not occur to Stegner that indigenous peoples and nonwhite immigrants of the nineteenth or twentieth century prospered amidst their own artistic, religious, sociopolitical, and cultural traditions. Nor did it occur to him that the body of writers from whom he formed generalizations about regional literature did not include any of those people, who were, after all, also writing and publishing between 1880 and 1960—say, Zitkala-Sa, Mourning Dove, Black Elk, D'Arcy McNickle, Josephina Niggli, Edith Eaton (Sui Sin Far), Hisaye Yamamoto, or Carlos Bulosan.

Stegner brought a very Anglo-centered bias to his reading of regional culture at precisely the historical moment when the civil rights movements called such bias into question. Thus, at the moment when the new regionalism is taking initial shape in identity, pathos, form, and the like, the dominant spatial field guiding this new literary school is one to which writers of color are generally averse, especially given that the various geopolitical imaginations of different civil rights movements offer such compelling alternatives. Writers of color will have every reason not only to mistrust this spatial field and see in it a kind of segregated preserve of white supremacy but also to conclude that western traditions are synonymous with white spatial prerogatives. In other words, to many writers of color (particularly the men), the geographic imagination of western literary history will be no different from that of the dominant geocultural imaginary.

Now, if writers of color are wary of white western spatialities, a contrary phenomenon is underway when it comes to the attractiveness of "other" spatial imaginations to young *white* writers. The new spatial fields generated by civil rights literatures channel powerful imaginative and political energies into what are, up to then, primarily white-imagined cultural geographies. The assorted new wests found in the works of writers of color offer novel lessons in alternative cartography—and the host of aesthetic and political possibilities such cartographies imply. This lesson in mapmaking supplements the lesson available to them in the legacy of Wallace Stegner. Thus, texts by writers like N. Scott Momaday, Tomás Rivera, Rudolfo Anaya, Frank Chin, and James Welch—even those of political bête noire Richard Rodriguez—become as much backbones for the new regionalist spatial consciousness as are the works and legacies embodied in the man (gendered language intended) of Wallace Stegner.[52]

By the late 1970s and into the late 1980s one can observe those alternative geographic imaginations directly enabling even Wallace Stegner's evolving evaluation of the current literary scene. By the late 1970s, Stegner's thinking about race would become more self-conscious. In 1979 interviews, Stegner reflects somewhat breezily that he is "vulnerable and ill informed on this Indian business."[53] He judges James Welch and N. Scott Momaday as "thoroughly good writers" who have "their hour in the sun coming."[54] By 1986, Stegner delivers a lecture series in which he begins to develop the differences between Anglo American, New Mexican, Asian American, and Native American histories and contemporary communities.[55] In that lecture series, Stegner also disclaims his cherished ideal of the West as a geography of hope.

Let us pause here to reflect on how much of a paradigm shift a disavowal of the "hope trope" is for all of the spatial fields that ultimately help generate the new female regionalism, for before the late 1980s, the "hope trope" is the logic underlying western criticism's theoretical predispositions, its anti-modernism, its white-centeredness, and its ambivalence about feminism. For most of his life, Stegner makes a case for the West as a cultural landscape upon which the nation writes its most American dreams. He calls the West "the youngest and freshest of America's regions, magnificently endowed and with the chance to become something unprecedented and unmatched in the world."[56] Western wilderness is "the geography of hope";[57] the western writer is innocent, optimistic;[58] the West as a region is "hope's native home."[59] The recurrent theme here, and Stegner implies this too, is "incorrigible hope." That hope was rallied over Stegner's own career against such varied threats as environmental ruin, cultural breakdown, and human vulnerability. In the *Los Angeles Times* book reviewer's arguments that open this chapter, one observes precisely this move to name the West as *the* spatial container of American optimism.

The "hope trope" indeed represents the major unspoken philosophical and epistemological commitments of western criticism, and as such, it has proven dear *and* strategic. Many western critics deploy the hope trope throughout the 1980s and into the 1990s to guard against poststructural theories of language and knowledge and the unsettling prospect of fractured postmodern life. In an era increasingly given over to poststructuralist thought, the hope trope is the theoretical premise upon which a reinvigorated humanist critical ontology can be built, one that reasserts the primacy of liberal humanism.[60] Critic Martin Bucco, as if offering a parting commentary on the last page of the landmark *Literary History of the American West*, remarks:

> Compared to the terrifying rhetoric of postmodern theory, western criticism still offers us the luxury of humane discourse.[61]

Bucco equates "western" with what is "humane." In *New Ground*, a book about western literature and the American canon, critic A. Carl Bredahl argues that western narratives offer a "corrective and balance to post modern despair."[62] Howard P. Simonson in *Beyond the Frontier* sees "placedness" as bestowing the security of belonging, human connection, social purpose—desires that signal a battle with what he sees as the disconnection and social chaos associated with postmodernism. And in several biographies of Stegner published since his death in 1992, biographers make use of languages of hope to narrativize Stegner's life, works, and Stegner's West.[63]

To be sure, the Stegnerian field can be mobilized toward liberal, humanist political ends. Stegner was a diehard humanist, himself, a believer in the knowability and holism of the individual, the efficacy of individual action, the reliability of meaning, the transcendentalism of art, the progressive nature of history. And yet it is also true that at his life's end, Stegner relented. Chastened by a lifetime of witnessing boom-and-bust economic cycles play themselves out always at the expense of environmental wisdom, chastened too by the knowledge that the West's history of settlement by conquest necessarily meant that one man's geography of hope was another man's geography of the *end* of hope, Stegner finally disclaimed the West as America's salvation. He became "more cautious," "more pessimistic," even declaring:

> the West is no more the Eden that I once thought it than the Garden of the World that the boosters and engineers tried to make it . . . neither nostalgia nor boosterism can any longer make a case for it as the geography of hope.[64]

No longer was the West a national Eden, the place where America's most beloved dreams came true. By the 1990s, Stegner had fundamentally rethought western literary history. Its speakers were multiracial. Its landscapes were often urban. He talked about western culture not as heroic but as "a cultural battlefield." Western character, he surmised, looking as much backward as directly into the eye of the postmodern storm, was more about "desire" (his word) than the satisfaction of desire.[65]

If by the 1990s western literary history has begun to be reformulated to account for racial difference, the same gains cannot truly and finally be claimed for gendered difference. The reasons for this are complex and will require some unpacking. Again, the spatial field's assumptions *at their best* are revealed in the legacy of Stegner; the spatial field's shortcomings are revealed there too. I have written about Stegner and "the woman question" elsewhere and wish to make a far more abbreviated argument here.[66] It begins from an acknowledgment that most of western criticism regards Stegner, more than do I, as "good on women's issues."[67] In western literary history, as Stegner mapped it, gendered conflict recurred as a defining western theme. He imagined women, in his own novels, not as symbols of entrapment but as complex characters with legitimate motivations and understandable needs; he imagined men as desirous of both western adventure and also domestic fulfillment. He readily grants, moreover, that Annette Kolodny "corrected a certain imbalance in Henry [Nash] Smith," as well as that the frontier often meant different things to women versus men.[68] If one takes together all of Stegner's writings on the literary west, one finds that western critical landscapes are consistently peopled by women writers, including Mary Austin, Mari Sandoz, Willa Cather, Ina Coolbrith, Virginia Sorenson, Dorothy Johnson, Maxine Whipple, Harriet Doerr, Joan Didion, Leslie Silko, Gretel Ehrlich, Annick Smith, Louise Erdrich, Linda Hogan, and Maxine Hong Kingston. On the level of simple acknowledgment that women writers indeed existed and influenced the spatial field, Stegner exceeds by every measure any other male rendering of the literary past. For this last reason, the Stegnerian spatial field *must* be counted as part of western feminist geographic imaginations. In a Stegnerian spatial field, women are historical subjects with integrity, legitimate needs and desires, agency. Like men, they influence the course of history. They matter.

Yet Stegner was not a feminist, and I conclude this because Stegner did not hold the fundamental feminist conviction that women are oppressed. Over the thirty-year period that witnessed the development of contemporary feminism, Stegner's own views on "women's issues" appear not to have changed very much; certainly he did not refigure the entire history of the West to accommodate the changes wrought by the *women's* movement. What truly changed, in my view, was his appreciation of just how self-centered masculine narratives can be in a male-dominated world (this is the pained burden of "Letter, Much too Late," to his long-gone mother). But even until his death, Stegner's sensibility about "the woman question" remained tied to Victorian gendered ideals, guided by a sense of male honor, virtue, and duty. He was reluctant to admit that society does not value women as much as it does men. Thus, while Stegner conceded that western literary criticism at times marginalized female literary history, he believed that women writers' most serious problems arose from *regional* differences, not gendered difference.[69] He cautioned feminist scholars not to make more of gender issues, as he put it, than was "really there."[70] Stegner's thinking about women's exclusion from western literary history was similar to his thinking about western writers' exclusion from American literary history. In both cases, he judged marginalization to be not the result of "real prejudice" (as he put it) but rather "cultural blindness" and cultural difference. And yet, Stegner could not help but notice that regional difference often *did* amount to regional domination. Indeed, this very point is absolutely central to his sense of the problems faced by western writers. He knew, too, that when it came to racial difference, that difference added up to a perception of inferiority.[71]

Why did Stegner fail to bring to gender relations the same dynamic political understanding he brought to race relations? As a man who held himself and other men responsible for their actions, who required of men that they provide for their families, respect their wives, take time for their children, not drink away the family supper money—as that kind of man— Stegner believed that other men, too, were honorable. He was precisely the kind of "manly man," an upholder of Victorian male virtue, that historian Gail Bederman has described at articulate length in *Manliness and Civilization*. That is, Stegner believed about gender relations what he knew was untrue for race relations: that good will and deeds between individual men and women made for harmony and mutual admiration.

Stegner could be generous about women's exclusion from western literary history because he did not, as do feminists, consider exclusion to be facilitated by broader, male-dominated cultural traditions and sociopolitical affairs. For Stegner, gender relations were an individual matter—something to be worked out privately, between man and woman. A good Stegnerian man (like many in his novels) would not violate a woman's sacred trust. The problem with an "honor women" response to "the woman question," however, is obvious enough. It permits no space for thinking about misogyny, male privilege, a restrictive, gendered division of labor, or the institutional structures (law, education, religion, family, culture) that house and enforce gender injustice.

The final and crucial point is that Stegner could evaluate gendered relations in Victorian terms because it worked toward other ends that were of enormous importance to him. The failure to theorize women's oppression *as oppression* maintains gender as one site upon which optimistic humanism is based.[72] People of "good will," as aware as they are that the West was settled by conquest, do not—indeed, cannot—sentimentalize race relations. American history has proven definitively that relations between individual men of different races cannot sustain the humanist ideal of brotherhood between all men. But by not conferring that same legitimacy upon *gender* oppression, the Stegnerian spatial field divests gender of its ability to negotiate power differences. Relations between men and women thus remain a site where the subject at the heart of the liberal humanist ideal—the civic-minded, personally responsible, individually ethical man (of any race)—can be his best self. And, if legitimate gendered difference generates inequities, one can depend on the character of the Stegnerian ethical man not to take advantage of the situation. Significantly, though Stegner disavowed the "hope trope" on racial and environmental terms, he kept it alive on gendered terms. This ambivalence about disclaiming forever the hope narrative and disclaiming as well the false notion that the goodwill of individual men can overturn the injustices women so often face *as women*, haunts the Stegnerian spatial field. *Women* are not implicit soldiers, or casualties, in Stegner's revised sense of the West as a "cultural battlefield."

In conclusion, if many of the male writers of this period can look to civil rights imaginaries and/or to the Stegnerian field for inspiration in their own remappings of western space, *women*, across race, will have a much harder time looking to those imaginaries when it comes to remapping the masculinist biases that pervade western spaces, including counterwestern spaces. If the Stegnerian field represents women, writes them as agents into cultural history, it also is fundamentally compromised when it comes to basic feminist questions. Compromised too are most of the geocultural imaginaries of civil rights literatures. Exceptions to this claim exist, the most notable being that of American Indian literary history. There, in female-centered origins tales and oral traditions, feminist writers have often situated a feminist-enabling contemporary imaginary.[73] But Chicanas and Asian American feminists, writers and critics both, have been far less affirmed by the origins stories that center those respective spatial fields. How, for example, does the alternative geographic imagination of Aztlán enable the articulation of gendered inequality?[74] Or, why the need for Maxine Hong Kingston's explicitly "*woman* warrior"?[75] Because feminist alliances with, and also critiques of, various civil rights cultural projects are well-known, I will not take this occasion to rehearse that ground. Rather the point is to stress that in their efforts to articulate themselves not only as people of color but as *female* people of color, Chicanas, Asian Americans, and sometimes Native American feminists link themselves finally not only to civil rights geographical imaginations but also to other spatial traditions, other spatial fields. And these fields quite definitively are *not* associated with the American West.

Two cultural imaginaries that lend themselves readily to the feminist spatialities so often observable in the new female regionalism—those of second-wave feminism, and finally, of postmodernism—pose (again) problems but also opportunities for the expression and development of western feminism. Increasingly, it will be the inability of *any* single spatial tradition to meet western women writers' simultaneous multiple needs, it will be the impossibility of, once and for all, laying claim to racial over gendered over sexual over class over regional identity that moves women writers ever more toward an embrace of the spaces and places of postmodernity.

Feminist Spatialities

Though second-wave feminism is an undeniable, obviously enabling, social and imaginative force behind the new female regionalism, I want to take a different initial approach here. I want to argue, first, that feminist thought as it was evolving in the mid-1960s presented its own set of spatial problems or biases for western feminist literary production. When one reads movement participants' memoirs or consults textbook documentary histories, one finds that the kinds of records assembled, the organizations studied, and the biographies most often narrativized are overwhelmingly those of northeastern intellectuals—whether black or white, liberal, socialist, or radical.[76] I myself am considerably invested in recognizing and promoting the political visions contained in this history and in no way wish to deny feminists like Shulamith Firestone, Betty Friedan, Susan Brownmiller, Robin Morgan, Ellen Willis, Jo Freeman, Barbara Smith, Michele Wallace, Eleanor Holmes Norton, or many others their role in constituting contemporary feminist history. I keep alive, in the classroom, the organizational history of women's liberation groups like Cell 16 (Boston), Chicago Women's Liberation Union, The Class Workshop (New York), DC Women's Liberation (Washington, D.C.), The Feminists (New York), The Furies (Washington, D.C.), New York Radical Feminists, New York Radical Women, Westside Group (Chicago), and WITCH (Chicago).[77] Neither would I undervalue the importance, for feminist philosophy and political evolution, of documents like "Bread and Roses," the "Redstockings Manifesto," "The Combahee River Collective Statement," or books like *The Feminine Mystique* or *Sexual Politics.*

Nonetheless, the above political and historical trajectory is hardly representative of the history of *all* of early contemporary American feminism, as is often claimed.[78] Ultimately, quite the opposite is probably truer: that is, that the above trajectory represents the politicized, avant garde exception to the broader rule of feminist conversion through countercultural influence. But more on that momentarily. The point, initially, is that second-wave feminism is conceived nearly wholly through a northeastern spatial field that privileges particularly defined kinds of political endeavors: the writing and circulation of treatises or books (which assumes knowledge of established forms of political advocacy), formation of feminist cells or women's liberation groups (which assumes faith in collective agitation), legal challenges to the State, direct action protest (in the form of demonstrations, street theater, etc.), as well as, of course, the more informal consciousness-raising groups. This spatial field reproduces or calls upon the intellectual and activist legacy of New England–based puritanism and early republicanism, and it echoes in symbolic association with the more radical of America's later movements for social change, including especially trade unionism, socialism, and abolition. All of which is to say that many of the conditions for representing both feminist and political issues grow out of, and are implicated within, existing spatial relationships and the respective political roles those relationships play in national political history.

Nor should we forget, as I argued earlier, that northeastern spatialities are vulnerable to (some) critique of white masculinity—already northeastern spaces have given up white men's sole claim to political enfranchisement and subjectivity, agreeing (problematically, to be sure) to share it with black men. This spatial predisposition is not lost on early 1970s feminists. When feminism takes up questions of difference, its "race talk" and sense of moral imperative about racial justice belongs fairly exclusively to the northern/ southern historical dynamics generated by the Civil War. Thus, even as the northeastern feminist movement expands its geocultural shape southward, and to some degree changes the dominant political landscape of that north/ south imaginary by peopling it with explicitly female and contemporary political issues, the ruling feminist geographical imagination retains its spatial and moral "center" in the northeast.

If taking strategic advantage of the above spatial openings amounts to a political coup for second-wave feminism, that victory comes with its own political bargain. For the result is that northeastern feminism distances itself from alternatively conceived feminist movements—especially those with far less choate political agendas (like cultural feminism), those with agendas not directly interested in women's liberation (like the western counterculture), or those with agendas not conceived through established black/white and north/south radical and spatial histories or civil rights genealogies (like the Asian American movement).[79] Western feminist historians have raised this point about regional bias in rather different terms; in the early 1980s, they insisted that the conceptual apparatus of American women's history pertained most often to northeastern women and that when it came to, for instance, western labor history, the history of western race relations, or the history of the ideology of separate spheres, northeastern biases revealed themselves quite apparently, and counterproductively.[80]

What I would focus our attention on here are the above mentioned "alternative agendas," agendas that often, as I see it, provide the contemporary political touchstones for early political consciousness among *western* women. While cultural feminism (and with it, claims of female moral superiority and close connection to nature) finds support in the northeast in the early 1970s, it garners a much larger audience throughout the West thereafter, particularly as it becomes joined and repeatedly refracted within various kinds of ecofeminist discourses. Countercultural identity and participation—in its many, many manifestations—shows a related developmental "curve" and becomes another crucial proving ground for western feminist formation and consciousness. However, it is a very different kind of proving ground, because unlike cultural feminism, the counterculture is often distinctly masculinist.

To date, though, little scholarly attention has been devoted to either topic. There has been some informal discussion, among scholars who focus on contemporary history, that the roles of cultural feminism and of the counterculture more generally have been understudied and underrepresented in feminist historiography. Indeed, especially since poststructuralism has remade the fundamentals of feminist theory, cultural feminism is out of academic favor so much so that in the late 1990s it enters intellectual debates most often as an example of theoretical and political naïveté.[81] This spatial and historiographical bias, as well as theoretical attitude, is something of an albatross for this study, however. It complicates thinking about western feminism on terms that are not inherently prejudicial.

Whatever one's ultimate judgments about the efficacy of countercultural or cultural feminist politics, it is crucial to remember that "the West," especially the West Coast, enters national politics in the contemporary moment precisely as marker *for* the counterculture. If one wants to teach the counterculture, what sources does one use? Perhaps the documentary film *Berkeley in the 60s*, or Joan Didion's essay "Slouching Towards Bethlehem"? Maybe the musics of Janis Joplin (a Texan turned San Franciscan) or Jimi Hendrix (Seattle-born and raised in Berkeley)? The dominant western geocultural field—given its cultural identity as the nation's dreamscape and its emplotment with radical individualism and shadowy notions of native-inspired mysticism—is "ready" for or receptive to those very kinds of individualistic, inchoate, or politically "immature" impulses that are conventionally associated with countercultural politics. If we view countercultural history in spatial terms, it is little surprise that flower children, hippies, surfers, the Beats, a good part of drug culture, feminist witchery, New Age spiritualism (including American Buddhism), as well as deep ecology and ecofeminism all play out their resistance politics primarily on *western* lands, in western parks (including city parks like San Francisco's Golden Gate), on western waves, within western imaginative geographic domains. What other space within the national imaginary would have been suited to, or could have tolerated, such a cultural task?

But if the West is regularly invoked as symbol of the heart of *national* social convulsion, what about the effects of countercultural movements on *local* western participants? This last question is the far more problematic to answer. Studies of popular culture confess the notorious difficulty of quantifying and analyzing countercultural phenomena.[82] And to date we do not have a series of memoirs by countercultural participants that are somehow comparable to those of radical northeastern feminists, memoirs wherein, say, cultural feminists map out their evolving political identities in western or ecofeminist or some other terms. For glimpses into these issues, one can look to literary production by a few California witches, or to poetry by some of the women on the periphery of the (mainly male) Beat culture, or, on mysticism, to early Chicana or American Indian women's poetry. Some studies have been done of contemporary gay and lesbian communities that shed light on northeastern/western regional difference.[83] And I myself am at work on a memoir focused on female participation in an overwhelmingly male, Southern California surf culture. But observations must remain suggestive and speculative until further studies are done. Certainly we can assume, however, that women did *find and make* feminist content from western countercultural impulses—one sees that process at work in the figure of Janis Joplin, to name just one countercultural icon, whose sexualized persona embodied the idea that raw female passion superseded conventional ideals of feminine beauty.[84] And one sees the often embarrassed outline of, and impact of, countercultural influence upon many of the narratives we will consider in the following chapters.

Female regionalists sense that countercultural politics are judged immature, protoradical, all personal and not political, escapist, and so on, but in order to *have* a story to tell, to find themselves as political beings so they can bring feminist sensibilities to bear on topics important to *them*, they must somehow recover those western-inflected parts of recent feminist history. This is no easy political task, however, because the terms of feminist politicism are set up against them. Still, evidence abounds that this effort motivates many writers, and often. For example, the 1960s drug culture and sexual revolution provide the contexts out of which Joan Didion fashions a rather peculiar feminist protagonist in *Play It as It Lays* (1970); those contexts have everything to do with the spooky, helter-skelter "moral" left behind at story's end. Or there is Maxine Hong Kingston's *Tripmaster Monkey*, a virtual countercultural encyclopedia. Though the center of that text, like the central personas of the counterculture, is a hip, male social critic, Kingston goes to some lengths to knock him at least partly off his pedestal, which gains her space to represent feminist countercultural presence in an otherwise masculinist movement.

Especially when it comes to female regionalists' engagement with environmental issues, cultural feminism has been an indispensably enabling political discourse. Consider Barbara Kingsolver's *Animal Dreams*. Though I am told by those who know her that Kingsolver disavows the label "ecofeminist," aware of its essentialist overtones and its reputation as naïve (does this anxiety about being dismissed as naïve sound familiar?), the feminism of her "new western" stories nonetheless speaks to readers because it relies on valuing female difference and using that difference to create effective environmental politics. Its reception thus intersects clearly with the gender ideologies underwriting cultural feminism. If cultural feminist thought underwrites white ecofeminism, it finds even more complex renderings among nonwhite feminist writers. To forward female-gendered, ethnic and racial politics, many feminists of color deploy representations of female nurturance, creativity, and female proximity to nature. They use cultural feminist discourse, that is, to mark out racial and cultural difference *between* feminists. Thus American Indian feminists recover female-centered tribal mythologies to create a "usable past" for contemporary feminist literary production but also to make the case that the gendered disgruntlements of white women's history cannot be imposed thoughtlessly upon Native history.[85] Chicana feminism, in its investments in figures like *la curandera* but also in its attention to rhetorics of female self-help steeped in mestiza mysticism, shows that it too wants to make, via gendered difference, points about racial difference and about the specificities of Mexican American cultural practice.

Now, having said all of the above, having argued that northeastern spatialities map onto dominant feminist thought a hostility or condescension to countercultural politics and cultural feminism, let me move on to concede that when the day is over and western women writers need feminist political friends, it is to northeastern spatial fields, including that of dominant feminism, that they most often turn. They do so, first, because the fact of female oppression is at the center of northeastern feminist spatialities. Where else, in all of the foregoing geographic imaginations, will one get a full hearing on women's issues? Moreover, by the mid-1970s, northeastern feminism commands (relative) clout. Not only does it produce strong, articulate, visible feminist leaders who stand at the head of an identifiable movement, but it rallies behind movement causes some very influential governmental agencies and high-cultural gatekeepers.[86] Thus, though an unflinchingly feminist book like Maxine Hong Kingston's *Woman Warrior* (1976) might be derisively panned by a prominent California intellectual like Frank Chin, Kingston nonetheless soars into the national limelight when the northeastern reviewing corps pronounces her brilliant, dazzling. As the *Nation's* reviewer John Leonard puts it, hers is a "poem turned into a [feminist] sword."[87]

Further compelling women writers' embrace of northeastern feminism are the *spatial* insights that imaginary produces, insights that become quite relevant to and participant in efforts by female radicals to remap the masculinism of western spaces. I am speaking here of early feminist critiques of the false dichotomy between public and private spheres or, indeed, of the many groundbreaking feminist analyses and practices originally conceived in spatial terms. The observation that women were "missing from" (placeless in) the national public landscape, that women needed "their own space" or "safe space" in order to know their own minds, that feminist politics had to do with challenging notions of what constituted "women's place," that feminists refused to concede that this was a "man's world"—all of these spatial conceptions of power gave fuel to the fire of western feminist consciousness. If feminist agitation claimed the right to *name* spaces and places that held meaning for women, to possess "a room of one's own," to "take back the night" (and with it the public space of streets, but also female sexuality), such a claim could be translated into western contexts, western spaces, western "frontiers."

Thus, when it comes to making a choice—and the persistent masculinism of many of the western literary men (across race) forces women to choose—individual female writers and, increasingly, female cultural production as a whole will engage multiple spatial fields. In the process of trying to resolve what otherwise might be felt as a kind of spatial "conflict of interests," writers produce a *new* spatial field over which to articulate western, female, multiracial subjectivity. This new imaginary holds eastern and western spatial differences, as well as the male spatial biases of many of the "alternative" geographies (like Aztlán), in some kind of productive political tension. Some women will deploy the geographic imagination of western literary history as it begins to shift in the 1980s. But for most feminists, there remains a conflict between extant geocultural imaginaries and feminist politics, and it is this conflict that leads writers toward an embrace of postmodern spatialities. Postmodernism—with its social spaces simultaneously of the local and global; spaces of inherent contradiction; spaces that mistrust metanarratives, that foreground difference, that hold multiple realities or space-times to be true at the same paradoxical moment—negotiates the various spatial divides that western feminists face.[88] Finally, postmodern spatialities are not as susceptible to the reinvention of the antifeminist border between "place" and "space"—which is my closing subject.

Place, Space-Time, and the Postmodern West

The American West—like most areas designated "regions" in the global economic culture of postmodernity—is a "place." And "places" produce cultural meaning only as they are distinguished from "spaces." What is the difference? A place is particular, definable, known. Its discursive opposite, "space," is by definition broad, inclusive, and that which, even if it connotes the specific (like, say, New York City or Paris), is much bigger than its particularity. Accordingly, spaces may *include* or subsume places. Places have no such prerogative.

In the national imaginary as well as in the Stegnerian spatial field (even if more ambivalently and on different grounds), the American West circulates as a promised land, site of innocence, site of redemption, a place where the world or the self can be transformed and perfected. As in days of old, contemporaries too turn to western places for retreat, renewal, solace. As a tourist destination, the West's commercial viability lies in its knack for transforming the above meanings into negotiable commodities. But commodities are, of course, very slippery constructions, and the *idea* of tranquil places may be as much of a "value for the dollar" as is the place itself. By bringing home and hanging upon one's wall a poster of Yosemite's Half Dome, of Utah's Arches, of crisp Southern Californian waves, of Oregon's rain forests, of Arizona's saguaros, or of Montana's sky or rivers, the memory of the places of the West may continue to provide emotional sustenance long after one's journey there has ended. Indeed, one need not physically journey westward to begin with; the imaginative journey alone may accomplish the healing task.

I mean to suggest through the above example that the cultural work of dominant western geographical imaginations continues to be, as it was throughout the course of American empire-building, a way to provide shelter from whatever storm is upon first the Old World, then the New World colony, then the new nation, then the modern nation, and now the postmodern and post–Cold War nation. What is noteworthy about the above notion of "shelter from the global storm" is the very gendered suggestion of the identity of place itself. Place, like western nature, enters contemporary representation in a female form. Western places, like women and nature, take care of people, feed them, nurture them when they are hungry, tired, or hopeless. They instruct the needy about how to tolerate that which cannot be changed. They heal; they nurse; they listen; they reassure; they care; somehow they love. Places point the way to new beginnings. Through it all, another day can be faced. Life is worth living.

When I argue that the West plays "place" to, say, New York City's "space," I intend no contravention upon the impulse driving Part I of this book—to call attention to the masculinist emplotments that dominate western spatiality. New York City's status as a "space" (even if it is also a place) owes to its relatively greater national power, to its relative economic, cultural, political, and social influence. The determined masculinism of most western spatial fields may indeed be a response precisely to the West's second-class status as place, for western men, including literary men, have long resented and resisted their comparative lack of national power. Within their own territories, where the various social hierarchies are less governed by outsiders, western men have devised spatial logics and structures that reflect their own needs and interests, and they situate themselves as police of "authentic" western spaces.

Landscape discourse plays a constitutive role in the mobilization of spaces and places toward masculinist spatial ends. The landscape commodities that I alluded to above—postcard images of pristine or "virgin" nature—sell the idea that irreducible, elemental, definable places exist and that those places *are* the American West. Further, the power of those images to suggest locatedness, to suggest placedness, has to do with their implicit femininity, their implicit boundedness, ahistoricity, inability to move. Place, like nature, is valued for its "beauty," its (relative) "purity," its ability to signal timeless "home." Resonant here are the links between masculinist visual ideologies that structure the onlooker as active, aggressive, possessive, desiring, and, of course, male, while they structure landscape or place itself as passive, static, acted upon, virginal, objectified, and, of course, female.[89] Within ideas about "place," then, are many of the masculinist assumptions and many of the visual ideologies and nostalgias that define dominant landscape discourse. Place, like woman and unlike space, anchors the world-weary to safe, secure, knowable moorings. Place does so because it is, itself, outside of History and Progress.

The landscapes featured in the following chapters invite interventions on precisely the above assumptions. The status of landscape as wild card, as open-ended discourse—*not* as a fixed or "authentic" or stable, boundaried thing; not as a homing signal; not as marker for the "beautiful" or seductively "pure"—is linked to a desire to expose this false equation of the local with the female, which is ostensibly distinct from the global. The goal is to map upon critical renderings of the new regionalism an acknowledgment of the *web* of social relations that is operative across *all* spatial scales—from the global to the national to the local to the personal.[90] Contained therein are issues of gender, race, sexuality, class, historicity, and so on. Only by such an acknowledgment will critics of the new regionalism catch up with *postmodern* landscapes, with what they do and mean for westerners as we negotiate a massively complex new century.

In *this* historical moment, the masculinist domination of western spaces and places has been fundamentally upset and is not yet reconsolidated. It may indeed be quite difficult *to* reconsolidate western spaces on terms that are historically familiar. I have already alluded to one important upsetting factor, postmodern spatiality, and the openings within it for multiracial, feminist claims upon space. Let me focus, in conclusion, on the postmodern sense of time that is embedded in the landscapes under study in this book. I take off here from what geographers call the "time-space compression" of postmodernity. This phrase refers to the fact that the advent of worldwide telecommunications and the interdependence of global financial markets have radically shrunken distances between the planet's peoples. David Harvey calls this process the "annihilation of space through time," by which he means that it's never been as small a world as it is today, that the experience of temporality has never before been so tightly compressed. As experimental physics has long hypothesized, time and space exist on a kind of simultaneous, multiple, yet paradoxical continuum. The absence, in postmodern culture, of traditional distinctions between space and time, the inability to claim, in linear time, notions of a single kind of "spatial reality" in which the observer is not also the observed, means that space is necessarily fractured and dependent on one's frame of reference.

Out of this fundamental instability, feminist writers have fashioned an empowered ethics of place/space-time. This new ethics does not always work in ways that some theorists would consider typically postmodern. For example, the "times" of the wests figured in the works I discuss below are decidedly contemporary but also, nearly without exception, stridently, even conventionally, historicist. The present presents itself as intelligible only in terms of multiple historical pasts (whether women's history, a history of conquest, nonwhite racial history, environmental history, or the like). Indeed, through the various spaces imagined by the women writers I present here, one feels many alternative histories spoken, sometimes barely audibly. Many voices, echoing within the same voice, compete for the speaking. We see again this notion of multiple, simultaneous "times" which, taken together, constitute some different historicity, more spatial than linear, but also not without historical chronology.

The "sense of place" dramatized in writers' landscapes shows profound locality and specificity, a loving feel for the details of particular places, but this passionate localism in no way separates the local from the transnational, whether that "transnational moment" arrives in economic, racial, gendered, or environmental clothing. In the final analysis, place is not a symbol of retreat from the larger complex or nexus of world affairs, politics, conflict, or issues but instead represents, constitutes, those same global issues. There are no easy "insiders" or "outsiders" in feminist regionalist discourse; boundaries that momentarily demarcate "authenticity" shift in the next moment, in response to a range of qualifying or complicating factors. Which means that to go to *this* "authentic" west is to traverse a place, which is also always a world-space, where *telenovelas* (Mexican soap operas) narrate feminist desire as much as trailer parks symbolize Indian communion with nature. Urban landscapes figure largely in this west, though it is not just the urban that is littered with postmodern symbolic content. So too is that most treasured spot in the dominant geocultural imaginary: the dignified working ranch, home to cowboy and cowgirl alike.

The last point to make before moving on, first to a spatial imaginary that might seem to many to be anything but western—that of Los Angeles—and then to that of San Francisco, is that the places and space-times of the new feminist regionalism are not familiar. Many western critics, I fear, will recognize little here to "locate" them in known territory. Suffering from a kind of sensory deprivation, with no established markers to light the path they've traveled down before, they may well rail at the goings-on. But I would request a hearing still, for if these landscapes are less well marked, that makes them no less legitimate. Indeed, familiar wests, many will concede, are spatial company that might better be left behind, permanently.

I confide, finally, a certain joyous glee in putting forward here the "bad girls" of recent western literary history, those who talk back, act up, show off, break rules of all kinds, succeed on something of their own terms without self-destructing—the very girls your mother or your brothers-in-the-cause warned you about. I've often thought that "bad girls" get a bad rap; so often they're out to prove how "good" they are, how much they care about forging some better ethics. Their stories, the landscapes on which they find and hear themselves, on which they recreate the western past and future, are the inside and out of this unfamiliar, multiply-timed, spatial-historicist west.

The West that emerged from World War II was, above all, a metropolitan West. Old cities expanded. Small communities became booming cities. . . . [B]y 1970, 83 percent of the people in the Mountain and Pacific Coast states lived in metropolitan areas. Four of the country's top ten metropolitan concentrations were in the West, and of the ten fastest growing standard metropolitan statistical areas (SMSAs) between 1970 and 1980, half were in the West.
—Richard White,
It's Your Misfortune (1991)

2

Urbanscapes in the Golden Land: California as Western Continuum

The City and the West

Few symbols stand in for the modern, modernity, and modernism as thoroughly as do those organized under the sign of "the city." Few urban spaces are as paradigmatically linked with the *post*modern as is the city of Los Angeles. In the continuing interest of naming the spatial terrains through which new female regionalists invent their wests, this chapter focuses on urban landscapes and California narratives. Such an emphasis aims to challenge that which is considered deeply, truly western—to let flood upon all of that authenticating dry land some blue-green Pacific water—and by so doing, to permit the opening up of new spaces through which to imagine nondominant westerners' relationships to western geographies.

In some critics' minds, this choice of initial frame and focus will disqualify me as a trustworthy western critic. As I have hoped to make clear already, critics have most often formulated the canonical landscapes of western literature through paradigms that reify rural wilderness, making the rural wild an implicit yardstick by which one measures the one, best West. In this critical canon, landscape rarely signifies city trees, urban public beaches, crowded metropolitan parks, or desert scenery observed from an air-conditioned car speeding down the freeway. Instead, critics favor relatively unpeopled expanses of prairie; they favor stands of Rocky Mountain pine whose quiet is broken not by human or machine chatter but by wind, whose big skies are interrupted not by jet streams but by passing clouds. Desert solitaire is ideal—meaning desert unshared, claimed for the individual. The preferred mode of transportation across these landscapes is by foot or on horseback. If one must give in to automation, let it be by that most authentic western vehicle—the dusty, rattling (never brand-new or car-wash clean) pickup truck.

I hope, sincerely, to be proven wrong in my worries about disqualification, for it is especially important, given the changing demographics of western society since 1945, to come to terms with the urban, and it does not speak well of the field, given those changing demographics, to resist such a reckoning. As many a new history of the new West shows, after 1945 most westerners live in cities.[1] Indeed, urban westerners today may well constitute the representative western subject. This fact has every kind of meaningful consequence for western critics. At the most obvious, when it comes to cultural production and literary critics' attempts to understand the very large body of text composed since the early 1970s, texts that regularly represent and are enabled by city life, a reckoning with the urban, not simply a repudiation of it, is surely inevitable.

I claim at the start, then, that urban life is as "authentic" to contemporary western narratives as is rural or suburban living, and I do so not to invert values of authenticity and inauthenticity, but to develop the idea that the opposition between the urban and the "true" (nonurban) west is an invested and symptomatic opposition.[2] The denial of the urban is as necessary to the traditional sense of western identity as is the affirmation of wilderness, for the persistent opposition between the urban and wild performs a complex kind of masculinist cultural work.

There are a number of pieces to this argumentative equation that require elaboration. To begin, one of the more obvious obstacles to acknowledging the West's contemporary urban identity grows from its historical non-association with Culture, or with the social amenities (or travails) that accompany cosmopolitan life. The West's claim to fame, its raison d'être, is as producer of nature, wilderness, and the "natural man." What I would settle our attention on here are the multiple, gendered significations (feminized Culture, the "natural man") that have produced the profound mistrust of the urban that resides in the deep heart of western discourse, and which, I am arguing, have played policing roles in the formation of western geographical imaginations. At root, the mistrust of the urban is one symptom of the antimodern/modernist dilemma I outlined in the first chapter. This dilemma, the reader will remember, more often than not expresses the kind of West, the kinds of spatial fields, found within both the dominant geocultural imaginary and Stegnerian literary history. The case I want to forward in this chapter recalls this gendered dilemma and argues that *women writers*, more so than their male counterparts, ally themselves with the general projects of modernity and postmodernity. They do so, I believe, because within both projects lie hopes of realizing female civil rights and political subjectivity.[3]

Western feminist critics of the modernist period may to some extent disagree with this claim, for their work on writers like Mary Austin or Mabel Dodge Luhan demonstrates those authors' considerable interest in primitivist as well as antimodern western spaces.[4] Indeed, one might well argue that women writers' antimodernism *anticipates*, or creates the discursive terms for, later canonical antimodern sentiment. But I am less certain. The scholarly record is so far from complete (take as examples the new material emerging on Mexican American and Asian American cultural produc-

tion that has not even begun to be incorporated into western literary studies) that, to my thinking, we cannot yet know.[5] And what remains generally
true for white writers may be untrue, or differently conceived all together,
for nonwhites, who themselves hardly comprise a unified group.[6] Until we
have a developed account of the many, many writers of the period—an
account that refracts not only gendered questions but also racial, sexual, and
subregional differences and which considers writers' relationships to formal
questions (questions to which writers themselves certainly attended)—the
critical record may be better left open.

Even without the antimodernist bent to western discourse, it is no easy
task for female writers to claim modern experience, or modern or postmodern cities, as liberating social forms and spaces. Women certainly cannot
handily revert to modernist discourse when they desire to emplot urban
landscapes with female-permitting narratives. That spatial privilege is reserved for men. Feminists in urban planning, literary criticism, geography,
art history, and philosophy have often remarked upon the masculinism of
discourses about "the city," not to mention the risks cities pose for women
who venture outside of spaces sanctioned as female friendly. As Teresa de
Lauretis observes, though Culture in western civilization is gendered female, in the "discursive space of the city . . . woman is both absent and
captive."[7] In the modern history of capital-W Western thought, including
radical Marxist and neo-Marxist thought, "great cities" like Paris, Berlin,
Vienna, and London remain associated virtually without exception with
"great thinkers," who also always turn out to be men.[8] If feminists have
made some intervention upon this genealogy (i.e., Woolf's London, Stein's
Paris),[9] the "great city" tradition remains profoundly gendered male, even
in recent influential renderings of postmodern cities that explicitly foreground issues of power, space, and urban life (like those of Edward Soja,
David Harvey, and Frederic Jameson).

An interesting departure from this tendency can be observed in the relationship of western literary men to cities. Given their ongoing love for
the wild and their preoccupation with negotiating many of the historical
changes folded into the notion of the frontier, western literary men have
generally *not* laid claim to western cities or urban spaces. One can point to
Jack London's San Francisco, Nathanael West's San Francisco or Los Angeles, John Fante's Los Angeles, or the like, but in all, I would venture, these
are more the exceptions than the rule. Wallace Stegner, a kind of ultimate

westerner to those who consider themselves "inside" western discourse, is not someone even remotely associated with San Francisco, though why should he *not* be, given fifty years' residence in nearby Palo Alto and the fact that most of his mature books depart from precisely that suburban locale to take up issues of civilization and historical change, change that often emanates from none other than 1960s-crazed San Francisco? Instead, in symbolic commemoration of the spaces Stegner considered both home and really western, the Stegner papers will be permanently held at the University of Utah at Salt Lake City. Moreover, when queried about the Stegner book they revere most, many historians and critics point to *Wolf Willow*, set not in San Francisco's contemporary South Bay but on the Canadian rural border of Stegner's childhood. This particular mustering of the Stegnerian legacy in a vague, nonurban/non-Californian direction isn't anomalous. Few, if any, of the canonical male writers of the literary west are situated in place or time via an association with western cities.

Because of the abandonment of urban spaces by dominant western cultural discourse and despite the profoundly masculinist and Eurocentric bent to the "great cities" tradition, the new female regionalists, I believe, find unexpected possibility in western urban imaginaries. Urban spatial fields, that is, offer writers something of a quirky feminist opportunity. First, urban imaginaries are not so "written over," claimed, colonized, and mobilized toward masculinist ends as are, for example, "wild western" spaces. I am not suggesting that male urban traditions do not in fact exist; that assertion simply is untrue, as will be apparent shortly, when we look at the most sustained urban narrative tradition in western literature: that of literary noir. Rather, the point is that northeastern intellectual men, like European high theorists, don't take western cities seriously.[10] Neither do western intellectual men. So when it comes to urban narratives, cultural gatekeeping is comparatively relaxed.

In asserting this notion that western cities are relatively unclaimed spatial fields, I mean to build on the "difference" I claimed for western literary traditions in Chapter 1. There I argued that an awareness of the new western female regionalism ought to nuance established discussions in American feminist criticism about women writers and public spaces. My point was that feminist scholars, in their efforts to locate and historicize the relationships between gender and the evolving spatialization of "the public," must attend to the ways these relationships change depending upon the spatial power relations invoked in those very same discussions. As I suggested in Chapter 1, feminist definitions of public spaces must inflect which part of the national imaginary a writer writes *from*.

I would advance the above claim for western difference by noting that western cities develop with far more female symbolic overtones than do the European "great cities" or even the early American cities of New York, Philadelphia, or, to a lesser extent, Chicago. If Paris or Vienna or London or New York embody monumental tributes to the modernizing logic of Enlightenment rational progress (or, later, embody critiques of that same logic), western cities are embodiments of a fallen "natural man's" dream, the necessary but regrettable outcome of the close of the frontier and the arrival of "civilization," which means, in western American discourse, the arrival of white women and the symbolic end of an era of male fraternity. A tragic, not heroic or progressive, narrative emplots the fact of western urbanity, and not just chaotic or time-compressed industrial modernity but also American white femininity are what is being mourned. The "spread-outness" of contemporary cities like Houston, Dallas, Phoenix, Seattle, Los Angeles, Denver, or Portland speaks further to the female-gendered architectonics that structure western urban spatiality. Although these cities possess skyscraping financial centers as part of their official downtowns, I would highlight instead the sprawling and decentralized spatial organization of these urbanscapes and thus their retreat from the phallocentric, built up, or, yes, "erect" skylines of northeastern and European cities. Indeed, the characteristic signature of the western city is precisely the fact that it *is* "spread out," takes longer to traverse, is not as organized around a single area—with all of the competing female-centered sexual imagery, erotics, and sensibility suggested thereby.

Having made a claim here for the non-role of western cities in the genealogy of both western and Great Western (including radical) thought, let me attend now to a very conspicuous exception: contemporary Los Angeles. Particularly in postmodern geography, some of the biggest names in recent intellectual history have centered their broad, exemplary readings of postmodern culture and economics directly upon the site of Los Angeles, the place, as Edward Soja notes (quoting the *Los Angeles Times* motto), "where it all comes together." Los Angeles has become, "more than any other place," as Soja sees it, "the paradigmatic window through which to see the last half of the twentieth century."[11] In its vast cultural diversity, Los Angeles has become that place where every world place *is*, symbol too of the new transnationalism that has revolutionized global capitalism. Regrettably, however, this "paradigmatic window," forwarded by these accomplished radicals, entirely neglects both the presence of women and the role of feminist resistance in any "reassertion of space in critical social theory" (the subtitle of Soja's *Postmodern Geographies*).[12] That neglect inspires something of a feminist call to arms.

In order to wage, on feminist terms, a struggle over who will represent and dominate both radical as well as western cultural politics, this chapter first intervenes on recent masculinist claims upon postmodern Los Angeles. I want to "mix it up" a bit, renarrativize what counts as "paradigmatic postmodernity" by framing critical issues in terms that take gender and feminism seriously. I want to add to the L.A. picture a few of the many women writers currently writing about postmodern Los Angeles, too.[13] One of my goals, in so doing, is to diffuse the hold that classic noir has on L.A.'s radical imagination, to make room in noir for more than class critique. Along the way, other parts of California, including Sacramento but especially San Francisco, come in for extended discussion. San Francisco, known today as a "sanctuary" city, home to the nation's oppressed, embodies a city identity and civic politics antithetical to those of Los Angeles. San Francisco's progressive activists seem to have embraced David Harvey's notion that "any political movement that does not embed itself in the heart of the urban process is doomed to fail in advanced capitalist society."[14] Thus, in addition to renarrativizing what counts as paradigmatic postmodernity, the second goal of this chapter is to evaluate the different feminist possibilities for cultural production offered by each geographic imagination and to speculate, finally, about the symbiotic relationship between California's biggest cities and the western geocultural imaginary at large.

California: The Great Exception?

In California postmodernity exists against a primeval landscape suffused with golden light. Landscape and light have defined the complex body of fate which, incubuslike, shapes our lives on the Coast.
—David Reid, Preface, *West of the West* (1989)

The main body of this chapter focuses on Joan Didion, Wanda Coleman, and Maxine Hong Kingston, all California writers who figure the Golden State in quintessentially urban but simultaneously western terms. Though the subjects these writers take up—Anglo nihilism in Didion, black ghetto life in Coleman, or the role of art in progressive, political, multiracial community building in Kingston—have not conventionally been deemed western, I will be concerned here to show that all of these writers' topics resonate with unmistakably western overtones. I pursue what may seem an obvious claim, because though these writers engage multiple discursive fields to tell their various stories, *western* discourse is a significant enabling imaginary that is usually overlooked or elided in critics' discussions. In addition to the racial politics of western cultural history, which I discussed in Chapter 1, another of the reasons for this critical oversight has to do with California's peculiar status in western studies.[15]

California, as most (non-Californian) critics and historians will tell you,[16] is conventionally deemed "west of the west." The "real" West includes the Rocky Mountain states, Idaho and Montana, and the Southwest. California is its own world, its own problematic, and knowing California myself from more than half a lifetime spent there, I understand this claim and cannot in good faith argue it completely away. California *is* unquestionably different from other parts of the west—whether one points to its economic might and corresponding political clout, its population density and diversity, its unusual history of class formation and politics, its home-base relationship to Hollywood, its enormously varied ecosystems, or its strange culture of hypercommerciality expressed so often through affinity for "the natural."

Though I grant all of the above, I nevertheless will dispute vigorously the notion of California as being west of west.[17] For the dominant California story, one that Joan Didion illustrates in all its complications, echoes the dominant western story in that it is, fundamentally, one of paradise lost.[18] The good days are always in the past—one sees this as early as Richard Henry Dana's 1864 reissue of *Two Years Before the Mast* (1840)[19] or as recently as critic David Wyatt's *Fall Into Eden* (1986).[20] This narrative of loss is a profoundly racialized story, a point made most clearly by the non-Anglo writers in this chapter, for not all Californians hearken back to some better or golden time in the golden land. It is also, in the final instance, a male-gendered story, another tale of the tragic "close of the frontier," a lament for the arrival of the urban and modern and female. It is my claim, here, that California's urbanism should be regarded, at least in part, as responsible for its "west of the west" cultural status. By naming urban California as *western, female-gendered space* and incorporating it into the west's various geographic imaginaries, I intend to unmask and disable the spatial bias that supports the anticivilization and anti-woman bent of "authentic" western topographies.

Let me alert the reader to a few final argumentative assumptions within my discussion of California culture. First, a major link between California and western narratives is articulated through representations of landscape. I would point out, further, the different subregional conventions that govern or shape northern versus southern California landscape discourses, and therefore the different social practices enacted through such conventions. Given its historical image as a curative mecca, Los Angeles circulates mostly within "natural landscape" conventions, whereas San Francisco's landscapes are allowed, at the outset, to blend both "natural" and "cultural" factors. Sacramento, as Didion and others too represent it, falls in between, but it ultimately leans toward "the natural," I will argue, in order to demonstrate its "authenticity" as a western space.[21]

Differences in subregional landscape conventions speak, not surprisingly, to the different city identities and political histories of Los Angeles, San Francisco, and Sacramento. Los Angeles is a kind of whorish, anything-for-a-buck city—the city, as Mike Davis notes, that people love to hate.[22] By contrast, romantic San Francisco is beloved, sure of both an urban but also a western identity. In its contemporary incarnation, San Francisco is a very liberal city, one that refuses many of the economic developments witnessed in Los Angeles. Sacramento, alas, never quite comes of urban age, a half-city, with both the charms and the anxieties appropriate to such a spatial status.

I begin with Joan Didion and set up her early novels as examples of two relatively homegrown western literary paradigms—that of the lost west and that of noir—which the new female regionalists contend with and, until recently, reject. I want to acknowledge immediately that Joan Didion is an exceptionally complex figure to claim in a study of feminist writers. The paucity of critical work devoted to Didion surely indicates how hard it is to get a handle on her work,[23] and the choice of her here as any kind of a frame for the analysis of later female writers comes after much deliberation. To begin with, she ruthlessly patronizes the women's movement and feminist philosophy in some of her White Album essays.[24] Her intense snobbery, apparent by nearly any litmus test one wishes to apply, renders her off-limits to critics with sympathies for the cultures of the nonrich. Didion is thus no instant candidate for radical or feminist endorsement. And yet, in Didion novels, if not in many of her essays or in her public person, she uses both modernist and postmodernist representational strategies, which join her, more than she might like, to feminist aesthetics and political projects. That is, if very few feminist writers would claim a usable past in the public person or white racialist pathos of Joan Didion, they nonetheless may well take from her style, her modernist and postmodernist revisions of western plots, something akin to feminist spatiality. In this conviction, I should note, I partly revise my own earlier judgment about these matters.[25]

The choice of Didion here as a genealogical frame serves another important purpose, that of cautionary tale. Didion's struggle to integrate female and western subjectivity, to make "west" and "woman" not mutually exclusive categories, and her simultaneous struggle to *refuse* feminist sensibility, identity, or philosophy, offers to the new female regionalists a paradigmatic lesson. Without an overt claim upon feminist spatial imaginaries, western female writers might well find themselves (as I think Didion ultimately does) without a spatial "home," without a lasting genre or form or literary anchor to which they might tie female western subjectivity.[26] Didion's career illustrates how very difficult it is to point out western female oppression while retaining an antifeminist public persona and antifeminist political commitments. The stubborn masculinism of dominant western geographical imaginations inevitably reopens whatever gap a writer has closed between "west" and "woman."

In the first of Didion's books considered here, *Run River* (1963), Didion writes with a nostalgia similar to that of many canonical literary westerns—a sense that the best, most colorful days are gone, that the frontier has closed, and without it, life can never be as good again. Yet, also like canonical westerns, even as she invokes the pioneer legacy, she deconstructs it. In *Run River*, further, I want to situate a significant moment in western female literary history: that of the shift from modernist to postmodernist form and subjectivity. What forces the shift, I want to argue, is Didion's persistent interest in the crossroads between western plots and female protagonists. Importantly, this crossroads is enacted, in spatial terms, by an increasing affinity for city narratives. By the time Didion's second novel, *Play It as It Lays* (1970), appears seven years later, postmodern formal strategies are fully in evidence, and deployed toward feminist ends. Her alliance with the most prominent of urban western narratives, noir, is in evidence too. *Play It as It Lays* tells a new kind of western story in which Los Angeles represents, in Mike Davis's words, the "nightmare at the terminus of American history."[27] But again I want to attend to the ways Didion's continual foregrounding of female subjectivity mediates what counts as L.A. nightmare or as nightmare's antidote, desire. I want to attend, too, to the efficacy of noir for articulating specifically female, urban western subjectivity.

Mourning the Loss of the "Real" California: Joan Didion's Lament

Didion's *Run River* and *Play It as It Lays* are urban and urbane narratives. Unlike most literary westerns, they do not tell tales of individual men's measures of self against the western wilderness. Nor are they stories of founding civilizations in new territories. Didion's are stories of civilizations founded and undergoing the pressures of post–World War II change. They begin from the urban premise. Most unlike literary westerns, they are stories of powerful women who are wildly, destructively sexual, who cannot hold themselves or their families together. As a rule, Didion is not an optimist; neither are her landscapes generally redemptive. These facts have made Didion unpopular among reviewers,[28] an anathema to western critics in particular, who see the West, as I argued in Chapter 1, as "hope's native home." Didion is one of the West's important writers, I believe, for she illustrates the instabilities of the dominant geographic imaginary; she exposes its rawest nerves, what it hates or rejects, and what it protects as its own.

The plot of *Run River* centers upon protagonist Lily Knight McClellan— whose husband Everett, in the first two paragraphs of the book, murders her male lover and then turns the gun on himself as solution to the family's problems. What has led to this magnitude of impasse is the book's central topic. Giving the novel much of its moral tension is Didion's representation of nineteenth-century pioneer ancestors, workers with a sense of what they wanted, juxtaposed against a representation of those pioneers' descendants: an aimless contemporary lot, who in spite of wealth and position are undone by their own flaws. Contributing to the tension is the presence, located "offstage" in this story, of an emerging sense among American women that there is something wrong, some "problem with no name," as Betty Friedan will coin it in *The Feminine Mystique* in 1963, the same year that *Run River* is published. That "problem" is ruining the lives of women who would have been thought to *have* no obvious problems (Lily is not poor, sick, unloved, nonwhite, or without children). My focus initially here will be on the novel's representations of the Sacramento river, for therein, I think, lies the more interesting and revealing discussions of the above topics. Therein, moreover, lies the *spatial* link between Didion's "offstage story"—the developing feminist narrative associated with northeastern spatial fields and women like Betty Friedan—and that which is more unconsciously coded western: "natural" landscape.

Didion once remarked that she set this first novel, *Run River*, in Sacramento because she was lonely for her native landscape. Living in New York City at the time, she missed

> the [Sacramento] river and the weather . . . the heat. I think that's the way the whole thing began. . . . There's a lot of landscape which I never would have described if I hadn't been homesick. . . . The impulse was nostalgia.[29]

This remark is a fitting starting place for our study, suggesting as it does the nexus of issues that cohere for western writers in and through landscape discourse and suggesting, too, Didion's anxiety that landscape is an illegitimate literary subject. As someone consummately savvy about high-culture conventions, Didion knows "overattention" to landscape is amateurish, an editorial lapse. Her problem, however, is that she cannot tell the California story she wants to tell without it.

In Didion's California narratives we see all that landscape can stand for—all the social, cultural, and political practices enacted through western "natural" topography. We see why "overattention" is mandatory, even if it threatens Didion's better high-culture sense. The natural narrative *is* California social narrative, in a more diffuse and symbolic form (though no less practical a form, I would add—practical in the sense of having a political effect). Landscape as a form of cultural practice is less defended and controlled, more revealed. All those things at stake in landscape discourse are unconsciously revealed too—political alliances, race and culture wars, the tooth-and-nail struggle for female psychic survival. Lastly, landscape negotiates the postwar contest over regional "authenticity," standards by which the "real California" (Didion's phrase) is defined.[30]

Although I will qualify this claim later, let me begin by noting that Didion's association of Sacramento landscape with nostalgia links her to dominant traditions in landscape representation that infuse western topography with a longing for a proud and romantic pioneer past. If *Run River* does not describe the Sacramento River in the direct, sustained, love-story way in which canonical western novels so often represent western lands, the river nonetheless pervades the story's symbolic center, bleeds out at the periphery, shows up in the title. It is the site of all the post-1945 changes that are *Run River's* subjects, including its feminist subjects. Upon the river's docks, within its boathouses, on its midnight beaches, the protagonist, Lily Knight McClellan, carries on her extramarital trysts. And the murder/suicide spawned by those trysts—the principal drama of the book—happens at moonless dockside, too. The river is also the site of metaphoric deaths. Not only will a brand of "respectable" female sexuality die at the water's edge, but so too will rigid distinctions between the ruling, middle, and lower classes. In the postwar period, the riverfront slips away from the exclusive control of the landed elite, as suburban tract homes, inhabited by the families of aerospace technocrats, now line the water's edge on either side of the McClellans' 17,000-acre spread. The changing face of the river serves as the most painful reminder to the rich that the old Sacramento is gone, and the new Sacramento will be led not by growers and gentlemen farmers descended from a pioneer lineage but by Cadillac dealers, real estate developers, and defense industry executives.

Didion's invocation of the river, river heat, river locals, river culture, river parties, down-river drives for summer auctions, river flooding, even river deaths simultaneously invokes a social topography that maps those who belong on the river and know its ways, those who implicitly "own" Sacramento, and those who are interlopers, inauthentic participants in the California story. Those who lay claim to the river—the Knights, McClellans, and Didion herself—are those to whom the pioneer myth offers a relevant usable past. Invoking their "authentic" relationship to the river invokes their lament for the coming of urbanization, for the dirtying of a clean dream, for all that has been lost in what Didion calls California's transformation from a "real" to a "manufactured" place.[31]

The river is racialized in this process and belongs not to the Mexican American men who manage the ranches and work the hops that grow on river-rich soil, not to the Okie migrant pickers, not to the domestic worker "China Mary," whose speech patterns suggest she is African American. The river belongs to the white elite—whether growers or technocrats. That is, the "real California" belongs to the white people who can afford to buy it, just as a century before it belonged to the white people with the means to dispossess others with competing claims. White landowners are the "authentic" subjects of Didion's California story; theirs is the "authentic" pathos written over the Golden State's history. By noting this lament, I also want to point out that the lament can and should be read simultaneously as a refusal of the present, explicitly a refusal of the various civil rights assaults on white supremacy that are brewing in the United States at this same historic moment. Landscape discourse, in this particular incarnation, thus enacts a white racialist social practice. It rearticulates the cultural logic of Manifest Destiny in order to consolidate the offensive against civil rights reforms and sensibilities.[32]

The white racialized river, as Didion constructs it, is symbol of the proto-urban, the California that is gone after 1950 and the arrival of the "new Sacramento." The river serves as palimpsest upon which Didion articulates a longing for the heroic western past, when men and women knew what they were about and set themselves the task of getting what they wanted. The loss of an historic Anglo mission creates Didion's particular regional pathos—one disillusioned and sad, nostalgic and impotent, with a vague but pervasive dread that "the good life" is possible only in memory and that all that lies ahead is declension and tragic error.

Yet nostalgia, in Didion's hands, is never a simple tradition-defending move, for Didion's tale is just as interested in the underbelly of things—in the way, for example, the Sacramento River in *Run River* consumes those who lay claim to it most. (Take as examples Lily's father, who, along with his mistress, drowns. Or Lily's sister-in-law Martha, who also drowns.) Even as Didion memorializes a proud pioneer past and would mobilize landscape discourse to deny civil rights claims upon "authentic" western identity, she also relentlessly exposes the contradictions and romanticization of that past. She indicts the idea that the westward urge was a clear-eyed historical mission undertaken by brave, honest, and persevering souls.

> [Lily and Everett] carried the same blood, come down through twelve generations of circuit riders, Bible readers, one obscure United States Senator from a frontier state a long time ago; two hundred years of clearings in Virginia and Kentucky and Tennessee and then the break . . . the cutting clean which was to have redeemed them all. They had been a particular kind of people, their particular virtues called up by a particular situation, their particular flaws waiting there through all those years . . . It had been above all a history of accidents: of moving on and of accidents. What is it you want, she had asked Everett tonight. It was a question she might have asked them all. (246)

The westering venture adds up to a long succession of accidents, of chance victories, latent problems, misguided ideals, especially the notion that "cutting clean was to have redeemed them all." There is finally no clean cut in *Run River*. The past follows everyone, and haphazardly, it surfaces; then all the chips must be cashed in. Unfortunately, when it is time to pay up for past debts incurred, contemporary westerners discover they have only Monopoly money.

What I want to recognize before moving on is that if, in the above assessment, we have an indictment of the white men of the western venture (circuit riders, an obscure U.S. senator), Didion also implicates western white *women*, too—the Bible readers—as a part of the problem. There is no deployment here of the image of the stoic pioneer woman who births uncomplainingly along the trail one day and buries a child or husband the next. In *Run River*, Lily Knight McClellan's mother is just as flawed as is her father, just as impotent. Moreover, the aimlessness of Lily's younger generation of 1940–50s westerners belongs equally to men and women, even if it is lived out in very gendered ways. I have written elsewhere on some of these gendered dilemmas[33] and here wish to emphasize that if one of the gendered dilemmas particular to women concern the consequences of sexual activity, especially pregnancy, one of the *solutions* to gendered dilemmas finds articulation in urban, not rural or natural, western spaces.

The second dramatic dilemma of *Run River* (following the suicide/murder) is generated by exactly this social space of gendered difference. Lily Knight McClellan is pregnant with a child that is not her husband's—a problem for any woman, certainly, but especially a problem in eras devoted to wartime duty and postwar American (cold warrior) family-building. Lily's resolution of the unwanted pregnancy is to abort this child, and she goes from half-urban Sacramento to indisputably urban San Francisco to do so. There are two points to make. First, *Run River's* lament for the coming of the urban is, finally, a partial or qualified lament. The partiality occurs where "western" meets "female" identity. *Run River* cannot side completely with a lost west pathos and rural bias that accompanies it, because with the urban comes certain female necessities or services, like that of anonymous abortion. Although even illicit and potentially unsafe abortions require access to money and are thus a very class-restricted service, they nonetheless represent one type of freedom or alternative to unwanted pregnancy for the woman who can pay. Lily is just such a woman, and the freedom or options that abortion offers to her, I argue, are very real. (Note that in Didion's books, it is rarely the women who ultimately are the suicides, and a case could be made for abortion as one of the social safety valves that enables female survival. To spin this safety valve observation differently, if Frederick Jackson Turner saw in the frontier a social safety valve that let off the steam of class conflict, the argument here is that in the "frontier" that came with the sexual revolution, abortion is a western safety valve that blows off the steam of gendered conflict.) Though the abortion receives subdued attention in *Run River*, especially compared to the abortion scene in *Play It as It Lays*, the logic that underlies it is unmistakable— abortion is a female civil right. Further, the city is the place where this fundamentally necessary civil right is available. Under the cover of metropolitan anonymity, Lily is obliged to ask no one's permission. In the city, Lily is accorded what is usually a male-only prerogative: a measure of bodily independence.

The second point to make is more speculative. I see this novel's chosen time frame, spanning 1938–59 but focused on the war and immediately postwar years, as a kind of temporal displacement, a compromise Didion strikes in order to remain true to her first desire, to tell something like her life story, which is a western story. Only secondarily does she want to tell a deliberately female story. The female story is secondary because such a story seems to suggest a female writer, and "female writer" to Didion means literary invalidism. It is secondary, further, because Didion wants no intimacy with liberalism or progressivism or any emergent feminist movement. To my reading, however, the "offstage story," that of the beginnings of the sexual revolution and the battle between the sexes, is as central to this text's portrayal of social upheaval as are the post-1945 economic and demographic changes that remake western spaces forever. And that is exactly the problem. Didion walks ground that cannot satisfy adequately the simultaneity or combination of the two stories. If she focuses on female-gendered issues and submerges western ones, she will not have written the Sacramento book she needs as a young writer to write. But if she disallows herself female sensibility, she has no protagonist. So the bargain is this: write a story in which the sexual revolution cannot dominate because the primary historical period under study is earlier, the war years. But what happens when the sexual revolution narrative won't stay put and threatens to blow apart the Sacramento story? Didion discovers a novel response: relocate the story to (what I have argued is) a sympathetic female space that is also less implicated in "real" western symbolism—that is, to the city. Then the Sacramento story can remain western at the same time that the female protagonist can survive the war between the sexes. Or, play one space against another.

I have spent time to lay out the above dilemma because I think it is one that illustrates many of the spatial dilemmas faced by the new female regionalists: how to find sympathetic spatial terrains upon which to narrate stories that are not forever choices between female and western (or counterwestern) sensibilities. What Didion does, and what many new regionalists will do, is to play one space, all the time, against others—in theoretical parlance, to enact performativity as a general spatial modus operandi. While some of Didion's dilemmas prefigure those of the new regionalists, some of her other conflicts, especially her antifeminism, are *not* representative of new regionalist sensibility. Indeed, I believe it will be the straightforward commitment to feminism by so many new female regionalists that ultimately forces the women's issue in western studies and makes the gatekeepers of western cultural production more self-conscious about the gender politics of "westernness."

If the coming of the urban (symbolized by the disfigurement of the river) is hard for Didion to accept in *Run River*, accepted it is by the time she produces the beaches and deserts of *Play It as It Lays*. There is no nostalgic impulse here, no half embrace of city spaces. In typical Didion fashion, she targets the heart of male narrative power—that of literary and film noir—and then locates herself within it. The literary product is a pale, bloodless picture not just of Hollywood but of the play-the-card-as-you-laid-it western sensibility, rearticulated now in postmodern terms. As a geocultural imaginary, Los Angeles provides the social space in which characters play out a kind of national "dare"—the high stakes game of western chicken. Acutely sensitive to gender politics, however, Didion reflects some of the female-gendered issues at stake in any game of chicken, in any postmodern, winner-take-all gambling scheme. But will noir get Didion anyplace, will it gain her any space, after all?

No Day on the Beach in Los Angeles (and Other Narratives of Noir)

L.A. is probably the most mediated town in America, nearly unviewable save through the fictive scrim of its mythologizers.
—Michael Sorkin, quoted in *City of Quartz*

Play It as It Lays, a National Book Award nominee, depicts the fast-paced Hollywood of the 1960s, a world where drugs, social malaise, sexual experimentation, upper-class malice, and excess abound.[34] The young protagonist, Maria Wyeth, a model and actress, is daughter of deceased parents whose life philosophy, garnered in their hometown of Reno, is that what comes in on the next roll of the dice will be better than what went out on the last roll—American optimism in its more reckless *western* form. In Maria's character, however, the go-get-'em-ness of her father is not only absent but somehow irrelevant. As she says, she has never made a decision in her life; she has no "knack for" things (19). Neither is she likely to make a decision, for "nothing applies" (2).

"Nothingness" and a confrontation with "nothingness" constitute philosophic dilemmas of the book, ones that owe large debts to L.A.'s film and literary noir traditions. Though some critics read Didion's nothingness through existentialist philosophy,[35] and though one could also read "nothingness" as a dialogue with the bohemian or leftist philosophical trends of the 1950s and 1960s, I read it, first, as shaped by *western regional* more than national or international philosophic trends, and next, by the spatial field of northeastern feminism. In the final analysis, I want to argue, Didion's landscape representations suggest that at the center of things is *not* nothing but rather oppressive and depressing social relations (including especially gender relations), which always seem to doom the fulfillment of female desire.

Let us briefly consider the regional history of noir. As critic David Fine recounts it, studio writers of the 1930s and 1940s, disillusioned by Hollywood's single-minded emphasis on the bottom line, inverted the "metaphoric shape" of paradisal Los Angeles by "transform[ing] the [myth of El Dorado] into its antithesis: that of the dream running out along the California shore."[36] The fabulous land of sunshine, orange trees, and youth thus imploded into its grotesque opposite—a land of shadows and depravity. This antimyth sensibility survived into L.A. fiction and film of the 1950s and, as cultural critic Mike Davis argues, appeared again in the 1960s and 1970s in a rearticulated and somewhat deradicalized form.[37] Certainly noir, in both literary and filmic forms, survives into the late 1990s. But in the main, our discussion here will stick to noir during the formative years of the new female regionalism, the 1970s.

While I am indebted to David Fine and inspired by Mike Davis, I would take both men's histories of noir, but especially Davis's splendid argument, in feminist directions that they do not pursue. To be sure, Didion's "nausea" (as Davis calls it) comes out of noir's twentieth-century rendering of the City of the Angels; Davis knows that cultural ground, at least in its classed configurations, better than anyone today. At the same time, as I see it, *Play It as It Lays* marks a new moment in noir genealogy (yet another genealogy that is virtually entirely male),[38] for it combines noir sensibility with feminist content and the early showings of feminism-linked, postmodern form. Thus where Davis implies a somewhat devolving (class) politic to the noir genre in this period (a claim I don't dispute), I see Didion's noir taking on new radical topics, namely feminism. This point matters when later I try to establish some historicist trajectories in the evolution of the new regionalists.

With the foregoing claims about Didion's gendered motivations in mind, let us revisit the protagonist Maria's confrontation with "nothingness." Certainly confrontations with "darkness" (if anyone can use this racialized language in any defensible way) are the signature sensibility of noir. And the "dark forces" are both within, interior to characters' own confused psychologies, as well as without, located usually in unequal class relations or within California's culture industry and its unprincipled pursuit of profit. But *Play It as It Lays* represents other kinds of "outside forces" that the *female* writer or protagonist must contend with—namely, male power and the power of the culture industry to oppress women or to mobilize representations of women in quite gender-specific and demeaning ways.

Maria's confrontation with "darkness," her belief that "nothing applies," is due in large measure to the thorough devastation that follows her abortion. Maria's abortion haunts this noir narrative poignantly, for after it, Maria has lost not one but now two children. (The first is "lost" to the unnamed but devastating condition that requires her permanent hospitalization.) The feelings of vague dread, of inexplicable "weirdness," which constitute so much of the pathos and emotional impact of noir, come most intensely to the fore, in Maria's case, after her abortion. Indeed, it is the abortion that sets the escalating personal crisis of the novel in motion. Much of the crisis pivots around the fact that the abortion is half coerced. Maria's estranged husband has threatened her with a custody lawsuit if she does not abort this new baby, and she knows she will not win. So the initial point I would stress is that Maria's confrontation with "nothingness," and Didion's own particular rendering of noir, owe a crucial debt to contemporary debates about women's reproductive freedom (generated in northeastern feminist spatial fields)—debates that would culminate three years after the publication of this novel in *Roe v. Wade*.

Didion's noir is hence inseparable from the gender politics of the sexual revolution, and as such, it respatializes the noir narrative away from the "tough guy" realism that is such a large part of the noir aesthetic in favor of a new noir, where issues of western regional identity meet up, in the spaces of the city, with issues of children (and the love of children), reproduction, and female sexuality. In this respatialized Los Angeles, bedrooms, nurseries, and female bodies compete for spatial presence with the more conventional noir settings of ports, warehouses, and "ethnic" slums. In this L.A., women begin to populate the city on something of their own terms. Headlining this cityscape are "miseries peculiar to women," as the narrator of *Play It as It Lays* names prescriptive standards for female beauty (61). Nowhere do these "miseries" show themselves as starkly as on L.A.'s famed beaches.

Let me narrow this discussion to focus on Didion's beaches, for though beaches are not a staple feature of noir, Didion shows them to be of special relevance to female noir. From the beginning, this novel's beach spaces are represented nearly always as symbolic spaces implicated in their own production. Part of Los Angeles's postmodern dilemma, *Play It as It Lays* suggests, is its investment in the cultural manufacturing of itself. This text seems to be a hall of mirrors, a maze of self-referentiality, for the movie the characters negotiate throughout the novel is itself a beach story named *Angel Beach*. Almost heavy-handedly, Didion situates a filmic representation of the beach within her fictional representation of it, the point being that beach landscapes are so saturated with images of themselves, mediated from so many angles, that the notion of the beach as a value-free, "natural" medium is absurd. This critique of "natural" Southern California beach landscapes opens onto an exposure of the very unnatural, or social, pressures upon women that create and feed their particular "miseries."

Beach spaces enact Maria's (and also Didion's) very female-gendered relationship to the culture industry. In the course of the novel, beach spaces are revealed to be fully permeated and structured by labor, gender, and sexualized social relations stacked in favor of the men who control the means of representation. Let me give an example. The production of the film *Angel Beach* happens from the male producer's own beach house. The beach is therefore no leisure space, no "natural" retreat from the stresses of city life. Rather it is the site of people's relations to the local film economy, a workplace, a kind of factory. By emplotting the beach with workplace struggles, Didion makes headway on the gendered labor concerns she cares about. Maria, as an actress, is worker, her husband/director Carter is middle management, and producer BZ is the boss, both controller of capital and of the final cut. Gendered logics structure the sexual politics of this workplace.

Maria has been instructed, not requested, by husband Carter to "come along and swim" (109) while Carter talks business with producer BZ, not because swimming is pleasurable or healthy but, the novel implies, so that BZ can get a look at Maria's goods, at her model's body in a swim suit. Afterwards, having assessed the "goods," BZ can decide whether or not to bank Carter for future films. BZ agrees to put up some money, apparently satisfied with the collateral security Maria's body provides. Maria's body is the commodity traded in exchange for capital investment. But husband Carter, not Maria, is the owner and manager of this collateral—that much is made clear when later, estranged from her husband, Maria can no longer find work.

BZ's beach house is also the site of some of the most provocative discussions in late 1960s fiction about power relations, gender, and sexuality. Again, in a saturated scene within a scene, BZ looks over Maria's "goods" as he simultaneously watches the dailies from this *Angel Beach* movie—a picture not incidentally in which Maria stars as the victim of a gang rape. BZ tells Carter that he is misdirecting the story behind the gang rape. The real story is that the "twelve cocks" are "doing it not to her but to each other" (110). With the habitual snideness of Didion characters, BZ wonders if Maria finds the fact of men doing-it-to-each-other interesting. Two issues are important here. One is that Didion takes the surprising tack (anticipating lesbian and gay studies) of framing the gang rape not only as an act of misogynist representation but one of homoerotics exposed. The second is to note that when BZ wonders if Maria finds male homoerotics interesting, Didion, in effect, is permitting space for another question: what constitutes female desire?

A complicated discussion about post-1960s California sexuality is in process here—and, significantly, it takes place upon beach spaces. I thus want to attend to the beach imaginary, more generally, as one of the most productive sites of sexualized bodies in contemporary American culture. For the engagement of beach landscapes in *Play It as It Lays* simultaneously engages a discursive field in which the sexual revolution is fiercely under negotiation. Beaches figure here, then, as a social space highly sensitized to the changing geography of desire so characteristic of this historical moment. Beach spaces produce a chaotic mix of trends and countertrends in American attitudes toward sexuality and body aesthetics.

Didion's beaches are full of repressed as well as expressed male homoerotics; they are geographies so saturated with masculinist sexual discourses that female desire can hardly be imagined. In these spaces heterosexuality and love are incompatible, sexual experimentation leaves men in positions of power, and same-sex love would be freakish were it not so pathetic. Nobody is winning the sexual revolution, though women are losing harder than are men. But masculine hegemony is far from monolithic: one man, the most powerful man in the novel, BZ, is a (married) gay man who ultimately suicides.

In the context I've suggested about the role of beach imaginaries in the production of sexual discourse, let me digress momentarily to discuss the contemporary blockbuster TV show *Baywatch*. I'm interested to ponder this show's immense popularity (it is the most widely syndicated TV network show in the world today), and to argue that its appeal owes something to the show's continual mobilization of beach spaces as "beautiful" social geographies. The appeal of *Baywatch* suggests that the Southern California beach imaginary offers many Americans—and a global audience, too—a kind of cultural topography upon which to imagine ideal beauty and sexuality. As a geography of desire, Southern California seashores thus "play" as enormously seductive and powerful social spaces. But what kinds of imagined bodies mostly populate these spaces? Men are white, ideally blonde, not bulky but muscular, youthful, implicitly potent, unquestionably heterosexual. Women are white, ideally blonde, thin but with defined muscles, busty, youthful, implicitly willing, and never a thought to their being other than heterosexual. Not very surprisingly, this beach imaginary is the site of the creation and promotion of very explicit kinds of racialized, gendered, and sexualized physicalities.

The spatial terrain of Southern California represented in *Baywatch* is different from that which preoccupies Didion, and the difference is accomplished by the contrary emplotments each narrative introduces upon the "natural" landscape tradition dominating the Southern California regional imaginary. Didion, through noir, invests her beach spaces with social relations, whereas, by contrast, *Baywatch* works within redemptive or "natural" landscape conventions. Its stories move from problem-to-resolution kinds of moral economies. Even if *Baywatch* has responded over the years to the changing status of American women during the 1980s and 90s and now displays not just female bodies for a male gaze but also male bodies for a *female* gaze, even if Gidget has grown up and women are now lifeguards and surfers too, the landscape discourse mobilizing these various changing representations remains essentially the same. The viewer is invited to participate, via a visual ideology of "the natural," in the construction of a landscape that looks upon the shoreline, waves, offshore bays, dunes, and the like, as objects of beauty, veneration, and, usually, virgin availability (which the good steward should "preserve"). And the spaces that accompany that visual ideology provide no enabling room for an abortionist's home clinic, for needy or disabled children, for female workers confronting gender bias and harassment on the job, or for female bodies suffering the many "miseries peculiar to women."

As a social practice, then, beach discourse in its dominant form produces the fiction of "realness," of being outside of representation, unadulterated, outside of history itself. One goes to this space to be healed, not to confront the world's injustices. It is this image that is commodified by any number of cultural industries, and with it, Southern California as a cultural geography on which can be mapped the possibility of cultural or personal renaissance, and social equality too (*Baywatch*'s lifeguards and surfers of both sexes). This image most links Southern California landscapes to those of the broader "authentic" west. And the "purity" of this image is what Didion always hones in on and makes problematic—at least almost always.

As an imaginary that promises that anything is possible, any situation redeemable, the beach seduces even Didion, albeit only briefly. The seduction comes where she is most vulnerable, where female desire is most at risk. And the space that articulates that "crossroads" of female desire is one where desires for motherhood overlap with desires for adult female companionship, including sexual companionship. As a way to fall asleep calmly, secure that she is protecting herself from peril, protagonist Maria imagines an idyllic domestic scene in a house on the water that she shares with her daughter Kate:

> The house was like none she had ever seen but she thought of it so often that she knew even where the linens were kept, the plates, knew how the wild grass ran down to the beach and where the rocks made tidal pools. Every morning in that house she would make the bed with fresh sheets. Every day in that house she would cook while Kate did her lessons. Kate would sit in a shaft of sunlight, her head bent over a pine table, and later when the tide ran out they would gather mussels together, Kate and Maria, and still later all three of them would sit down together at the big pine table and Maria would light a kerosene lamp and they would eat the mussels and drink a bottle of cold white wine and after a while it would be time to lie down again, on the clean white sheets. (113)

Here the beach is constituted via its dominant form, as "curative mecca," not as Didion usually represents it in the novel, full of oil scum and sand flies (64), home to toxic shellfish (114).

Very significantly, this moment of the "curative beach" does not invoke a classic, masculinist visual ideology of the "natural" to emplot it. Didion is after something else all together, tied in to the "crossroads" desire I noted above. On Didion's "good beach" live mothers who cook while daughters do their lessons. After lessons, mother and daughter pass afternoons together gathering mussels for supper. At dinnertime, mother and daughter dine with a father figure who cares (a figure otherwise absent in the book). Adults sip wine and partake of adult pleasures, yet it is an environment not exclusive of a child's well-being too. This little family goes to sleep at night between fresh sheets, presumably children dream contentedly, and adults do whatever the night has moved them to do, and everyone awakes healthy and secure the next morning, happy to do it all over again.

This is an exceptionally important fantasy for this book and for my argument, because it highlights the exception to the "nothing matters" rule that dominates Maria's psychology. The exception is Kate, Maria's brain-damaged and institutionalized daughter. As Maria tells us on the book's opening pages, what she "plays for" is Kate (2). If anything "applies," it is Kate, her love for Kate, her attachment to Kate. At book's end, Maria says now that she knows the "answer" is nothingness, she can make some plans. She can even, it seems, make a decision. And the decision is this: "(1) get Kate, (2) live with Kate alone, (3) do some canning" (209). When all else fails, Didion suggests, and decent men are nowhere to be found, women can still live out meaningful lives with the children in their charge, the children they love. This hope constitutes one deep longing within the constellation of desires that form "female desire," and it is a hope that repeatedly finds expression in new western feminist sensibility more generally.

The beach as a site of redemption holds out, if only momentarily, the possibility of idyllic mother-daughter domesticity. Upon it, disoriented mothers like Maria become self-possessed enough to cook, can, and provide homes for brain-damaged daughters like Kate, who then recover their wits, able again to learn and thrive and run down sandy paths that lead to tidal pools. Upon this utopic seashore, fathers are not obstacles to female bonds, nor are daughters obstacles to mothers' sexuality and satisfaction. The dilemmas that come between mothers and daughters in a misogynist world, that is, are here absent. Dilemmas about gendered divisions of labor that disempower mothers in the home *or* in the marketplace are absent too, as are the layered complications (for determining "the real") that the realm of representation adds to any "picture." But this is only a dream, Maria knows all too well, for the next several lines narrate Maria's acknowledgment that "the still center of the daylight world was never a house by the sea but the corner of Sunset and La Brea" (114). It is the urban and social that is the subject of landscape representation, after all, Didion concedes. One cannot evade the compromises of the contemporary world by invoking therapeutic, "natural" beach spaces; they cannot patch over the unique problems women face or satisfy the particular desires (including the desire to love children) that make up *female* desire.

A number of concluding remarks are in order. Part of the attractiveness of the genre of noir for Didion is that it resolves some of the gendered contradictions inherent within the "lost west" story. It permits not only ironic critique but outright pessimism about the folly of the entire western experiment. Noir further promises, in its embrace of the spatial field of the city, some openness to female-gendered subjectivity, some openness to the emplotment of female-inspired western narratives. Noir suggests a potentially conducive terrain, then, for imagining stories that suit a westerner concerned with female protagonists. But noir has its own gendered problems, and even if Didion is no outright friend to feminism, she nonetheless is a woman writing about highly sexualized female protagonists, and those facts make the gendered dynamics of noir impossible to ignore. If studio greed and exploitation of writers is one central theme of male noir narratives, Didion's representation of studio politics shows that hack writers are not the only vulnerable workers in the quest for studio profit. Being *female* in that system constitutes yet another vast realm of exploitability. Exposing and resisting attempts to exploit women—and that is the cultural work ultimately performed by this novel—is a relatively new radical politic for a narrative tradition historically inclined toward class critique.

Concluding remarks are in order, too, about Didion's relationship to and deployment of postmodernism. As I suggested at the beginning of this section, Didion's noir shows early signs of the link between feminist content and postmodern form. This link works in several somewhat internally contradictory ways. In its more obvious uses of postmodern formal strategies, *Play It as It Lays* is an easy read (unlike, say, Maxine Hong Kingston's *Tripmaster Monkey*). It is very, very fast, suggestive of the "time-space" compression that characterizes postmodern urban sensibility. Much of the text is, indeed, not written text but blank spaces on mainly "bare" pages. We get three, very short, first-person stories, which introduce the larger third-person story of Maria. At novel's end, the first-person story of Maria interrupts the concluding sequences of the third-person story of Maria, and the last word is given to Maria in her first-person form. Though one could meditate a great deal on the issues suggested herein, the point here is that the novel puts forward a narrative structure very much in keeping with the idea of multiple narration, or ruptured subjectivity, for which postmodern narrative is famous. One could legitimately conclude that any of these various narrative voices is equally true, and that truth, therefore, ultimately is relative. No omniscient metanarrative, no "final" word on Truth is possible.

More complex engagements with the postmodern can be identified in this text, too. One works through landscape discourse, wherein Didion registers a postmodern emphasis on the representational rather than the "real" status of landscape, and by so doing, accomplishes a feminist intrusion into what is otherwise a masculinist discourse about "natural" nature. Yet right on the heels of this revisionist moment, Didion encourages feminists to question how much they should celebrate the representational and the constructed, because she attends so thoroughly to the crucial matter of who controls the means of representation. In the tension between these two poles—where postmodern ideas about the constructedness of meaning meet up with the continuing problem of the economic conditions under which meaning is produced—Didion prophesies current theoretical disputes about the efficacy of postmodernist epistemology for feminist visions of social justice.

I have teased out some of Didion's competing engagements with both noir and postmodernism in order to chart some beginning genealogies that are relevant to the new female regionalists. Didion's engagement with noir is not one that will "catch on" among later, especially white writers, even though, as I have argued, she opens that form in the early 1970s to feminist deployment. Having said that, however, I want to note an important recent exception, found in the new genres of mystery and detective novels currently being written by nonwhite writers.[39] In some basic way, texts like Lucha Corpi's *Eulogy for a Brown Angel* (1992) and the many novels of Michael Nava and Rudolfo Anaya take literary inspiration and form from noir. Indeed, so many Chicano/a writers today are publishing detective/mystery tales that the Chicano/a Crime Writers Association (CCWA) was recently founded. I would also call attention to a recent novel by Lisa See, *Flower Net: A Thriller* (1997), a narrative that seems to take noir transnational, and to a growing number of female sleuths, found in novels by Abigail Padgett, Earlene Fowler, and J. J. Nance. Generally, however, new regionalists do not embrace noir as a directly enabling sensibility or genre. Apparently, it is just too difficult to work within noir's very masculine preoccupations. Or perhaps Didion is too ambivalent a "feminist foremother" to lead a feminist assault on noir herself, one that would open it more completely to new plot lines that join urban, female, and western narratives.

But some of the openings in noir—for instance, its dialogues with the sexuality of the city and with postmodern formal strategies as well as postmodernist philosophies about representation—indeed appeal to the new female regionalists. These openings are incorporated into the center of the new regionalist enterprise, even if the borrowing is unacknowledged. But the terms of their incorporation, I want to insist, have traveled a rupturing distance from their origins. The kinds of cities one sees in the remaining texts surveyed in this chapter represent a very new kind of city whose spaces are novel in terms of both American and western cultural production. What's new in particular are the different *racialized* gendered subjectivities that are so self-consciously a part of regionalists' urban and western spaces.

This subjectivity enables one, retrospectively, to highlight the most hidden but racialized story of all, that of Didion's own Los Angeles beaches. With palpable meticulousness, *Play It as It Lays* attends to the role of beach spaces in the construction and negotiation of gendered and sexual identities. At the same time, again with palpable meticulousness, it does *not* attend to the role of landscape representation in producing dominant, Anglo racial subjectivity. I use this notion of "meticulous silence" because the California years Didion is writing about witness the Watts riots, the Chicano Moratorium, the emergence of the United Farm Workers, and the formation of the American Indian Movement, as well as a broader national civil rights movement and the assassination of Dr. Martin Luther King Jr. All of these movements reveal the racialized power structures that dominate American cultural and political life. By shunting these social developments to the spatial sidelines, Didion's text keeps the Hollywood "picture" white.

Didion's whiteness is thrown into stark relief as we look at urban territory as represented in the late 1970s by Los Angeles poet Wanda Coleman. Coleman demonstrates how white a space the Southern California regional imaginary is—how segregated and Anglo the discourse of beach representation remains. After Coleman, it becomes quite clear how much Didion's beaches, and those very popular beaches of *Baywatch* too, articulate segrega-

tionist social and spatial practices. Segregation has the convenient consequence of granting spatial mobility rather exclusively to L.A.'s white population while disciplining black people to Watts or East L.A. where they
ostensibly belong, always signifiers for an urban or social narrative, never
signifiers (in *western* discourse, that is) for "the natural."

Black Los Angeles and Wanda Coleman

The Los Angeles I know, the way I grew up in it in the '50s, doesn't exist in literature yet. . . .
Everybody I know is writing about Hollywood or Orange County or Beverly Hills, but they are
not writing about the Los Angeles that I grew up in [Watts]. So in a sense I have a stake here. I
like cars, I like driving, I love the freeway. I am very much a product of the environment, but I feel
like I am trapped here the way you feel like you are trapped in any kind of ghetto, any kind of
prison. You just don't have the choice [to leave], you don't have the option.
—Wanda Coleman, Los Angeles Times interview (1982)

After Rodney King and the 1992 South Central riots, I doubt many Americans would depopulate Los Angeles of its black citizenry.[40] Over the last
twenty years, in fact, in both popular and governmental discourses about
American cities, African American populations increasingly "just seem to
go with" urban territory. Historian and urban planner Dolores Hayden
notes that the racial composition of America's cities has changed dramatically since the 1970s (white populations comprised 70 percent of the top ten
cities in 1970 and had dropped to 40 percent by 1990).[41] In popular political
discourse today, rhetorics of the "inner city" suggest the tensions of American race relations at the same time they burden the "inner city" with every
major social problem (crime, violence, poverty, drugs, underemployment,
family instability, illiteracy, etc.) that plagues national, not just "inner city,"
culture.

The above remarks announce this section on Wanda Coleman because, I
want to underline, African Americans come into contemporary western
discourse already signifiers for an urban or social narrative, already signifiers, arguably, for that which is postmodern, too. What more apt image of
postmodern chaos and social insanity than the burning of South Central, at
least if one views it from some "authentic" landscape of westernness? This is
especially true since the flames, smoke, and looting so often consumed the
businesses and homes of the very same residents who set the blazes going.
To the extent that the urban and the postmodern (not to mention the Cal-

ifornian) are generally regarded in western criticism as antitheses of the "real" West, African American peoples and cultural production habitually meet up with western geographical imaginations on the fringes of what constitutes western identity. (Might this hint at why western literary critics, unlike western historians, have written so little on black western writers and at why black scholars are not at all present in professional groups devoted to western literature?)

Let us return then to the previous assertion. If few Americans after the riots would depopulate Los Angeles of its black citizenry, it also remains true that the riots still may not have populated Los Angeles on terms that are both black and western, not to mention female. That is, granting that Los Angeles is populated by African Americans is an altogether different matter than is spatializing western terrains in ways that circulate African American female cultures and historic presence within western spatial fields.

Wanda Coleman, as both a public figure and a poet, is interested in precisely the above task. To say the least, then, Coleman brings a different perspective to the California myth of mobility, beautiful people, and sun-drenched days. She brings a different perspective to L.A.'s antimythical or noir cultural tradition, too. Unlike Joan Didion, that consummate Californian, and in spite of being also (in her own words) a "native," Wanda Coleman is no insider. As Coleman wryly lamented in "Malice in Movieland," an early-1990s (pre-riot) poem, after twenty years of writing, even after winning an Emmy for her screenwriting work on *Days of Our Lives*,[42] she still cannot get inside the movie business, even though she "gives good meeting . . . and turns emotional lead into literary gold."[43] As the sexually suggestive poetic image insists, Coleman "performs" both as woman writer in a male-gendered culture industry but also—and this is the historical burden of black womanhood[44]—as a sexualized, black woman worker. But no matter how good she "gives it," it's never good enough to make her a real power player. Don't take it personally, though, the poem's executive speaker tells her—meaning, don't take it racially. However, race, of course, always matters, a fact demonstrated yet again when, during the South Central riots, the *Los Angeles Times* approaches Coleman for an insider story. Miraculously, after the riots, Coleman is offered a semiregular column, titled "On the Town," a tremendous boon to her career, which she eagerly accepts.[45] Coleman comes into a broader local and national purview, then, on the heels of the South Central riots, when some of the powers-that-be suddenly notice, for the first time, that there is not just an articulate African American who can speak about the riots but a woman who is also a writer. And she's been around over twenty years, already. Imagine that.

Coleman's reputation as a writer has grown steadily within L.A. since the early 1970s, when her work first appeared. She has written volumes of poetry as well as reviews and columns for various Los Angeles papers.[46] She has cohosted a radio program, released CDs of her poetry recordings, and won both National Endowment for the Arts and Guggenheim fellowships in addition to the Emmy noted above. Most recently and visibly, Coleman's column for the *Los Angeles Times* has widened her audience and secured her literary prospects. So why, then, in a cultural climate hospitable to black women writers, is Coleman virtually unknown outside of Los Angeles?

My argument, to put it simply, is that Coleman falls through the spatial gaps. The literary territory she inhabits confounds the spatial assumptions of the various geographical imaginations she might be expected to call upon to fashion her tales. As I argued in Chapter 1, African American geographical imaginations most often work between southern/northern poles. That spatial imaginary quite effectively and immediately evokes the legacy of slavery, as well as black cultural adaptation and resilience in the face of it. By deploying the northern/southern geocultural imaginary, African American writers narrate race relations in the present through spatial conventions that simultaneously keep alive America's slave-trading past.

But the north/south inclination of black geographical imaginations also renders a poet like Wanda Coleman out of place, seemingly bereft of a cultural logic (meaning a *spatial* logic) that might explain her "L.A.-ness." As evidence, consider that until recently, Coleman has not been taken up by African American Studies.[47] Her critical marginality must be seen at least partly as an outcome of her unusual status as a black poet who is identified exclusively with the West Coast. Coleman herself has made this point when she says, "I'm from the West Coast. Most black writers come from the South or the East."[48] She also has noted, "Unfortunately, if you want to be taken seriously in this nation, you have to be sanctioned by the skies of the East Coast."[49] Coleman's comments, demonstrating as they do an explicit critique of northeastern regional chauvinism as well as an awareness of the north/south imaginary that dominates African American literary culture, are an indication of the raised consciousness, and confidence, that the new regionalist movement has brought to western writers.

Thus Coleman might expect to find some comprehending audience, or some better spatial "home," amidst western geographic imaginations, right?

Unfortunately not. Centered as they are on the westering experience, on stories of mountain men, covered wagons leaving civilization behind for the great American wilderness, on searches for the "big rock candy mountain," the dominant western imaginary charts its principal historical drama in eastern/western terms. To the extent that nonwhites figure in this drama, they are American Indians and, to a far less common extent, Mexican Americans or Asian immigrants. Where, in traditional western geographical imaginations, is there any room or historical logic for representing or understanding the L.A. of Wanda Coleman or Walter Mosley, the L.A. of Rodney King or the 1992 South Central riots? For that matter, what critical tradition sustains any kind of California "girl," or imagines Southern Californian women as other than beachy nonintellectuals?

In order to speak, Coleman must create some new literary landscape, some new western cultural space—but out of what? What new plots, aesthetic philosophies, or narrative strategies will articulate the *im*mobilities that govern Coleman's, and her female poetic subjects', relationships to western spaces? How, in a culture given over to the car and the (mistaken) assumption that all bodies move equally easily through space, is Coleman to represent characters whose less moneyed mode of mobility is walking, or riding the bus?

Of all of Coleman's poetry, let's look at her first collection, *Mad Dog, Black Lady* (1979), for here is the raw and revealing initial attempt to join urban with western with black with female with California stories. What holds all of these stories tentatively together is the L.A. story, but *this* L.A. we haven't seen much before—not on TV, not in movies, not in either literary or film noir. As a collection written during the 1970s, *Mad Dog, Black Lady* provides a comparison to Didion's Southern California of approximately the same period. Like Didion, Coleman takes up the seedy underbelly of things. She writes about the culture industry as well as the pimping, whoring, and struggling to survive that characterizes female life for her poetic protagonists. In more ways that one might first allow, Didion and Coleman have something in common. But their sisterly struggle ends where female identity meets up with racial and economic status. Coleman's women are black. And poor. They were born poor, they work and yet remain poor. Short of a miracle, they will die poor.

Because Coleman lives in the heart of a regional economy beginning to undergo the transition to a postmodern economy (recall that theorists have dubbed Los Angeles *the* window onto the global marketplace), Coleman senses earlier than do most commentators that during the early 1970s a profound cultural shift, which is additionally an economic shift, is underway. Coleman's earliest poetry can thus be read as something of an enraged response to that shift, to what David Harvey calls capital's revamped, more flexible regimes of accumulation.[50] Coleman anxiously witnesses the arrival of the new service sector, which will come to be the majority employer of the nation's disadvantaged, especially women. By the mid-1970s, Coleman sees the writing on the wall; she anticipates the decline in decent jobs for the nation's underclass that comes with globalization, and she worries that the consequences of these declines will be catastrophic for the residents of her hometown, Watts, and for black America generally. Indeed, it is this historically specific brand of underclass formation, put in motion by the forces of globalization that produces Coleman's particular postmodern, working-class, poetic stance.

This changed economic environment seems to require new strategies of political resistance. Theorist and critic bell hooks offers a related observation: "Militant [1960s] protest was [ultimately] stifled by a powerful, repressive postmodern state. . . . It [thus] has become necessary to find new avenues to transmit the messages of black liberation struggle, new ways to talk about racism and other politics of domination."[51] For hooks, new resistance strategies include what she calls "radical postmodernist practice," through which voices of ignored or marginalized peoples are made audible. For Coleman, growing up in the shadow of media-dominated Hollywood, new resistance strategies are linked to asserting a black presence in representation at large and, importantly, to claiming and naming western spaces. These are the various political projects of *Mad Dog, Black Lady*.

This "black los angeles," as the last line of Coleman's first poem, "Where I Live," calls it, is one of bullets and blood, of helicopter surveillance and drive-by shootings, of (gangbanging) Crips and Brims, of soul radio, of always, always hustling to make the rent. More to the point, *this* Los Angeles is one where black women go about their daily lives. What is immediate about Coleman's poetic world is the degree to which it problematizes the cultural assumptions usually evoked by the West, western landscapes, California, or even Los Angeles as the genre of literary noir creepily presents it. The controlling metaphors and antimetaphors of the region, to use one of Didion's favorite phrases, "do not apply." There is no unlimited possibility here in Coleman's poetic landscapes, no upward mobility, no beautiful or redemptive vistas, no Stegnerian geography of hope. Coleman's poetic subjects are trapped in urban L.A., prisoners in a polluted environment that is world-renowned for curative climates and individual freedom.

When the famous Southern California sun might shine down on Watts is hard to say, for *this* California happens at night, on dark street corners, in smoky barrooms, upon the gray-black asphalt landscapes of the embattled ghetto. If the emphasis on "darkness" and images of pool halls or street corners echoes some of the recurrent images of both film and literary noir, the protagonists of Coleman poetry in general do not. The various speakers of this particular poem, for example, are the anonymous black women whose daily lives happen beyond society's or noir's notice—the "old black woman up the street . . . [who] collects the neighborhood trash and begs kindness in doorways" (13), the nightclub barmaid who suffers "flesh bruised from niggahs pinching my meat and feeling my thighs, my ears full of spit from whispers and obscene suggestions" (13), the "insane old bitch next door beating on the wall, scaring the kids" (14).

If these women stand in, at least at first glance, for The Black Ghetto Woman, Coleman's point is not to reinscribe racialized and gendered stereotypes, which would only render these women again invisible. Rather, the net effect of the poem is to demonstrate that, no matter what outsiders might think, the "black ghetto woman" is not finally or exclusively a victim. Neither is she somebody's stereotype. The speakers of "Where I Live" live in Watts, yes, that place of bullets and blood, of choppers overhead and slumlords, that place controlled by forces distinctly *outside* of Watts. But the social spaces of Watts are not experienced only on outsiders' terms. This play between insider and outsider statuses works its way throughout the poem, producing the sudden surprise and rebellious release at poem's end.

"Where I live," the poem begins, is "at the lip of a big black vagina birthing nappy headed pickaninnies every hour on the hour" (13). Coleman's language here crudely reproduces southern white supremacist ideology. Black women are reduced to (presumably monstrous) "big black vaginas," and they birth not children to be loved and raised into productive maturity, but instead an endless stream of (presumably stupid and lazy) "nappy headed pickaninnies." Deliberately opening this poem via racialized, gendered, and regionalist (southern) clichés—the kind of imagery through which Coleman might expect an outsider to judge the Watts community— suggests the hate rhetorics about black families and black women that black peoples labor under. But there's more here than an evocation of black suffering. Coleman twists these hate rhetorics to her own ends and in so doing makes a larger point about what it's like to be on the inside of Watts looking out. We get "hamburgerfishchilli" smells, a scene in which Mexican American low riders (not just white/black tensions) threaten black safety. We feel the aggressive homophobia of local sexual politics, the colors of an old woman's permanent "dress" of loneliness, and, of course, the constant—a struggle for black female survival and integrity.

As the reader reads on to the poem's end and finds that the crude line "where I live / at the lip of a big black vagina" repeats and indeed frames the final brash poetic moment ("she's the baddest piece of ass on the west coast / named black los angeles"), the lingering aftereffect is less one of racial or female suffering than of adaptation, survival, and a sly, confident, and defiant victory. If Coleman begins by invoking the stereotypes harassing her and her black female subjects every day of their lives, she ends by exposing and redefining these same stereotypes and locating within them the entirety of African Americans in Watts—women at the head, that is, of Southern California's black community.

Against insurmountable odds, against even a foe as powerful as a pimping welfare state ("the county is her pimp"), the various black women workers who are Coleman's speakers *become* black Los Angeles. Coleman makes herself and black womanhood the principal subjects of L.A. cultural geography. This Los Angeles is not the one that outsiders pity or condemn. This Los Angeles (again, here, links to Didion) is one in which women persevere according to their own rules and with some amount of self-respect intact. In other words, this is an altogether different space, one with different meanings than those conventionally assigned to "Watts" or black Los Angeles. If black women are made into whores by a welfare state that exacts motherhood as the price of a food stamp, if they have to "put out" to eat, then, by God, they'll do the job right, and at the end of the work day they'll stand up and be counted. No shamed slinking into the shadows here. After all, theirs is the baddest piece of ass on the West Coast.

This sassy emplotment of Los Angeles geography maps an alternative moral economy onto spaces that otherwise do not feature black women as presences within the city's landscapes. It does so, moreover, in ways that are affirming and that account for, in nondepreciatory ways, the historical sexualization of black women's bodies. Suddenly, women's experiences of space—*their* nighttimes, individual indignities, and graces—find their ways into "the black story," the "Los Angeles story," the "California story," and so on. Coleman lays claim to multiple territories at once, and though none of them alone provides her an enabling logic from which to speak, all of them deployed at once permit her the last word. The "I" figures of this poem completely transform the geography of Los Angeles proper by integrating a feminist Watts into Southern California urban history. This black Los Angeles is female, sexual, victimized by any number of circumstances, but still fighting, raising children and seeking pleasure, and going on about the daily business of life on something like self-devised terms.

The above consideration of city spaces should not be concluded without pausing to consider the kind of spatial field that the city represents for urban ghetto dwellers who cannot leave. As critic John Jeffries has argued, blacks "have rarely found 'the city' to be a place of refuge" from what he sees as parochialism or racist surveillance.[52] Historian Dolores Hayden draws on James Baldwin to make a similar point. Baldwin writes, "I remember my first sight of New York. . . . You know—you know instinctively—that none of this is for you."[53] I understand both sentiments, and want therefore to note a qualification to my earlier argument about the opportunity that new female regionalists find in the spatial fields of western cities. As Coleman clearly demonstrates, her poetic subjects have no choice but to remain in city spaces. Their entrapments are not the result primarily of psychic or gendered logics, as is the case, for example, for Didion's Maria. They instead are prisoners of poverty, and economic disability goes hand in hand with racial and gendered oppression.

But I would also argue, as critic Carolyn Mitchell has argued about Ntozake Shange's work,[54] that Coleman's women outlast, if they don't entirely transcend, the problems that city spaces present them. Thus I will insist too, even having made the above qualification, that although city spaces may not always be enabling spaces from which Coleman articulates stories that are simultaneously black, female, and western, *rural* or *wild* spaces enable black feminist presence even less. And it is this polarized choice that faces all western women writers, whatever their race. It comes with the western imaginative territory, whether one likes it or not. So, given the unavoidable dilemma, I return then to argue that city spaces are an enabling imaginary for articulating black feminist existence. Coleman's own evolving career as an artist, who comes into relative prominence only on the dubious coattails of the 1992 South Central riots, supports such a claim.

To illustrate the above points from a different angle, I turn here to two beach poems from *Mad Dog, Black Lady*, which demonstrate the racialized character of natural landscape conventions and show Coleman's attempts to reorient California narratives so that by definition they do not exclude black narratives. Coleman's beach poems comment on California beach culture as, first and foremost, white leisure culture and demonstrate the coercive social practices that "natural" landscape conventions encourage. But they also execute Coleman's own politics of difference, her exercise of the (bell hooks–compatible) postmodernist strategy whereby unplaced peoples suddenly take or insist upon some new place, and the black liberation struggle is therefore articulated and advanced in new and original terms.

The first beach poem I'll consider, "His Old Flame, Lady Venice," tells the story of a black woman in love with a black man. The man has been run off Venice Beach by racist, young white men sometime in the past. The poem narrates the day when the banished black man returns with the speaker and they walk the Venice Beach boardwalk together, bumping into his old acquaintances, rekindling memories of old times, and, in the process, reawakening this man's desire to return. In choosing Venice as literary subject, Coleman represents one of the most urbanized and unabashedly commoditized beach geographies in Southern California. Visitors to Venice Beach stroll not with their sandals dangling from their fingertips, their feet feeling sand or the rush of the water onto shore, but rather they stroll (or skate or jog or skateboard or rollerblade or bike) down a miles-long stretch of concrete boardwalk, lined on each side with vendors. Among a million other things, these small entrepreneurs sell accoutrements of "beach experience"—visors, sunning oils, sandals, sunglasses, postcards of Venice Beach, pricey bottled water, beach wear, beach gear, health food. One need never get sand between one's toes to have a "beach experience," is my point. The beach, in this picture, is site of, and for, American consumer culture—surely not what Wallace Stegner had in mind when he said western landscape was the force against which Americans forged national character.

But what is being consumed? One "product," Coleman suggests, is a very classed and racialized form of leisure culture, in which the sexualized white body is not just representative but prescriptively normative or "natural" to beach spaces. To fit within the social geometry of Venice beach, then, one must somehow "be white." All of the old friends whom the poetic speaker encounters are implicitly white. They enact a distinctly white, bourgeois lifestyle as gourmet cooks, paddle tennis and chess players, jazz connoisseurs. This poetic world, bordering as it does on the collection's surrounding poetic renderings of Watts bullets, blood, hunger, and rage, registers a profound mismatch, rupture, collision. Clearly, we are now in white social space where the sun shines, tanned (darkened) skin is a status symbol, everyone is healthy, and the police are friends.

By this poem's end, the speaker realizes that the man she loves is himself in love with a leisure beach culture that not only is racialized white but exacts a kind of prescriptive homage to bourgeois culture, and to white *bodies* in particular. Not just any white bodies will do. The preferred bodies are featured on Venice Beach postcards—bikinied young women or the pumped-up white men on rollerblades. Blondeness sells well, too. The speaker's male lover is willing to "pass"—at least culturally—in order to partake of beach culture. He is willing, perhaps, to be exoticized. But the poem's speaker won't pass with him; she'll give up the man before she stoops that low. Coleman genders the beach female ("Lady Venice") to mark this man's multiple betrayals—his "other woman" is the white, bourgeois body culture unfolding along that bizarre stretch of coastline known as the Venice Beach boardwalk.

Now, if the above commoditized beach landscape is very obviously em-plotted with racialized cultural values and thereby critiques, even parodies, "natural" landscape conventions, other Southern Californian beaches are less so. It is these that come in for comment in Coleman's "Beaches. Why I Don't Care for Them" (121). The poem's first lines speak clearly to the destructive effects that this racialized imaginary exerts on one teenage girl's self-esteem:

> associations: years of being ashamed/my sometimes
> fat, ordinary body. years later shame passed
> left a sad after-taste. mama threatening to beat me if i
>   got my hair
> wet. curses as she brushed the sand out, "it's gonna break
>   it off—it's
> gonna ruin your scalp." or the tall blond haired gold-bronze
>   muscled
> life guards who played with the little white-ones but gawked
>   at us like we were lepers
> *sound. the water serpent's breath: a depth as vast as my hatred*

The poem's speaker recalls the adolescent anxiety of misfitting with beach beauty conventions. She is fat, ordinary. But most of all, she is black. Her hair doesn't look right (meaning it doesn't look white) when it is wet, and her mother, in a perverse attempt to protect her from racial humiliation, threatens to beat her if she gets it wet. The Adonises of the sand, lifeguards, "gawk" at black beachgoers, suggesting that they don't belong there, that blackness is a physically grotesque disease, like leprosy. These experiences add up to an association of ocean sounds with a vast hatred, a hatred of racialist attitudes that demean black people and colonize beach geography, putting white people and firm bodies in positions of power, authority, and ownership. As the title says, the speaker doesn't "care for" this beach, where white beauty and power reigns.

But, when the beach is "cold, hostile and grey," the speaker feels "kin to it." "Or at night," she tells us, it talks to her. Here, the speaker remakes the beach in ways that are not waterlogged by images of white surf culture, hard-bodied bathing beauties, or summery, coconut-oiled days. Coleman's "black los angeles," recall, is that of Los Angeles at night, "darkened." In this region associated with lightness, sunshine, and whiteness, "dark" people cannot lay claim to the day. But Coleman refuses spatial erasure. In a move that breaks new ground in the formation of African American geographical imaginations, Coleman claims the darkened California daytime (the grayness of the water on a cold day) or the California night as black geography. In that space she can enact stories that work from different spatial assumptions and biases. There she spatializes Southern California social relations so as to liberate people, like those from Watts, who are not otherwise able to move about freely in the regional imaginary.

The poem's speaker tells us she prefers the "poor man's beach," a beach she can "darken":

> . . . where bodies echo my chromatic scheme from
> just-can-pass to pitch-tar-black, at home among fleshy
>   rumps, tummys,
> thighs, breasts jiggling a freedom our hearts will never know
> *sound. eternal splash. a depth as vast as my love*

The last line quoted above, "*sound, eternal splash. a depth as vast as my love*," is italicized, linking it to the previously italicized line, "*sound. the water serpent's breath: a depth as vast as my hatred.*" These two lines superimpose differently racialized beach geographies and evoke vastly different feelings in the poem's speaker. One line, suggestive of the dominant narrative constructed by white people with themselves as normative examples of beauty, creates self-hatred and rage in the poem's speaker. The other, constructed by Coleman as poet, posits the chromatic range of black people's coloration as normative. Fleshy, jiggling bodies are normative, too. Narrating a geography that accepts, values, and is defined by blackness and by bodies not hardened by exercise and low-fat food creates in the poem's speaker an association of ocean sounds with vast love. She loves this ocean now, because she has written it as a mirroring and affirming social space for herself and others like her.

The poem closes by imagining an ocean, and a literary narrative about the ocean, that is neither racialized white nor regionalized in exclusively northeastern terms:

> . . . in my fantasy i would challenge the ocean
> a feminist ahab stalking the great white whale. harpoon it
>   and ride down
> down to meet davy jones, content, for my america dies with me.
> *sound. swoosh swoosh the scythe. a depth as vast as my vision*

The challenge Coleman poses is to kill off the "white maleness" that the whale represents to her as African American feminist artist and to kill off the dominance of *Moby Dick* and the bias toward New England culture in American literary history. These deaths, the poem implies, would enable the emergence of a vast and new visionary space, one that the speaker could "learn to like." Perhaps, as Coleman's closing lines suggest, on such a new landscape, the poem's speaker and her male lover might survive and prosper as a couple. Perhaps there the speaker's lover will no longer cheat on her, as he has, implicitly in the poem, earlier. She might even trust him enough, as she says in the last line, to "let you teach me how to tread water." Were the whale dead, the speaker, a nonswimmer—symbol of her ultimate nonsafety on beach geographies dominated by a white-male imaginary—might entrust the black man with her emotional life. Part of Coleman's alternative world, as I read it, is one in which black men stop treating black women like whores. On darkened beaches populated by bodies that jiggle, relations between black heterosexual men and women are freed of the demoralizing pressures that white supremacist culture exerts on black life and love. But that world is possible only when a broader, white supremacist, and male-dominated social world is upset and meets with Davy Jones, at the ocean bottom.

Let me draw together some of the new spatial terrains that Coleman's poetry represents and charts. At the broadest, it puts Watts on the literary map of both Southern California and African America and links California to black *and* western *and* feminist narratives. We begin to see, from Coleman, how Los Angeles might be spatialized when nondominant subjects' relationships to space occupy the center of analysis. One apparent spatial fact is that of restricted mobility. We do not see Coleman's poetic subjects ritualistically traversing one after another of Los Angeles's freeways, for example, as does Maria in Didion's *Play It as It Lays*. They do not end up in the desert at day's end, or in any other location where they might be a solitary black person. Not only do they not have the money (one notices in Coleman's poetry a real first: Los Angelenos who ride the bus), but they do not possess the spatial license or right. The *last* sensible spatial behavior is to be conspicuously visible in a white area: such visibility attracts racial harassment. Thus blacks are "contained" within Watts, restricted to Watts. The waitresses, barmaids, prostitutes, destitute elderly women, welfare mothers, and other women workers who comprise Coleman's poetic subjects live out their lives within extremely small and circumscribed spaces. They come and go within very plotted routes (like those of buses) in which their movements are already predetermined and approved. The observation to make here, finally, is about limited or controlled access to the city.[55]

Not only is access limited by race, but the ways that women move through space in Los Angeles, particularly in the degree to which movements are embodied, are different from the ways that men move through space. Feminist geographers use issues of the body, and of subjects' embodiments, as overt points of departure for many discussions about gender and space. They insist that it is only white, privileged men who escape the marking of nature upon the body. All other subjects (including nonwhite men) enter space and representation in embodied form.

Although Coleman certainly attends to the ways black male bodies are marked and visible and therefore also vulnerable, I am interested here in female bodies, and the ways their representation reorients recent theoretical renderings of Los Angeles. Both Didion and Coleman write women who bleed, birth, vomit, weep, smoke, negotiate sex, get on and off buses, and eat. They suffer coerced abortions, bruised thighs from groping pinches; they suffer ears full of spit from drunkenly whispered obscenities, black eyes from S/M practices that leave men holding the belt afterwards. These women work and live in contexts that always figure them as bodies, bodies to hustle or demean or praise or photograph or ignore, but bodies nonetheless framed within patriarchal visual ideologies that make Woman the object of male commentary, pleasure, or erasure. If one reads any of the "big books" on Los Angeles and postmodernism, the eschatological list above should reveal something of what is missing. The subjects in, say, Soja's L.A. seem to have to no bodies at all, which means only that they have (predominantly white, straight) male bodies and that their male narrators are unconscious about the privileges of masculinity.

Coleman's and Didion's renderings of Los Angeles suggest, by contrast, the embodied nature of any spatial relation. Los Angeles as a spatial field deserves special scrutiny on the topic of body culture, for the city is so invested in the production of ideal, sexualized bodies, *white* bodies in particular. The Los Angeles women that Coleman and Didion articulate do battle for female self-respect in a regional culture that is geared, perhaps more so than nearly any in the world, to the manufacture of cultural images about women that are, by and large, racist and antifeminist. One cannot depart meetings with Coleman's and Didion's Los Angeleses without some reckoning, finally, with the materiality of bodies as they move through and invent the sociality of space itself. In the final analysis, each writer's repopulation of Los Angeles geography radically changes how critics might make sense of Southern Californian spaces. The longings, trials, accomplishments of women take center stage in this renarrativized, female Los Angeles. The feminist philosophies conveyed via Didion's "miseries peculiar to women" and Coleman's "baddest pieces of ass on the west coast" no longer seem so foreign, thereafter, to what constitutes either L.A. or paradigmatic postmodernity.

I'd like to close this discussion of Wanda Coleman by teasing out some of its implications for contemporary female literary history. Though Coleman becomes (relatively) known only in the 1990s, I forward her here as an early example of the evolving new female regionalist sensibility. Readers will recall that the new regionalism as I have described it in Chapter 1 develops in the late 1960s when (mostly nonwhite) writers like James Welch, N. Scott Momaday, Rudolfo Anaya, Frank Chin, Gerald Haslam, and many others begin producing and publishing poetry, story collections, and novels that fundamentally reconfigure the imaginative spaces of literary westerns. Add to these civil rights–inspired geographical imaginations those of the Stegnerian bent, and the combination is a whole new generation of western writers who will come at western landscapes with fresh minds and political intentions (writers like John Nichols, Ivan Doig, Norman Maclean, Richard Rodriguez, and William Kittredge, to name just a few).

Female literary history, however, proceeds according to a slightly different time line, blooming and maturing later. By 1973, when the male side is in full swing, the female side is barely up and on its feet. Poetry is the dominant product (only the most luminary of writers, like Silko or Kingston, are close to putting out novels), and the primary producers of it are nonwhite writers. I thus forward Coleman here as early example of the new female regionalism in its formative years. Coleman is very much a creator of and "on to" the regionalist impulse well in advance of its commercial debut in the mid-1980s, and this is in spite of the consequential fact that her interest in writing about Los Angeles creates, from the beginning, a distance between herself and the audiences and critics who promote and gatekeep black literature.

This genealogical point is crucial to establishing the complex origins of the new female regionalism, for in Coleman's engagement with Southern California as a regional imaginary, one can see the broader "first wave" struggles of many nonwhite, western female poets of the 1970s (for example, Leslie Marmon Silko, Lorna Dee Cervantes, Ana Castillo, Paula Gunn Allen, Janet Campbell, Wendy Rose, Joy Harjo, Angela de Hojos, Carmen Tafolla, Estela Portillo Trambley, Marcela Christine Lucero-Trujillo, Jessica Hagedorn, Mitsuye Yamada, and Karen Tei Yamashita). Like most of them, Coleman feels herself to be bereft of traditions that express female, feminist, and western (or counterwestern) relationships to American space. But unlike them, Coleman cannot readily deploy civil rights geographical imaginations to situate her racial relationship to western spaces. She cannot readily deploy the spatial field of Aztlán, for example, to situate her racial relationship to the West and, through it, to American literary culture at large.

As poetic influences, Coleman names "the same white males who have influenced everybody else": Charles Olsen, Charles Bukowski, Pound, Poe, and Shelley.[56] Her most important literary mentors, Nathanael West and Bukowski, show unmistakable connections to Los Angeles literary landscapes. Though she locates herself in the "deeper culture of the black church and the black blues tradition," as a poet, Coleman says, "I am a whole new animal. I don't see myself in terms of a tradition." I would agree. Coleman is a "new animal," who charts new imaginative territory. But so do almost all of the new female regionalists. There is no tradition that enables any of them an easy voice. They all have and take allies.

As I have repeatedly insisted, one of the allies of which Coleman takes full advantage is that of the emerging new sense of space available in postmodernist culture. By creating new cultural spaces of black presence where none existed before, Coleman heeds bell hooks's call to make neglected or suppressed voices of American culture heard, to make difference a political virtue, instead of a stigma. Coleman practices hooks's "politics of difference" insofar as she locates, makes visible, a very unplaced, invisible American population, that of working women meeting each new day from within the Southern California ghetto.

Less obvious points should also be made about Coleman's engagement with postmodernism. One aspect of postmodernism, implied already, is that the new global economic structure, discernible in American culture after 1973, shapes indelibly the forms that self-representation and community representation assume. At the cultural heart of this new economic order is the idea of *simultaneity*: the idea, for instance, in financial terms, of markets taking upward or downward cues from factors that are at once both local and global. Simultaneity also describes what it is to be somebody like Wanda Coleman: to be at the same time, and indivisibly, black, female, poor, a Californian, an urban westerner, inheritor of geographic imaginations both western (with east/west spatial affinities) and African American (with north/south spatial affinities). The constant conjunction of these identities, in fact, defines the postmodern condition, the sense of occupying multiple spaces simultaneously (in the Einsteinian sense), and the impossibility, therefore, of being able to hold stable a single, objective identity (like race) from among other competing and equally compelling identities (like gender or class or regional status). In conclusion, these spaces of simultaneity that Wanda Coleman's poetry appropriates and charts are crucial ones for new female regionalists. They permit women writers to emplot western landscapes and identify themselves as western citizens on terms that don't forever reverberate with some version of a Sophie's choice.

Northern California with Tripmaster Kingston

Sojourners no more but. Immigration got fooled already. You not be Overseas Chinese. You be here. You're here to stay. I am deeply, indigenously here. And my mother and father are indigenous. Native Sons and Daughters of the Golden State. Which was the name our ancestors made up to counteract those racists, Native Sons and Daughters of the Golden West.
—Wittman Ah Sing, in *Tripmaster Monkey*

The narration of San Francisco presents a different set of challenges and problems for writers and critics. Unlike Los Angeles, Northern California's main city is neither curative mecca nor a city intellectuals love to hate.[57] It boasts a long history of "homegrown intelligentsia" that L.A. lacks, a history in which intellectuals are not perceived to be owned or corrupted by the profit-driven film industry.[58] The role of the San Francisco Bay Area in California and national mythology is different, too. As the urban seat of the mid-nineteenth-century gold rush, the gateway to the Mother Lode, San Francisco *as a city* overflows with the sense of romance usually reserved for the nonurban frontier West. From the beginning of its economic development and its popular representation in the mid-1800s, San Francisco is characterized as a city in a class of its own, a symbol of beginnings and possibility—above all, like the West itself, of hope.[59] The first of western cities—different from, without being inferior to, eastern cities—San Francisco is a privileged western space, one that, from its inception, is cosmopolitan yet simultaneously "authentically" western. But if its special allure grows out of a romantic, nineteenth-century, frontier identity, the city's principal "landscape" nonetheless is cultural. San Francisco's black oaks and eucalyptus, its foggy coastline and bay, its surrounding low hills—though full of "natural" beauty—are implicitly conceded, from the beginning, to intersect with a thriving economic and cultural center.

When it comes to representing nature, this difference in northern versus southern landscape conventions allows Northern California writers not only to resist the nature-as-redemption narrative but very often to take up, through cultural landscapes, questions of American and western *history*. Thus, it is the cultural, not the "natural," landscape that directs the ways that Maxine Hong Kingston approaches her various literary projects. All of Kingston's books—*Woman Warrior* (1976), *China Men* (1980), and *Tripmaster Monkey* (1989)—take up the cultural landscapes of Northern California to talk specifically about Asian American history. All of these books trouble a solely romantic narration of the regional imaginary. But it is *Tripmaster Monkey* that I'll focus on here, for the novel locates us squarely in the contemporary Bay Area, home to the nation's countercultural revolt, a revolt that ultimately has a great impact on the development of new regionalist political sensibility.

Maxine Hong Kingston needs little introduction to most critics of contemporary literature. Since her writings first appeared in the mid-1970s, Kingston has been extraordinarily well-reviewed, particularly in the northeast. She is the subject of an array of scholarly critical work, much of it taking up the exemplary courage of her no-holds-barred feminism, her particular deconstructive brand of cultural nationalism, or her rivalry with misogynist Frank Chin.[60] One valuable critical lens—that of western woman writer—is generally missing from Kingston's critical reception. Although this is changing, Asian Americanists as a rule have not regarded the relationship of Asian American literature to western literature as an important subject.[61] And, criticism of western literature, though it is beginning to claim Kingston as a western writer, has not integrated Kingston as an Asian American into definitions of western American. All of Kingston's work, as I noted above, is decidedly western, however, and the most self-conscious example is *Tripmaster Monkey*.[62] In it, Kingston aims to write herself into American literary history, but more explicitly into that of the American West, especially California.

Tripmaster Monkey opens with Kingston's protagonist, Wittman Ah Sing, taking a wild and wacky walk through one of the nation's most celebrated city parks: the Golden Gate. The book's initial line locates this story both regionally, in San Francisco, and also spatially, in Golden Gate Park—which is what I'll call a "mixed genre geography." By "mixed genre," I mean it is emplotted by both a "nature" and a "culture" narrative. Golden Gate Park is large enough and "wild" enough to be a naturalist retreat: one finds woods of eucalyptus, pine, and black oak. At the western edge of the park one finds Ocean Beach, too. But this is not a natural retreat to be confused with Southern California's landscapes. The mention of eucalyptus, pine, and black oak identify this as a specifically northern tale, because, as the narrator notes, "those three trees together is how you tell you're in northern California and not Los Angeles" (6). Simultaneously, Golden Gate Park is also figured as a "cultural" landscape—home to the Academy of Sciences, Steinhart Aquarium, the Japanese Tea Garden, the Shakespeare Garden, the Andrew Wyeth Museum, and the Conservatory—which is to say that Golden Gate Park is a site for the creation and promotion of different kinds of public histories.

As an already emplotted cultural space, then, the park is useful to Kingston for the particular cultural work she has in mind, namely, the invocation of recent histories performed upon Golden Gate Park's topographies, especially those of the various countercultural movements that comprised West Coast radicalism in the 1960s. Why this recall should occur in 1989 (the publication year of *Tripmaster Monkey*), many years after the last of the flower children have grown up and tended other gardens, is a topic I'll return to later. For now, the point is that *Tripmaster Monkey* opens by recalling the park's radical recent history, marking it as a notorious geography of contest, a site that enabled the enactment of many different kinds of social struggles. Crucially, however, the social struggles that Kingston maps upon park geography defy the more commonplace imagery of the countercultural scene.

In Golden Gate Park, so the most popular historical memory goes, the flower children blew bubbles, strummed guitars, and communed on such subjects as the nature of love, peace, and power. Located adjacent to the intersections of Haight and Ashbury Streets, where music stores, head shops, and coffeehouses served as meeting grounds for the newly arrived, the park provided a kind of overflow space in which to carry on the business of the counterculture: rocking out, dropping out, dropping acid, or ridding oneself of what was then often called "middle-class Freudian hang-ups."[63] What Kingston's Wittman adds to popular memory is a broader sense of just who constituted this incredibly diffuse social movement. If above I've described the "center" of the park's guitar-strumming counterculture, Kingston gives us its (supposed) liminal fringes or edges. Wittman, in his wacky walk through the park, does not meet up with hippies handing out flowers. Instead, he traverses the outer, less-traveled regions of park spaces and encounters there a psychotic, white, homeless woman; a recent Chinese immigrant family; and two black men—one of whom, like the white woman, is destitute, the other of whom is accompanied by a Doberman pinscher that he continually assaults with misogynist language. By peopling the park with figures who embody the movement's shortcomings—its racial and class bias as well as its overreliance on the notion of the personal as political—Kingston recreates Golden Gate Park culture so as to expand the political contours of the movement, making it more genuinely inclusive of issues of poverty, racial injustice, women's status, and the like.

Wittman should not be distanced too much, however, from the "center" of the goings-on, even if he enters spatial representation on its edges. For Kingston does not narrate Wittman as equally liminal to the other liminal figures mentioned above. Instead, these other figures serve to affirm his own sense of *belonging* to the counterculture, of being an authentic participant. The clearest example is the disjuncture between Wittman's own Chinese American identity and that of the "F.O.B." ("Fresh Off the Boat") Chinese immigrant family. Wittman's characterization of this immigrant family implies not shared history but his own transcendence of that history, his Americanness and sense of "knowing better."[64]

> The whole family taking a cheap outing on their day offu. Immigrants. Fresh Off The Boats out in public. Didn't know how to walk together. Spitting [sunflower] seeds. So uncool. You wouldn't mislike them on sight if their pants weren't so highwater, gym socks white and noticeable. . . . Can't get it right. Uncool. Uncool. (5)

The specific strategy Wittman deploys to express Americanness, we should note, is that of being "cool." "Coolness" links Wittman to the counterculture *and* to the bohemianism of the 1950s Bay Area Beat scene. Wittman wants his readers to know that he understands cool from the inside. He knows what it looks like, what it acts like, what it isn't and what it is. He's the real American item, so much so that he is privileged enough to become a beatnik, not some newly arrived F.O.B., trying to get things right. He's a fifth-generation Chinese American; he's been in California, he wants the reader to know, longer than most. And as early as, say, Didion's own pioneer family. (Kingston, like Didion and Coleman, makes yet another claim upon nativity.)

Golden Gate Park serves as a kind of port of entry, then, into the center of radical contemporary history. At that center, this text argues, is the role *culture* plays in the negotiation of radical history, the role culture plays in radical political struggle. The park acts as a transitional space for Wittman, where he makes the distinction between an F.O.B. immigrant identity and those identities that he will carry with him once he leaves the park: that of UC-Berkeley graduate, playwright, beatnik, and hip, literate, cultural revolutionary. The park acts as a transitional space for Kingston, too, for it functions as the site from which *Tripmaster Monkey* will stage its own interventions into American and western American literature. The counterculture, I am arguing here, spatialized over the topography of Golden Gate Park, is another originary site for the creation of the multiraciality and feminism of the new regionalism. Once Wittman exits countercultural space and moves into San Francisco's broader downtown and then on to Chinatown, he elaborates his sense of what California and American literatures have been, but, most importantly, what they ought to be.

Wittman himself—Chinese American hippie whose name signifies his authenticity as a national subject by aligning him with the quintessentially

American poet Walt Whitman—will be the first and central literary figure of the book. But Kingston spends time distinguishing this American artist from others. Wittman is not "el pachuco loco," not some crazy dude like (presumably) the legendary "Brown Buffalo" Oscar Zeta Acosta, Chicano accomplice in the escapades of new journalist Hunter S. Thompson. What los pachucos locos *do*, the narrator tells us, is commit suicide—the fate not only of Acosta but also, we are reminded on page one, of Hemingway. Wittman rejects suicide. In the first ten lines, then, Kingston evokes just what context she writes from: she is writing about Great Literature (she drops a reference to *Lolita* in the first line), American literature, and masculine literature—Walt Whitman, Hemingway, and the Beats, including Chicano Acosta.

But if American literature is Kingston's broadest context, western American literature is the literature she really zeroes in on, for it is the literature of California in particular, she believes, that is most relevant to Asian American history. As I noted above, California literary history comes into play once Wittman leaves Golden Gate Park, boards the city bus to Chinatown, and begins to read poet Rainer Maria Rilke aloud to fellow bus riders. As Wittman reads, he daydreams about what he considers an ideal job: becoming a reader of literature to passengers on the western railroads, a more romantic reading forum for Wittman than the city bus. If he were reading to train passengers, he tells us, here is what he would read:

On the train through Fresno—Saroyan; through the Salinas Valley—Steinbeck; through Monterey—*Cannery Row*; along the Big Sur ocean—Jack Kerouac; on the way to Weed—*Of Mice and Men*; in the Mother Lode—Mark Twain and Robert Louis Stevenson, who went on a honeymoon in *The Silverado Squatters*; *Roughing It* through Calaveras County and the Sacramento Valley; through the redwoods—John Muir; up into the Rockies—*The Big Rock Candy Mountain* by Wallace Stegner. Hollywood and San Elmo with John Fante. And all of the Central Valley on the Southern Pacific with migrant Carlos Bulosan, *America Is in the Heart.* . . . And he had yet to check out Gertrude Atherton, and Jack London of Oakland, and Ambrose Bierce of San Francisco. And to find "Relocation" Camp diaries. . . . He will refuse to be a reader of racist Frank Norris. He won't read Bret Harte either, in revenge for that Ah Sin thing. Nor *Ramona* by Helen Hunt Jackson, in case it turned out to be like *Gone With the Wind.* (9–10)

To the extent one can speak of a "canon" of California literature, this list includes its most revered figures before 1970: Steinbeck, Saroyan, Muir, Stegner. It expands that list to include the radical Beats, Twain, the unlikely Stevenson, the quirky Fante, and unionist and (the one nonwhite writer) Filipino Bulosan. There are some writers whose reputations continue undecided: Atherton, London, Bierce. There are writers yet to be read, like Japanese Americans, on the internment camps. And there are writers rejected by Wittman as racists (Norris, Harte) or as sentimentalists (Jackson).

Through this list Kingston foregrounds what she intends as her own cultural interventions. Kingston makes it clear, through Wittman, that she too "want[s] to spoil all those stories coming out of and set in New England Back East" (34). The reason to do so is to "blacken and to yellow Bill, Brooke, and Annie" (34). So this is first a critique of regional chauvinism, an expression of tiredness with "all those [eastern] stories" which center national historical and literary narratives away from any engagement with western geographical imaginations. But it is next a case for the Americanness of Chinese American identity and cultural production, for the "yellowing" of classic figures in American cultural history, and the case will be made by invoking both western racial and regional history.

Repeatedly Kingston links Asian American history with western American economic, social, and cultural history. The most developed example is the production of the play-within-the-novel, *Journey to the West* (a conglomeration of Chinese folktales and legends), which is staged as a western American cultural event, very much in the Beat tradition and open to anyone who wants to be part of its improvisational process. This move—whereby *Tripmaster Monkey* locates its multiple racial, national, and genre identities on the site of what might be called Beat *process*—suggests to me that at its political roots the new regionalism is infused with western counterculturalism. Wittman exhorts, "There is no [exotic] East here [in America]. West is meeting West. This was all West. All you saw was West. This is The Journey *In* the West" (308). Certainly Wittman means that Chinese Americans are "westerners" in the global sense, meaning west of the Far East. But he means even more that these particular Asian Americans are western Americans—not New Englanders, southerners, midwesterners.

Although there are numerous examples one could choose, one of the most telling indications of the text's claim upon western regional identity is Wittman's embrace of western regional physiognomy. He declares, "these eyes are cowboy eyes with which I'm looking at you, and you are looking back at me with cowboy eyes. We have the eyes that won the West" (314). Here, in an explicitly anti-essentialist move by Kingston, the narrative refuses to locate Chinese American racial identity in the body, especially not in the eyes. In so doing she challenges both the orientalist representation of Asian eyes as inscrutable ("They think they can't see into these little squinny eyes") at the same time that she questions the wisdom of founding contemporary Asian American cultural politics upon essentialist notions of racial identity (312). Neither will she concede that cowboy eyes are, by default, white people's eyes. Cowboys—mythical western figures—were a multiracial lot, she asserts, as is the production of *Journey to the West* itself.

Tripmaster Monkey makes inroads into western American literature by adding Asian America to its cast of literary characters, but it also demonstrates the limits of that literature—its inability to represent *women's* wants, needs, and experiences. Though Wittman is the book's protagonist, he is not, cleverly, the book's dominant voice. That role is occupied by a mischievous feminist narrator who, through her depiction of and distance from Wittman, reveals the masculinist ideals that guide his sense of himself, his role in the world, and his understanding of women. What we learn is that Wittman, by and large, knows very little about women, nor does he listen (at least at the beginning) to what women tell him about themselves.

Again, many examples come to mind, but the general statement one might make here is that the narrator repeatedly reveals Wittman's internal workings about women he finds attractive, only to pull him up short in the actual exchange between Wittman and whatever woman is in front of him. The earliest example in the book is that of the date between Nanci Lee and Wittman, in which the narrator gives extensive narrative vent to Wittman's need to be admired, even adored, by a woman in order to secure his manhood. In typical fashion the narrator comments, "O Someday Girl, find him and admire him for his interests. And dig his illusions. And laugh sincerely at his jokes" (14). While Wittman is tripping along on his own thoughts, telling Nanci his life story and half convincing himself that his Someday Girl is right now about to announce her undying affection, the narrator shows us Nanci Lee *not* as mirror for Wittman's self-reflection (her role in Wittman's eyes) but as subject in her own right. They duck into a bookstore together, and while Wittman (in his own mind) gives Nanci enough time to notice on the racks a play of his that has recently been published, Nanci strikes up a conversation, in French, with two other men in the store. She never will look over at Wittman's play. Instead, the bookstore scene turns not into a conversation about *him* as artist but toward *her* as artist, and toward the particular difficulties Asian American actresses face in trying to find roles not limited to oriental prostitutes or plain-faced peasants.

A similar dynamic operates in the narrator's treatment of the relationship between Wittman and Tana, the white woman who marries Wittman to save him from the draft. They are about to have sex for the first time, and the narrator again sets up Wittman for a big surprise. Here Wittman is, eager and hopeful and very much charmed by Tana's apartment to which he is intimately admitted, when suddenly she tells him matter-of-factly, "Darling, I've been thinking. The next time I get it on with a man, I set ground rules" (153). Too stunned to counter properly, he says instead, "Go on." Tana's ground rules amount to an acknowledgment, first, that "Making love is my idea as well as yours. This isn't just your idea, okay?" (153). This woman is a sexual subject, not a mirroring other for Wittman's discovery of himself. The other ground rule, according to Tana, is that "we can each of us cut out whenever we feel like it" (154). The narrator gives us Wittman's response as, "Damn. She beat him to it. Outplayed again. He was the tough-eyed one who had been planning to let the next girl know point by point what she would be in for entangling with him" (154). What has been accomplished by this exchange, and by the exchange above between Wittman and Nanci Lee, is a leveling of the gendered playing field. *Tripmaster Monkey* hence can proceed as a feminist text whose central protagonist (ostensibly) is a talented, lovable, and very narcissistic young man. But as is true in almost all trickster contexts, a competing protagonist always can be heard whispering her own story, and this story gets craftily forwarded alongside Wittman's and finally, even, eclipses it.

By arguing that this feminist voice eclipses Wittman's own, I wish to call attention to a feminist project that rarely takes center stage in discussions about this book or about the counterculture more broadly: the remaking of masculinity. In the above episodes, Kingston's feminist characters actively engage in the reform of male behavior and expectations. And in that effort they get a lift or assist from counterculturalism. The counterculture freed men from some of the more conventional and prescriptive gender roles *they* suffered under. It sanctioned men's long hair, flowered shirts, bell-bottomed pants, and open-toed sandals. In effect, the counterculture blessed a renovated male identity associated with the effeminate.

Tripmaster Monkey's critique of masculine self-absorption is thus more than a discussion of gender and interpersonal relations, art, or sexuality. It develops into a critique of the masculine bias that adheres in contemporary definitions of Asian American cultural identity. That identity, shaped in large part by the leadership of writer Frank Chin, is, in Kingston's opinion, fatally militaristic, racially separatist, and essentialist. All of these attributes, the text argues, ultimately favor the radical men who have invented them. Through them, men control who women love, who women take as political allies, and how women self-define (i.e., are you a feminist or an Asian American?). Moreover, the "effeminate Asian American man" that is so preoccupying and shaming a figure for a writer like Frank Chin (and for Wittman, too) is, from Kingston's perspective, not such a tragedy after all. Indeed, the "feminized" Asian American man may well be an alternative model of western masculinity to embrace.

Kingston rejects masculinist-militarist terms as the only viable ones on which to found ethnic identity or political strategy. In place of them, she forwards an antiseparatist, interracial, feminist, and pacifistic vision of progressive cultural nationalism. This alternative is most visible in the play-within-the-novel, *Journey to the West*. There Kingston converts Wittman's (Frank Chin–like) focus on Gwan Goong, the masculinist Chinese warrior as leader of Asian Americans, into a focus on peace.[65] In so doing, she also refigures the hypermasculine identity so much in favor among cultural revolutionaries—whether Malcolm X, Piri Thomas, Oscar Zeta Acosta, N. Scott Momaday, Ishmael Reed, or Frank Chin himself. Indeed, if men wish to leave behind the colonialist and racist exploits commonly associated with the counterculture's enemies, Kingston suggests, why not turn the counterculture's openness to the female into a powerful political ally in the search for peace? Men of color need not advocate for themselves within racist contexts by celebrating warrior rituals and casting women as fodder for masculine renewal or power consolidation, Kingston insists. At the end of the play's production, the narrator ponders the new world that might result from remaking militaristic masculinism; she ponders as well the possibility of feminist-pacifist politics. "Whatever there is when there isn't war has to be invented," the narrator muses. "What do people do in peace? Peace has barely been thought" (306).

I want to return to a point I gestured toward before—namely, why, in 1989, Kingston musters a history of the counterculture of the 1960s? What kind of cultural work will such a deployment of radical history accomplish? Related to this question is another: Just what kind of narrative is *Tripmaster Monkey*? This text is wildly complex and wide-ranging. It is inflected with a

distinctly postmodern sensibility, as its profound cultural busyness, its im-
plosion of high/low cultural boundaries, and its preoccupation with the
status of representation demonstrate. But more to the point, what kind of
novel puts forward a communal *play* as the most valued form of art? Both of
these questions are related to broader issues in which I am interested, issues
concerning the role of California as a geocultural imaginary for feminist
cultural politics.

Certainly one could offer Reaganism and the explosion of neoconserva-
tism in the 1980s as explanations for Kingston's enactment of Bay Area
progressive cultural history. At a time when the political tide rushed in with
a ferocious rightist backlash that surprised even hardened radical cynics,
Tripmaster Monkey supplies a kind of life jacket for drowning progressives. It also revisits the countercultural movement from vantage points not
widely represented before: those of a Chinese American cultural nationalist
as well as his feminist critic, who envision ethnic community-building on
quite different cultural terms. One could suggest, further, that the new
western history, taken together with the new literary regionalism, has created by 1989 a cultural environment quite receptive to a Maxine Hong
Kingston and quite interested in the historical role that culture plays in
movements for social change, and that Kingston simply seizes the cultural
moment and writes toward that audience.

I have another explanation in mind, however. It has to do with what I see
as Kingston's desire to combat the ascendance of Los Angeles as the dominant California city in the late 1980s as well as her desire to displace Los
Angeles's vision and embodiment of postmodernity in favor of those of San
Francisco. For political reasons, that is, *Tripmaster Monkey* wrestles away
Los Angeles's place in cultural history; and the grounds it works from to
make this political challenge are those of culture, especially cultural *forms*. I
offer two examples. First, one senses throughout the novel that Kingston
repeatedly toys with but also displaces the cultural form most associated
with the city identity of Los Angeles: noir. *Tripmaster Monkey* opens onto a
kind of noir setting, for we get the fringe underworld of Golden Gate Park—
its psychotics, violent misogynists, and painthead teenagers spraying sew-
age pipes with half-intelligible graffiti. The park also is a site of suicides,
especially male suicides. Moreover, Wittman and the narrator possess between them an encyclopedic database about Hollywood movies and cine-
matic history, including specifically film noir, and ruminations on the culture industry certainly appear repeatedly. But very quickly Wittman moves

away from the "darker sides" of Golden Gate Park and also from any suggestion of literary or community suicide, and through these moves, I want to argue, Kingston denounces noir aesthetics and politics and works against a Nathanael West narrative of western declension. After the opening chapter, we don't see a sustained flirtation with noir narratives again, because Kingston is busy constructing her own preferred cultural forms, especially that of the experimental play.

The biggest reason for Kingston's investment in the play as a cultural form, as I see it, is the play's emphasis on *performance*, and Kingston's preference for a politics of performance over a politics of representation. Can one begin to see the emerging critique of Los Angeles's culture industry unfolding here? The play as a cultural practice permits Kingston to suggest that cultural production can reform society only if individuals or groups *perform* their politics. It isn't enough simply to represent them. This is a devastating (though hardly surprising or novel) portrait of Hollywood and its liberals, suggesting as it does that they do more representing than performing of left, or liberal, political causes. Plays require more from their audiences, Kingston suggests, and that requirement is a good one. Movies are too consumable; they don't ask audiences to participate, to think, or, finally, to act.

The notion of performativity is critical to Kingston's anti-essentialist racial and gender politics, too. As has been recently suggested by critic Josephine Lee, "plays and playwrights make performance, dramatic form, and audience response inseparable from the meaning of race and ethnicity."[66] *Tripmaster Monkey* demonstrates precisely this sense of enacting, of dynamically performing, gender and racial and sexual identities as one goes along. And the liberating benefits of such a theory of political identity, its ability to tolerate the complicated political subjectivities operating in a postmodern era, are in evidence all through the text. For instance, Kingston writes a stridently feminist book, though its lead character is a (sometimes sexist) man. Her central female heroine, Taña, is a white woman, though this is a tale explicitly devoted to exposing orientalist thought and to promoting Asian American feminism. Wittman repeatedly makes a claim on western identity, wears old brown Wellington cowboy boots, speaks of himself as having "cowboy eyes." In the play-within-the-novel, we get many other such "crossover" identities, including one of the more dramatic: a pioneer woman, wearing a poke bonnet and leading workhorses, who turns out not to be white, as one expects, but African American and a runaway slave. Going further yet, the woman is revealed to have "a Chinese face" (297). In all of the above instances, racial, gender, regional, and political identities are most deliberately not located in the body, not based on essentialist premises, not static, fixed, or frozen in history. Rather, identity is contextual, immediate, conferred, performed, subject to change, subject to manipulation by individuals and groups on terms they themselves formulate. The performance is never separate from the meanings of categories like "western," "man," "woman," or "race," for the performance enacts the specificity of those meanings in that time and place. This process of identity formation contrasts fundamentally with that which characterizes Hollywood's, where the reliance on image, especially static image, reduces that genre's capacity, or so Kingston seems to suggest, for subversive narrative. Can one imagine a major-studio feature film, other than a parody, whose cowboy star is Chinese American?

San Francisco, then, "home" to Kingston's play-within-the-novel, presents an alternative cultural model to the cultural form of the film promoted by Los Angeles. Kingston embraces it as a model for California's postmodern and twenty-first-century political future. The text of *Tripmaster Monkey* resurrects, in 1989, the historical memory of America's 1960s counterculture wherein Berkeley plays midwife to the Free Speech Movement and San Francisco's left-leaning local government supports nearly every kind of progressive cause. It protects gay and lesbian culture, is committed to prolabor as well as feminist and antiracist politics, celebrates avant garde artistic productions, and tolerates miscegenation. Kingston deploys this history as a reminder of San Francisco's current progressive political character. See, she seems to say, the leftist and high culture that Bay Area counterculturalism spawned has weathered the neoconservative storm relatively well. It certainly has produced a more equitable model for community than any other *Southern* California city can offer.

Kingston is not alone in her assessment. More than a few political commentators have claimed for San Francisco the singular status of the nation's "most progressive city," even "the temporary capital of the liberal wing of the Democratic party in the United States."[67] San Francisco's progressivism stems, it would seem, from its ability to control and restrict the penetration of international finance capital into the local economy. More so than most western communities, since the 1970s, San Francisco's loose coalition of slow-growth advocates has successfully maneuvered local political processes so that city policies generally favor tight control over local real estate development and land use. By mobilizing a combination of populist, liberal, and environmental political tendencies into what urban historian Richard DeLeon calls an "anti-urban regime," the local slow-growth movement displaced the pro-growth, urban status quo that had developed in the wake of World War II and taken root by the 1960s. The anti-urban regime took further advantage of the 1980s crisis in international finance capital and commercial real estate to disrupt the notion that the city's economic role in the new postmodern economy rested on providing communications services between local corporate interests and transnational firms pursuing business with Pacific Rim nations. Thus, up into the beginning of the 1990s, San Francisco achieved what many western towns today strive still to achieve: some relative measure of autonomy from the forces of economic globalization and corporate will.[68] All of these facts distinguish San Francisco's identity from that of Los Angeles.

The above political context provides the prideful urban setting for *Tripmaster Monkey*'s vision of civic identity, as well as the political backdrop for the final optimism of this text, for what at times is its impulse toward the utopic. The concluding chapter of the novel is a nearly chapter-long soliloquy (located again on the site of the play-within-the-novel) on the demasculinization of the Asian American man, on the need for a better name for "Chinese Americans," on the rage that orientalist discourse inspires in those who are its exoticized objects, and on the consciousness-raising of Wittman as a self-absorbed man and heterosexual domestic partner. By book's end, a politics of interracial and intraracial coalition is in place, and a radically anti-essentialist politics of performance is in place, too. Orientalist discourse is reconstructed, and Wittman becomes not only a pacifist revolutionary but a domestic partner willing to play the role of "wife," at least half of the time. In other words, all of the text's major philosophical and political problems see optimistic resolution. The argument here is not that *Tripmaster Monkey* is utopic in any facile way—and this distinction is important as we move on to the next chapter. Its idealism is not simple-minded. Nonetheless, the text values and means to inspire idealism and hope. It recovers from counterculturalism some of the more idealistic goals of that movement. These are powerful political tools, Kingston suggests, useful in the battle against the late-1980s, Reagan-dominated political climate and useful too to battle Los Angeles's example of noir-inspired "darkness." Perhaps most importantly, in the cultural form of the play as well as the progressive urban environment that San Francisco embodies, feminism as form, pacifist vision, and enacted antiracist politic is possible.

California as Western Continuum

This chapter offers a California-based illustration of the book's fundamental working premise: that the discourse of landscape is crucial to the production of western and American knowledge. Joan Didion and Wanda Coleman take up "natural" landscapes (including beach spaces) and Maxine Hong Kingston focuses on cultural landscapes because all three write within and through conventions of landscape representation that are attached to particular regions of California. In order for any of these writers to tell their stories, they engage regional narratives that explicitly frame, constrain, and enable the kind of story ultimately told and the kind of landscape representation deployed to tell it. Even when there is overlap in subject matter, each writer's connection to southern or northern California makes the difference in how she frames her particular western subject matter. In support of very divergent political agendas, then, each of these writers mobilizes landscape conventions in order to refashion interregional culture and to alter the terms by which western knowledge is known.

My task has been different with the southern versus the northern Californians, for southerners inherit a tradition of landscape representation that conditions readers and writers to figure the beaches as carefree, sunny, "natural" topographies. In order to resist that narrative and to write about L.A. as each of them knows it, both Didion and Coleman deploy a noir aesthetic, though certainly Coleman is far less of a classic noir writer than is Didion. But noir comes with its own problematic biases, which Didion and Coleman struggle differently to engage. In the final analysis, both Didion's and Coleman's repopulations of Los Angeles geography radically change what counts as western space and "paradigmatic postmodernity."

Northern Californians are not as culturally embattled as their southern counterparts. San Francisco is a literary center, its civic image is romantic and secure, and its writers take up "culture" questions very directly—they don't need noir to do it. And yet challenges come with northern landscape conventions too, for the romance plot written over Bay Area culture threatens to displace the less celebratory features of local history. By writing about the travails of Asian American identity—including orientalism, sexism, and racism, all indicators of life's unequally distributed hardships in the charming city of cable cars—Maxine Hong Kingston contests Bay Area culture as one that is all frontier romance, smoky cafes, refurbished Victorian homes, and city lights reflected on water.

I have also been concerned in this chapter with the ways that interregional tensions produce competing notions of urban California and the rest of the West. If we were to reframe the premises about California that usually inform western studies and consider not "how is California different" but instead "how is California linked to the same issues that dominate the western problematic," we might begin with a different set of questions. First, how do these two subregional landscape binaries reinforce each other? Or, put differently, what relations exist between California landscape traditions and the larger dominant emplotment of the western spatial field, especially its emplotment as redemptive space?

First, how do subregional landscape binaries reinforce each other? By ghettoizing the urban narrative, making it stand in for that which the "authentic" (Edenic) west is not, the dominant western imaginary (and Stegnerian literary history as well) uses Los Angeles as a kind of "fall guy," a geographic imaginary where urban life can be talked about precisely because it is rigorously contained. San Francisco thus plays "west" to Los Angeles's "antiwest" and continues as the Eden of western cities, able to mobilize in its own favor both culture and nature narratives.

The concluding point is that together, the sum of these subregional narratives consolidate many of the tensions within the dominant western geocultural imaginary at large. On the one hand, Los Angeles's example illustrates the West's boom-or-bust mentality and the consequent historical displacement and/or exploitation of the vulnerable. Los Angeles illustrates the West's role in the production of American white racialist and masculinist subjectivity and power blocs, too. On the other hand, the San Francisco example embodies the West's utopic possibilities, or the "hope trope," and its support of liberal individualism, including the individual desires of women and/or peoples of color. Considered in this light, "California" is a kind of unacknowledged spatial continuum on which are mapped various parts of the western problematic. San Francisco performs the role of leading the nation in new avant garde directions (a progressive renovation of Turner's safety valve thesis), while Los Angeles serves as handmaiden for late industrial capitalist and hypermaterialist culture, a culture some westerners might disdain but one that nevertheless is the bedrock of national economic wealth.

The above tensions, however, are hardly unique to California; they reflect the broader preoccupations of the geocultural imaginary and of western history. What more *western* story (either past or present) can one think of than the battle between slow growth and raging development? For that matter, what could be more western than Wanda Coleman's portrayal of L.A. as the "darkest" side of American capitalism juxtaposed against Kingston's faith in western possibilities and American radical idealism? Isn't western mythology rife with this same ambivalent tension between imperial exploitation and the hopes of democratic reform?

This chapter, in a roundabout way, has deconstructed the wilderness bias that underlies conventional definitions of the West, in order to forward new definitions that jibe with the very metropolitan environments in which most westerners find themselves today. Yet the strength of this emphasis is also a limit to the extent that the writers discussed in this chapter do not figure landscapes as regenerative or spiritual resources and thus are not representative of western texts at their presumably most pure and seductive. It is the task of the next chapter to discuss two writers who are beloved by western critics and who are hands-down claimed as western writers: southwesterners Barbara Kingsolver and Leslie Marmon Silko. What is it about them that makes them so popular? The next chapter introduces Part II of this book, a series of chapters on gender and some of the "master" landscapes within the western problematic.

Part Two

Gender and
the "Master"
Landscapes
of Western
Narrative

*Americans are constantly
discovering nature, and through
it, or so they think, themselves.*
—Richard White, "Discovering
Nature in North America"

*For most Americans it is
perfectly consistent to drive a
thousand miles to spend a
holiday in a national park.*
—Ramachandra Guha,
"Radical American
Environmentalism and
Wilderness Preservation"

3

Sidestepping Environmental Justice: "Natural" Landscapes and the Wilderness Plot

Bleached-white bones, Indian ruins, mountain sage, dry heat. An earthen world of adobe homes, little rain, the spare expanses of desert hills. Metaphors of infinity. Of God. Of nation. By most standards, these images capture America's "real" Southwest—the high desert outside of Santa Fe, immortalized in the paintings of Georgia O'Keeffe. The popular renderings of Arizona's deserts complement those of New Mexico's: more Indian iconography, glowing cholla, twisted saguaro, yipping coyotes. Both sets of representations figure the nonhuman world as the dominant feature of southwestern cultural identity. That identity is articulated through vast, relatively unpeopled, wilderness landscapes. And it sells, to this nation of nature discoverers, as hot and salty as the McDonald's french fries one can buy at every third or fourth Tucson streetlight.

These days, the wilderness Southwest is as often a part of popular representations of the region as are the geological anomalies preserved as national parks: the Grand Canyon, the Painted Desert, the Petrified Forest, and Monument Valley. Overrun as the parks are with tourists and recreational vehicles, the Grand Canyon itself plagued by air pollution, helicopter tours, and an overrafted river, the otherworldly images noted above, floating freely apart from population and economic centers, preserve a "purity" that would seem to be missing from many of today's western spaces. Indeed, O'Keeffe's own Southwest, if interrogated at all, could be a symbol less of "purity" than of ultimate contamination, for her ranch in Abiquiu, which houses the studio where she did her best work, is located just twenty miles north of Los Alamos, the infamous birthplace of the A-bomb. The whole Southwest is, in fact, as one critic curtly puts it, "rock-hard urban" and has been for a hundred years.[1] It faces distinctly urban challenges. Though it is not the task of this chapter to revisit the antiurban bias that permeates things considered "really southwestern," a case study of this western subregion surely proves the point.

I want to begin from a different angle, however, one that lets us take up one of the most entrenched master narratives of the broader geocultural imaginary—that of the wilderness plot. First, some questions. Why is the dominant trend in representations of the Southwest so invested in exoticized and depopulated imagery? Certainly the Southwest was not always viewed through this romantic frame.[2] Why, in the twentieth century, is it a touchstone for things "natural" and "western"? One might formulate any number of plausible (if economistic) speculations about the importance of this image to the tourist, to the defense and retirement industries, or to real estate developers. Simply put, there is more money to be made by representing the Southwest in mystified terms.[3] But why do "serious" writers and critics, leaders in American critical thought, participate in and therefore, often, perpetuate this trend? It is an unlikely alliance, for most western intellectuals, especially environmentalists, adamantly oppose the kinds of developments advanced by the above industries.

That intellectuals (including, often, ecocritics) perpetuate this trend is one contention here. Consider the representations of nature that govern books deemed classics of literary environmentalism: Mary Austin's *The Land of Little Rain* (1903), Aldo Leopold's *A Sand County Almanac* (1949), Edward Abbey's *Desert Solitaire* (1968), Barry Lopez's *Desert Notes* (1976), or Terry Tempest Williams's *Refuge* (1991). There are other titles one could offer here, including the two I will take up later on in this chapter: Leslie Marmon Silko's *Ceremony* (1977) and Barbara Kingsolver's *Animal Dreams* (1990). Book publishers and writers, and even sometimes critics too, trade on symbols of western "virgin land" in ways not completely unlike those of real estate developers. Exoticized book jacket covers and subject matter aid writers and their marketers in the sale of their ostensibly "authentic" western product: namely, untrammeled nature. What book cover comes to mind that characterizes Tucson, say, as a connected series of mini-malls? And yet, wouldn't that make the environmental point in more trustworthy terms than does, say, the cover of Kingsolver's *Animal Dreams*, which pictures a shadowy and magical desertscape, animal-shaped clouds, coyote figures, and cactus in the foreground and, as background, an anonymous woman whose dark hair and colorful sarape suggest American Indian identity? And that book cover is by no means an isolated example. Go through your own personal library to verify just how dominant this "great unpeopled outdoors" motif is.

The profound misgivings I have about the above trend will alert readers to the fact that I come down more on the social ecology side of the Green movement's current debates between social ecology and deep ecology, though I believe that neither side ultimately presents a coherent program of ecological liberation, as ecofeminist Val Plumwood skillfully demonstrates.[4] To my mind, the reasons to come down more on the social ecology side have to do with the various race, gender, class, and First versus Third World politics that frame and, more consequentially, *limit and control* what gets discussed in contemporary discourse about "the environment."[5] But the goal here is not to revisit this debate—especially given how devoid it usually is of feminist content—as much as it is to note a different, under-investigated, but pertinent phenomenon: the relationship between ecocriticism and regionalism, especially the new *western* regionalism.

A first fact is that the tendency by writers to represent "natural landscape" is probably one of the dominant, if not the most dominant, landscape practices in evidence among the most visible of new western regionalists today. Certainly it is one of the most widespread *critical* practices. Indeed, when many readers pick up this book, whose title announces some relationship between women, writing, criticism, landscape, and the West, they may be surprised or disappointed to find that it lacks any celebration of, or reverence for, nature. I could have written a book, for example, that followed in the footsteps of a text like *Circle of Women* (1991), a recent anthology of western women's writing edited by Kim Barnes and Mary Clearman Blew. Though *Circle of Women* problematizes much of masculinist western mythology, it too seems to rely rather unconsciously on the central idea that "natural" nature exists and is deeply revealed in western spatial fields.

But in order *not* to reinvent every kind of western stereotype—that the Rocky Mountain West and the Southwest are the "real" west, that the red/white paradigm characterizes western race relations, that the urban west is a west to be shunned, that western womanhood means perseverance against all odds, or that "natural" nature provides trustworthy or "neutral" ground upon which to figure alternative social visions—I have proceeded down a very different path, a path which from the start argues that critics should bring a great deal more critical distance to "western nature" than is often the case. I want to consider up close the political implications of a too-willing embrace of narratives about "natural" nature. Some of the critical ground I must enter and challenge, therefore, is that of ecocriticism, where the best work on western nature and its relationship to culture is currently undertaken.

Ecocriticism is that recent branch of literary studies committed to the representation of environmental issues in literature and culture. Thus far, it focuses a good bit, though not exclusively, on nature writing.[6] In nature writing, as one founding critic puts it, "the world is alive again . . . seen precisely for what it is. . . . Good nature writing . . . recaptur[es] the child's world . . . before fragmentation."[7] This quotation sums up a view of nature that is holistic, fragmentation-transcendent, "innocent," and transparent, while it simultaneously sums up a vague environmentalists' agenda: the desire for a more "real" or environmentally sane life can be found in simpler living and a retreat from a postmodern world that decenters what ideally should be the "whole" self. In the West's wilderness spaces, ecocritics generally believe, these desires find consummation. Ecocriticism inherits from western cultural history a love of, even obsession with, "pristine wilderness"—which is to say that it inherits a general but pervasive inclination toward what we call today "deep ecology." It inherits, too, the political biases that come with that territory.

This high premium put upon maintenance of "pure" wilderness, I want to argue, often predisposes critics and writers to conceive their ecostories through what I call a "wilderness plot." Critic and writer Frank Bergon has recently made use of the term "wilderness aesthetics" to describe the complex mix of literary, religious, and scientific impulses at work in American nature writing.[8] Though I find his formulation persuasive, my own goals here, as I hope will become clear, are different, and thus I pursue the term "wilderness plot." It is my argument that the wilderness plot dominates the western "environmental imagination" generally (to use Lawrence Buell's term).[9] That plot, in fact, writes the ecostories that readers read and writers write, even if, as my case studies of Silko and Kingsolver argue, writers had other plots equally in mind. The plot, in formula terms, usually contains the following: a love of wide-open, "wild" spaces; a penchant for the mystical, which is also the "natural," American Indian; the suggestion of redemptive possibility; a disavowal of the industrial or technological; and representations of woman as nature. This is thus a discussion about dominant landscape discourse and the ways in which that discourse emplots quite specifically what supposedly are "new" and "alternative" western spaces. Before we move to an analysis of the wilderness plot at work in the writing of Leslie Silko and Barbara Kingsolver, some of the links between ecocriticism and the wilderness ideal need to be established.

The Wilderness Ideal and the Wilderness Plot

The rhetorical practice of environmental history [and this is true too for nature writing] commits us to narrative ways of talking about nature that are anything but "natural."
—William Cronon, "A Place for Stories"

What is the wilderness ideal? Certainly the shifting historical meanings attributed to "wilderness" have been thoroughly investigated by American scholars.[10] Less has been written, however, about the wilderness as *ideal*, or its influences on western narrative or environmental politics in particular. In common political and literary parlance, the ideal holds that large tracts of undomesticated land provide an antidote for modernity, a site where people can return to their deepest, wildest selves. Wilderness is a refuge that must be guarded in order to maintain the biodiversity of planetary life forms *and* what believers might call human dignity and spirituality. In a representative remark in 1960, Wallace Stegner said that without the preservation of wilderness, humans have no reprieve from the "Brave New World of a completely man-controlled environment."[11] Years later Stegner clarified another of the ideal's dimensions: "Looking a long way is not a social experience," he said. "It's an aesthetic or even religious one."[12] Wilderness, in American nature discourse, is a nonhuman, extraindustrial, spiritual topography of humbling otherness, where biodiversity and the sacred coexist, a reminder that "man" is not all-powerful.

But who *is* this "man"—this central, tropic figure of deep ecology—in need of the humbling reminder that he is not all-powerful? He certainly is not, say, a nonelite man from a Third World nation. For that man is under no illusion that he is all-powerful. Indeed, as Ramachandra Guha makes clear in what has become something of a landmark essay in Third World criticism of American environmentalism, the policy of "wilderness preservation" lends itself *not* to this man's greater humanity but rather to his further economic exploitation and vulnerability. Using the example of his own native India, Guha demonstrates that setting aside large tracts of wilderness land in the name of conservation ethics has the gravely injurious result of redistributing land control away from the majority poor who work it and toward the rich.[13]

If we shift continents and consider conservation ethics in an African context, the point is sharper still. For if, recalling Stegner, a Kenyan or Tanzanian national looks a "long way" into preserved wilderness, namely a game reserve, what he is likely to see is not some form of godliness that restores his frayed modern nerves but instead white nonnationals on safari holiday! The preserves are a kind of Ultimate and Last Great Wilderness, and it should tell us something that they cater overwhelmingly to white Europeans and Americans. Julia Martin puts it this way: "The majority of South Africans have reason to find [North American] environmental friendliness unpalatable, tasting as it so often does of white privilege and forced removals. . . . Environmentalism as conservation ethics has been a significant element in colonial and apartheid policy . . . as people have been forced off their land to make way for game reserves."[14] As an environmental goal and policy, then, wilderness preservation enters the global green movement with an acute First World blind spot. We'll come back to the fact that one wonders, in all these discussions about "man's" need to be humbled, about just where the world's women are.

Now, as I've already noted, the environmental movement has a particularly intimate relationship with western cultural history. Thus it is no accident that ecocriticism, as an emerging scholarly field, originally took shape from within the Western Literature Association (WLA).[15] Indeed, the newly constituted Association for Study of Literature and the Environment (ASLE) initially held its administrative meetings at WLA annual conferences, and WLA continues to sponsor specific topical plenaries. It is no accident, moreover, that a majority of nature writers are western writers, because the West as a region continues to circulate quite broadly in American culture as symbol for "the wild" and "the natural."

American environmental history shows its own regionalist bent. The majority of the most prominent of the new western historians—William Cronon, Richard White, and Donald Worster—are in fact environmental historians. William Cronon has recently addressed environmental history in much the same spirit as I here address ecocriticism: he worries about the deep ecology bias that seems to infuse "authentic" ecopolitics.[16] Although much controversy surrounds Cronon's take on, as his 1996 essay is titled, "The Trouble with Wilderness," and indeed although the most thoughtful opposing response comes from the ecocritic Michael Cohen, I weigh in on Cronon's side.[17] I think he is right that environmentalists generally are, as the essay is subtitled, "getting back to the wrong kind of nature."

Cronon begins with the premise that contemporary environmentalism is "itself a grandchild of romanticism and postfrontier ideology."[18] The frontier era viewed wilderness as a space capable of reinvigorating masculine virility while staving off the emasculating tendencies of "feminine" civilization. The man who used wilderness for these purposes, Cronon points out, was usually elite, a white man with the resources to vacation in western territories. As the frontier "closed," Cronon goes on, that same man nevertheless retained the frontier experience by supporting a preservationist political agenda. That is, the desire to retain a masculine imaginative preserve, a kind of perpetually open and renewable frontier, played a motivating role in constructing "wilderness" as both environmental policy and cultural ideal. The ideal promised that in wilderness, twentieth-century Americans might find respite from the complexities and chaotic changes of twentieth-century industrial and urban life.

The "trouble with wilderness" as ideal, according to Cronon, is that it offers "the illusion that we can escape the cares and troubles of the world in which our past has ensnared us."[19] It contains within it an intense tendency toward the ahistorical, and the history that falls away from believers' consciousness is that of the gendered, classed, and imperial contexts out of which the wilderness ideal emerged. Further, "wilderness religion," as the environmental historian Dan Flores calls it, encourages environmentalists to idealize big wild spaces, which, most consequentially, are usually *not* the actual places that people call "home."[20] Thus "nature," in this western narrative, is no pristine or asocial "pure" or "authentic" space. Nature is not "natural" at all. Instead, nature articulates what Cronon calls a "peculiarly bourgeois form of [masculine] antimodernism."[21] Nature serves as template upon which the elite male speaker speaks self-absorbed dreams.

Rethinking the tie between environmentalism and the wilderness ideal within western discourse accomplishes the overt task of bringing social ecology into more effective dialogue with western environmentalism. Impatient with deep ecologists who see preservation of native biodiversity as the globe's single most pressing political issue, revisionists point out that humans have always altered nature in order to survive.[22] Humans are not, de facto, nature's enemy. Less overtly, and perhaps more radically, rethinking this tie brings a heightened sensitivity to the role that gender plays in ideas about nature and the West. The need to be a solitary soul on the planet—the illusion at the heart of the wilderness ideal, Cronon reminds us—derives from romantic, western frontier mythology and supports a male-gendered mythology in which wilderness is a topography that produces something like "real masculinity." To the degree that western cultural history is the unofficial backdrop for much of today's environmentalist counterculture, ecological liberation theories retain a huge male bias, much like that bias that permeates the region of the West itself.

It is within this general intellectual, regional, and political context that the two books I want to consider here are critically received: Leslie Marmon Silko's *Ceremony* (1977) and Barbara Kingsolver's *Animal Dreams* (1990). Both these books are widely read, taught, and talked about by western critics. Silko's *Ceremony*, in particular, is accorded canonical status in both American literary and western literary circles. An unspoken consensus about both books exists: they get the West somehow "right." What is it about them that is so self-evidently and "authentically" western? I contend that their "westernness" is established by the books' dialogues with the wilderness ideal. Each is a kind of environmentalist's novel. Between them they take on the horrors of nuclear warfare, global warming, and toxic waste disposal. And both books are part of the revisionist trend in environmental thought, for they connect environmental with human exploitation. This is to say that they evidence a "feel" for deep ecology at the same time that they are quite aware of the driving premise of social ecology: that human exploitation of humans causes human domination of nature. And finally both of these texts engage questions of gender, nature, and western cultural history, so they would seem to speak to feminist issues.

But both narratives engage many of the most hallowed tropes of the signifier West *and* the wilderness ideal: an antimodern and antitechnology bent, redemptive landscapes, Native American mysticism, wide open spaces, and utopic possibility. And it is this engagement, particularly in the case of Leslie Silko's *Ceremony*, that puts these texts into a cultural orbit that is much, much larger than the texts themselves. Silko's *Ceremony* comes in for discussion first, for critics' reception of this book alerts us to the kinds of cultural ecowork that can be gleaned from a text that engages many of the features of the wilderness ideal. Silko's text appears in the late 1970s, when environmentalism temporarily wanes and public attention shifts from the many Environmental Acts of the mid-1960s and early 1970s to the economic issues that will preoccupy American politics throughout much of the 1980s. Using *Ceremony* as a point of departure raises provocative questions not only about the indebtedness of the wilderness ideal to Native American culture (a topic that politically conscious scholars cannot concede often enough) but, more problematically, about the presence of that ideal within Native thought, and its reinscription into what otherwise is assumed to be "resistance literature." It also raises issues about ecocriticism, its relationship to primitivism, traditional gender relations, and class prerogative.

Ceremony—What Makes Tayo Well?: Nature as Postmodern Therapy

Silko's is the New West, not the Old, as any number of critical essays make clear.[23] At the book's opening, mixed-blood protagonist Tayo is suffering from World War II battle fatigue. Having been released from a psychiatric hospital in Los Angeles, Tayo has returned home to the Laguna Reservation in New Mexico, but he is hardly cured. He is haunted by the memories of his years in a Japanese POW camp and haunted too by the memory of his brother's death in the Japanese jungle. He does not sleep. He cannot eat. He rants. Without some kind of curative intervention, Tayo will die. His step-mother and step-grandmother summon Betonie, a medicine man who lives outside of Gallup, in the hope that a Native ceremony will restore Tayo's mind and health.

Betonie's ceremonies are also very much indicative of the New, not the Old, West. Betonie works his magic as much through telephone books, old newspapers, and Coca Cola–advertising train calendars as he does through the expected items in a medicine man's bag: dried sage, various hairs, spirit-invoking chants, and pagan ritual. His wisdom about race relations, that not every Indian is a friend to Tayo and not every white person is an enemy, is New Western too. In the end, Betonie's contemporary ceremonies enable Tayo to integrate the old traditions with the postwar New West. And pre-cisely because he has melded old and new, Tayo heals. Thereafter, he refuses the destructive paths of violence and alcoholism taken by his local buddies who are also veterans. He returns to the reservation a well man, now a community storyteller, a leader who embodies the new consciousness nec-essary for Indians to survive the atomic age.

Silko's West clearly takes a resistance-to-the-traditional line. Thus, my own argument, that *Ceremony* illustrates one of the most traditional com-ponents of Old Western narratives in its deployment of the wilderness ideal, seems, perhaps, an odd one. Though I concede that Silko deconstructs many of the myths of the Old West, she does not, in my view, deconstruct one of the most trenchant: the wilderness ideal. And this is not a choice she makes twice: her *Almanac of the Dead* completely disallows a "wilderness plot" reading, and this may be one reason for its vast unpopularity among critics, particularly western critics. One might speculate, even, that Silko wrote *Al-manac* in outraged response to critics' "feel good" reception of *Ceremony*.[24]

The point is that the wilderness ideal overlaps rather significantly with what is popularly conceived as a "classic" Native American cultural world-view. Of course I do not suggest by this that there is one "Indian" view of nature. Instead, what is at issue is that western narrative in general, south-western narrative in particular, is infused with mysticism from the literary start, and this infusion in some basic way cannot escape being a cross-cultural appropriation of Native cosmology.[25] Though Silko might position

Ceremony within the emerging new American Indian literature and not within "southwestern literature," and though her works draw explicitly from Pueblo storytelling traditions and Pueblo ideas about history and landscape, the book nonetheless owes much of its authority to the bigger cultural fields of "the West."[26] And here is where the complications become most serious. For western critics, all too willing to consider Native Americans ideas about nature as some kind of final "authentic" word, not as socially and culturally entangled discourses, do not generally problematize *Ceremony*'s representation of nature.[27] Quite the contrary: *Ceremony*'s landscapes are deeply familiar already, for they echo many of the most beloved features of westernness.

The *healing wilderness*: a first signal that the wilderness ideal is in operation. Landscape and a reconnection with the earth return Tayo from the land of the dead, what the narrator calls the "invisible," to that of the living. All of Tayo's healings—the recovery of his mind, the stilling of the soldiers' voices that haunt his dreams, his resurgent physical strength, his ability to love and make love, his remembrance of the "Old Stories"—these very social and cultural abilities are generated, in *Ceremony*, by his return deeper and deeper into the *natural* world. Tayo "sink[s] into the elemental arms of mountain silence. . . . the voice of the silence was familiar and the density of the dark earth loved him" (201–2). By becoming one with the earth's sounds, movements, cycles, heat and cold, and logic, Tayo becomes "visible" again (104). The sound of grasshoppers, the shifting light on sandstone bluffs, the water in arroyos, the desert cholla and piñon nuts, the star-filled skies—all of these natural elements mediate the corrupting aspects of a post-bomb society and their destructive impact upon Tayo. The last quarter of the book is a rush of scenes in which the "magnetism of the [earth's] center spread[s] over him smoothly like rainwater" (201). The earth "pull[s] him back, close to [it], where the core was cool and silent as mountain stone" (201). He remembers, finally, that "we came out of the land and we are hers" (255). His dawning sense that he "might make it after all" comes as he absorbs the multicolored, beauteous sunrise (237).

The natural world in *Ceremony*'s cosmology provides a corrective to the emerging culture of a world capable of destroying itself. And it is here, in the novel's representation of nature as able to rejuvenate, redeem, restore sanity and right relation to self, to local community, and to global community, that *Ceremony*'s "nature" so dovetails with that of the wilderness ideal. For landscape, in the wilderness ideal—and here we see a clear link with deep ecology—is never "background" or "context." The "nature narrative" *is* the narrative. Landscape is as central a protagonist as Tayo; without landscape there is no Indian or western pathos, no cultural geography that supports a redemption process.

Sign number two of the wilderness ideal: *sacred nature.* Like most tales of purification and salvation, *Ceremony* is infused with metaphysical meaning. Tayo's redemption goes deeper than simple restoration of sanity. It is spiritual and transcendent, and it is the land and nature that mediate Tayo's relationship to the spirit world. The redemption process is not only about Tayo's personal trauma, nor even the trauma of Navajos, Lagunas, Hopis, or Mexicans, who live under Gallup's bridges in tin lean-tos amidst broken bottles and raw feces. What is at stake in *Ceremony* is a tale of *global* redemption. For the moment anyway, the recycling of the Old Stories has saved the planet from the "witchery" of worldwide nuclear holocaust. As does the dominant geocultural imaginary, *Ceremony* evidences a rather intense utopianism, one that parallels the strident optimism that is one of the most common (ostensible) western regional characteristics. Again, the "hope trope" is revealed to be a structuring feature of "authentic western" culture.[28] Silko's tale thus converges with western exceptionalism; the notion of the West as a kind of "last stand" of (Anglo-European) possibility. If the West is home to nuclear insanity, it is also home to global recovery. It has its problems, yes, but it remains the nation's, even the world's salvation.

But the "natural" side of *Ceremony*—and here is the break with deep ecology and the bridge to social ecology—turns out to be inseparable from its social (storytelling) side. For Silko's landscapes are always *storied* landscapes; she makes no claim for a "natural" or nondiscursive nature. Landscape, in fact, is the medium through which Tayo knows narrative itself— oral narrative, that is, in the form of the Old Stories. An example: "[Tayo's] protection was there in the sky, in the position of the sun, in the pattern of the stars. He had only to complete this night, to keep the story out of the reach of the destroyers . . . and their witchery would turn, upon itself, upon them" (247). At its heart, *Ceremony* enacts a ritual that believes that the act of storytelling—narrative process—can undo evil forces and thereby save the world from self-destruction. Silko stories *are* the planet; they are read through *nature as text.* Often throughout the text Tayo speaks about stories in ways that sound much like the basic premises of discourse theory. He understands "the way all the stories fit together . . . to become the story that was still being told" (246). He speaks of language in material terms, as "hav[ing] substance," like "pebbles and stones" (12). Sentences, in the fading tongue of the Pueblo elders, are "involuted with explanations of their own origins" (34). The Old Stories, by book's end, are implicit within his own. Tayo's story is part of a broader story, a story that has always been told and which now enters the global story and cleanses the world.

The relationship between Silko's landscapes and ethnicity-affirming, antitechnological, and antinuclear political projects seems obvious enough. But what are their relationships to western literary environmentalism or nature writing? Though this relationship may not be entirely obvious, it should not be underrated, because it is crucial to the text's prominence in classrooms and scholarly discussions, even when those discussions are framed through a multicultural organizing theme. First, consider that *Ceremony* features a "back to nature" story that is free of skyscrapers, smog, strip malls, traffic, suburban homes, TVs, and Wonder Bread. Tayo is horse wise, sleeps and makes love with mysterious Ts'eh under the stars, eats piñon nuts off the ground, chops wood for the morning coffee's fire. He even, by using the Old Stories, befriends a mountain lion. *Ceremony*, via its representation of holistic Native culture and wilderness reservation lands, is a kind of environmentalists' utopia. It permits critics and readers the imaginative experience of a world where Europeans' alienation from nature is absent. The reservation provides a dramatic setting for ecoreaders to reenact the love of open land, the encounter with wildness and the "ways of Indians," the mystical relationship to "Mother Earth" and to sexualized and willing American Indian female figures, and the possibility of economic self-sufficiency—all of which are various features of the wilderness ideal. Because Silko opposes rigid adherence to the traditional, however, and continuously insists on the ceremonies' adaptability to change, because her representation of Indian life is complex and quite often rigorously unromantic, the text can be simultaneously claimed as one that brings literary environmentalism into a new era and lays out what a "progressive landscape" might look like, a template for a new kind of 1970s radical environmentalism.

And yet, this landscape is as much old as new, for it resonates clearly with the traditional significations of "the West." Silko's narrative is powerful and popular not just because her instincts as a young writer of a first novel are deft but because it coincides with dominant representations of the West and of nature in the West. It can be deployed for some of the oldest kinds of cultural work performed through western discourse: the idealization of Native culture and the use of that culture as antidote to modern or postmodern problems. Even though critics acknowledge the misery inflicted upon the land and indigenous people as a result of conquest, the more dominant critical "spin" has to do with what *Ceremony* teaches us about life in the present and how to make peace with the present. Part of the lesson, unmistakably, is a "back to nature" lesson. This lesson is particularly compelling because, as the last chapter highlighted, the 1970s mark the transition of the West into America's most urban region. My suggestion, then, is that environmentalists' love of Silko's "progressive" landscape owes at least in part to the ways that landscape can be mobilized as a narrative of redemptive possibility, a goldenseal kind of salve for 1970s western urbanism.

Tellingly, many of the pressing environmental issues of the 1970s are irrelevant to this text: the struggles for the Clean Water Act (1973), the Clean Air Act (1973), and the Endangered Species Act (1973); the perennial efforts to curb grazing rights in order to prevent soil erosion (and the problems that result from erosion); the campaign to regulate application of DDT and other toxic pesticides. The novel's setting in the years immediately following Hiroshima and Nagasaki enables environmentalists to claim its antinuke message as a relevant reminder for the 1970s–1980s peace movement. But the final environmental embrace here is far more diffuse. It is about counter-cultural "lifestyle," and through that lifestyle, environmentalist identity. *Ceremony* sells a way of living, a structure of feeling: holistic, "natural," mystical, sensual, extraindustrial. By reading *Ceremony*, one connects with Green consciousness and with the ostensibly "Greenest" culture in history: that of North American Indians. That connection resonates profoundly because it is very much in keeping with what "the West" as signifier and commodity has sold since Europeans began representing it. The wilderness plot, in full ahistorical swing, has enabled a broader cultural appropriation of some of the text's most subversive features.

Finally, within the field of western criticism, the canonization of *Ceremony* and the ascendance of the wilderness plot as a preferred way of reading and teaching the text performs the cultural work of reasserting a humanist, metaphysical narration of nature at precisely the moment that poststructural ideas about language make a serious impact upon the American intellectual scene. Silko's *Ceremony* could be (though it generally is not) deployed by poststructurally minded critics in order to advance the notion that language speaks people and nature—that is, that language produces human society rather than being a product of that society. Silko, indeed, is herself quite invested in the idea that the Old Stories speak the storytellers and the land. Narrative, as I have already noted, is sacred to Silko, for as long as the Old Stories are alive, so also will be Native history.[29] Instead, however, Silko's representations of a rejuvenative landscape are deployed as part of a broader humanist tradition within western discourse that figures the Americas as a promised land, a site of redemption from European decadence, a place where Edenic innocence is again at least remotely possible, where the effects of modernity might be remedied, where the mind/body split will be healed (but not with the more profound social consequences that would go with such a healing).

The fact that this tale comes from an "authentic" Native voice serves to legitimate further the humanist project at a moment in American literary history that is fraught with racial conflict and separatism. *Ceremony* comfortingly reassures readers, and challenges racial separatists too, that racialist thought does not generate global evil. Rather "witchery" is the problem, and it transcends racial hierarchies. As the medicine man Betonie says, not all whites *or* American Indians are friends, or enemies. Ironically, however, the fact is that Silko's holistic ontology depends for its credibility upon the notion of the "authentic" Native voice, for that voice in American history *is* the voice of nature.[30] Moreover, Silko herself, in a biting attack on Louise Erdrich, shows her own commitment to the idea of the real, and the real and the ethnic are tied to nature.[31] With Silko's implicit blessing, then, the new environmental literary canon writes nature as a place of "authenticity" *and* a place of the American Indian. These "places" provide imaginative links to the transcendental, and the rhetoric of transcendence and "the real" are, of course, fundamental to humanist thought and deep ecology. The inevitable primitivism of this philosophy, its class bias, its reinscription of traditional gender roles, its remasculinization of discourses about sexuality (in an era of relative female sexual empowerment), become more evident as we turn now to *Animal Dreams*. Kingsolver's book demonstrates the degree to which the "progressive landscape" that *Ceremony* establishes can provide a narrative that both embraces and flees from history at the same time or, in postmodern fashion (at least according to Jameson), embodies history as style.[32]

Animal Dreams—What Makes Codi Well?: Consuming the Racial Other

Unlike Silko's, Kingsolver's prominence depends upon the emergence of the mid-1980s commercial boom in western literary regionalism. As such,

Kingsolver is representative of many, even most, of the writers popularly and critically conceived of as "new western feminist regionalists." Since 1987, Kingsolver has published three novels, a book of stories, a nonfiction book, a collection of poems, and a recent book of essays.[33] Though she and Harper & Row have quite skillfully marketed not just her work but also her public persona, as of mid-1998 hardly a single critical article had appeared about Kingsolver's novels or stories.[34] Book reviewers (including such luminary writers as Ursula Le Guin, Margaret Randall, and Jane Smiley) are quite taken by Kingsolver generally (overly taken, I will argue) and have praised *Animal Dreams* as an honest and ambitious book about postmodern community in all its layered complexity.[35] Appearing as it does during the "Year of the Environment" in 1990, *Animal Dreams* illustrates a different moment in America's green movement than does Silko's *Ceremony*, and a different wing of the movement—ecofeminism. It raises a related set of green problems, however. It is to explore these issues that we take up Kingsolver here.

But first let me more deliberately locate Kingsolver, and the many Anglo regionalists whose work roughly parallels hers, in the broader developmental current of the female side of the new regionalist movement. I have offered thus far a genealogical trajectory in which Joan Didion, Wanda Coleman, Maxine Hong Kingston, and Leslie Silko represent the founding or "first waves" of different impulses within this new geocultural imaginary. I have posited various civil rights and feminist imaginaries at work in the 1970s in the emerging spatial field, including, with Silko, that of contemporary environmentalism. One could add any number of names and political issues, moreover, to this "first wave" list, to be sure.

The cultural phenomenon of someone like Barbara Kingsolver, however, marks a pivotal transition. By the mid-1980s, a series of factors converge to produce what is today commonly—and, I hope to have demonstrated, *inaccurately*—conceived of as the heart of the new female regionalism. One watershed factor is that the new western history rather suddenly finds itself in a very media-covered controversy over the interpretation of the western past. Although the various schools within western history had been rewriting some of the field's founding assumptions since the early 1970s, it is only in the late 1980s that these disparate schools unify into anything like a public history movement. Importantly, the evolving availability of new *literature* helps historians make their various cases about the changing regional sensibility observable in the west of the 1980s. By the same token, new western literature piggybacks on the sudden "jackpot" that apparently is hit when the new western history goes public. Nowhere is this truer than in white women's literature, which is just happening upon the scene at the moment that the new western history sparks national debates about issues of western gender and race relations, the environment, western culture, and so on.

Publishing houses in the northeast move quickly to cash in on this controversy. They sign and thereafter vigorously promote a new and next generation of white women writers like Kingsolver, Terry Tempest Williams, Gretel Ehrlich, Pam Houston, Mary Clearman Blew, Teresa Jordan, Kim Barnes, Kate Braverman, Judith Freeman, and Alison Baker. Some of these writers (especially the poets) have been at work since the mid-1970s, but most find their real starts in the early to mid-1980s. Novels, not surprisingly, are the preferred commercial product. At a crucial and public developmental moment, then, white women's literature is the "new kid on the block" in the regionalist movement, and this fact is mistakenly read as the "soul" of the movement, rather than being read as its more classic and, I would add, relatively less threatening expression.

Less well known is the fact that publishing houses at the same time also begin to pick up and reissue crossover books by nonwhite writers like Chicana Sandra Cisneros and Chicanos Gary Soto and Rudolfo Anaya. Originally published by noncommercial presses, their novels, poems, and short story cycles appeal to both a "new western" and a "multicultural" audience. In the 1990s, this crossover niche continues, and longtime writers like Ana Castillo, Pat Mora, and Victor Villaseñor achieve for the first time a national audience and market. Newer crossover writers like Denise Chavez, Louise Erdrich, Cynthia Kadohata, and Fae Ng find a relatively willing commercial marketplace for tales that draw both regionalist and multicultural audiences into the big-house fold.

I have digressed here somewhat to emphasize how nonwhite is much of the cultural and publishing phenomenon surrounding the new regionalism. This is a critical point, as we shall see, for this literary movement is often characterized, summed up quickly or in microcosm, by a work I referred to earlier: *Circle of Women*, the anthology edited by Kim Barnes and Mary Clearman Blew. If one wants to offer a thumbnail sketch of the movement, its writers, or their combined visions, it is tempting to cite this text's introduction, with its gestures toward a radical new West defined by community, multiracial tolerance, interdependence, and an ethics of environmental preservation. I do not take issue with any of these aspirations, and this text's emphasis on what it calls "spatial narratives" overlaps with my own. Nonetheless, I want to point out how much *Circle of Women* can potentially be mobilized or read via what I have called in this chapter a wilderness plot.

Just as California landscape conventions are already always emplotted with tensions about the role of the urban and culture in western discourse, so too are southwestern and Rocky Mountain landscape conventions saddled with questions about the status of nature, the "authentic" West, and women and men's relationship to nonhuman nature. *Circle of Women* only partially departs from, or seems aware of, this broader cultural mapping and context. Thus, though indeed it questions the dominant geocultural imaginary—and Chapter 5 focuses on this fact by looking at Blew's *All But the Waltz*—*Circle of Women* retains structuring assumptions that I have hoped to debunk: that the red/white racial paradigm characterizes western race relations; that rural, ranching, or small-town landscapes are at the center of western experience; and that western women endure, stoically. Thus, I quite deliberately do not locate the heart of the new female regionalist literary history in either the Rocky Mountain or southwestern regionalist tradition, because to do so, it seems to me, is to unwittingly recenter geographical imaginations via white-dominated cultural logics. Both of those traditions ultimately would erase some of the very new and actually alternative landscapes and analytic principles at work in new regionalist discourse: that red/white paradigms nearly always work to white racialist ends, that cities are not antithetical to western subjectivity, that there's more to western womanhood than long-suffering grit, and that a multiracial and feminist western criticism can be achieved only by rethinking "nature."

Having said all of the above, let me return to Barbara Kingsolver and to a topic of enormous investment for most white western feminist writers: ecofeminism. As readers may have observed, feminist scholarship plays a relatively modest role thus far in this chapter. I note this last fact because, on the one hand, it underscores the general inattention of feminists to environmental issues as well as the underdeveloped state of the field. It also suggests, on the other hand, the "bad reputation" that ecofeminist thought has in an epistemological climate dominated by antiessentialist theory. Ecofeminism is associated quite commonly with "cultural feminism," and the latter, with its claims to women's moral superiority and female "intuitive" capacity, is rather thoroughly discredited.[36] Yet it is ecofeminists, or adherents of what Val Plumwood would term "critical ecological feminism," who consistently put nature on feminist agendas and point out the relationships between the domination of nature, the Western world's worship of reason and science, and the domination of women.[37] Plumwood argues that it is ecofeminist philosophy today that might straddle, and even resolve, the social ecology/deep ecology debates. As I noted earlier, it is not the goal of this chapter to take up these debates directly, and I will not here focus on conflicts internal to ecofeminist thought, of which there are many. In general, however, I want to express support for the project of critical ecological feminism and to participate in its refinement. Feminist thought definitely needs ecological feminism, for without it, feminists risk basing their own models of liberation upon the continued domination of nature.[38]

What I do want to focus on, however, are some of the suggestive links between ecofeminist politics and discourses about the West. Although no history of the regional inflection of this movement yet exists, I would venture to say that ecofeminist thought, like environmentalism in general, owes something significant to western cultural history and to the Native American–inspired mysticism associated with things considered "authentically western."[39] Many of the early 1970s ecofeminist conferences met in Northern California, and much of current ecofeminist scholarship and the leaders in ecofeminist thinking, as well as the bulk of the movement's interest in pagan witchcraft, continue to emerge from the west.[40] The Bay Area in particular is a kind of American home to ecofeminist activism, publishing, intellectual life, spirituality, and culture. And, as I noted a moment ago, the "natural" landscapes of the Southwest and the Rocky Mountains are imaginative wellsprings for nonacademic ecofeminist epistemology. This is not to say that ecological feminism is unknown outside the West; such a claim is untenable. Rather my interest here is to consider how the pitfalls of ecofeminist thought are pitfalls that rest in part with its too uncritical partnership with "things western." For reasons that I hope will become clear, Kingsolver's *Animal Dreams* provides a very useful case study of the ways in which westernness unconsciously overlaps with some of the slipperier parts of the ecofeminist impulse.

Of all of Kingsolver's books, *Animal Dreams* is the most popular. It is probably also the most simple. Although Kingsolver's writing is characteristically upbeat, *Animal Dreams* is all the more so, and in a western context, this quality has a definite positive impact on the book's critical reception. Among readers, *Animal Dreams*, like Silko's *Ceremony*, strikes a "western chord" that is complex, unconscious, and very dear. I argue that

that chord is tied up with the wilderness ideal, however much Kingsolver tries to dismantle that ideal. Winner of the 1988 Western Spur Award, *Animal Dreams* revolves around two sisters whose intimately connected lives suddenly take divergent paths. The protagonist, Codi, returns home to the fictional village of Grace, Arizona, to care for her father, the country doctor, who suffers from Alzheimer's. Her real reasons for going to Grace, however, are that she doesn't know what else to do with herself. Though she has finished medical school, she does not want to practice medicine. And she no longer wants to be companion to her male lover of ten years. Codi's sister, Hallie, however, is not so purposeless. As an agronomist and activist in the 1980s anti-intervention movement, Hallie goes to revolutionary Nicaragua to offer her services as an agricultural consultant to the Sandinistas, Nicaragua's revolutionary government. Hallie aids Nicaragua's farmers as they reconstruct the country's agricultural economy. Hallie and Codi correspond by mail, and the novel's interest in American contemporary politics takes off from the different life choices each sister makes.

Once in Grace, Arizona, Codi trips into an old love with whom, at age fifteen and unbeknownst to him, she conceived and then miscarried a baby. She trips, too, into a local environmental disaster. In search of gold and molybdenum, the owners of the local, now-defunct copper mine have run sulfuric acid through the mine's tailing piles. The acid has leached into the town's water supply, threatening to poison the orchards, which are the single self-sufficient aspect of the town economy. The novel develops an ecofeminist story in which the town's women band together and—by way of their folk art—succeed in thwarting the mine's efforts to divert the orchard's water supply. Meanwhile, Codi's sister is killed in Nicaragua by the U.S.-funded contras (the novel is dedicated to the late Ben Linder), throwing Codi into hopeless despair and threatening her newly sparked relationship with her old love.[41] The story resolves with Codi's decision to risk love again, her new pregnancy, and her permanent return to Grace and to the commitments of community, new teaching job, love, and motherhood.

The above deracinated and deregionalized plot line, one that could happen anywhere in the United States, is so far not a very commercial or sexy story. It certainly captures no compelling political imagination, at least not like the kind of political imagination that emerges once the story is drafted through a western tradition—and this, of course, is the book we read. The point is that the regional inflection is quite nearly *everything* to this tale, even if it seems to come "naturally." *Animal Dreams*'s beginning and end locate the reader in the Southwest not by way of mentioning the specific locale but instead more amorphously, by way of Spanish names and paganized Catholic–American Indian ritual. The first chapter, "The Night of All Souls," enframes this novel through the Latino version of Halloween. This is a region, we are to understand, marked, as is Silko's world, by a belief that supernatural forces are a part of daily life and culture. The two sisters of the novel, Cosima and Halimeda (names later shortened to Codi and Hallie), little girls in the opening sequence, are looked upon by their father as they sleep. They've been up in the town cemetery all day, bringing flowers to the townspeople's graves: *cempazuchiles* (marigolds), flowers of the dead. The father, Homero, muses that his girls' "cheeks and eyelids [are] stained bright yellow from marigold pollen"; he smells "the bitterness of crushed marigold petals on their skin" (4).

The above representations define the Southwest through somewhat wispy images of Spanish-flavored rural and mystic earthiness. Kingsolver's representation of the high desert landscape grounds the reader in equally "classic" regional terms:

> Grace is made of things that erode too slowly to be noticed: red granite canyon walls, orchards of sturdy old fruit trees past their prime, a shamelessly unpolluted sky. The houses were built in no big hurry back when labor was taken for granted, and now were in no big hurry to decay. Arthritic mesquite trees grew out of impossible crevices in the cliffs, looking as if they could adapt to life on Mars if need be. (8)

This "wild" landscape is otherworldly; mesquite trees seem able, explicitly, to survive on a planet other than the earth. The "walls" or borders of this town are red canyons. The air is clear and healthful. Fruit trees thrive in spite of their agedness. Though it immediately becomes clear that Grace's inhabitants don't have much money, neither do they suffer apparently for its lack, because their air is clean, their houses endure, they grow their own food, and remain unburdened by the State.

As the story progresses, the western and wilderness plots thicken. Codi's old boyfriend, Loyd, turns out to be Apache, Navajo, and Pueblo. And Grace itself is a town settled, so the story goes, when nine Spanish sisters (the Gracelas) sailed to the New World to marry gold miners. In front of Grace's town hall are horse tie-ups, if no horses. Loyd's dog acts not like some city mutt but like a Jack Londonesque "real dog," whose wildness and self-respect is intact. Billy goats and chickens crowd the courtyards of Grace's homes. At local bars, Grace's people dance a Mexican-spiced Papago polka called Chicken Scratch. Again, as in *Ceremony*, lovemaking is done out of doors. Afterwards, Loyd and Codi sleep in the back of Loyd's pickup, under the stars, the dog between them. The list goes on. This is a picture chock-full of markers of the "authentic" West: primitivist culture, smatterings of Spanish words, lots of animals, Indian reservations and rituals and pre-Columbian ruins, healthful air, sensual living, and exotica such as the marigold-stained cheeks of children. Notably, the desert landscape is the sublime *high* desert, one that escapes the blistering heat of Tucson or Phoenix. Steeping with the metaphoric smell of westernness, this landscape awaits the classic western plot: one of individual self-discovery and ultimate healing. Codi, at novel's end, will be alienated neither from self, community, nor nature.

But this wilderness narrative is not without its qualifications. Codi's return to Grace on board an unromantic Greyhound bus opens the book's second chapter and permits *Animal Dreams* to give the reader a competing overview of Codi's hometown, one that displaces romantic western rurality by disturbing the wilderness plot. This rural community is not removed, we will learn, from broader urban and social trends. The novel's concerns and "feel" are unquestionably contemporary. The language the narrator of *Animal Dreams* speaks is colloquial, voiced in the talky style of much 1980s American women's fiction. And that narrator takes for granted a readership who understands the culture of lesbian-influenced, contemporary, progressive, heterosexual women who wear butchy Billy Idol haircuts and have male "lovers," not boyfriends. Bumper stickers on Grace's cars feature the Alcoholics Anonymous motto "One Day At A Time." Satellite TV dishes occupy a prominent place on Grace lawns, where the high desert foliage grows up around these symbols of the new, postmodern information age. And since the copper mine closed down, Grace's (male) citizens depend on the railroads for employment. Without urban commerce, without the railroad to connect urban with rural economies and provide cash income from railroad employment, Grace's inhabitants cannot buy shoes or clothes, cannot pay their cable TV bills, cannot buy beer or gas or, in an AIDS-contaminated age, condoms. This is not a pastoral or timeless landscape. Grace does not exist independently of urban industry, fiber-optically transmitted mass media, American leisure culture, or the epidemic of AIDS. Kingsolver's narrative exists indisputably in history, and that history is self-consciously postmodern.

Dreams refigures in postmodern terms the antiurban/antimodernist bent that infuses "things western" and also "things environmentalist."

Less obviously, what the wilderness narrative offers (and what "the West" as an American myth has always offered) is a fantasy topography upon which Kingsolver can try out her own solutions to contemporary political dilemmas. The central dilemma of *Animal Dreams* is community.[47] How does an educated, progressive, professional, western woman make a home and sustain a community in a hypermobile superhighway of a postmodern urban economy, in which willingness to relocate is often the prerequisite of professional and personal opportunity? *Animal Dreams*'s implicit answer is to cultivate the ground where you stand. This seems a reasonable enough position, one in keeping with the adage of many progressive movements of the 1970s and 1980s: think globally, act locally. The problem here, the hitch, is that Grace, Arizona, as a signifier for "western towns," resembles nothing that most readers are likely to recognize as "home." The ecological problems faced by environmentally committed Grace citizens do not dialogue with those finer *or* grosser environmental dilemmas that most westerners face. Grace's problems are too obvious, concrete, and solvable. Like Silko's book, relevant environmental issues aren't finally at issue in *Animal Dreams*.

If one truly means to set contemporary western life within a meaningful environmental context and talk about community, why doesn't Kingsolver set this tale in Tucson, where she actually lives? Or in any other southwestern city, where the overwhelming majority of the region's people live? Why don't critics fall in love with *those* tales? The point here is not to ask a writer to write a different book, the book the critic wanted her to write. (It should be granted that Kingsolver does locate some of her other tales in Tucson.) Rather, the aim is to get at how one of the master narratives within western narratives, the wilderness ideal, takes Kingsolver (and critics too) in a certain direction, a direction that is fundamentally at odds with her (and their) own political commitments.

The wilderness ideal is attractive because it enables readers and writers to generate alternative landscapes on which to enact the particular causes that drive their works. The problem with alternative landscapes, though, is that they are not bias-free. In the case of *Animal Dreams*, they end up being explicitly *not* alternative, because the idea of the west as a tabula rasa is one of the oldest of all tropes to govern western tale-telling. With it comes one of the most regressive kinds of symbolic constellations: a love of rurality and wild country overlapping with Indian fetish, the possibility of innocence or redemption, and representations of woman as nature. With it comes primitivist representations of society and of humans' relationship to land. And, most problematically, the plot drives ahistorical narratives. *Animal Dreams*, though it remakes part of the wilderness ideal, and thus refuses some of the narrative's imperatives, nonetheless capitulates to others. The breaks in the text's ecopolitical agendas grow from its failure to break with the most troubling aspects of the wilderness ideal.

By manufacturing an artificial and rural place against which to test ecofeminist politics, *Animal Dreams* drafts environmental policy for areas that are distant from most southwesterners' actual homes. The high desert fantasy landscape of Grace conveniently sidesteps the question most middle-class desert-dwellers face in the 1990s: how to live with the heat. Does an environmentalist permit herself air conditioning? It consumes a colossal amount of energy. Gas too, if one uses it in the car. And speaking of cars, is it one or two for the professional family? How about a swimming pool, that frequent sight in many Tucson neighborhoods? Silko's character in *Almanac of the Dead* has one.

In Grace, the climate is so temperate that *Animal Dreams* and its readers do not struggle with the above or other more serious environmental questions. Class, racial, and rural/urban politics do not complicate environmental standoffs and broader discussions of environmental justice. Native Americans and developers or corporations do not unify against environmentalists, as they do, say, in Santa Fe and, increasingly, in other smaller western towns. Nor do Native Americans, in the interest of economic survival, volunteer reservation lands as sites for gaming or nuclear waste disposal.[48] In Grace, the good guys and the bad guys, the environmental battle lines themselves, are simple. It's a "poor folks against Capital" econarrative, with feminist nuance and primitivist flavor.

Animal Dreams promotes the same romantic image of the Southwest that draws people to Sun City or to the many lush, golf-course developments on the outskirts of Tucson. This image causes southwestern cities to expand to a hundred thousand times the population that the desert's water supply deems sound.[49] However inadvertently, *Animal Dreams* is a cultural product that sells the same mystified Southwest that real estate developers sell, and Kingsolver—and her readers, too—congratulating themselves all the while for their environmental awareness, do not see the production of the wilderness plot as part of the environmental problem.

Because the utopic and pastoral impulse available in the wilderness plot has not been disciplined, the tale's progressive politics implode. Consider: Grace is a place where racism is a rather glib nonissue: "Here the Hispanic and Anglo bloodlines got very mixed up early on, starting with the arrival of the Gracela sisters. By the time people elsewhere were waking up to such ideas as busing, everyone in Grace had pretty much given up on claiming a superior pedigree" (57). The problem with this representation is not simply that it promotes the notion that Grace, unlike any other place in the world, transcends racialist thought or racism. Nor is it that Apache Loyd is the one subject in the book who is not a decentered subject—the Indian again as the nation's remaining holistic man, in this incarnation a man able to handle a butchy, postmodern, emotionally trying woman. (And never without a break in his composure, despite his history of alcoholism, childhood traumatic loss, and racial oppression?)

The problem—or, rather, the symptomatic aspect of this representation—is that this text is thoroughly preoccupied with racism, racial politics, and intercultural difference. Anglo Codi dialogues earnestly with her own anti-Indian racism. The narrator, too, sets up one scene after another that permits the narrative to show its sensitivity to the ways in which racialized ideas easily lend themselves to racist ideas. When reading this text, one feels the overwhelming presence of antiracist work undertaken by some progressive white feminists of the 1980s (especially those who, like Kingsolver herself, were active in the anti-intervention movement). Indeed, the narrative figures the biggest racist in the book to be its progressive protagonist, Codi.

This last painful point is telling. I read *Animal Dreams*'s narrative of racial harmony against the grain and see it, as I see the environmental story, as a flight from history, enabled by *Animal Dreams*'s half-break with the wilderness ideal. The history the tale flees is recent feminist history. The female world in Grace is relatively conflict-free, a utopic representation indeed, given that progressive feminist communities of the 1980s redefined themselves, as the 1980s progressed, no longer through sisterhood but through *difference*. Feminists, especially those of the antiracist Solidarity Movement, grew increasingly and painfully conscious of the irreconcilable differences that separated women and cast fundamental doubt on the (white) feminist ideal of sisterly unity.[50]

It is as though the primarily Anglo Solidarity Movement did not offer enough sustenance or hope or narrative possibility for the ideals Kingsolver held true, and thus, rather than dramatize that—the painful story of the disillusionment of humanist-based, female activism—Kingsolver "went southwestern," into the cultural imaginary of New Mexican ancient pueblos, Native legend, simpler economies, awe-inspiring landscapes. There she drew upon a different but also important political legacy: ecological activism. In this regional and political imaginary, Kingsolver could probe the possibility of interracial love and successful grassroots environmentalism. There too, she could voice her discontent with the notion that feminism means female achievement. For this novel figures Codi's status as medical doctor not as something to take pride in, as an achievement, but rather as a kind of problem. In *Animal Dreams*, achievement alone does not guarantee happiness. Neither does unchecked individualistic freedom. It is female-gendered values like connection, community, commitment, and motherhood that add up, in the end, to a meaningful life.

The "possibility" offered by the wilderness plot finally constrains and limits the book's vision. The desire to take stock, through the character of Codi, of contemporary feminist culture is derailed by an inability to represent non-utopic female battles. And while *Animal Dreams* speaks with much resonance about the inadequacy of female achievement as the end-all goal of feminism, this critique is at the least ambivalent, at the most disingenuous, for Kingsolver's own public persona speaks worlds to the satisfying aspects of female accomplishment. Not only that, but is Kingsolver's solution to embrace motherhood, small-town life, and less demanding work environments? The desire to take stock of racism is constrained too. Surely progressive feminists are not the most dangerous enemy nonwhite peoples face in America! Nor are Native Americans—who live predominantly in urban areas *outside* the Southwest, most especially in Southern California—the West's last "whole" people.

By not breaking with the markers that underlie an "authentic" wilderness plot, Kingsolver misses the constructed nature of her own tale and of her own self as postmodern phenomenon. She can travel the United States as "progressive artiste," appear on important policy-shaping news programs like *NewsHour* with Jim Lehrer, advocate environmental sensitivity and responsibility, and embody in her own public persona the opportunities women can sometimes find (usually in cities). All the while, however, because she packages herself through symbols of "the authentic," Kingsolver, as cultural phenomenon, remains transparent. Not as savvy as westerners must be to survive the realm of commodity aesthetics, Kingsolver is swallowed up by a force more powerful than she is, a force quite skilled at selling the West to its new ecospokespeople.[51]

Southwestern kitsch—of which *Animal Dreams* is a version—is available today, depending on your pocketbook, at Nieman Marcus, upscale art galleries, museum gift shops, Crate and Barrel, K-Mart, Barnes and Noble, and, yes, your radical feminist bookstore. This last fact should not be so shocking, for what escapes commodification in the 1990s? Still, ecological feminism does the cause of environmental justice no favor by resolving ecological crises in romantic or western or "saleable" ways. Nor does it ease the tremendous mistrust between white and nonwhite feminists when white feminists appropriate, with truly astonishing unconsciousness, the symbols, cultures, and religiosity of Native American or mestizo peoples. White progressives, once and for all, ought to find some other than an "Indian way" to "feel natural." Because when all of these features emplot an "environmental narrative," one cannot, finally, enact the connections between human and environmental exploitation that a writer like Kingsolver knows so well add up to environmental justice. This is, at the least, an irony; at the most, a quicksand of intellectual complicity. In the midst of all this exotica and consumer possibility, one isn't thinking about the odd claim that poverty (in particular female poverty) in Grace isn't such a big deal after all; traditional gender relations have apparently smoothed away all of Grace's rough edges.

De-idealizing Wilderness

Over the last twenty years, literary environmentalism has played an important role in producing the evolving green consciousness of westerners, and some of the most prominent of the new female regionalists have been at the head of this movement. Yet clearly, some of the values that go with literary environmentalism need significant revision. By relying upon wilderness preservation as a self-evident environmental goal, environmentalists deny the gendered, classed, racialized, and imperial histories from which the wilderness ideal sprang. The most troubling consequence of environmentalism's "flight from history" is that environmentalists fail to idealize the environments that most Americans, including themselves, actually inhabit.[52] By not idealizing their own homes, environmentalists neglect the ecosystems in which their daily lives are lived.

It is this last point, environmentalists' flight from *urban* history, that has been the major problematic of this chapter, one that ecocritics must begin to address regularly in literature that focuses on small-town environmental issues. This flight, I have argued, leads western critics, already predisposed to the antiurban, to emulate texts that provide representations of "authentic rural western lifestyle." A politics of style (versus policy) leads critics away from many of the issues important to global survival. This kind of ahistorical and antimodern narrative, deployed to establish the "real West" and infused with features of the wilderness ideal, is a trend I have called the "wilderness plot." And it is this plot, I believe, that enmeshes ecocritical discourse, with deafening irony, in the most problematic parts of postmodernist culture. Moreover, damningly, it links ecocritical discourse with antifeminist discourse.

To the extent that the wilderness ideal informs western literary environmentalism, a social justice philosophy in which both nature *and* people matter is muddied and finally undermined. Thus, environmental justice, in its broadest application, is sidestepped. Global environmentalist policies based on an ethics of reduced consumption and wilderness preservation assume a First World economic privilege that nonwhite poor people around the world usually lack.[53] Environmental agendas that put biodiversity and the protection of rainforests ahead of basic human rights are agendas that themselves are implicated in broader imperialist and racialist political projects. This version of environmentalist thought becomes yet another cultural product whose export disables not only environmental justice in other bioregions but human rights justice, too—hence, Max Oelschlaeger's term "green fascism."[54] The crucial link between human *and* environmental exploitation is obscured as the long the ideal goes uncritiqued, and the relevance of Green consciousness to other liberation philosophies is obscured as well.[55]

But what is salvaged? Why do critics care for books that are so invested in contradictory politics? By retaining the wilderness ideal, no matter if half-modified, ecoreaders preserve that which seems to be deeply, truly western: rurality; the promise of harmonious interracial bonds between Hispanics, Natives, and Anglos; the promise of unoppressive motherhood; female empoweredness in wilderness contexts and in heterosexual partnerships; pagan mysticism; and redemptive nature. Authenticity and hope emplotted yet again. Writers and ecocritics mystify their own roles in the production of the exoticized Southwest, which in turn sidesteps not only issues of class in the production and consumption of western wilderness as recreational or spiritual commodity but also the very issues of environmental justice that drive literary ecopolitics. Finally, when women writers emplot their tales with half-qualified wilderness narratives, they reinscribe masculinist identity back upon western spaces. The wilderness plot undermines a just environmentalist imaginary, and a feminist imaginary too.

If "authentic" western landscapes ultimately support antifeminist political projects, what kinds of nonurban landscapes lend themselves to less problematic discursive legacies? Chapter 4 was conceived with this question in mind.

4

Queering Heterosexual Love: Trailer Parks, *Telenovelas*, and Other Landscapes of Feminist Desire

Mapping the (Western) "Desire Which Is Not One"

Desire.[1] Hardly a catchword of western studies. Whether it's too high-falutin', too hard to historicize, too psychological, or somehow just "too French," I don't know. But critics and historians aren't particularly interested.[2] Given that discussions of desire have captured a significant segment of the scholarly imagination in literary criticism and historical studies at large, the disinterest is all the more notable. One might go so far as to call this silence in western studies about questions of sexuality, sexual mores, sexual license, and the more amorphous realm of desire itself a conspicuous silence. "Conspicuous" because as a land of dreams, of El Dorado, of Edenic Paradise, western geographical imaginations locate their origins quite provocatively in what I call here *topographies of desire*.

As a cultural imaginary, the "Wild West" began as a place where desires of all kinds—taboo desires especially—found imaginative expression and release. In nineteenth-century popular iconography, "western wilderness" was not only a proving ground for American know-how, but also a cultural space where forbidden sexual liaisons were rumored to take place: those of white men with Indian or Mexican or Chinese women, of men with men (a less acknowledged event), and of white men with "virgin land."[3] In "wilderness," white men crossed the color line; they felt out (even if they also denied) the seductions of homosocial worlds. In it, they indulged fantasies of lawlessness too—the perverse pleasures of violence against one another, against Natives and Mexicans and Asians, against white women and the feminized landscape. Part of what made the Wild West wild, part of its "lure," was the availability of the sexual unknown.

By the turn of the century, and owing to the larger "crisis of masculinity" that is the subject of recent gender studies scholarship, the above cultural imaginary produced many of the defining images of the new twentieth-century ideal of "virile" (versus manly) American manhood.[4] Consider Buffalo Bill's Wild West Show, the Turner thesis, Frederic Remington's art, Teddy Roosevelt's "the strenuous life," and the popularity of *The Virginian*.[5] Historian Gail Bederman's work on Victorian-turned-cowboy Theodore Roosevelt, especially his advocacy of white procreation, is particularly relevant to this discussion.[6] According to Roosevelt, white citizens should reproduce as a matter of national honor; otherwise, the nation's "virility," its very blood, would become "mongrelized," diluted. The space that permitted American white supremacists to imagine a relaxation of Victorian sexual self-restraint and control was none other than the American West. Roosevelt's "strenuous western life" came to include what in the Victorian years was unthinkable: affirmation of the public display of white male sexuality.[7] Not surprisingly, however, the status of female sexuality remained "private," too taboo an idea even for a space that tolerated taboo pleasures. As a topography of desire, then, western spaces "came of age" in the twentieth century via an erotic emplotment that was simultaneously masculinist, heterocentric, nationalist, and white supremacist.

This last point is the point of departure for our discussion here. For if the new dominant geocultural imaginary effectively jettisoned or foreclosed representations of female sexuality, western women writers themselves have never consented to that foreclosure. Indeed, sexual relations, including the elaboration of *female* desire, is from the outset at dead center of western female literary traditions. And the enabling mechanism for that tradition is landscape discourse.

Feminist criticism of the literary west has certainly been alert to the link between narratives of nature and female desire and has investigated parts of female literary history fairly thoroughly. Annette Kolodny's work remains the trendsetting work here. Kolodny demonstrates that white women's "promotional" literature of the 1830s–60s formulated an alternative discourse about western nature, through which women writers took their readers west.[8] The writers she considers (some of which are surprises as westerners) are Caroline Kirkland, Mary Austin Holley, Eliza Farnham, Margaret Fuller, Alice Carey, Caroline Soule, E.D.E.N. Southworth, and Maria Susanna Cummins. In their fictive worlds, the land was home to a dream of hearth, garden, and community. They searched not for the Big Rock Candy Mountain. But theirs was not only an alternative discourse; it was a counterdiscourse that broadly critiqued the idea that female-gendered nature ("virgin" land) was there for the taking. This critique challenged white men's right to exploit both the land and women's bodies. It alerted women travelers to the trials that awaited them in westering spaces, in the hope that to be forewarned was to be forearmed. And the critique also implicitly (even if unevenly) sanctioned indigenous peoples' land claims. Not only, then, did women's production of a counterdiscourse about nature give rise to an alternative and more pro-environmental nationalist program, but it defined desire not through a masculinist or capitalist (exploitive) libidinal economy, but through some more diffuse and multiple geography of pleasure. This alternative vision of desire is one in which indoor and outdoor spaces are not dualistically opposed, in which dealings with both nature and indigenous peoples do not always go the way of domination, and in which the needs of family and individuals coexist.

The alternative economy of desire that Kolodny documents—written via a discourse about nature—sets the paradigmatic stage for women who write about the West later in the nineteenth century and into the twentieth. Consider Mary Hallock Foote, whose gentlewomanly propriety forbade her to write publicly about childbirth in the wilds, birth control, or sexual identity, but who nonetheless was driven by her western experience to write about these topics at great length in personal correspondence to her longtime, female best friend.[9] Or consider Mabel Dodge Luhan, who loved both women and men, wrote of fondling women's breasts, and was married four times, the last time to an American Indian man.[10] Or think of Willa Cather's eroticized landscapes, like those in *Song of the Lark*, which link artistic creativity to representations of the female body and land, and which express something of Cather's frustrated lesbianism.[11] This alternative vision can be seen also in Mary Austin's works, especially *Cactus Thorn*, which, though written in 1927, was not published until the 1980s, in part because of its explicit sexual content and the grittiness of its understanding of the gender politics of heterosexual sex.[12] And there is Edith Summers Kelly, not a writer conventionally considered "western" but one who nonetheless writes a western book, *The Devil's Hand* (1925), a book about two female farmers in Southern California, the less "manly" of whom feels a new libido out West, which she explores explicitly with her male Hindu neighbor and, implicitly, with her female partner.[13]

The above writers illustrate some of the trends apparent in a second period of enormous literary production by women, beginning in the early 1880s with the works of Mary Hallock Foote, Helen Hunt Jackson, Ina Coolbrith, Sarah Winnemucca Hopkins, and Maria Amparo Ruiz de Burton. It continues through the 1890s, and by the end of the First World War includes Gertrude Atherton, B. M. Bower, Mary Austin, Willa Cather, Mabel Dodge Luhan, Sharlot Hall, Mary Corbin Henderson, Sui Sin Far (Edith Eaton), and Zitkala-Sa. Certainly this group of writers does not represent the West in any one, uniform way. Nor is this an exhaustive list. I have mentioned these writers because they are writers about whom critics know a fair amount.[14] But they are not writers who have yet been incorporated into a synthetic, feminist conceptual framework or broad literary history.

If anything like a critical consensus exists about narratives of nature and female desire, it finds expression in the collection *The Desert Is No Lady: Southwestern Landscapes in Women's Writing and Art* (1987), edited by Vera Norwood and Janice Monk. Following upon the heels of Kolodny's work, Norwood and Monk expand critics' understanding of the links between landscape and sexual discourse by attending to the complications that racial difference poses for established western feminist paradigms. Feminist critics address some of the Anglo modernists, like Mary Austin and Mabel Dodge Luhan, as well as some more contemporary writers, Chicanas and American Indian women writers, in particular.[15] Notwithstanding important differences between writers, critics generally forward the claim that both Anglo modernists and contemporary southwestern writers of color (Pat Mora, Denise Chavez, Rebecca Gonzalez, Gloria Anzaldúa, Leslie Silko, Luci Tapahanso, Joy Harjo, and Paula Gunn Allen) conceive nonurban western landscapes as spaces that are feminine, sensual, and full of spiritual knowledge. They are sources of tribal or mestiza female power, metaphoric landscapes for the integration of human and nonhuman nature in an alienated industrial age.

I have offered the above sketch of feminist critical renderings of the landscape/sexuality connection both to acknowledge my indebtedness to this tradition and to clarify my departures from it. My interest in this chapter is not to expand critics' sense of how women "see" nonurban nature, how they write homoerotic, autoerotic, or satisfied heteroerotic impulses upon it. Rather, this chapter asks whether wilderness or rural space can *ever* be a place for feminist erotics, given that the "wilderness = sexuality" equation usually adds up to one or another version of the wilderness plot I laid out in Chapter 3. Although desire is, in theorist Catherine Belsey's words, "always derivative, conventional, already *written*," it nonetheless seems all the more foreclosed by the phallocentrism of the wilderness/sexuality alliance.[16] As symbolic trajectories go, then, this one is a very tricky one to maneuver toward feminist and antiracist ends. Further, in the postmodern period, women writers may indeed have other and better discursive and political options.

As I suggested in the last chapter, Leslie Silko's *Ceremony*—with its mystical and sexual Ts'eh, a figure who is part woman and part nature but all spirit—can be subsumed rather easily as an "authentic" part of the dominant cultural imaginary in part because male desire and development, even if racialized in American Indian directions, remains the central story. The "mystical Indian" tradition persists, as does the invisibility of desire for Indian women. The same kind of compatibility holds for Barbara Kingsolver's *Animal Dreams*. The feminist inflections of her tale fold uncomplainingly into the dominant imaginary, for the female protagonist's struggles resolve in ways that are startlingly conservative and romantic. Before I offer what I would claim as more trustworthy landscapes of feminist desire—found in the works of Pam Houston, Sandra Cisneros, and Louise Erdrich—let me spend a little time remapping some of what I see as the connections between gender, western spaces, and desire. Along the way I hope to suggest critical practices and food for thought that might help the field resist the seductions of the wilderness plot.

Let me begin with a broad thesis. From the 1830s on, women writers seem noticeably more invested in representing sexuality than are their male counterparts. There is something about western "wilderness"—its association with a topography of desire, I believe—that has tempted, even finally required, women writers to locate within it their own fantasied pleasures. Because the trope of "wild landscape" is a symbolic trajectory emplotted by European, and later American, male desire and prerogative, women must first expose it if they are to avoid being its victims. But to then go further and to survive with any kind of female subjectivity intact, they must re-emplot it.

This claim that canonical male writers do not foreground sexuality as a paradigmatic topic is a big one, for if a more virile and masculine sexuality was newly sanctioned at the turn of the century by the dominant cultural imaginary, why should twentieth-century male writers *not* write, and write aggressively, about it? The answer to this question is more involved than I can explore fully here, and I have spoken to these issues to some degree elsewhere.[17] But the short response is that canonical male writers (and later literary critics) show real ambivalence and skepticism about Teddy Roosevelt's "man's man." They are not nearly so sure as is Roosevelt that Anglo-Saxon masculine power and raw energy ought to take the nation into the twentieth century. Which is to say that canonical literary westerns distinguish themselves from, and to some degree refuse, the masculinist privileges permissible within the dominant cultural imaginary.[18]

Let me further complicate this argument by refusing to attribute even to the dominant cultural imaginary total policing power on sexual matters. Throughout this book I have argued that a pervasive white male–centeredness dominates western geographical imaginations, and while I do not relinquish this claim, I nonetheless want to recognize that this "mythic West," so often held responsible for the most regressive of politics, does not stand still or operate in categorically fixed ways.[19] For example, although classic myth-producing texts like Cooper's *Last of the Mohicans* or Wister's *The Virginian* do indeed perform very conservative cultural works, they are also shot through with all kinds of subversions of and challenges to white and male supremacy, female sexlessness, Indian "savagery," environmental ruin, the invisibility of women of color, the heterosexist imperative, and so on.[20] From the outset, the primary producers of mythic discourse shaped a complex, dialogic narrative as much full of tension, dissent, self-doubt, and taboo desire as it was a triumphal narrative of Christian heterosexual progress in the western wilds.

Put differently, if a text like *The Virginian* consolidates the new twentieth-century, heterosexual, masculinist imperative, it also nurtures the struggle against that imperative. Though *The Virginian* would seem to mark the watershed moment from which a new, more entitled breed of masculinity is stamped onto "things authentically western," *The Virginian* also lingeringly preserves the bonds between the Virginian and Steve and, more deep and formative still, between the Virginian and the "tenderfoot" narrator.[21] The point here is that contained within dominant, twentieth-century, western geographical imaginations is both the justification for a new male power bloc as well as a longing for love and comradery between men, a love not defined (or less defined) against the backdrop of male power over women. Thus mythic discourse, though it can be deployed toward misogynist and racist ends, is also a potentially radicalizing influence upon literary westerns. It affords male writers and popular audiences an imaginative arena in which to claim and celebrate bonds between men, even as the frontier "closes." It affords female writers, as we shall see, license to imagine desire in ways that please *them*.

Having allowed for the possibility of dissent and contradiction within dominant cultural imaginaries, I want to be clear that overall neither the "mythic" nor the Stegnerian geographical imagination represents *female* desire. Female sexuality—indeed, most features of female subjectivity—are on the whole a noninterest. Although female desire might seem a topic in, say, popular culture's famous images of the frontier prostitute, the focus is less upon her as subject than as object of male fantasy. Prostitutes are generally cardboard characters who serve the more important plot interest of masculine development and maturation. The most plentiful representation of nineteenth-century women in popular iconography, the pioneering white woman, is a woman who is imagined to have or take few pleasures.[22] She is worn out by children, cooking, chores. Her face is besmudged with mud. Her husband has the free run of wilderness, while she is contained within domestic farm spaces. She is stoic, stalwart, dependable, hard-working, loyal. However "positive," these are hardly metaphors of passionate abandon. One cannot easily imagine such a woman opening her legs to anything but the agonies of childbirth. Representations of *non*white women are just the opposite—always sexualized: the willing squaw, the sweet-scented señorita, the pleasure-giving "oriental."[23]

And yet, neither can dominant geographical imaginations fully prohibit the representation of female desire. Because they are imaginaries already steeped in articulations of taboo male desire, they offer women writers, too, a chance to narrate taboo topics. There is something seductive about western spaces, outdoor spaces in particular, that have appealed a great deal to women writers. Certain "tendencies" come with the dominant imagination and with its ruling landscape ideologies. Western nature (unlike, say, the more gothic or naturalist conventions of landscape representations associated with other American regions) permits, even prompts, discussions about sexuality and sexual experience. And this sexual narrative always "lurking," if you will, in western outdoor spaces is an opportunity that women writers seize upon in order to fashion their own visions of desire.

With the above frame surrounding the landscape/sexuality link, let me quickly revisit female literary history so as to pave the way for our discussion of contemporary writing. As I argued above (building on Kolodny's work), as early as the 1830s women writers produced western landscapes whose logics of nation formation stressed settled community over continually expanding empire. Such an alternative national program contested the dispossession of indigenous peoples, favored limits on exploitation of natural resources, and, finally, imagined an economy of desire that is ultimately relational, reciprocal, and comparatively restrained. By the 1880s, female-penned landscapes continued to support alternative economies of desire such as these, while speaking with increased directness to the imperial uses to which landscape discourse and the symbolism of "the West" were mustered. As the turn of the century neared, specifically at issue was the sexualized character of Theodore Roosevelt's new nation.[24] We begin to see as early as the 1880s, then, an overt discourse about female sexuality emerge from within western women's writing. It puts out its own vision of a sexualized nation to compete with that of Roosevelt. But in the women's vision, sexuality is not linked to an antimodern version of the "authentic West," nor to Anglo-Saxon racial purity. Rather, female desire is linked to the broader project of modernity. And this alliance will enable western female discourse, throughout the twentieth century, to withstand and challenge some of the most antifeminist parts of the western problematic.

The evolving discourse about female sexuality, which women writers have produced since the early settler days, accomplishes several critical goals. It reveals the pivotal role that sexual discourse (articulated through landscape representation) plays in the process by which the region is gendered and racialized. It rejects a masculinist sexual discourse in which men's pleasure is the only pleasure that counts. And, in a myriad of ways, it invents and practices female desire. In the twentieth century, women's preoccupations include those that Kolodny argues are so much a part of settler women's writings: a worry that environmental exploitation is foolhardy and a desire for permanent homes and communities. But fantasy, for twentieth-century women, is expressed increasingly in erotic, not domestic, terms.

Tellingly, twentieth-century women's narratives do not articulate erotica via the dominant imaginary's nostalgic pathos. Their own fantasies are comparatively contemporary, tied in implicitly to the advance of women's rights and female autonomy created by various political openings of the twentieth century—that of "the new woman," of suffrage, of female economic independence during the Second World War, of the early civil rights movements, and the anticipation of the 1960s–70s sexual revolution. Female fantasy, then, is increasingly linked in the modernist period to visions of a just State. Even in feminism's quiet years—during the "doldrums" between the winning of the vote and the awakenings of the 1960s, years when public sexual expressiveness for women risked severe social censure— western women writers invested heavily in the symbolic *close* of the frontier, for there a viable female-centered desire could be imagined. (Think, for example of Jean Stafford,[25] and the Joan Didion novel *Run River* discussed in Chapter 1.) Unlike western literary men, women writers have shown little desire to return to Victorian gender prescriptions. They find more erotic possibility finally in the new, not the old, West.

The above sketch of histories of desire in western discourse is intended to provide a beginning, somewhat general context for the multiple and contradictory trends influencing new female western regionalists on the topic of sex and sexuality. One of the most significant legacies I have tried to foreground—embedded in landscape discourse and representation—is this discussion about gender, sexuality, and the nation. The female writers who precede the current period have fantasized a good bit about what women want and how exactly they want it. Importantly, part of what they want has nothing to do with sexuality per se and everything to do with the conditions under which sexual activity takes place. The discussion of sexuality is thus also an implicit discussion of female independence, economic autonomy, or female bodily safety. That is, this discussion ultimately links the discourse of female sexuality to various discourses of the nation. Issues of citizenship, reproductive rights, female education, and economic security—different components of female civil rights—are issues entirely relevant to some new economy of western female desire.

When it comes to the contemporary period, sex, sexual desire, and sexual politics are *the* recurrent topics of western women writers[26]—not the only topics, but unquestionably preoccupying and entirely pervasive topics that transcend the many race, class, and subregional differences that divide the new regionalist movement. For new female regionalists, the desire to speak of desire is never a luxury, for issues of sexuality and the body are inseparable from the fundamental experience of femaleness, including female oppression. As I have suggested above, female dignity can be assured only if the ostensibly "personal" and "private" matter of sexuality is linked to a sympathetic and enforcing State. Never before in recent history will the State seem as responsive to feminist demands as it seemed during the legislatively minded 1970s, when the bulk of contemporary feminist legal reform became new law.[27] These reforms coincided, importantly, with many of the Environmental Acts mentioned in Chapter 3. The point is that during the formative years of the female side of the new regionalism, both women's and environmental issues found progressive redress in national policy-making, a fact that further consolidated the link in western female discourse between feminist sexuality and a politicized representation of nature. Certainly western feminist criticism of the 1980s reflects this larger cultural and political milieu.

Let me now turn to the writers who are the ultimate subjects of this chapter—Pam Houston, Sandra Cisneros, and Louise Erdrich—and to the alternative landscapes of female desire they produce. Theirs are landscapes that I believe evidence relatively reliable feminist projects, for they ultimately resist reinscribing traditional representations of woman or of primitive others. These writers do not locate female desire in a "redeemed" or re-emplotted nature narrative; they do not, that is, narrativize nonurban nature through a wilderness plot. Indeed, I have chosen these writers, and framed my own critical presentation of them, to enact a different logic of mapping female desire upon western spaces. *Telenovelas* (Mexican soap operas), trailer parks, female solidarity, demystified American Indian culture, even the symbolic site of American national identity are all cultural geographies, cultural "places," for the expression of feminist desire, which includes antiracist political commitments. To my mind, *this* kind of new regionalism (versus that embodied in a text like *Circle of Women*) best accomplishes the cultural work of forwarding a truly *alternative* new West. These texts, as the Beatriz Colomina epigraph encourages, do not reinscribe within feminist sexualities more conventional emplotments of western space.

She Wants It All (Pam Houston's "Problems")

There really isn't much truth in my saying cowboys are my weakness; maybe, after all this time, it is just something I've learned how to say.
—Pam Houston, *Cowboys Are My Weakness*

With the above line, Pam Houston, in the title story of her sassy first collection, *Cowboys Are My Weakness* (1992), disclaims the very premise that her combined narratives work in and through. Within the story's logic, Houston, who is herself the autobiographical protagonist, has just secured the love of a "real cowboy" who'll be waiting to take her dancing should she ever return to the Montana ranch that she's leaving. Having achieved, now halfway through the story collection, a feat she's imagined to be the central motivation guiding her deepest desires, Houston suddenly, in a complete and unexpected reversal, declares:

> I started to think about coming back to the ranch to visit [cowboy] Monte, about another night dancing, about another night wanting the impossible love of a country song, and I thought: This is not my happy ending. This is not my story. (125)

On the verge of realizing her own plot, Houston realizes she has allied herself with an incompatible script. It has written *her*, her desires, her moves, her angsts, and it has done so, she determines, wrongly. The country and western song, which figures woman as victim and man as brutal or inexpressive, is not her song after all. The possibility of ranch life with cowboy Monte does not add up to the happy western ending she's dreamed of.

Cowboys aren't really her weakness. Implicitly, something else is. Why would this writer—one whose sudden and controversial literary prominence depends upon her representation of feminist heroines who desire quite unfeminist men—deconstruct her own reason to be? If this story is not *her* story, what is?

Pam Houston made a splashy entrance onto the western literary stage in the early 1990s by putting out a series of wild stories about smart, sexy, feminist women who always fall for, and into the bed of, the wrong guy. Not just any guy, but—gasp—one of the most idealized men in American masculinist discourse: the cowboy. A man who, by definition, a true feminist disdains. Hollywood wanted to option this book. And Houston herself—brilliantly blue-eyed, blond-haired, soft-spoken, and youthfully girlish—has become something of a media delight.

As a hunting and river guide, mountain climber, snow camper, and horsewoman, she embodies female accomplishment in the most masculinist of genres: that of adventuring. She has written widely about her own wilderness treks for magazines as different as *Elle* and *Women's Sports and Fitness*.[28] In the two years after her book's publication she gave a whopping 300 readings (almost one every two days). To attend to her sudden opportunities, she took time off time from her Ph.D. work at University of Utah's English Department.[29] Since then, she has edited a book of essays on women and hunting and is currently at work on a novel and a screenplay.[30] Houston would seem to be at least a contender for feminist admiration, but she is not. The reason is because, in the minds of most feminists, she is masochistic, quite stupid for a smart woman, an example of the kind of woman whom many in the 1980s called "a woman who loves too much" (based on the best-selling, self-help book by the same name).[31] It is this last category of pathological desire that I want to explore here first, for I believe that Houston's text explores it too, and does so not incidentally, and quite provocatively, through western wilderness landscapes.

The unavailable man: Houston's favorite. Her heroines—chasing into western wilderness after boyfriends who are cowboys, hunters, river shooters, sheep trekkers, dog breeders, horse breakers, you name it—end up, by the conclusion of most of her stories, disappointed and lonely. Her type of man undergoes a kind of automatic meltdown when he hears words like "monogamy" or "commitment." He balks, stalls, laments past relationships gone wrong, goes out of town to clear his mind, and usually, by the way, to sleep with other women. Unfortunately, it is secure, committed relationships, Houston's heroines tell the reader, that they want more than anything in the world. In the final analysis, the heroines blame themselves for getting involved with what the self-help movement would call "inappropriate" lovers. "What is my problem?" her protagonists miserably ask themselves. "I must be crazy, a total lunatic. I never learn my lesson. It's me, not these men, producing my unhappiness."

Feminist critics and most reviewers agree that these women indeed do have problems. As one puts it:

> [Houston's] female narrators hardly deserve the name protagonist, since they rarely initiate action but rather follow along behind the men they keep falling for. . . . After a dozen of these stories, one wants to shake the women by the shoulders and shout, "Wake up! Put on your clothes! Get a life! See a therapist!"[32]

The same critic reports that some readers have been so infuriated by Houston's characters that they have written her to complain and to accuse her of retarding feminism fifty years![33]

To be sure, this story collection instructs the reader to evaluate it in pathological terms: as tales of self-destructive women who are "addicted" to the need for male love, pathologically driven to excuse the inexcusable. One press release even calls Houston the "Annie Oakley for women who love too much."[34] Twice this story collection portrays scenes with psychiatrists in which characters reveal the deep pain they suffer from unrequited love. Midway through the collection, a "recovery" narrative emerges. In "You Talk About Idaho," the protagonist tells us she is going on her first date without a drink. She muses, moreover, on the ability of liquor to ease the awkwardness of getting to know a new man. Though she never states it, we assume the protagonist considers herself an alcoholic. But alcoholism isn't the only, or even the primary, problem here. The real issue, or so it would seem, is "codependence." The codependent narrative finds its most explicit and sustained expression in the collection's final story, one which features two strong and sympathetic female characters, each of whom is partnered with an unavailable man. The narrator talks about their situations through, again, the rhetoric of codependence, from which they are trying to recover. That language echoes the language of an earlier story, "Dall," when the antihunting narrator, disgusted with herself for making excuses for her boyfriend's sheep-hunting habit, exclaims with alarm: "This is wanting to love somebody too much" (101).

The pathology frame through which these stories announce themselves, and which reviewers and critics seem to take at face value, is one I want to resist here. The reason to resist it is twofold. One, this text ultimately refuses to resolve its psychological dilemmas in conventional terms, and indeed it charts a different outcome or recovery narrative for women who "love too much." Two, the kind of desire that most reviewers seem to judge "appropriate" to feminist politics ends up feeling, at least to this reader, somewhat less expansive than one would hope for.

The most persuasive reason to reevaluate these stories in other than exclusively pathological terms is because after midpoint in the collection (i.e., "You Talk About Idaho"), heroines do indeed "fix themselves"; they do evidence mental "healthiness"; and, here is the biggest hitch of all in the pathology narrative, it doesn't matter. Love affairs still go wrong, even when protagonists are not codependent. Men still see sex as sex, and women still see it and want it as love; and even the men who can "talk feelings" are posturing, doing so to lure earnest (and recovering) women into bed. In an outcome that undercuts the progressive narrative that informs so much of American feminist clinical psychology, "healthy" women do not necessarily get what they want. Women who know when and how to "set limits" (the codependent's supposed cure) are not assured of decent or mutual relationships. No matter that these feminist women remake themselves and "work on" their self-esteem, they nonetheless live in a world where men usually do not meet their deepest needs.

If we problematize the critical frame that judges these to be stories about "sick" women who pathologically "need" their own pain, then what critical space is opened? And what are these stories alternatively about? Part of the critical space opened concerns the relationship between the West, feminist narrative, and topographies of desire. Houston's stories offer an opportunity to consider the relational context in which contemporary straight women and men imagine love and sexual activity to occur. They are stories, as I read them, about feminist desire in the context of contemporary postmodern culture. If one wants to consider any of these to be neurotic or dysfunctional tales, their dysfunctionality owes not to women characters' "neuroses," but to the fact that feminist desire in a misogynist world makes all the players play against themselves: there is no winning hand. As critic Cynthia Schraeger has pointed out, the "successful" ending to the self-help book *Women Who Love Too Much* is middle-class marriage.[35] That is, whatever its empowering qualities, *Women Who Love Too Much* ultimately teaches women to better adjust to gender inequalities, not to challenge them. And the self-help movement of Al-Anon (populated overwhelmingly by women), which is the unmentioned organizational backdrop for codependents' recovery, is as much about acceptance of relationship travails as it is about ending bad relationships or changing the cultural logic that creates the *kinds* of relationships in which women so often find themselves.

Houston's tales, however, refuse to consummate a conventional romance plot in terms that reinscribe middle-class femininity. Recall that this story collection concludes with a tale of two women. This frustrates readers' expectations, as *Jane Eyre* frustrates readers when she leaves Rochester, because it does not resolve the plot formulaically. There is no "happy" ending, for there is no conventional "recovery." Why? Because pathology is finally not the problem. The problem has more to do with the seemingly contradictory desires for female security and attachment but also, and simultaneously, the desires for female liberty and erotic experience and satisfaction.

The book's opening story, "How to Talk to a Hunter," is addressed to "you," a gesture toward Everywoman. Though it talks about the differences between men and women, and reviewers pick up on this difference theme and reinvent it in their own readings, the story's net effect is to demonstrate men and women's psychological *similarities*. Women do not hold a monopoly on self-destruction (men self-destruct too); men are not the only ones who are emotionally skittish (women are equally so). This is less a story about men letting down women than about contemporary people who are so afraid of emotional entanglements, whose life histories are such collages of past love affairs, that they cannot bond securely or permanently.[36] Houston's characters, both male and female, live in an environment of intense mistrust between men and women, of profound insecurity about the efficacy of heterosexual love. Even what might appear to be an act of stability, one in which hunter and narrator trim the Christmas tree, is not one that connects them. Instead it puts into play the destabilizing presence of "Christmases past," when trees were trimmed with other sweethearts. At story's end, the narrator and hunter make love under the trimmed tree, yet the closing feeling is not one of love realized but of independence threatened. Should the narrator attach herself to this man, who eventually will sleep again with his other woman? When the rewards are so scant should she compromise her freedom?

Indeed, female independence and autonomy are as much central concerns of this collection as is the desire for commitment. One must listen hard to hear this independence narrative, however, for, as I noted earlier, the permanence desire gets top billing both in the text and in reviews of it. Nonetheless, freedom is as much a feature of this representation of female desire as is connection. Several stories, in fact, begin by talking about heroines who are "lured out of" happy single lives. Linked to independence are characters' senses not only of personal liberty but of sexual liberty, the opportunity to feel out many partners' sexualities, to experience one's own sexuality as it responds to different people and settings. Always, when relationships end, a not-to-be-underestimated consolation prize follows: narrators return to individualist living, and this return is accompanied by a quiet but nonetheless profound sense of relief.

What better place to play out a desire for freedom, independence, and varied sexual experience, and to play out the conflict between those desires and that of committed union, than the wilderness spaces of the American West? Houston chooses the ultimate American testing ground of the nation's most powerful subjects—white, able-bodied, young, straight men—to write a tale about female angst, self-determination, strength, and a kind of open-ended sexuality. In a space traditionally defined by white women's absence, where indeed white Victorian womanhood *is* a form of pathology that threatens to destroy what is "authentic" about the topography itself, she writes a sequence of stories about white female presence, especially sexual presence. Her characters evidence competence, physical prowess, agility, endurance, overall athletic accomplishment; and, always, they tumble in and out of beds of every makeshift kind. Though these women agonize over needing more nurturance, they definitely don't agonize over lackluster sex. Which is to say that if they aren't getting some of the things they want, they *are* getting others.

Most importantly, these women adventure. But Houston is less out to make a case for women as capable "frontierswomen" than she is to write them into the American adventure genre. For, finally, notwithstanding their pursuit of men, her characters are more in pursuit of the adventure itself—whether into northern Alaska tundra or white-water rivers in Utah. They hunger for the adventure, whatever it might be, because the adventure keeps them sharp, alive, growing, intense, and, most of all, erotically "fit."

This text's version of erotica, however, stays well clear of the wilderness plot. Although Houston's characters traverse actual wilderness—the Alaskan outskirts, the removed isolation of desert Utah, the highwater rapids of western rivers—no wilderness plot is invoked to give meaning to the journey. Houston's "natural" landscape differs from, say, Kingsolver's in its lack of Indian mysticism or Hispanicism. She rehearses no tale of exotic ritual or cosmic redemption. Instead, the text maps relatively original social relations onto the western wilds, original in the sense of their unwillingness to make use of so many classic symbols of the "authentic western moment." In Houston's wilderness we get blood sport, sex between white women and men, simmering conflict as well as actual fisticuffs between white women and men, and no final "everything worked out after all" (meaning marriage is on the way) ending.

Significantly, as I mentioned before, this book closes with a tale of love between two women. Not a sexual love, the narrator notes, though, she muses, it could have been. One woman is horse trainer, one is rider. The trainer, ultimately, dies a female death—of breast cancer. But this sad (if at times tryingly New Age) story is not tragic finally, for in female friendship, the narrator has found a new power and happiness. Female solidarity and companionship has infused the protagonist with a new sense of self-worth, one that implicitly won't chase anymore after the impossible love of country and western songs. This is a curious ending for a book that tantalizes readers because of its appeal to an ostensibly widely shared cultural experience: attraction to the rugged American cowboys. Not only is there no marriage plot here, there is no heterosexual coupling. There is no sex, no cowboys, no weakness. There aren't even any men.

What kinds of reversals have occurred such that Houston both claims and displaces the most classic of western landscapes of desire: cowboys, wilderness, and adventuring? Why is Houston both a seductive media darling as well as an object for feminist intellectual derision? My claim here is that this text doesn't play the western "game" on its own terms. If cowboys aren't finally Houston's weakness, neither, for once, are Indians. This frees her to imagine western spaces by way of some other, relatively newer, and less formulaic desire—namely, that of a smart, searching, vulnerable, and very sexual female protagonist from New Jersey who winds up at story's end conspicuously and thoughtfully single.

The novelties of Houston's resituated western tale for our discussion of feminist desire are that she claims, upon the space called "western wilderness," an animalistic (her word), driven, primal, adventuring, feminist erotica. But the terms of the notion of "primal" refuse a pathological label and refuse also to flirt with primitivist imaginaries in order to be "deep." The desiring women of this text want nurturance from men, they need to trust men. They want oral sex and intercourse and fast love and slow love and lots of partners. They would be willing to take just one, too. They like the smell of men impressed upon their bodies, lingering in their hair. But the fulfillment of their desires is equally tied to female freedom and independence, to female solidarity, and to women's abilities to fight back—quite literally—if men disappoint or abuse them. This is not a representation of desire beholden to middle-class marriage as the symbol of "resolved" female wants and needs. It is not tied to a feminized nature. And even if this desire also desires women, it is not necessarily linked to lesbian love as a kind of final "escape hatch" from misogyny, gender difference, or the challenges of heterosexual love and sexuality. Desire here, finally, is variable, open-ended, adventuring, without conclusion.

Wicked, Wicked Sister Comes "Home": Sandra Cisneros's *Woman Hollering Creek*

To have a lover sigh mi vida, mi preciosa, mi chiquitita . . . *I wanted to say so many things [to him] but all I could think of was a line I'd read in the letters of Georgia O'Keeffe. . . . Flavio, did you ever feel like flowers?*
—Sandra Cisneros, "Bien Pretty"

In Cisneros's final story in *Woman Hollering Creek*, the protagonist of "Bien Pretty" echoes both the longings and the conclusions drawn by most of Cisneros's female characters. When it comes to the bottom line of decisions made about halfway romances, women tell their men, "I love you, honey, but I love me more" (163). Thus, Cisneros, a woman whose book-jacket biographies repeatedly dub her "nobody's wife and nobody's mother," stays true in this fourth book[37] to her continual fictional message: Chicanas should not compromise, shouldn't "settle." They should hold out for the true thing, for "feeling like flowers." Failing that, they should retreat with dignity from questionable relationships. As one (fictional) Barbara Ybañez of San Antonio, Texas, confides to La Virgen de Guadalupe, "I've put up with too much, too long, and now I'm just too intelligent, too powerful, too beautiful, too sure of who I am finally to deserve anything less" (118).

As unlikely a comparison as it might seem, *Woman Hollering Creek* very often reads like *Cowboys Are My Weakness* without the pathological overtones. Both collections feature recurrent stories of female disappointment in heterosexual love; often the men are romantic cultural figures. For Houston, they are Anglo cowboys. For Cisneros, they are Mexican revolutionary *charros*, like Zapata, whose silver-tooled belts and studded black pants are part of the seductive spell, or they are exoticized Mexican Indian nationals, men whose features are hyperbolically Mayan. These men function for Chicano identity much as cowboys function for white identity: as symbols of "the authentic" and of the national. The comparison is an important one, which I'll return to, for it is not accidental that both writers pursue questions of feminist subjectivity, sexuality, and female solidarity through dialogue with these heavily symbolic figures, whose own cultural meanings are inseparable from western spaces. This comparison also forces the further refinement of this chapter's beginning assertion, for western spaces are not just always already sexualized, but they are sexualized in racialist ways. By intruding upon our earlier discussion of Anglo-centered topographies of desire with Sandra Cisneros's work, and by directing our attention to Texas, where Cisneros now makes her literary home, we can take up some of the fault lines within both the dominant cultural imaginary and within feminist sexual geographies too.

Woman Hollering Creek is Chicago-born Cisneros's first book to be set in Texas, and her decision both to locate herself permanently in San Antonio and to devote this story collection to the Chicana voices of that broader regional locale exemplifies the hold that South Texas, in particular, exerts on Chicana feminist imaginations. The region itself, to its contemporary women writers, symbolizes a female and sexualized ethnic identity—a kind of "authentic" Chicana feminist homeland.[38] Like many South Texas Chicana writers (Gloria Anzaldúa, Pat Mora, Evangelina Vigil-Piñon, Angela de Hoyos, Carmen Tafolla, Rebecca Gonzalez), Cisneros emplots the regional space of South Texas with sensual, eroticized narratives. Cisneros's Texas is a space that is open to "brown desire"; indeed, brown desire is not just thoroughly mapped onto the region's cultural identity, but brownness also draws Cisneros's women to particular kinds of brown men. Brownness is its own erotic landscape. For Cisneros, then, the space of Texas offers itself as an erogenous zone. It is infused with a Latino/a historical past, with Chicano/a ethnicity, with the deep, rolling rhythms of the Spanish language, and finally with feminist possibility.

Importantly, unlike Anzaldúa or Pat Mora, Cisneros is far more interested in South Texas as a symbolic landscape than as a literal desert or borderlands terrain. Her concerns do not center, for example, on the recovery of lost land or on protesting local histories of Mexican dispossession (as do Anzaldúa's). Nor does she valorize the wild plants, herbs, cacti, or desert animals of South Texas in order to keep alive an alternative *curandera* philosophy that supports Mexican American female mental, spiritual, physical, and sexual health (as does Pat Mora). By locating her claim to the South Texas spatial field upon its cultural, not physical, landscapes, Cisneros is able to take up not only questions that inhere in that spatial field but also questions newer to it.

In *Woman Hollering Creek*, Cisneros parts company with many Chicana literary subjects. First, her interest in female sexuality centers on heterosexuality. She also comments on the discourse of Chicano cultural nationalism, especially its reliance upon the romantic figures of the *charro* and the Mexican Indian national.[39] In her view, both these figures contribute to maintaining normative heterosexuality, which has everything to do finally with upholding both a masculinist Anglo West and also a masculinist Chicano nation. Mexican American women and their desires rank low on the priority list of both nationalist projects, and *Woman Hollering Creek* thus begins with a sense of imperative. New stories need to be told, it argues, and it sets out to tell them.

One of those new stories is the (ultimately straight) female's sexual coming-of-age story.[40] Thus *Woman Hollering Creek* opens with "My Lucy Friend Who Smells Like Corn," a story of Mexican American sisterhood that is charged with homosocial attraction and intimacy. The protagonist and her friend Lucy are deeply, physically bonded. They are rebellious and pranksterish, too. As the girls enter puberty, they turn toward boys, though they also discover that, as girls, they are marked as second-class citizens. The several stories of second-class citizenship that follow, however, are never those of helpless victimization, an important point in a narrative that continually features situations in which girls and women indeed are brutally victimized. Girls outwit parents or nuns who would control female sexual expression. In one story, they evade the clutches of a serial killer, and thus outwit even death. We begin to have a sense early on of the kinds of desires that make up feminist desire for Cisneros: female-identified sensuality, a sense of trickster playfulness, wit, and an unwillingness to play the role of victim Other to an oppressive Subject. As invested as Cisneros is in the recovery of Chicana sexuality from historical erasure, however, she is nonetheless not invested in a idealized portrait of female desire—one that can do no wrong. Sometimes, as in "Never Marry a Mexican," passion plays drive women to crazed despicability, and women exact cruel, intense, and victimizing revenge. Overall, however, Cisneros's Tejana protagonists are moving toward some more self-realized ends, ones in which they act in their own best interests.

Romance figures quite prominently in this particular vision of female desire. The title story of the collection, "Woman Hollering Creek," is about a battered woman's resistance to her husband/abuser, but, interestingly, the story does not begin with the man's beatings. It is framed instead through what Cleofílas, the protagonist, wants, what she hopes for, what—in her own special world of fantasy and daydreams—she's imagined her life might ideally become. When she, a Mexican woman from a small village, meets him, a Mexican American man from "*el otro lado*" (the other side of the border), a man who has a good American job and financial prospects, he seems to her a windfall of unthinkably good fortune. This man will deliver Cleofílas from small-town boredom and take her off into new American worlds, where she can dress up, as do the women in the *telenovelas* (Mexican soap operas) she watches everyday. The narrator tells us "what Cleofílas has been waiting for, has been whispering and sighing for . . . is passion" (44). This passion is of "the kind the books and songs and *telenovelas* describe when one finds, finally, the great love of one's life, and does whatever one can, must do, at whatever the cost" (44).

The rhetorics employed in this discussion of passion, we should note, are those of popular soap operas but also those of literature, too—meaning, potentially, those of high culture. The point is that this moment articulates not just Cleofílas's desire for the dreamy and dramatic style of heterosexual courtship displayed in Mexican soap operas (a style even more overblown than U.S. English-speaking soaps), but it also articulates this text's own production of a romance plot. A kind of genre-bending is going on here, where Cisneros embraces popular romantic drama and wants to include it as part of a "high literary" aesthetic and emotional sensibility.

What soap plots and the soap gestalt offer is emotionality. They sanction female expression of feelings, but even more they represent male emotionality. Men cry. They profess love, loyalty, lust. They bring flowers, they fight for the woman they want, they apologize. Obviously soaps are engaged in intrigue and deception, and they represent many unsavory, even terrorist, men. Nonetheless, they put romance *first*. As U.S. television commercials frequently advertise, soaps picture "love in the afternoon." And it is not only women who work in the home to whom soaps primarily speak. Cisneros suggests that soaps get Mexican American female desire "right" in some basic way. They put sweet-smelling, freshly shaved, attentive men on women's imaginative doorsteps. That is, they make available objects of *female desire* such that women can enact the principal drama—the viewer's experience of female passion, the feeling out of the depth and range of women's most intense longings and hopes.

Based in part on the kinds of desires stirred up in Cleofílas by *telenovelas*, Cleofílas marries this Mexican American man and moves away from her family to an American border town in Texas. It isn't long before Cleofílas's new husband begins beating her. Cisneros situates this battering story within a broader social context in which violence against women is so prevalent that it seems normal. Indeed, one of Cleofílas's husband's friends is rumored to have murdered his wife. Cleofílas worries that the rumor is true, because the newspapers, the narrator reveals, are

> full of such stories. This woman found on the side of the interstate. This one pushed from a moving car. This one's cadaver, this one unconscious, this one beaten blue. Her ex-husband, her husband, her lover, her father, her brother, her uncle, her friend, her co-worker. (52)

Interestingly, in a narrative setting dominated by male power, Cisneros refuses to grant speaking space to the abusive husband. Indeed, as if turning the tables in order to avenge misogynist narrativity, Cisneros rarely permits men to speak for themselves throughout this story collection. Instead, she shows men's actions, words, and feelings only through women's responses to them. Quite self-reflexively, Cisneros controls the means of representation, the objects and subjects of the narrative gaze. Cleofílas thus remains the subject of Cisneros's story, even as her husband's beatings degrade her and threaten to harm the unborn child she is carrying.

At the doctor's office, during a prenatal sonogram, Cleofílas breaks down and begins to cry. She knows she must acknowledge her husband's abuse. Her attending and responsive Chicana technician calls one of her *comadres* (a trusted friend) who agrees to help Cleofílas escape and return to her family in Mexico. The two Chicanas apparently cooperate in a kind of working-class underground railroad that aids Mexican women in trouble who are too shy or afraid or who don't know how to act in their own best interests. Cleofílas packs her bags, and with one child in hand and another on the way, she flees. But not without satisfying a question that has punctuated the story again and again and one that is quite relevant to this study: How did the creek running behind her house get such a funny name, the name "La

Gritona" (Hollering Woman)? Everyone Cleofílas asks does not know—that is, until she asks Felice, the woman who, in her red pickup, has come to drive Cleofílas to the bus station where she'll board a Greyhound for home.

Felice herself is a shock of a woman to the more reserved Cleofílas. She not only owns her own pickup truck, but she is not married. And she is vulgar, and loud. What kind of a woman is this? Cleofílas wonders, both enchanted and alarmed. In this moment, driving away from her battering husband, the meaning of the creek's name dawns. She has puzzled before over whether the "hollering woman" cried out in anger or pain. But now, she suddenly is aware, in the presence of this wild woman Felice (a name that translates into happiness/congratulations), that as they cross the river, her own voice is newly full, what the narrator describes as "a long ribbon of laughter" (56). She is ecstatic with the sound of her own rich, laughing ebullience.

The passage over this female-gendered creek serves to liberate Cleofílas into a particular kind of freedom: the freedom to laugh, to play, to hoot and holler, not just defensively or protectively with anger or pain, but pro-actively with joy, energy, happiness, something like the state French feminists call "jouissance." It is this complex bliss, I suggest, that encapsulates part of Cisneros's version of feminist desire. Significantly, it comes in the presence of another Chicana and a Chicana-named creek. Cisneros's particular offering to the region's feminist imaginary is not just a longing for female homosociality, then, but also for joy, the joy of Chicana solidarity, as well as the joy of self-respecting behavior. The creek, La Gritona, becomes a landscape upon which Cisneros locates an ultimate passion, like the kind Cleofílas has wanted, like the kind the *telenovelas* promise, one for which she will do anything: a passion for her own Mexicana and Americana self.

It is significant further—in the context of Chicana literary and mythological history—that this figurative landscape called La Gritona is also the antithesis of the mythic La Llorona, the lake-woman who is forever crying. Cisneros's revision of Mexican female cultural history is one in which the story of female joy and strength wins out over the story of female victimization and regret. La Gritona shouts her own joy and strength. She liberates a victimized woman from terrorized captivity, a woman who flees with her children and dignity intact. By contrast La Llorona weeps, eternally, for her children are lost, her race betrayed. She is alone, shamed.[41]

This river, La Gritona, this Spanish-named and mestiza-racialized space of joy, is also the symbolic meeting place where the road to and from Mexico runs—a cultural, if not literal, borderland. This is a particularly difficult meeting place to negotiate in Mexican American literature and cultural life in general. If the bicultural nature of Chicano/a identity and the fact that the "mother country" is so close to the U.S. gives rise to the richness of Chicano/a ethnicity, these factors also are sources for much of its angst. The above moment of joy Cleofílas finds when traveling between the New and the Old World is more an ideal moment than a representative one. Generally, throughout this collection and also in Chicano/a literary history, the moment of direct engagement with Mexico or Mexican nationals is far more ambivalent, conflicted, and fraught with the pain of being rejected by "real" Mexicans, who see "'Mericans" as a compromised breed of Mexican. These difficulties add up to a losing battle to balance Mexican with American identity.

It is this desire to possess the withheld—to unify what is a ruptured binational identity—that motivates the most graphic erotica of the collection, "Eyes of Zapata" and "Bien Pretty." Here I want to make the second part of my argument about Cisneros's vision of feminist desire: that it is entirely caught up in longings for a different narrative of the Chicano/a (and later I'll show, American) nation. In both "Eyes of Zapata" and "Bien Pretty," female desire is narrated upon the body of men who are Mexican nationals, ones quite deliberately more Indian or mestizo than Spaniard. The point here seems to be both to mythologize a Mexican nationalist cultural hero, one who displaces the American cowboy or other figures of Anglo derivation, and simultaneously to displace Spanish colonial history and the political problems that colonialist legacy presents for contemporary Chicano/a cultural nationalists, who overwhelmingly want to tie their contemporary racial genealogy to indigenous, not colonialist, history. This Indian or mestizo hero is one whose national *and* racial identity is not in question, not splintered. Again controlling the means of gendered representation, Cisneros frames the men in both stories as objects of the female gaze, and what the female sees is this:

> I put my nose to your eyelashes. The skin of the eyelids as soft as the skin of the penis, the collarbone with its fluted wings, the purple knot of the nipple, the dark, blue-black color of your sex, the thin legs and long thin feet. For a moment I don't want to think of your past nor your future. For now you are here, you are mine. (85)

This man whom the protagonist, Inéz, describes here is none other than the great General Emiliano Zapata—revolutionary, lover, peasant hero, romantic *charro*—undressed now and revealed in his lovely, blue-black nakedness. Inéz delights in Zapata asleep; it allows her to do what she is unable to do otherwise: possess him. Part of what possession means to her is fulfillment of the simple desire not to let her roving beloved go. This scene allows the narrator to follow the above erotica with an evocative representation of the *charro* figure in Mexican cultural history. Inéz examines Zapata's "black trousers with the silver buttons . . . the embroidered sombrero with its horsehair tassel, the . . . Dutch linen shirt . . . the handsome black boots . . . tooled gun belt and silver spurs" (85). Zapata is larger than life, mythic, a stunning, beautiful, flamboyant, powerful man, who—and here is where he becomes problematic and where the story pivots—treats Inéz shabbily. She cannot decide, as she says, what she is to him—whether she is "sometime wife, lover, whore, which?" (105)

This passage—in which strong, intelligent, dignified women are reduced (in their own eyes) to something like whiners, or women who cling—is reminiscent of those parts of Houston's *Cowboys Are My Weakness* where Anglo cowboys' inexpressiveness and failure to commit foster insecurity and self-loathing in Houston's female characters. Both men embody the classic prerogative of male heterosexist culture: they are entitled to many women, and, indeed, their masculine status depends on the graceful exercise of this prerogative. Part of what is at issue for both Cisneros and Houston is the bind this heterosexist prerogative puts women in. If women partake of the dominant culture's premiere example of masculine beauty, they must pay an ultimate price. For however much Zapata pleases Inéz—and we are to understand that he pleases a great deal—he will also fundamentally disappoint. This no-win scenario defines the dilemmas of female desire in sexual discourses dominated by a masculinist heterosexist logic.

Although Cisneros controls the means of representation, and creates her female characters always as subjects, she cannot construct a male figure who gives women what they want. Zapata cannot give it, because he refuses to reckon with female political realities. As Inéz tells him, "Don't you see? The wars begin here, in our hearts and in our beds. You have a daughter. How do you want her treated? Like you treated me?" (105) That is, "revolution" means something different to her than it does to him. It includes gendered sexual politics and requires transformation of social structures that empower male sexual subjectivity at female expense. This gendered difference complicates a shared national and political identity, and it also forces what I earlier called Cisneros's desire for a different narrative of the nation.

Ultimately, Zapata cannot be a nationalist hero for a woman like Cisneros, for the kind of figure he symbolizes cannot resolve the dilemmas she faces about Mexican American female national subjectivity. Indian Mexico—as imagined national community—will not satisfy the binational and bicultural identity crisis that Chicanas negotiate.[42]

The second story I want to consider, "Bien Pretty," brings the gendered complications closer to home, out of Mexican revolutionary history and into the U.S. and postmodern period. The progressive Chicana protagonist, a painter named Lupe, has been dumped by her Chicano sweetheart, who leaves her for a white woman. In this collection of stories, there is no racialized solidarity among Chicano men toward Chicanas. Mexican American men will do what they want in America, marry in or out of their ethnic and political communities. It is as if the history of gendered struggle seen between Inéz and Zapata has been transplanted to and reinvented upon American soil. Among contemporary cultural revolutionaries, the men remain, as did Zapata, the battle's victors. So contemporary protagonist Lupe has been shamed, and to recover she hightails it out of San Francisco and takes up residence in San Antonio. Lupe's new digs in San Antonio are of the grooviest kind, and Cisneros takes the opportunity afforded by the very self-conscious southwestern style of these new digs to comment on contemporary professional Chicano/a progressive artists and intellectuals.

Lupe house-sits for a "famous Texas poet who carries herself as if she is directly descended from Ixtaccíhuatl." This poet has a Ph.D. from the Sorbonne. Her husband is an "honest-to-God Huichol *curandero*" (139). This cultural power couple are away for a year on a Fulbright, and Lupe, licking her love wounds, resides now in their turquoise home close to the historic King William District of San Antonio. We learn quickly of the many Mexican cultural artifacts that decorate and animate this home: pieces of Oaxacan black pottery, a signed Diego Rivera monotype, a replica of the goddess Coatlicue, a Frida Kahlo altar, a seventeenth-century Spanish *retablo* (139–40). Lupe sleeps upon an iron bed with mosquito net canopy. The sheets are of Egyptian cotton, the bedspread of eyelet lace. This house mixes high cultural artifacts like these with a fair amount of kitsch: strings of red chili lights, a star-shaped piñata, a Texana chair upholstered in cow skin with longhorn horns for the arms and legs (139–40). High culture and popular and mythical histories thus characterize both the literal and more figurative or broader cultural "home" of these prominent academicians and artists. This home implicitly includes the protagonist Lupe herself, who, recall, is a painter.

Beneath all the funk, lace, silver, and obsidian exist, relentlessly, Texas cockroaches. Like everything else in Texas, the roaches are bigger than big, excessive. The presence of these scuttling obscenities ushers in the love affair of this story, for the exterminator whom Lupe calls upon to solve her bug problem turns out to be none other than Flavio, the "bien pretty" man who will make Lupe "feel like flowers." How, we might inquire, is this romantic stage set by so unlikely and unromantic a premise? How is it the man whose job it is to kill roaches ends up being the conduit to a sighing and ecstatic female pleasure?

The site here for the romance plot is, again, the Mexican Indian, whose national and racial identity, like that of Zapata, is (supposedly) stable, unsplintered. Cisneros returns to this figure of the Indian man, but this time she emplots this female landscape of desire with a new kind of consummated climax. We are told from the first that Flavio has "the face of a sleeping Olmec, the heavy Oriental eyes, the thick lips and wide nose, that profile carved from onyx" (144). Indeed, Lupe wants to use Flavio as a model for a painting in which she updates the classic representation of the Prince Popocatepetl/Princess Ixtaccíhuatl volcano myth. We see not just primitivist discourse about "the Indian" at work here, but Orientalist discourse, too. Flavio is exotic, "authentic," "classic" enough even to serve as a mimetic double for Prince Popocatepetl.

Flavio consents to pose, a romance evolves, and Lupe, of course, falls in love. Flavio's lovemaking Spanish stimulates in Lupe something like an experience of the very "essence" of Mexican culture—its family intimacy, its love for children, its warm days, open windows, peopled kitchens, smells of masa, shawled *viejas* (old women). After Flavio, she muses, she can never again make love in English. Flavio is a romantic, a realist, but also a kind of wise man. The power of his intellect as well as his personal charisma rests on the easy way he moves between telling stories of a humble exterminator's workday to commenting on "grand topics" like the nature of time, all the while embodying a broad Latin American cultural identity. Flavio loves, as he says, "pure tango," meaning classic tango (150).

Flavio also, however, wears Reebok tennis shoes. The point is that Flavio serves this story's desire to both represent and critique the various strategies most often operative in current efforts by Mexican American intellectuals to establish both political and racial subjectivity. When Lupe tells Flavio that his Reeboks and Izod T-shirt make him a "product of American imperialism," his response is, "I don't have to dress in a sarape and sombrero to be Mexican . . . I *know* who I am" (151). This simple statement might well be read as a critique of all of the story's characters' desires to deploy heavy Mexican Indian symbolism to "authenticate" their own Mexican American identities. Not only is the recourse to Mexican Indian identity a flawed political project, Cisneros implies, but it does not finally redress female oppression. Punctuating this point is the fact that there's little time to explore any of these questions or even lingeringly to relish this new love affair before Flavio—the beautiful, the delicate, the exquisite lover, delivers the punch line: he has two wives and seven sons in Mexico, and he must go. Flavio, it seems, is not so different from Zapata when it comes to the exercise of masculine prerogative—even if he makes no pretense to revolutionary consciousness.

Conclusions? On the topic of "feeling pretty" as a *woman*, as Cisneros terms it (137), the likelihood is great that the symbolic body of the Chicano nation—located upon the Indianized features of the Mexican man— will not sustain Chicana feminist pleasure. How does Cisneros close this story, the concluding one of the collection and thus her final comment (for this book anyway) on female heterosexual coming of age in postmodern times? By having Lupe the painter revise the mythic volcano image so that Prince Popo and Princess Ixta trade places, Cisneros takes what revenge she can on the patriarchal power structure underlying Chicano masculinist cultural nationalism. After all, the narrator says, "Who's to say the sleeping mountain isn't the prince, and the voyeur the princess, right? So I've done it my way" (163). In parody of the Chicano/a mystification of a proud, pre-Columbian, Indian past and in an act that seems to cut down to size the grand phallocentric preoccupation of nationalist discourses, she calls the revision "El Pipi del Popo." Cisneros, ever true to form, always insists that she will direct the mode of representation in ways that suit her. By story's end, the now twice-dumped Lupe has recovered her self-respect, and the book triumphantly announces a Walt Whitmanesque exuberance for life.

What?! The reader demands here, a *Whitmanesque* ending? Why does *the* celebrity of Chicano/a literary culture conclude a discussion of feminist desire and Chicano/a cultural nationalism by invoking Whitman? My argument is that through Whitman, Cisneros claims American literary identity, cultural radicalism, and open-endedness on questions of sexuality. If Mexican American cultural politics fail to deliver on women's issues, Cisneros suggests (as do many of the new female regionalists) that she'll take her chances and locate her own political allegiances more in the northeastern cultural mainstream, where women get a relatively better hearing. Further, Whitmanesque cultural space would seem to be more enabling of the kind of *jouissance*—joy and energy—that Cisneros marks as a central feature of Chicana feminist sexuality. Lupe *will* be happy, she decides, "Just because it's today, today, with no thought of the future or past. Today. Hurray. Hurray!" (165). These last moments of the book recall the earlier discussion of *telenovelas*, and, taken together, they begin to sketch the relevant arenas in which female wants must be accorded some respect. *Telenovelas* present romance, male emotionality, and attentiveness as key to the kinds of relationships women crave, as key to female passion.

But this exuberance, even as it is linked to Whitman, is also located in the figure of *urracas* (grackles), common birds outside Lupe's windows. These birds are feisty, dark, loud, messy—certainly not birds of genteel admiration. Like Chicanas, *urracas* are of New World origin. With a thus distinctly American *and* western American signature—one optimistic and feisty but, echoing Los Angeles poet Wanda Coleman, "darkened" and made more democratically female—Cisneros closes this book. She has declared herself, in unmistakable terms, an American artist.

In conclusion, I want to be clear that the terms of "Americanness" are yet in the making, not secure or already known. But I do think Cisneros's text ultimately crosses the racial literary divide and invites its readers to do the same. By so doing, it forges some new, miscegenated, nationalist space that can accommodate nonwhite feminist demands. It does not rely, as do so many western cultural imaginaries, on appropriations of "authentic" Indian identity (and erasure of, in this case, Spanish colonialist history). Until the day that Cisneros's heroines find men who'll both respect them and make them "come undone like gold thread, like a tent full of birds," they'll embrace the joys they find in Chicana solidarity (28).

Love Medicine: Coming Home to the Postmodern, or Louise Erdrich's Revision of the Romantic Western Indian

At the beginning of *Love Medicine* (1984), middle-aged June Morrissey is more than down on her luck. Sitting in the stall of a bar bathroom, June feels worn out, life itself is worn out, hope for something better has faded. Something—a man mostly—has got to be different, she tells both the reader and her drinking date for the night. And yet, even if something or even if he is not different, she'll make it, she realizes quietly. She's past the worst of things—she no longer worries about the outcome of her life. Underneath her worn clothes and heavy makeup, June is pleased to feel that "all her body was pure and naked." It is only her "skins [that] were stiff and old" (4).

When, predictably, her drinking companion drives them outside of town at night's end and climbs drunkenly on top of her, when it is over in less than a minute and he passes out heavily, June lets herself out of the car. She decides to walk home, toward the reservation. She will not return to town or its bars. Even as snow begins heavily falling, even when "her heart clenched and her skin turned crackling cold," she finds peace in the idea that the pure and naked part of herself will carry on. As the snowy storm comes on, burying her slowly beneath it, June "walked over it like water and came home" (6).

This opening scene—from which unfolds a series of stories of a big, extended family—gives us some initial clue about the degree to which female desire is usually fulfilled in Erdrich's fictional world. Interestingly, though June's story frames the tale and sets in motion the telling of the family sagas, June's is nonetheless a submerged story. We get snapshot vignettes of June as a child and adolescent. We get a bit of the splashy impression she made upon her young niece Albertine. But in all, June's longings, her happinesses, her dreams, go unfathomed. Erdrich's representations of landscape, especially its emplotment with Native American social history, offer a partial picture of June's place in the community. But June remains, as do the exact circumstances of her death, shadowy, half-realized, tragic. This, in short, is Erdrich's comment upon feminist desire, at least as it is tied to traditional representations of Native American life.

It will be in the figure of the enticing and street-smart Lulu Lamartine and the kinds of Native landscapes Lulu represents that alternatives to tribal and female suicide emerge. For Erdrich, nontraditional "nature spaces" are emplotted with the possibility of feminist sexual satisfaction and self-respect. Without an embrace of the new, it seems, the question, "was it good for you, too?" will continue to mark whose pleasures are at the margins of sexual discourse.

Love Medicine is not devoted to any single protagonist, story, or even to a single gendered or racialized story. For that reason, it is a remarkably difficult novel to read. It is hard—and this is part of what it teaches readers—to keep people distinct from each other. As the late Michael Dorris noted, the series of books of which *Love Medicine* is the first is a kind of continuing community narrative—one, moreover, that is not focused on "contact with the outside," as is most Native fiction, but rather on the community's internal relations.[43] One critic calls Erdrich's narrative technique "the tribe as collective protagonist."[44] It tells men's and women's stories with equal grace and interest. It tells stories of full bloods, of mixed breeds, and of whites. It is not individualist in any sense of the term. It is not even clear that the text of the novel will remain in its present form, given that it was expanded and reissued in 1993.[45]

In spite of the above, June Morrissey's presence, however fragmented, exerts an enormous influence on all the other characters' lives. Her death is the single most important event that drives the novel's characters to re-evaluate their pasts, and to grow and change. Though her own story appears nowhere but in the first six pages of the novel, she is everywhere. Yet even though she is everywhere, she does not of herself add up to a graspable presence. Here is the novel's most ambitious undertaking—to articulate a story that refuses coherent telling. For the story, in some serious part, is the story of female desire. An exploration of its discontents and satisfactions is a continuing feature of the community's identity.[46] The story of female desire is also the story of the kinds of landscapes that will ensure Native American survival. The two—female desire and the tribe's relationship to nature—are mutually dependent, because without Indian survival there is no hope for Indian women, and without an embrace of postmodern landscapes, there is no hope for either.

The world of *Love Medicine* is tough and hardscrabble; life on the North Dakota reservation is dominated by brutal winters, by the relentless demands of child raising, by gossip, alcoholism, and poverty. In this context, female desire (and often male desire, too) is the first thing that goes—a luxury few can afford. Women's hopes for sweetness or fidelity in romance, for female honor, for satisfying sexual love, for possibilities for their children, for rest and respite, are hopes profoundly compromised and constrained. Even so, perhaps *because* of the pressures keeping them at bay, those same hopes remain softly and stubbornly alive, providing much of the energy and pathos that drives Erdrich's work. Many critics remark upon the ultimate hopefulness of the novel and locate that hope in the healing power of love medicine. I am less convinced of the story's hopeful character. It seems as much tragic as hopeful, and the search for love medicine remains as much a search as a certainty. Sadly, the recent tragic and scandal-surrounded suicide of Michael Dorris adds credence to this last claim, it would seem.[47]

A demythologized landscape is also a central part of this decentered narrative. The reservation pictured here is no undeveloped wilderness where a preindustrial people live out a holistic, wholesome, nature-loving life. This reservation is polluted by twentieth-century trash and constant signs of urban blight—burned-out automobiles, beer cans, trailer parks, broken-down plastic and aluminum lawn chairs, abandoned children, Indian-on-Indian violence. Our first introduction to the reservation is by way of a car bouncing along its bumpy, pothole-ridden, lots-of-deferred-maintenance roads. This is a landscape despoiled, a landscape that does not, as does Leslie Silko's in *Ceremony*, enable its tenants to run cattle or sheep and thereby potentially to secure a living from the land. Instead, Erdrich represents reservation life in ways that work profoundly against the mythologies about Native Americans that make up the dominant cultural imaginary.[48] This reservation has all the problems of advanced industrial life with few of that life's benefits. It is a kind of symbolic trash heap for what society at large throws away.

Even standard claims upon nature, like Native hunting of deer on reservation lands, are overturned. June's ex-husband, Gordie, hits a deer on a darkened road and decides to haul it home in the backseat of his car and butcher it. The deer turns out to have been only stunned, however. When the deer recovers and suddenly pops into Gordie's rearview mirror, Gordie, in a panic, bludgeons it to death with a crowbar. There is no bee pollen offered to the deer's spirit, no cloth over its face, no prayer of gratitude, no feathers tied to its antlers. There is just a bloody mess left behind, staining the car's upholstery.

June's and Lulu Lamartine's very different responses to the landscape of late-twentieth-century Native life reveal Erdrich's sense of which ways of living ensure survival, which ways flirt with doom. And they reveal very different kinds of female desire. From the beginning, the narrative frames June as a character who knows "wild nature." She survives her own mother's death (the mother chokes on her own blood while the two of them are alone together in the woods) by eating pine sap until her father finds her many days, or even weeks, later. Her aunt, Marie, who cares for June once her mother is gone, says of June that "the woods were in [her] . . . just like in [Uncle Eli] . . . she had sucked on pine sap and grazed grass and nipped buds like a deer" (65). Indeed, Marie observes that June looks nothing like either of her parents, that she seems descended instead from "what the old people called Manitous, invisible ones who live in the woods" (65). In her relationship to the wild, June is something of a spirit of days past, when tribal culture was less divided from its cosmological worldview.

As she gets older, June comes under the tutelage of her Uncle Eli. She grows as good as he is at hunting, carving wood, and bringing home birds for supper. In the community that *Love Medicine* portrays, Uncle Eli is a "real old-time Indian," who "knows deer good enough to snare" (28). In fact he is the last man on the reservation who actually can snare a deer, the living embodiment of an Indian past that will be extinct once he is gone. Eventually, June moves out into the bush with her uncle; he is the solitary parent figure whom she tolerates. In this narrative, both June and Eli are connected as ones who have, as is said about Eli, a "second sense" for the wild (57).

June and Eli embrace a history that is fast fading, and that history is intimately tied to people's traditional relationships to the land. As symbolic figures, Eli and June invoke tribal memories of the era before European conquest, when people took their daily sustenance from the land around them. In those days, the tribal memory goes, Indians "knew" nature, felt it, responded to it in some kind of "natural" way. As niece Albertine says about her aunt: June would "know a storm was coming. She'd [know] by the heaviness in the air, the smell in the clouds. She'd [get] that animal sinking in her bones" (9). June is as much animal as human; the two are not divided. She is a pre-Enlightenment subject, one for whom the split between nature and culture is, in some ultimate way, never effected. When June "comes home," in the opening scene of the book, she comes home not so much to the contemporary reservation as to a representation of "nature as it was in the old days." June comes home to a time when Native peoples lived freely on the land, when they were well fed, proud, when women (like June herself) did not find themselves hustling "boom[town] [white] trash" for a drink, for a meal, or in hopes of some different and better future (8). She goes home to a mythic Native past, leaving the trappings of modernity in town, and in that past she finds her most dignified self.

In Erdrich's world, a nostalgic relationship to nature is finally a relationship that kills, however; it is suicidal. Like Leslie Silko, Erdrich believes that a rigid attachment to a romantic past spells doom for Native peoples. That past is gone with the land. Endless longing for it comes to nothing. Those who survive are those who adapt, who accept change, who somehow integrate the past with present, retaining the old ways, but in new and different and, finally, *modern* fashion. Indeed, as long as Indians fetishize that longing, both writers suggest, they unwittingly play into the notion that Indians are "vanished" along with the "pristine" land, and no one need heed the presence or needs of contemporary reservations or urban Native peoples.

Moreover, a nostalgic relationship to nature precludes thinking about feminist desire. And here is where Erdrich parts company with Silko, for Erdrich is quite interested in the question of female-imagined and feminist sexuality. In Erdrich's novel, women are not doubles for a female creative spirit in the universe, as is Ts'eh in *Ceremony*. They are not sites for the development of masculine identity and self-love. Erdrich's desiring women are not symbolic or abstract, not mystical herb gatherers. They are not all-nurturing. They don't perform miracles. They're flesh, blood. They want things. They complain when they're disappointed. Their pleasure matters to them, as it does to Erdrich; their pleasure is a narrative presence.

June's desires, like the landscape of the past she embodies, are fainter, much harder to hear, than Lulu's. Erdrich listens for the gurgling of June's voice like she is listening to someone who speaks from under water or from a great historical distance—June's longings are muffled and diffused by the vanishing relevance of the symbolic topography she inhabits. We get one direct statement, when June is in the car with her night's date, and the heater suddenly blows hard as he fumbles with undressing her.

> She felt it [the heater] open at her shoulder like a pair of jaws, blasting heat, and had the momentary and voluptuous sensation that she was lying stretched out before a great wide mouth. The breath swept across her throat, tightening her nipples. Then his vest plunged down against her, so slick and plush that is was like being rubbed by an enormous tongue. (5)

What is telling here is both the kind of sex act this suggests she wants—it is disembodied, the actor behind it degendered, neither male nor female but just tongue and mouth—but also that the man on top of her is in an utterly different world. His world is enabled by a masculinist and racialist sexual discourse, where white men get what they want, and women of color, as symbols of exotic difference, provide it. "Oh God," he moans to June, "it is good" (5). The narrative line Erdrich follows with is, "He wasn't doing anything, just moving his hips on top of her" (5). The narrator here reveals a classic gendered split about what "it is good" means. To him, "it" is thirty seconds, ejaculation, a heavy sleep. To her, "it" is the fantasy of a giant mouth and tongue and, significantly, some reprieve from racialized gender politics that create the desperate feeling of being, as June puts it, "totally empty" (3).

But no reprieve is at hand. June has seen "so many [men] come and go," we are told in the first ten lines of the book. This one will be but another. Indeed, things never will be different for June or any other woman as long as men are the only subjects of the narrative of sexual desire. Though the narrator is on June's side, represents her desire momentarily, and shows up the man's "doing nothing," the man is the one who ends up satisfied. The weight of him as he sleeps on top of her—as if it is the weight of the erasure of female desire itself—makes June feel "frail." She is grateful when she remembers to "pull herself back together" (5). This opening representation of a sexual encounter is one in which the man snores contentedly away in a postorgasmic energy crash, while the woman pulls herself together, hoists her pants up, fastens her bra, and walks into a snowstorm, for the last time.

What a relief when Erdrich gives us the unlikely feminist heroine, lovely Lulu. Lulu Lamartine, Erdrich's counterexample to June, is absolutely not about to put up with the kind of man that sends June to her grave. Anybody who had to ask *her* "Was it good for you, too?" would not have the chance to ask again. In Lulu, Erdrich narrates not just an alternative representation of female desire but also an alternative representation of Native relationships to nature and social history. The antithesis of June's aging "dryness," Lulu Lamartine is all curves, wetness, and gleam; she is alluring, sly, effective, proud. Even as she grows on in years, Lulu seems dewily young. She has eight sons, each with a different father. She is a happy woman, by her own telling, who has not shed but one afternoon of tears in her life—long ago when but a girl. Part of what defines Lulu's difference from June is that she is not represented as a woman with a "traditional" or wilderness-capable relationship to nature. Lulu, instead, is a modern woman, whose immaculate, cheery, knickknack-filled house is surrounded as much by car hulks, oil pans, and gas cans as by the petunias for which she's envied.

Lulu describes herself thus:

No one ever understood my wild and secret ways. They used to say Lulu Lamartine was like a cat, loving no one, only purring to get what she wanted. But that's not true. I was in love with the whole world and all that lived in its rainy arms. Sometimes I'd look out on my yard and the green leaves would be glowing. I'd hear the wind rushing, rolling, like the far-off sound of waterfalls. Then I'd open my mouth wide, my ears wide, my heart, and I'd let everything inside. (216)

Lulu is a woman with "wild ways" who embraces her own desire, who opens her mouth upon the world, lets it in fully. She's had her men, but as she says, she's loved them too. How is that "bad"?

Lulu is the object of nearly every man's desire on the reservation. Why? Because, as Nector Kashpaw says, Lulu could "contain him." Nector loves her in a very deep and sexual way because she experiences him at his fullest; she is full enough herself, that is, to handle him. Nector remembers:

> Climbing in her bedroom window, I rose. I was a flood that strained bridges. Uncontainable. I rushed into Lulu, and the miracle was she could hold me. She could contain me without giving way. Or she could run with me, unfolding in sheets and snaky waves. . . . I could run to a halt and Lulu would have been there every moment. . . . And so this continued for years. (100)

In this passage we see Lulu enacting the role women so often fill in sexual relationships: they enable and contain primal masculine feeling and neediness, including the discovery and expression of masculine erotic power. But this passage also reads quite against that moment earlier in the book between June and her unnamed date. For though the reader takes in Nector's sexual storm with Lulu through Nector's eyes, the narrative effectively permits the revelation of *her* sexual "rise," her energy and facility and depth. Hers is a power or sexual subjectivity not conceived in "power over" or "power under" terms. Nector's rapture, we can bet money, is not at Lulu's expense. Instead, this love affair keeps them *both* coming back because of its reciprocity. Mutuality governs this economy of desire—mutual expression of primal but also mature needs, the needs of adult men and women to know themselves and others in moments of intense erotic power and pleasure and vulnerability which also then adds up to an energizing kind of intimate security.

Given that Lulu, like the reader, knows the truth about the emotional quality of these sexual storms, Lulu holds her head high, even if the community regards her as something of a common slut. The narrator holds Lulu in high esteem, too. But female pleasure is never free—sexual women always have to pay some impossible price, and Erdrich's is no feminist utopia. Nector Kashpaw not only is a married man, but, in spite of his love for Lulu, he betrays her. It is in her response to Nector's betrayal that Erdrich demonstrates the kind of defiant relationship that Native women must forge with tribal society if they are to survive, desire intact. As tribal leader, Nector

Kashpaw lends his signature to a proposal that permits the tribe to sell land upon which Lulu's house sits. She will have to move. The council thinks of her as a weak adversary, given her reputation. And now that Nector himself has betrayed her, the council imagines her defeated.

However Lulu will not leave, and she takes on the voice of political historian to make her case. She and her Chippewa ancestors have been relocated enough in their lifetimes, she intones—from the Great Lakes, moving, moving, moving, ultimately settling in North Dakota, doing what they were told. She will never move again, she declares, especially if the factory to be built upon her land will make Indian trinkets! When Lulu threatens a packed tribal council meeting with a series of paternity suits and threatens too to reveal the fathers of her sons (who sit fidgeting nervously next to their equally uncomfortable wives), the council relents, and she keeps the land her house sits upon.

At this crisis moment in the text's depiction of community relations, Erdrich lays out her own resolution to tribal troubles. As do Pam Houston and Sandra Cisneros in each of their respectively racialized literary traditions, Erdrich brings to this moment an alternative moral and political logic, one different from that which is more conventionally witnessed in American Indian literature. This tale's resolution ultimately links community survival (embodied now in Lulu) with the preservation of female desire and also the willingness to "do business," as it were, with some branches of the postmodern economy.[49]

Lulu's tidy little home has, not so mysteriously, been burned to the ground. She has nowhere to go. But again, rather than leave the reservation and repeat a political history of racial displacement, she and her sons refuse to be cowed and instead sleep on site in the burned-out hulks of cars that surrounded the place. As Lulu calls it, they are "living like wild animals." Now at the visible center of the reservation's conscience, Lulu and her boys' homelessness shame the community and disgrace her neighbors until, in an act of community conscience, the people build the Lamartines a new, permanent home. On the new homesite, which is better than the old (not, as is so typical in American Indian history, worse), an invigorated, multiplying "Lamartine camp" develops. Wives, children, in-laws, cousins—all live surrounding the new house in trailers and old rusting cars. One of Lulu's boys becomes a contractor—the symbolic link to a contemporary, post–World War II economy—and he hires on his brothers, who in turn support the whole extended family.

The way the Lamartine clan survives—all "bastard" children, "black sheep" of the tribal community—is by embracing the postindustrial age. They build houses, participate in the general development and suburbanization of the West. This kind of labor, if backbreaking, is also, significantly, lucrative. And the monies generated by this family-staffed construction business are a real boon to the Lamartines; because of them they experience a noticeable rise in economic status and a rise in community status too. The Lamartines become, by the novel's conclusion, not only relatively respectable, but they also reformulate the terms through which respectability might be achieved. This is no simple "sell out" or "assimilationist" resolution, however. For the figurehead of this new economic philosophy, who even in retirement "felt the liquid golden last days of my oats" (229), is the matriarch, Lulu, still sowing her oats even at the old folks home in town. Who else should be also living there but Marie, the wife of Lulu's great love Nector Kashpaw. The two women, in true and unanticipated testimony to "love medicine," become friends in the closing pages of the tale. Again, that is, we find female solidarity at the core of both feminist desire and plots of community rupture and resolution. In the final instance, women's relationships with one another *must* figure positively in order for heterosexuality ultimately to please women.

Sex and the New Female Regionalism

This chapter has grouped together the texts of Houston, Cisneros, and Erdrich to demonstrate what kinds of western sexual spaces trouble masculine indifference to female desire. The investment here has been to make the case that, regardless what beginnings one chooses, spaces themselves are mapped, in sexualized terms, terms that themselves negotiate racial and gender politics. The texts considered here reframe altogether the notion of "wild space." Not so surprisingly, very often the "wildest" landscape of all, it turns out, is a social landscape. Here all the tenderness, cruelty, chaos, and folly of the wilderness of human relationships is in full relief.

I have taken some of my own pleasures in forwarding an against-the-grain argument about Pam Houston's *Cowboys Are My Weakness*. I value Houston's willingness to lust after and also love the quintessential romantic figure of western mythology, the cowboy, and to try to settle the score with him in what I see as honest ways. It seems to me that it does feminists little good to refuse on principle his attractions. These moves are of course tricky at every turn and suggest why Houston's stories are so internally embattled and also why they create a great deal of embattled ambivalence in reviewers whose feminist sympathies would seem to dictate a response of instant distress. I myself have never really had a cowboy love, and I bet I'll live to regret it.

I also applaud in Houston's text the waging of a subtle battle with one of the more sacred topographies of white male desire: that of the adventure landscape. It is there, in the "wilds" of this forbidden topography, Houston implicitly argues—where men construct themselves as raw and "real," at their Robert Bly best—that the fight for women's right to desire, and for the substance or content of desire itself, should be waged. Western wilderness *is* a "final frontier" of white male privilege, a cornerstone of masculinist western and national discourse. Houston's women in no way will leave that spatial field exclusively to men, but they are not going to locate their *own* pleasures unproblematically within it either. Which means that this text's attitude about female sexuality is something like: why shouldn't women want sex, need sex, just as men do? And why shouldn't they pursue intense sexual experience without suffering a pathological label? The text's attitude also asks: but why shouldn't they want it differently too? Indeed, why should women want sex on terms set up to empower men? Houston's text disempowers the logic that continually reinvents masculine subjectivity as synonymous with western sexual subjectivity.

If Houston is a kind of "bad girl feminist," Louise Erdrich is a "bad girl Indian." Her tale of North Dakota reservation life, when compared to Leslie Silko's set in New Mexico, is not likely to be claimed by environmentalists as any kind of exemplar of a "natural" way of life. To be sure, Silko's reservation in *Ceremony* could easily be read, like the spaces that surround Georgia O'Keeffe's work, as site of ultimate nuclear contamination—a far more catastrophically polluted environment, in fact, than is Erdrich's reservation. But it generally is *not* read that way. The point here is that Erdrich's reservation refuses emplotment by the wilderness ideal, and part of its refusal grows from its interest in representing women and female desire in nonexotic or mystical terms. The feminist morals to Erdrich's stories are linked, importantly, to nature—but not to a privileged "natural" or transcendent nature. Instead, Erdrich's reservations are blighted by twentieth-century industrial trash—tires, abandoned cars, old trailer parks. Ironically, or perhaps because this spatial field is of less interest to masculinist discourse, it is these landscapes that are the sites for postmodern female desire. In Lulu Lamartine's cheery, non-Indian-signifying, little home exists one of the most self-conscious and *satisfied* female beds in all of American Indian fiction. The men, like Nector Kashpaw, fortunate enough to share this bed with Lulu, enter sexual discourse and representation on *her* terms. Yes, Lulu tells Nector, he may crawl through her open window in the deep of the night and she will take him and love him, but he must make it possible for her to let him in by loving her in return, showing her romantic favor, by submitting his body to her lilac powder because she likes its smell and the smell it casts into her lovemaking-scented room.

If Lulu's bed is a warm one, it will cool down quickly for the man who does not give Lulu enough to keep her happy. That is, her fidelity or availability is no sure or automatic consequence of sexual relations. Here—in the space of renovated heterosexual, racial, and gender relations—one finds, or at least can look with hope for, love medicine. Erdrich's extended tale, of which *Love Medicine* is but Book I, is a continuing "wild space" within American Indian discourse, because it refuses to adhere to the romance myths that surround "the Native American" and it refuses to silence female desire.

Like Houston and Erdrich, Cisneros ruffles more than a few prominent feathers within Chicano/a studies. Her "bad girl" status is earned because, so the informal attitude goes, she shows a "too commercial" kind of racialized identity. Her texts are too easily co-opted by non-Chicano/a cultural gatekeepers and are mobilized toward political ends that are "too mainstream." I hope I have suggested my own reasons for disagreeing with this evaluation of Cisneros's work. As I argued, Cisneros's "wild space" is at first glance the state of Texas. One character in *Woman Hollering Creek* says, "Texas! They still lynch Meskins down there. Everybody's got chain saws and gun racks and pickups and Confederate flags. *Aren't you scared?*" (142) Yes, the truth is, the protagonist is scared. She knows very well that Mexicans were the losers of the War of 1846 and of all the undeclared wars upon Mexican citizens since. But, for Cisneros, Texas as *cultural landscape* offers seductions that are well worth the risk. One benefit is the Chicana feminist imaginary of South Texas. Through it she can give voice to Chicanas' continual struggles to satisfy their longings, to their good times, too. There she can get closer to the mythic Chicano/a landscapes of Aztlán, which were distant from her Chicago birthplace. Finally, however, Cisneros breaks with one of the fundamental aspects of this regional and ethnic imaginary, for she takes an unequivocal stand against a Chicano/a genealogy that relies on the "authentic" Mexican Indian national as a foothold of progressive Chicano/a politics. Not only are the race politics of this operation suspect, completely eliding as they do the *dual* colonial heritage of contemporary Chicano/as (both colonizer and colonized), but the gender politics reinscribe masculinist heterosexism and male supremacy.

I have suggested that Cisneros articulates something of a new "wild space" upon the South Texas regional imaginary, a space linked to Whitmanesque, exuberant Americanism. This Americanism is very much in process of invention, not complete. But Cisneros's American exuberance, her Chicana *jouissance*, should not be easily reduced to the literary "mainstream," because the particular energy of her revised portraits of female desire are so thoroughly linked to cultural forms like Mexican soap operas, to Chicana female solidarity, and the dark, feisty *urracas* of her collection's final pages.

Let me conclude by noting that none of the narratives featured in this chapter tells a single story of feminist desire. They each have different political and narrative projects, different visions of desire. And yet certain similarities suggest themselves. All of these texts represent women who are not permanently partnered at the text's close. It is not accidental that by refusing the redemptive wilderness plot, feminist desire does not—as it does, say, in Barbara Kingsolver's stories—end with the implicit words "happily ever after." The absence of texts or plots that figure heterosexual marriage as a landscape of feminist desire suggests, then, that new female regionalists are wary of consummating western feminist sensibility through invocation of a marriage narrative. Indeed, there come to mind few new western texts that enact this kind of consummation; the marriage plot, it would seem, is not at the forefront of what's being written today. Heterosexual unions that do get narrativized in positive (if not central) terms often cross the color line (e.g., Wanda Coleman writes in *Native in a Strange Land* of a third marriage to a Jewish man, Jeanne Wakatsuki Houston in *Farewell to Manzanar* figures her Anglo husband James Houston as a pushing-off point for exploring Japanese American identity). Most of these cross-racial relations are between a white and a nonwhite partner, rarely between two nonwhite partners. The message here is that women are forging some new narrative of heterosexuality, one not dominated by masculinist desire, or by the monoracial, suburban, nuclear family, or by other "normative" outcomes of straight love and/or lifetime companionship.

That fact should not suggest, however, that these new narratives feature unhappy endings. Rather, the terms of "happy endings" have been redefined. In them, "happiness" is figured as a context of open-ended possibility, of continuing desire. This "wanting something" pathos is not attached to any specific sex act or emotive state. Neither is it attached to a particular relationship status (i.e., being single or alone is not stigmatized), nor is female intimacy haunted by homophobic fear. Indeed, the new heterosexual narratives evolving here are both produced and empowered by lesbian culture as well as by contemporary debates about queer identity. New female regionalists import the relatively heightened expectations for relational satisfaction associated with lesbianism into their own, new, sexual geographies—hence the chapter's title, "queering heterosexual love."

The "wanting something" pathos of the new regionalism rotates around a constellation of related things: a desire for sex acts centered on female pleasure; a desire for an erotica of nurturance, romance, and security, none of which would be at the expense of female power or respect for women; and a desire for freedom—the freedom, that is, to call the whole thing off when women don't get what they ought to get, the freedom to change the rules of the game if the game turns out to be fixed. This new feminist desire locates itself not in the past but in the unromantic, chaotic, miscegenated, postmodern present—the present of trailer parks and telenovelas, of profoundly psychologized discourses about female sexuality, of "consumed" and commoditized desire. All these visions of desire are underwritten by and absolutely depend upon a broader, state-protected, civil rights apparatus that (at least officially) censures violence against women as well as sanctions female autonomy, female efforts at self-improvement, and female reproductive rights.

Finally, all three texts, to differing degrees and in different ways, long for homosocial community among women. All of them end with visions of female solidarity. None explicitly figure this desire in terms of lesbian sex, even if lesbian sexuality is not precluded. Though this is not explicitly a topography of homosexual desire, neither is it one that is heterosexist. There is little of Judith Butler's "heterosexual matrix" here, little of Rich's "compulsory heterosexuality," or of Monique Wittig's "the straight mind."[50] Instead, new western landscapes of desire have been "queered," divested of the automatic ability to confer normative or virile heterosexuality.

Western landscapes, in this changed imaginary, are neither securely male nor female but instead may be androgynous or indeterminate or transgendered. Their gendered identities, indeed, seem less important than the fact that the spaces themselves remain fluctuating, oscillating, receptive, seductive. It is the challenge of the concluding chapter to link this politics of feminist eroticism to a politics of twenty-first-century American (post)nationalism.

National identity is always consciously characterized by both a historical and geographic heritage. . . . The symbolic activation of time and space, often drawing on religious sentiment, gives shape to the "imagined community" of the nation. Landscapes, whether focusing on single monuments or framing stretches of scenery, provide visible shape; they picture the nation.
—Stephen Daniels,
Fields of Vision (1993)

5

A Good Country Is Hard to Find: Journeys toward Postnational Landscapes

Queer nations, Aztlán, a trans-nation of overlapping borderlands.
Mormon country, God's country, the heart of Zion National Forest.
Survivalist territory for various Idaho or Montana or Utah neo-Nazi
   "patriots"—today, the Freeman. Yesterday Timothy McVeigh. And the
   Unabomber—an anti-industrial Nation of One.
An environmentalists' nation of sacred preserved wilderness.
A pan-Indian State of autonomous reservations, governed by tribal law.

The American West was born out of a desire to imagine, enforce, enact new nationalisms. It continues to serve this role in American cultural and countercultural life. The claim that western mythology provides the nation's founding myth, that the West circulates in American culture *as* America, is a fairly broadly accepted claim in western studies.[1] Therefore I will be less interested in remembering the Alamo, as it were, than in considering the role of landscape discourse in the production of nationalist subjectivity. I begin from the premise that landscape provides national subjects, including marginalized subjects, a space in which to project themselves and their desires. Through landscape discourse, the destiny of the desiring national subject is made manifest.

Though all of the writers surveyed in this book have, by virtue of their engagement with western spatial fields, commented on national history as well as America's political past and future, I have not yet focused on the nationalist narratives that always already emplot western landscapes and western stories. This latter task is at the center of this final chapter. I spell out first the "patriotic" or imperial ideologies that characterize dominant landscape traditions—and which sustain the racial, gender, and heterosexual bias of that tradition in its production of a national citizen subject. Then I move to make sense of the nationalist and postnationalist plots at work in new female regionalist literature today.

Leading the Nation from the Patriotic West(ern Landscape)

Let us review the ways that western literary criticism has dealt with the issues this chapter addresses. As I suggested in the Introduction, the narrative of nation that pervades western landscape discourse is one about which critics have been consistently self-reflexive. They have devoted considerable scholarly effort to analyzing the fact that descriptions of westering lands were first set into written form by European explorers, for whom New

World topographies were very different than any they had encountered before. The prairies, deserts, and arid lands of what are today's West and Midwest, critics note, defied European Romantic notions of "natural" beauty. The geologic formations found in western geographies could not be faithfully expressed through the language of Wordsworthian sublime vistas, for "sublime" was part of a language that named forested and well-watered pastoral spaces. The West was dry, often treeless. Thus, some new form of landscape perspective had to be invented. Western European influence, especially British Romantic influence, created the imaginative context for dominant American attitudes about landscape, critics conclude.[2]

But Old World aesthetic assumptions and social values ultimately were adapted to accommodate New World conditions, topographies, and, especially, political imperatives. Many studies are particularly interested in the "Americanness" of New World responses to landscape. On what grounds did Americans claim western landscape as a feature of national identity and history? What about the relationship between new landscapes and New World character and cultural values? And how did that landscape in turn shape Americans' particular creativity?[3]

In investigating these subjects, critics foreground the role that landscape representation plays in nation-building political projects, which includes explicitly the formation of the New World's "new man." David Wyatt describes this project in *Fall Into Eden*, an investigation of literary California that is probably the most elegant of western landscape studies:

> In agreeing to read the face of the continent as a measure of its destiny, the young country proposed to the world that the images of a nation could be grounded in natural as well as in political, cultural, and military history.[4]

By naturalizing the images of imperial expansionism projected onto western landscape, Wyatt argues, by reading these images not as representation but as physical "fact," western landscape discourse produced manifest destiny as a "natural" political development, part of a cosmic, godly plan for the budding America.

To say, then, that critics have been aware of the nationalist narrative that emplots western landscapes is to grant that criticism of western literature acknowledges that "natural" landscape is a socially constructed category infused with cultural meanings and values and thus subject to political deployment. Indeed, western critics have been alert to these meanings (as am I) precisely because in them so often are found objectionable, regressive, or exploitive political tendencies. Critics see both themselves as intellectuals and the literary histories they produce as liberal political interventions into the "mythic" or dominant geocultural imaginary.

But this awareness goes only so far. If in the erudite and poetic landscapes of someone like David Wyatt, we see no denial of conquest, no gloss on the bloodiness of the subject, we also see where critics' self-reflexiveness stops, who critics imagine their audiences to be, who they think "Americans" are. In the very next sentence following Wyatt's assertion of the sociality of landscape, he writes: "California acts as the site for such [existential] discoveries because her landscapes, beautiful, looming, and austere, remain a dominant fact in the experience of her culture." Moreover, he writes, it is a

> regional belief . . . that one always acts in concert, for better or for worse, with natural fact. In this California intensifies the national myth that America has been set apart from the beginning by its freedom to test itself against the unmediated. If landscape has meant one thing to Americans, it has meant innocence, and the ways in which we make use of it—the ways we fall into it or make it fall—constitute a telling record of the price we are willing to pay for experience. (206–7)

After a previous discussion in which Wyatt self-consciously notes the Old World ideas mediated by New World landscape, after his awareness that those ideas might support a nationalist project of imperial designs with all the power plays implicit in such a project, Wyatt genders California's landscape female. In so doing, he implicitly reinscribes the protagonist of this narrative of nation as white and masculine, and he plays out the consequences of that gendering in the next lines by gendering national goals, too, in white and masculine ways. America is a site of "freedom to test oneself against the unmediated." As goals go, that one hardly counts as universal, for white women's lives in eighteenth- and nineteenth-century America were circumscribed by paternal and sacred authority, family responsibility, and by notions of female propriety. Nor were indigenous populations or Mexicans preoccupied with testing themselves against the unmediated. Their tests came in the form of fighting disease, other tribes, the U.S. Army, and waves of settlers. How could landscape have meant innocence to them?[5]

Wyatt's unconsciousness about both race and gender bias causes him to read and to produce blatantly racialized and gendered representations of landscape without any apparent awareness of that fact. In a chapter that

Wyatt entitles "Muir and the Possession of Landscape," Muir "penetrates" and "enters" the natural paradise of Yosemite. Indeed, Wyatt argues that Muir's "stories are nearly always of penetration." What Wyatt does not notice is that this romance narrative and sexual fantasy genders the explorer/citizen subject male, the land (and object of the citizen/subject) female, and the sexual attraction heterosexual. Man is sexual actor, woman is passive recipient, the national sex act is intercourse. It all adds up to "possession." The power relations enacted through both Muir's, and now Wyatt's, representation of landscape keep the white male citizen subject, well into the 1980s, on heterosexual top.

I regret seeming to single out Wyatt's study for special criticism, for it is a beautifully written, learned study from which I have learned very much. But it's fair to ask in what spirit critics now use the royal "we," especially when, after Kolodny and civil rights scholarships, no one needs reminding that the "we" in "we the people" meant quite exclusively property-owing, white men and that the "we" who were excluded have been trying to recover a place within the institution of public citizenship ever since. As critics, shouldn't "we" reaccustom ourselves to hearing the *kinds* of narrative of nation, the kinds of national identity, that get written by us upon western spaces? For only then—when critics take far less for granted what constitutes "the nation" and national subjectivity—will we be able to hear the many, many competing claims made for nationhood upon western lands.

Since it is through culture that the subject always becomes a citizen,[6] and since whatever else a State may be or do, it is always territorial,[7] we should attend to the specificity of the national identity that is being constructed and maintained in critical discourse about landscape and the nation. A landscape ideology whose dominant features are limitlessness, expansiveness, fresh "virginity," optimism, awesomeness, grandeur, a space of forever receding horizons, a landscape in which immigrants see themselves (in Wallace Stegner's words) as "single," "separate," "vertical," and "individual"[8] is a patriotic landscape powerfully implicated in colonialist rhetorics and ideologies. For the "New World" is not new to the indigenous peoples, nor do clan-identified American Indians (or Mexicans or white women) see themselves vis-à-vis the land as "separate" or "individual." The history suggested by "fresh" and "vast" landscapes is initially that of European immigration to North America and, next, that of northeastern expansion westward. Of course, both migrations are entirely colonialist projects, for only by superior force are inhabited lands brought under new ownership. Landscape discourse, in this incarnation, is an accomplished tool of both European, and later American, imperial designs. It produces a national body politic in which an Enlightened, white, heterosexual male, embodied in the abstraction of John Q. Public, is the representative citizen subject.

This above rendering of the national landscape is not one designed to include a female citizenry, female suffrage, or classic "female" values of hearth, home, and community. Neither does it include the kind of state that might make possible a desiring female citizen subject, of the type I nurtured in Chapter 4. Instead, in one of the oldest renditions of "the patriotic," western nature is associated with the female body. This depiction of the national (western) homeland as (white) femininity embodied requires its male citizens to rush to "her" defense when "her" virtues appear in danger of "violation." So often the motivating drama of westernness concerns the "imperiled female" whose virtue must be protected from "savagery." The drama's moral (and national) resolution—"preserving" female sexual integrity—has the convenient consequence of killing off Indians and expanding Anglo empire at the same time that it reinscribes ideal femininity in terms of chastity and family dutifulness. The institutions of citizenship, heterosexuality, and patriarchal governance thus remain securely bound together,[9] mutually supporting discourses wherein the only decent or American thing for a "man" to do is to usher the women and children off of the battlefield or the sinking ship first, for women, like children, are weak and in need of protection. The duty of the head of the heterosexual family and nation is to look after them, to fight on behalf of the "mother country," the "home" land. And indeed, the "American" thing for a woman to do is not to get in the way, not to interfere with masculinist control of the nation and its citizen subjects.

Of course this national love affair with the individualist citizen subject is changing, being reshaped in more communal and less militaristic terms. The world Americans live in today is post–Cold War. The economies within which workers trade their labor are transnational. Further, the influence that feminist thought now exerts on the national imaginary should not be underrated. Not only does feminist presence in universities, government, business, law, the American corporation, and other arenas create a need to revise old notions of who is "an American," but feminist epistemology has also produced new visions of the State. These visions overlap, however unintentionally or ironically, with the new, more flexible roles of the state in transnational economic contexts. The new *norm*, that is, is a more complex, decentered conception of statehood and of political subjectivity. New western female regionalists retain desire as a fundamental category of U.S. citizenship. Landscape discourse does the cultural work of articulating, but now in deterritorialized terms, the national desires of these western female citizen subjects.

Nationalisms and the Multiracial Female West

Nations within nations, nations within citizens as well as citizens within nations, nationality as a segmentable and comparative quality rather than either as an absolute possession or lack . . .
—Michael Moon and Cathy Davidson, *Subjects and Citizens*

The nationalist plot already written upon western landscape is a tricky and complex issue for women. As I've already noted, "the nation" in both western and American discourse is no exception to the general global rule: it is a female-gendered entity whose true subject is a noble warrior. Thus, to entertain nationalist plots, women must read against themselves, identify with representations that marginalize them, or they must become what Judith Fetterley calls "resisting readers."[10] Many women writers, therefore, have a very uneasy engagement with nationalist discourse. They sense that "the nation" by definition is not about themselves.

During much of the period that this study surveys, the dominant meanings of American nationalism suggest a conservative or imperial politics and call to mind that kind of American patriot who applauded the Gulf War, voted for Reagan and Bush, and worried about the "moral downfall of America." Moreover, repeated civil wars in Central America (wars in which the United States backs distinctly antidemocratic leaders) make many of the new regionalists acutely reluctant to deploy the very term "America," given its more general and imperialist deployment as sign for the United States, not the Americas hemisphere.[11] If in the past the West has often provided an ironic but nevertheless widely cherished imaginative site whereupon a "better nation" might be articulated, by the contemporary period the West not only embodies its own regional problems, but it seems like a symbol of all that is wrong with America. The West represents the nation's cultural contradictions—its suppressed history of imperial aggression, its "rape" of the land, its commitment to nuclear proliferation and to economies based on defense industry spending. The land of "beautiful and spacious skies" where "freedom rings" is also a crafty police state that needs no iron curtain because it has the more flexible "tortilla curtain" to monitor the Mexico/U.S. border. Thus, because of many kinds of liberal and anti-imperial political commitments, most of the new regionalists shy away from direct engagement with "nationalist discourse," preferring to formulate political interventions in other ways.

And yet (and this is my western application of the central insight of so much new theoretical literature about the formation of nationalist discourses), even as subjects traditionally marginalized within western visions of the nation, female regionalists have nonetheless laid claim to nationalist thought in order to articulate themselves through the status of the desiring citizen subject.[12] As Homi Bhabha has argued about postcolonial subjects, it is often minority writers who self-consciously deploy the language or symbols of nationalist discourse in order to disrupt and rewrite a signifying system that has historically produced them as "Other."[13] Regardless, the nationalist narrative embedded in the plot of "westernness" is an inescapable story, one with which all writers who represent western landscape, minority or not, must finally contend. Just as sexual relations are already figured in the ways western space is organized, just as gendered and classed relations are inherent in the notion of "wilderness space," or as femininity emplots western urban space, so too do western landscapes already connote nationalist projects.

Given the male and white bias that defines the very terms of national subjectivity in western discourse, it has fallen to feminist critics, often nonwhite, to figure out the role of gender and race in the making of western nationalist landscapes. The work of Kolodny and of Norwood and Monk have provided key analyses that evaluate gendered difference in white peoples' evolving relationship to the "West as America." Nineteenth-century, white, women writers, especially New Women like Mary Austin and Mabel Dodge Luhan, used western spaces to envision new kinds of national possibility. To them, possibility aligned itself more with community-based and ecology-friendly nationalist subjectivity than with one based on (white male) autonomy or an imperial Statehood.[14]

Nonwhite, female nationalist thought has its place in mid-twentieth-century women's writing, too. Tey Diana Rebolledo argues that in the New Mexican desert landscapes of the 1940s and 1950s, New Hispaña writers like Fabiola Cabeza de Baca or Nina Otero Warren envisioned a redeemed Hispaño-mestizo national identity. That is, these writers made use of the nationalist plots (including colonial Spanish plots) already written into western spatiality to figure themselves not as Americans but as Hispañas. A term that included racial, national, linguistic, female, and regional identifications, "Hispaña" suggested the pride of being a citizen of imperial Spain and speaking high Castilian Spanish but also the distinctiveness of New Mexican regional identity. As Hispañas, then, these genteel ladies laid a claim on American nationality, a claim and legacy so complex that it has been largely rejected by Mexican American women writers of the civil rights era.[15]

Thus, though there exist alternative feminist nationalist narratives upon which contemporary women writers might draw to imagine new postmodern landscapes, there are nonetheless huge cultural and historical gaps that new regionalists must negotiate. Mary Austin's "alternative West" was the relatively undeveloped desert West of the late 1800s and early 1900s. In Austin's socialist and ecofeminist vision, the "alternative nation" could be founded upon Native American–based mythicism and communalism. It might support a national ideal that valued shared wealth, limited industrial development, and respect for nature, for women, and for indigenous peoples. Though certainly one sees echoes of that vision in the work of many new regionalists, Austin's is not a nationalist project with great relevance for a postindustrial capitalist economy, one in which limited development is generally a moot question and in which computer literacy is a skill necessary to the most basic service industry job. Today, workers enter markets in which race, gender, and nationality continue to define one's role in the global economy. Most people, including "natural" Indians, live in cities; their children go to day care; the poor receive federal assistance (though decreasingly); and very few people grow their own food. The landscape of Austin's West is gone; the landscape of Kingsolver's West is fantasy. The landscapes of Fabiola Cabeza de Baca and Nina Otero Warren aren't applicable to people who don't own land and who won't or can't claim a high-Spanish colonial identity.

At their broadest, new regionalist narratives work instead from the notion that nationalism is, in Benedict Anderson's widely quoted phrase, "an imagined political community," considered to be both sovereign and limited.[16] Quoting Ernest Gellner, Anderson argues, and new female regionalist literature concurs, that "nationalism is not the awakening of nations to self-consciousness: it *invents* nations where they do not exist."[17] That is, nationalism is less a political than an anthropological process; and it is profoundly various and constantly in flux. In current theoretical discussions, "nationalisms," the plural term, often substitutes for the singular "nationalism," even when the concept is being used to indicate subjects of the same nation. Phrases like "nations without a state," "transnationality," "binationality," "performative nationality," and, perhaps most often, nationality as "hybridity," "inbetweenness," and "a form of social and textual affiliation" speak to the dynamism of new definitions forwarded in recent cultural theory.[18]

This chapter is informed by all of the above discourses, and indeed, I consider the new western regionalism itself to be a part of the burgeoning revision of nationalist thought. Consequentially, the primarily male side of this literary movement emerges during precisely those years in which Watergate shames the nation, adding insult to the humiliation suffered in Vietnam. The belief in American global supremacy plummets to an all-time low. Yet even as American men suffer emasculation as a result of these blights on the nation's virility and honor, the male writers of new regional literature will not enable the nation to sidestep this moment of reckoning. They will not deploy "authentic" landscapes of westernness in an effort to create a new, post-Watergate reconsolidation of masculine power. Although these same male writers mistrust the postmodern and all the values that seem to accompany it, they generally oppose what I have called here patriotic western landscapes, and thus quite willingly entertain a more "feminine" revision of the West and the nation.

The timing of the appearance of the female side of the new regionalism is linked just as consequentially to a crisis in the national body politic. In the post–Cold War moment, women's literature, fundamentally opposed to militarist-based visions of citizen subjectivity, answers the general call for a new vision of the American nation in a one-superpower world. What I want to trace is an evolving historical trajectory, starting in the mid-1970s, that charts changes in feminist conceptions of the nation. One of my arguments is that narratives of the nation inhere in feminist landscapes, even when they seem absent. What exactly might constitute a feminist and/or "ethnic" state? In the mid-1970s this question was considerably easier to answer than it had become by the early 1990s. Recent discussions of nationalist affiliation have deconstructed the notion of the nation so thoroughly that one wonders whether nationalist discourse can any longer be considered a useful counterhegemonic narrative or social practice.

Always I am interested to explore, as Stephen Daniels puts it, the "connection between landscape depiction and historical narration, including narratives which put historical identity into doubt" (8). The three books investigated here are autobiographies, a genre that gestures toward both historical and literary narrative and identities. They were chosen without a conscious decision to mimic Daniel's formulation. The choice to study autobiography, however, reflects the connectedness between landscape depiction, historical narration, literary sensibility, and the promotion of nationalist projects. I also attend to the ways that nationalist ventures are so often associated with sexual attachment or feeling. How do these women writers persist in this trend? What kinds of discourses of desire are spoken within their narratives of nation?

Welcome, National Subjectivity; Farewell, Manzanar

Few American stories begin at so profound a rupture or disjunction in narratives of nation as does *Farewell to Manzanar* (1973), an autobiographical narrative about one Japanese American family's internment during World War II at Manzanar, a desert relocation camp in central California. The story of the disintegration of Jeanne Wakatsuki Houston's family during their internment at Manzanar, it is also, significantly, the story of young Jeanne's flowering. She is but a child, age seven, when her family is forcibly removed from their lives as boat-owning fisherman in Long Beach and "relocated" north to the California desert camp with 10,000 other Japanese Americans. As the days and months in camp turn into years, we witness both the ongoing tensions to which interned Japanese Americans at large are subjected as well as the particular griefs and adjustments of Jeanne Wakatsuki's individual family. In a POW context, where one might imagine all expression of "American" symbolism would leave a bad taste in internee's mouths, we see a quite opposite cultural process at work, especially for young Jeanne. The camp—however much it curtails Japanese American civil rights—ultimately serves as site for this girl's articulation into female subjectivity, and this subjectivity is deliberately American.

This story is told in straightforward narrative style. It is rather a short tale, divided into three segments that essentially track before, during, and after the author's stay at Manzanar. Wakatsuki Houston tells the reader at the outset that she needs to come to personal terms with this part of her life. The only way she can do so, she determines, is to recount a good deal of the daily details of life at Camp Manzanar. This documentary-like format thus gives the book some of its social history identity. Indeed, this text is generally deemed more appropriate for social history than literary analysis, a view that the text itself encourages.[19] Moreover, I have learned from under-graduate students that the text is now often read in public high school classrooms and thus is deemed to be at a level of literary difficulty appropri-ate for high school students. I want to challenge this way of reading this text, which I believe underestimates it. One way we can see the very compli-cated female and ethnic subjectivity under construction here is via the text's interest in landscape discourse. Representations of the desert surrounding the Owens Valley desert camp play a critical role in figuring Jeanne Wakat-suki's emerging female American self, and they demonstrate how national-ist and feminist narratives can articulate themselves in some quite subtle and cautious ways. By contrasting this early regionalist narrative by Wakat-suki Houston with the work of the second writer we study, Gloria Anzaldúa, we see something of the changes that nonwhite women have undergone over the last twenty-five years in their strategies for laying claim to national belonging and political enfranchisement.

In the book's first section, when protagonist Jeanne has not yet broken faith with her father, the narrator represents landscape in ways that critique classic western tropes. Initial pictures of the desert show its "billowing flurry of dust and sand," which is whipped into something like a pelting rain by the wind (14). The camp, these descriptions suggest, is dry, hard, bleak. The only "erect" structures on this otherwise flat topography are the tents and hastily built, black barracks that will house the detainees. The desert plains surrounding the camp stretch on for many miles, uninhabited and uninhabitable. An escape attempt would be suicide. These beginning repre-sentations of the desert are not joyous, liberating, spacious, or mystical—the classic moves in southwestern landscape representation to connote either a "western" or an "American" moment. This picture, instead, is cluttered by the trunks and baggage of the thousands of prisoners who have been sud-denly uprooted from settled and often prosperous lives. The desert land-scape does not free the internees, and were they to flee imprisonment, it indeed would kill them. The desert landscape, at text's beginning, does the double work of literal and imaginative policing. The geographical imagina-tion of the desert is off-limits to America's American POWs.

Something is happening to this family, however, that will change the girl protagonist's relationship to the landscape that surrounds her. During the book's first section, the father slowly slips from his unchallenged status as patriarch. The family unit falls apart. They don't eat together. They cannot maintain familial cohesion. First, the father is detained for nearly a year in a different camp in North Dakota. When he is reunited with his family at Manzanar, his spirit has been broken. He's lost some central core of his dignity, for good. At this point, Houston narrates the father's history, and the reader learns of his elite background: he is of the samurai class, and immigrated to America in the early twentieth century because his family had fallen on harder economic times. Given that he is a prideful man who thinks grandly of himself, he decides to try his luck on Gold Mountain. Houston portrays him as "a nipponese frontiersman," a jack-of-all-trades who can cut timber, make dentures, sing Japanese poems, argue a court case, or carve pigs, depending on the need. "Whatever he did," she says, "had flourish" (42).

However, if the father figure has much in common with representations of jaunty, vain, arrogant, talented, and enormously enterprising Anglo western men who dreamed big dreams, and who complain of victimization when things don't go their way, he is also differentiated by race.[20] That is, though Houston locates him in western discourse, his location also serves to reveal the instabilities or fault lines within the discourse. Though he is educated, bilingual, and trained in law, when Jeanne's father moves to the United States, he ultimately decides on farming because there he can better skirt the limits imposed upon him by a racialist marketplace. But the depression hits, and after several years of drought, the farm folds, and he must send his children into the fields to pick field crops or else the family will not survive. After the depression, when the family's finances are at last rebuilt and seem secured by a family fishing business located on the Southern California coast, something happens again: Pearl Harbor. His two commercial fishing boats and his car are confiscated. Of course nothing is paid for them. Then come several years in relocation camps. And, the narrator notices retrospectively, he is getting too old to start all over again.

Poignantly, it is the father's emasculation that opens a narrative space for the girl protagonist's empowerment *and* for her deepening "Americanness." By the end of section 1, the father has definitively sided with those Japanese Americans who, when forced to sign the resented Loyalty Oath, argued that it was better to sign than to be detained longer, humiliated further. Which is to say he has declared himself, at least formally, an American (not a Japanese American). And yet, even though he has denounced connections to Japan, he deeply laments that loss and indeed feels a nationalist affinity more for Japan, finally, than for the nation to which he has pledged loyalty. Tellingly, that deeper loyalty and nationalist sentiment are expressed in his attachment to Japanese landscapes and Japanese attitudes about landscape. The first section closes as the father weeps while he sings the Japanese national anthem, which is a poem-song in which the imagery of nature symbolizes a man's relationship to the State. At the center of the poem-song is a stone, which can be read either as the nation or a man's life—either way, it teaches that endurance is worthy and ultimately results in the stone becoming much bigger and more beautiful than it was originally.

Section 2, significantly, announces itself as "Manzanar, USA," and from this section the young protagonist will depart to the final third section as an independent, even if wounded, American girl. This "American" section opens through a discussion of desert landscape. For the next twenty-five pages, which also mark the physical center of this autobiography and the center of the conflicts between father and daughter, the landscape narrative repeatedly articulates protagonist Jeanne's own emerging national and gender ideals. This is the very compelling and nearly crazy section of the book, where the reader learns of the stunningly contradictory lives Japanese American adolescents lived in the camps. They are POWS, and of course they know it. But they also celebrate themselves in their high school yearbook as regular American kids. They convene Boy Scout meetings, plan campwide sock hops, form a marching band, replete with baton twirlers—starring, of course, Jeanne Wakatsuki herself, baton twirler extraordinaire. All of this invocation of American wartime pageantry is sandwiched, repeatedly, within narrative passages about the desert and also the mountains.

Increasingly, Houston narrates father/daughter differences through American versus Japanese conventions of landscape perception. Jeanne's family, by now, has moved to a better part of the camp. This camp area has trees, and as the seasons in camp come and go, the father tends to his garden and his trees, while the daughter forays outside of camp grounds on hikes and overnight stays in the Sierra Nevada. About these explorations Jeanne says: it was there that she began to look for "that special thing I could be or do for myself" (79). In the very next line, we learn of Jeanne's decision to take up baton twirling. Baton twirling, as she puts it, is "unmistakably American," her ticket of admission to American adolescent culture. The landscape narrative thus is used here to express a desire for individualism, for that "special thing" a girl can do or be for herself. This kind of desire, juxtaposed against Jeanne's father's sense of appropriate Japanese girlhood (daughterly modesty, duty, grace, and passivity), impels Jeanne down a path of self-realization that is sure to meet with her father's disapproval. In those same pages, Houston contrasts her baton twirling with other tried and less American activities recommended by her father: ballet and, especially, traditional Japanese *odori* dancing. She hates *odori* dancing and in this section repeatedly repudiates her father's desire that she be more of a Japanese than an American girl—that she not smile so much, for example. In yet another gesture to belong, Jeanne wants to join the Catholic church, which has a mission in the camp, a move her father furiously prevents. In implicit retaliation, she returns to baton twirling, "hating" her father, as she says. She throws the baton into the air, watches "him" twirl, catches "him," and throws "him" high, again and again (71). That is, she appropriates the symbol of masculine and paternal authority, the patriarchal penis, and manipulates it toward her own subversively American and female ends.[21]

While Jeanne is empowered to rebel by the American sensibility she attributes to local landscapes, her father, in contrast, is empowered to endure by the Japanese sensibility he attributes to local landscapes. He builds a rock garden, pares his trees, tends succulents, and lays stepping-stones up to their barracks' door—all of which lends the camp, the daughter notes, an "oriental character." That is, her father's relationship to camp culture and to the immediate natural world is articulated through an expatriate Japanese cultural nationalism. The same holds for his relationship to California's Sierra Nevada. He walks in its dry creek beds and enjoys it. He carves myrtle limb driftwood into benches, table legs, and other furniture. He paints watercolors. When he looks at the snow-capped peaks of distant Mount Whitney, what he sees is a very Japanese kind of inspirational symbol. "The tremendous beauty of those peaks . . . represented those forces in nature, those powerful and inevitable forces that cannot be resisted, reminding a man that sometimes he must simply endure that which cannot be changed" (71). In terms of visual ideologies, what could be further from the Archimedean worldview of dominant landscape discourse than this?

The narrative that overlays traditional American landscapes is never about endurance. It is about bigness, grandness, possibility, exceptionalism, transcendence, perseverance, moral imperative. Humility is very, very rarely part of this trope. The daughter's own statement that upon that same topography she might do or be some special thing shows how far away she has moved from the father figure. Landscape representation enables Houston to figure movement that is too profound for the narrative to tolerate otherwise, because it rests, in part, on the poignant renunciation of the father.

In the final section of this autobiography, when Houston returns to Manzanar years later with her non-Japanese American husband and three children, she figures yet another kind of nationalist moment, and again it comes through representations of landscape. Houston is standing in what remains of one of the camp orchards, and on a gust of desert wind she suddenly smells the sweetness of lingering fruit blossoms. She hears, too, the voices of her mother, her father, and of other former prisoners. The final section is titled "Ten Thousand Voices" to make this point: that those voices remain in the land, as do the stepping-stones prisoners used to decorate their home entrances. In particular what she finds drifting on the wind is the memory of "a rekindled wildness in Papa's eyes" (141). That "wildness" is associated with her father's capacity for defiance, and in 1973, when Houston writes this narrative, it is a capacity she wants to claim as part of a renovated American identity: one both Japanese and American, one where the latter does not erase the former. In the context of the broader racial politics of 1973, this goal is predictable and understandable enough.

But if Houston ultimately desires a binational nationalism, through landscape discourse she enacts a recurrent primary allegiance to the American. I believe she does so because within "the American" lies hope for imagining *female* national subjectivity. Such a hope seems somewhat forestalled otherwise in the closing gestures of the book. And this *gendered* part of the "ethnic plot" is the stickiest, the hardest to justify in 1973, when feminist women suffer a great deal of derision from radical men about "women's liberation." So Houston diffuses the feminist urgency of this narrative, even as she puts it in motion. The "diffuser" is landscape discourse, a seemingly innocuous kind of "filler" or literary device in a tale conceived otherwise through the genre of documentary.

But landscape is finally no "filler." It permits Houston to work out the gendered dimensions of the Japanese American problematic, and the text closes with no resolution, only tensions. Part of the conflict between father and daughter comes from the daughter's unwillingness to be a "Japanese woman," at least on her father's terms. She will not be an *odori* dancer, with (as he desires) aristocratic and hyperfeminine values. And yet, when she performs the American alternative of leading the band as baton twirler, she is seen not as "American," she discovers, but as "Asian." A painful lesson follows, whereby Houston learns that "Oriental [women] can fascinate Caucasian men" and that, in the end, that kind of gaze is "just another form of [female] invisibility," very much like that encouraged by her father (117). The text indirectly puzzles over how she might express any desire that will not ultimately be co-opted. As a high school girl, Jeanne wears a low-cut sarong and wins the homecoming queen competition, only to realize that she has simply replicated orientalist stereotypes of the geisha. She remedies this by wearing to the homecoming dance a high-necked, white dress fit for the most austere Southern belle. And yet, as she walks down the queen's runway, she knows this too is not her. Meaningfully, this is the scene that ends section 2 of the book—the section that explores Houston's post-camp engagement with American ideals. This ending suggests the inability of *any* nationalist discourse in 1973 to represent her desires at the same time that it suggests the centrality of issues of sexuality and gender to all narratives of nation.

Houston finally opts to represent the links between gender, sexuality, and national subjectivity in the conjoined forms of American motherhood and defiant ethnic identity. This is an ambivalent choice, clearly, because many loose ends go untied as a consequence. And yet, because the choices she faces are impossible and also male-defined (torn between sexualized geisha, *odori* dancer, militant Asian American radical, or virginal bride), Houston charts what is perhaps the most respectable course available to her in 1973. The final nationalist landscape here is one that displaces paternal authority, advocates female autonomy, reveals the white racialist bias inherent in notions of citizenship, and equivocates or sidesteps questions of sexuality while simultaneously raising them.

I do think that Houston is "on" to something, though. She is "on" to who is *not* signified in narratives of nation. Though the mother figure in *Farewell to Manzanar* occupies a powerful role in the autobiography, she does not participate in any of the discourses of landscape—Japanese, American, or Japanese American—which tell the story's nationalist tale. If young Jeanne, or adult Jeanne as well, struggles for visibility in any of the above imaginaries, her mother is thoroughly invisible, her own narrative of nation entirely untold and apparently untellable on the terms that exist to choose from here. This point serves as a caution, I would suggest, a reminder that Houston's final figure of American motherhood is one that she claims rather than be left out in the nonnational ether altogether. The landscape of defiance that characterizes Houston's revisitation of the crime scene is one very clearly at work in the "third country" that Gloria Anzaldúa writes about, the southernmost 100-mile stretch that makes up South Texas, what Anzaldúa calls "the borderlands."

Gloria Anzaldúa's "Third Country"

The border is not an abyss that will save us from threatening otherness, but a place where . . . otherness yields, becomes us, and therefore [becomes] comprehensible. . . . Whether we want it or not, the edge of the border is widening, and the geopolitics [of it] are becoming less precise day by day.
—performance artist Guillermo Gómez-Peña, San Diego, 1986

In a funny way, Anzaldúa's *La Frontera/The Borderlands* (1987) is received somewhat like *Farewell to Manzanar* in that it is an autobiographical text whose literary import is not the primary focus of critical commentary about it. Anzaldúa's *La Frontera* is claimed by Chicanas, lesbians, and many theorists, including those of queer theory, postcolonialism, transnationalism, and Chicana literature. It is used widely in women's studies, Chicano/a studies, and even in some American literature survey classes. Her notion of "borderlands liminality" is regarded as one of the book's most valuable theoretical contributions, and I include it partly for these reasons but especially because any discussion of women, landscape discourse, sexuality, and nationalism is obliged, at this moment in cultural history, to draw Anzaldúa into its purview.

The "borderlands" that Anzaldúa narrates are not just geographic but also sexual, linguistic, psychological, spiritual, and political. As a lesbian, Anzaldúa is shunted to the borders of a homophobic and heterosexist society. As someone whose first language is Spanish, she lives on the linguistic border of an English-speaking society that considers Spanish (versus, say, French) a language to be unlearned. As an outsider in both U.S. and Mexican culture, an alien on either side of the border, Anzaldúa argues that the psychological health of new mestizas depends on their ability to live *sin fronteras* (without borders), to become a crossroads where multiple selves can harmoniously coexist. Borderlands consciousness values racial cross-fertilization and cultural complexity; it refuses dualistic thinking; it is the consciousness, Anzaldúa believes, that Americans (not just Chicanas) need to be able to negotiate the twenty-first century. This is the template from which Anzaldúa's new nationalist thinking takes shape, and it echoes throughout Chicana studies.[22]

When *La Frontera* appeared in 1987, as critic Tey Diana Rebolledo puts it, Anzaldúa captured on paper many ideas that were "in the air."[23] After its publication, many Chicanas felt a great relief in seeing their multiply constituted subjectivities finally articulated. Anzaldúa's book has become a classic of Chicana studies because it creates a usable past for contemporary Chicanas, one that links both Spanish and Anglo colonial legacies with contemporary gender roles that constrain Mexican American female freedom. It retrieves a female-centered, mestiza matrilineage that might guide today's Chicanas in spiritual, psychological, and political matters.

La Frontera is also an exercise in alternative nation-building. It deconstructs the classic Anglo and/or Spanish colonial narrative that dominates southwestern and Texas history. It provides a new narrative of nation for what it calls a "third country." At the "third country's" nationalist center live borderlands inhabitants, who speak mixes of Spanish and English, practice a collage of Catholicism and paganism, love people of the same sex, and believe in humans' primal tie to nature.

A driving universalism simultaneously informs this alternative narration of nation. Anzaldúa's "third country" refuses entry to no one. So, in the final instance, hers is a nationalist program that fundamentally rearticulates the terms of nationalist belonging, for it would erase the borders of any single or discrete imagined political community. Even if borderlands consciousness provides the cultural and social logic for Anzaldúa's vision of twenty-first-century nationalist thought, this is not a narrative of nation that is ultimately conceived in territorial or spatially contained dimensions. It is far, far more diffuse than that. And this move away from spatially specific forms of national affiliation (what many theorists term "deterritorialization"), I argue, is generally representative of new female regionalist visions of the postmodern nation-state.

Since some of what I'm saying here about Anzaldúa is well known by critics and theorists, and since Chicano/a studies may well be on the verge of a paradigm shift *away* from its current emphasis on borderlands studies,[24] let me take a different approach, by beginning with Anzaldúa's representations of South Texas landscapes, particularly her portrayal of South Texas as an agricultural farm belt. These are the images that frame this book's two parts: the introductory "manifesto" portion (part 1) and the sequence of poems (part 2). These images articulate the book's anti-imperial politics as well. Thus, as I did with Jeanne Wakatsuki Houston's, I will read this autobiography more as literature than as theory or social history.

A direct focus on landscape representation, I think, tells critics something we don't already know. Namely, it permits us to pursue the contradictions that inhere in the various new nationalist discourses available in *La Frontera* and to pursue them somewhat more self-consciously than they have been so far. To the extent that the critical narrative that surrounds Anzaldúa's reception is nearly unanimously celebratory, critics risk introducing Anzaldúa's unconscious confusions into their own nationalist formulations. The best, most useful, and most complex parts of this book, I think, are not the overtly theoretical ones but rather the poetic ones. The poems demonstrate the rupture that characterizes the text and that the text tries to contain. Importantly, this is the same rupture that new theories about the phenomenon of nationalism also struggle to comprehend and express.

Part 1 of *La Frontera* begins with a Statement of the Problem, which also includes a Statement of the Solution according to Anzaldúa. Anzaldúa's solution is that the new mestiza must live *sin fronteras*, must develop a subjectivity of the crossroads. The problem, as Anzaldúa sees it, is this: the people who live in South Texas, where the First World grates against the Third, live inside *una herida abierta* (an open wound) that bleeds. Every day the inhabitants of the borderlands negotiate the First/Third World culture gap, and it drives them half crazy. Are they Mexicans? Are they Americans? Can they self-respectingly locate themselves anywhere in a national imaginary?

The problem, further, is that the lands originally possessed by the Mexicans of the region are gone, and with them is gone the ranching culture that was the backbone of South Texas's distinct regional (and Mexican national) identity. After the Mexican-American War, Mexican Americans in South Texas eke out a living as best they can in the new economic and cultural context, changed and controlled in the twentieth century by corporate agribusiness. But Anzaldúa, ever hopeful that justice will prevail, repeatedly exhorts, "The land will be ours again!" This kind of inevitable triumphalism remains to the end and articulates both the rupture and the gesture to contain that rupture, that I noted above. In other words, landscape discourse is central to the various efforts of part 1 to deconstruct as well as to reimagine nationhood as we know it.

Then comes part 2, which presents a series of poems in which the reader experiences the pain of racist, sexist, and homophobic suffering and is positioned in such a way as to be forced to take a politically progressive moral stand against racism, sexism, and homophobia. Presumably, after having read the poems and experienced the resignation that so many of the poem's speakers articulate, the reader can return to part 1 for a sense of What to Do. The point I'm making here is that this book functions, on the surface, very simply. There's a social problem, which has a knowable and achievable political solution. Ironically, however, if one reads this book through representations of landscape or focuses on landscape as social and nationalist discourse, one may well conclude that the fundamental problem about which Anzaldúa writes—the problem of the changed physical landscape that has come about from the demands of big-business farming—is probably without remedy.

This book is all about lost land, that is, stolen land—and with it, stolen identity and history. Anzaldúa's own family's land has been seized as a result of Anglo American conquest, so she has personal history at stake. But she also tells a broader regional and racialized history of dispossession and disenfranchisement. Landscape discourse provides a medium, then, for Anzaldúa to narrate pre-Anglo, Mexican national identity, which is tied to regional and cultural identities too. Landscape, for her, "pictures" a historical moment in which South Texas peoples controlled, to some extent, a satisfactorily mirroring narrative of the nation. From this originary point (and I don't suggest it is unproblematic, for she consistently exposes the gendered hierarchies at work in Chicano/a geographical imaginations), Anzaldúa then exhibits the *changed* agricultural landscape in order to critique the consolidation of a new national and economic power base: that of Anglo American capitalist agribusiness.

The first poem in part 2 uses both of these landscape traditions to frame what is finally a third strategy at work in this text: the mapping of mestizo/a concerns onto South Texas's cultural imaginary. The poem "White-wing Season" tells the story of midwestern white men who come to a South Texas mestiza's ranch to birdhunt. The poem depicts a fairly widespread regional custom whereby small ranchers in South Texas generate cash by allowing out-of-staters to come on their land for a day's sport. This custom also suggests some of the racialized economic realities that govern today's small ranching enterprises: they have little access to capital and must raise cash by whatever means possible, including the comprising one of permitting Anglo men access to their land.

The speaker of "White-Wing Season" is not only financially hard-pressed, but she is a Mexican American woman doing business with white men, which is, the poem suggests, full of other potential dangers and compromises. Anzaldúa is quite skilled in her simultaneous rendering of sexual politics with class, racial, and regional politics. Making the gendered politics of this transaction clear, Anzaldúa features the ranch woman doing her laundry when the hunters arrive. The speaker takes their dollar bills in what seems a somewhat shady or shamed transaction, as if the speaker were whorish. The speaker tries to ease her conscience all the while by reminding herself that the money will reshingle her worn roof. Making explicit the distance of women's culture from blood sport, the speaker remembers a bird she once shot with her brother's rifle. The image of its "small opened bill/blood from its mouth" suggests maternal tenderness toward the fallen bird. Her early memory of hunting is not infused with the thrill of the hunt, the victory of game taken, but of the bird's smallness, helplessness, its bleeding pain. The speaker returns then to her laundry, which again juxtaposes the "cleanliness" of women's domestic realm over that of the men who have gone off for their bloody fun. Indeed, the relative quietness and cleanliness of her domestic tasks (she "shakes out the wrinkles / snapping the sheets") offer a damning contrast to what the hunters will do: "fill the silence and the sky / with buckshot" (102). But of course, the speaker acknowledges to herself sadly, she is implicated in the birds' deaths, for just then the shots ring out, and bird feathers fall upon her roof, literally "reshingling" it. The men, as is customary, offer her part of their take. In silence, they drop two birds on her washboard. Her supper does not sit well in her belly, however, and the final rebuke seems to come from nature itself, for during the night it rains "gentle as feathers." Her roof has now been reshingled twice with the natural resources of the region: first bird feathers, then rainfall. Such is the life, and Anzaldúa's comment on the life, of South Texas ranch women obliged to provide for themselves as best they can.

Another poem in part 2, "Cultures," echoes the resigned pathos that appears in the best, the least formulaic, of this section's poetry. And again, the poetic voice works out its story upon South Texas landscape. The poem's event is a simple one. A daughter has been instructed by her mother to dig a hole into which they will dump and recycle the family's trash. But a tension holds the poem tightly together, and it is a tension that results from the many different cultures being imagistically figured in this poem. The first "culture" is South Texas ranch culture—a parched, cheerless life from which, in these poems, there is little reprieve. The girl hits "the hard brown earth" with the pick axe and shovel. She "pick[s] at its dark veins, disinter[ring] a rotting tin can" (120). This is no beautiful or romantic "recycling" narrative, where organic matter redeems those who recycle it. Instead, the girl unburies what is dead and committed to burial but not yet gone, that which does not finally recycle very well—the aluminum trash of days gone by, cans of Spam, Coke bottles, rubber-nippled baby bottles. The artifacts of contemporary consumer culture cannot be easily disposed of. They refuse to die. The simple act of recycling—part of the agrarian tradition that South Texas knew before Anglo conquest—is thus impossible. This ranch's ecosystem has been permanently polluted by an American consumer economy.

The gendered culture that governs ranch life is corrupt too, for as the daughter "swings," "shovels," "lifts," and "sweats," her brothers stand coolly by. This, the daughter/speaker comments, is "woman's work and beneath them" (120). Making the point further, Anzaldúa situates the recycling hole underneath the family clothesline. Apparently it is women's duty to keep both the family clothes and the family's traditional connection to nature "clean" too. The girl notices "the cultures spawning in Coke bottles / murky and motleyed" (120). She notices the "crossed posts [on the laundry line] / crucifixes over earlier graves" (120). But neither scientific culture (that spawning in the Coke bottle) nor religious culture (symbolized by crucifixes) will amount to anything redemptive. Faith is here absent. In the closing stanza, the daughter remarks that though her mother claims that rotting trash "replenishes the soil," nothing has ever grown on these plots but "thistle sage and nettle" (120). There is nothing to believe in anymore in this tense, culture-compressed, multiply valenced world. And without even faith in the afterlife to save these ranchers, they will become something like trash themselves one final day.

Themes of resignation, poverty, gendered hardship, loss of a way of life, cruelty, and injustice are common to this series of poems. Certainly there are poems that celebrate resistance—indeed, that get political results from resistance. There are ones that describe mystical experience, too, and the healing that comes out of battling with one's own "dead rats and cockroaches" (164). But more often the poems are about psychic disintegration, brutality, persecution of minorities, human malice. They are painful reading, for the violence they depict is so immediate.

But Anzaldúa is unwilling to end this book with anything less than a triumphal narrative, where resistance defeats injustice. Thus, the penultimate poem, "To live in the Borderlands means you," is a poetic rendering of the general message of part 1's manifesto. It is written in the language of repeated imperatives: "To live in the Borderlands means you / are neither hispana india negra espanola . . . / [it means you are] forerunner of a new race . . . a new gender . . . [you] put chili in the borscht . . . resist the gold elixir beckoning from the bottle . . . you must live *sin fronteras* / be a crossroads" (194–95). This is a sequence of poetic instructions that coach borderlands inhabitants in the skills of survival. But this poem leaves out one significant aspect of part 1's manifesto: the land. This poem does not operate through the progression of landscape imagery. Land is a nonissue, and landscape discourse is absent. No comment accompanies the absence.

The word "borderlands" in this penultimate poem means everything, indeed, except the South Texas land seized by Anglos. We should note that by the end of the book, one of the motivating backdrops of part 1's manifesto as well as of part 2's poetry has been rendered silent. The reason for this, I think, is because the land is gone, period. No amount of radical idealism will get it back. Even if, by some revolutionary or millennial miracle, the dispossessed were refunded their rightful titles, industrial agribusiness has transformed the South Texas landscape so much so that it can never return to the dryland farming system that existed until the 1930s. The ecosystem has been permanently altered, and nothing will restore it to its previous state.

I want to speculate here, then, about the relationship between nationalism, landscape discourse, and the two parts of the book, the poems and manifesto. I said at the outset, the seeming relationship is one whereby the reader returns to part 1, the What to Do section, after having read part 2, the Experience of the Problems section. I also said that critics and theorists do not focus on the poems.[25] The structure of the book, then, as well as its critical reception, leads readers always back to the manifesto, and to its repeated claim, which is also its last line: "The land was Mexican once / was Indian always / and is. / And will be again" (91).

A consideration of the landscape discourse operating—or not operating—in the poems offers a different conclusion. The land will not be Indian or mestiza land again. And confronted with the problems that the poems lay out, to suggest that it might be otherwise is beyond naïve. This perspective helps us make better sense of the text's extreme focus on "the struggle is personal" narrative, and why Anzaldúa forays so often into the need for Chicana psychological health. The struggle is personal only if the land will never be returned. For one must make enough peace with the irreversibility of conquest, the irretrievability of lost land, so as not to be consumed by rage or powerlessness.

This last point is crucial because it clarifies the ground upon which Anzaldúa seems to want to build her new nationalist enterprise but does not quite yet know how. What makes it hard to know how to formulate this new nationalism is that it does not correspond to any kind of recognized spatial referent: not land, not even the (deterritorialized gay) body. This is a narrative of nation without conventional or counterhegemonic territorial "mass." It doesn't match up with any actual or literal space. The final investment here (in the final poem, "Don't Give Up, Chicanita") is in universalist and feminist mysticism, in the power of revolutionary praxis and insurrection, and in—yes, here it comes—Indianness.

At the last minute Anzaldúa, unable to stake out this new nonterritorialized ground after all, reverts to that most utilized figure of Chicano/a geographical imaginations: the ancient, dignified, pre-Colombian Indian. To be sure, Anzaldúa's usable past comes not through the male warrior but instead through female genealogies: Mother Earth, the "pride of being *Mexicana-Chicana-Tejana*," which overlaps with "our Indian woman's spirit" (202). But this is finally an ending that looks more backward than forward; it reentrenches nationalist narratives in established paradigmatic patterns as much as it breaks those patterns. *La Frontera* flirts, but does not finally consummate its intentions. It is scared off, awed perhaps, by the implications of its own love affair with a postmodern state and/or narrative of nation. Thus, as I argued earlier, while *La Frontera* illustrates the general rejection by new female regionalists of spatially specific forms of national affiliation, *La Frontera* embodies regionalists' ambivalence and fears, too. For different reasons, we see a similar project under construction in Mary Clearman Blew's *All But the Waltz*, the final book considered in this chapter.

By arguing here that Anzaldúa's text is "scared off" from fully inhabiting its own imaginative terrain, I don't mean to suggest that other writers or theorists fully, courageously, or joyously inhabit that same terrain. Perhaps, given the bravery of Anzaldúa's "third country"—a nation that welcomes "the squint-eyed, the perverse, the troublesome, the mongrel, the mulatto, the halfbreed, the half dead" (3)—Anzaldúa's final "the personal is everything" message is a wise one. For the pressures exerted upon an Anzaldúa type of subjectivity require tremendous internal fortitude. To survive, when the land will *not* be returned, and to find satisfaction, without recourse to Indian mythologies *or* to assimilation, now these are indeed challenges.

In closing, let us look at a text that, like Kingsolver's *Animal Dreams* or Silko's *Ceremony*, circulates with an unmistakably western identity. Where do overt interventions by white women into the wilderness plot and into classic masculinist narratives of nation fit, finally, with postmodernity?

Where Now?: A New Anglo West, by Mary Clearman Blew

Mary Clearman Blew's autobiography, *All But the Waltz: A Memoir of Five Generations in the Life of a Montana Family* (1991), is a fitting final book for this project. Many critics might have viewed this tale, and the Rocky Mountain school of new regionalist writing of which it is representative, as a natural place to *begin* my survey of this literary movement. However, by situating it at the end of this study, I mean to argue for its indebtedness to civil rights-inspired geographical imaginations and thereby to reformulate some of the informal assumptions currently operating in western studies about the origins of the new regionalism. The new regionalism did not begin with the Ivan Doigs and Norman Macleans of recent literary history. It began in murkier cultural waters but waters nonetheless linked to the changing social tides created by the civil rights movements and contemporary feminism. All of these social justice movements have in common the longing for a revolutionized State.

As I've argued throughout this chapter, this longing is expressed through landscape representation in quite complex and often unguarded ways. Blew's *All But the Waltz* is one example. Like Anzaldúa, Blew invokes the landscapes of particular places in order both to locate her western story as well as put into motion a narrative of nation. Like Anzaldúa, Blew does so while at the same time disturbing the link between the nation and territorial boundedness. In the final analysis, however, Blew does not simply reinvent a classic, but now feminized, "American moment" upon Montana's western lands; unlike Anzaldúa, Blew's nationalist narrative ends up far more open, diffuse, and spatially deconstructed. Blew breaks fundamentally with civil rights nationalist geographies and charts what seems to me a very searching and responsible course for someone who, like her, is born and bred into white spatial prerogatives and (to a lesser degree) white national prerogatives.

Mary Clearman Blew is a woman raised on a homesteaded Montana ranch, one whose upbringing took place always in what she might call the tragic shadow of the cowboy myth. Today she is an English professor and writer, having left behind permanently the everyday routine of ranch work and of ranching culture as a defining daily lifestyle. Blew is one of the most self-conscious spokespeople for the Rocky Mountain female regionalists, as her brief but substantive introduction to the anthology *Circle of Women* demonstrates. During the course of the writing of this book, the Rocky Mountain Anglo regionalists in particular have come full circle and are now commenting upon their own literary movement to wonder: what kinds of stories shall we tell to replace the parts of those stories we no longer hold true?

> [If] we no longer believe the old narratives that told us how our per-severance . . . led to the settlement of the West, or even [believe] . . . in the settlement itself, knowing . . . about its cost in bloodshed, and destruction of the natural environment, then what of our present and future? How are we to understand our lives, and the place were we live, and how are we to bring up our children . . . without the support and connection and meaning of stories? Where do we turn?[26]

This indeed is one of the central issues that *ought* to occupy writers whose commitments are those stated above. To that difficult question, Blew's auto-biography offers a great deal of food for readerly thought. Blew's *All But the Waltz* is a stunningly sad book, unsentimental, driven. The women and men in this book endure. They expect no one's sympathy. As the title promises, Blew narrates the history of her own Montana family, which arrived to homestead in 1882, when Montana was yet a territory. We learn about the great family patriarchs, the women who married them, the changing land-scape of Montana's agricultural industry as years of failing banks and bad weather shrink the state's financial base. This family, like their neighbors, come through deaths and drought and occasional prosperity. Some are edu-cated, many are not. Some, like Blew's father, never stray farther from the ranch than would a wayward cow. Always they work. We learn about births, courtships, about breaking horses, shearing sheep, about the hardships of Montana winters and one set of parents who make their children run behind moving wagons to keep them from freezing.

Blew writes beautifully, in the quiet lilting way that canonical western novels are beautiful. Part of what enables her to write as she does is that there is something profoundly secure about the narrative's claim to the land, something unshakable, (ostensibly) earned, certain. As if commenting on that security, the autobiographical child, Mary, who is the protagonist at book's opening, makes a telling claim twice in the book's first pages. The child sits at an evening supper table lighted by a kerosene lamp. She ner-vously imagines that she hears skittering pests or bogeymen in the shadows that the light casts upon the cabin's far wall. But then she comes back to her-self to remark, "I am safe" and, a moment later, "I am here, safe at the center" (4). One cannot imagine a self-referential comment about either "centrality" or "safety" made so early (if made at all) in the tales of so many women writers this book has surveyed. Certainly, for example, not in Gloria Anzaldúa, Sandra Cisneros, Jeanne Wakatsuki Houston, or Wanda Coleman.

What is going on here? What enables Blew's seemingly flawless opening writing and her deep feeling for the landscape? My argument is that this narrative announces itself through a tradition of landscape representation that is very tied into the dominant geocultural imaginary's narrative of nation. Listen to the tale's initiatory lines: "In the sagebrush to the north of the mountains in central Montana, where the Judith River deepens its channel and threads a slow, treacherous current between the cutbanks, a cottonwood log house still stands" (1). This landscape *belongs* to its narrator—she holds it completely in her hand, there is no apparent problematic relationship. Hers are familiar markers of the Anglo national imagination: half-wild western wilderness, female-gendered nature, the solitary log cabin. This is both a pastoral but also an adventure picture, simultaneously quaint and serene and yet romantic and dangerous. It is, in other words, an American landscape, fully emplotted with notions of the "New" World, colonialist imperative, and masculine bourgeois antimodernism. Indeed, the question the narrator poses in the novel's first moment—is it possible to believe in anything but today?—is itself sandwiched in the deep middle of a meandering, river-like sentence about the Judith River. It is an Anglo American question, pressed inside an Anglo American landscape. This book makes all the initial tropic gestures of a canonical western American story.

Until, that is, it announces itself as also female. The minute this announcement comes, this all-American tale problematizes its claim to center stage and "reality." The next story in the book's opening sequence is one in which the girl-child witnesses a sow and her piglets stranded on an island midriver and sure to drown, for the river is on the rise. The adult woman who narrates the pig's story remembers this as a moment when her child-self came to know that she too could be vulnerable, that her center could be as instantly imperiled as were those of the mama pig and her frightened babies.

Further decentering the subject, who in the initial pages of the book claimed to feel securely at the plot's center, Blew demonstrates that as an adult woman, she cannot remember finally whether the sow on the river was an event she witnessed or merely a bad dream. When, as an adult, she mentions to her father the place where the pigs drowned, her father is embarrassed. *It never happened,* he tells her. *You don't know what you're talking about.* By the end of the book's initial chapter, the adult narrator cannot say for sure whether the sow and her piglets drowned or whether she only dreamed that they drowned. Interestingly, though, Blew will not be put off. Dream or fact, she says, "the sow on the river is my story" (11). And her story *begins*, I want to argue, by laying out both her connection to and distance from dominant nationalist landscape discourse.

Let me make clear here the connections between landscape discourse, dominant discourses of the nation, and white female subjectivity. As a white pioneer, Blew can lay claim to both a nationalist landscape and a "center" in landscape, because that landscape narrates both her own family's home-steading history and more generally whites' relationship to the land. That is, she begins, as this tale begins, "centered" in a history that narrates Anglo expansion as legitimate and "natural" historic fact. And yet, because she is also a woman, her claim to subjectivity is not certain. It can be challenged by male (in this case, her father's) authority. Indeed, it is her father—a real cowboy, remember—who functions in this story as enforcer of the daughter's distance from authority, her distance from some unquestioned claim upon landscape *as* a form of western and national knowledge.

Like the pigs, Blew is marooned within both western and landscape discourse. The "treacherous" Judith River, it turns out, will turn on and consume the inhabitants of the land who cannot navigate it, who are vulnerable. Like the pigs, Blew herself is vulnerable. As we will see later in this memoir, the kind of nation this landscape and system of knowledge supports does not nurture women like Blew, who disavow paternal authority, who refuse to concede that their dreams, even if they depart from the "reality" of dominant forms of western knowledge, are nonetheless *their* stories—stories they will continue to believe and claim and, importantly, stories they will pass on to their children.

Blew becomes all the more infuriating to her father by questioning him repeatedly about the sow on the river. She becomes what her grandfather might have called "an uppity woman," the kind of woman that she in fact is, if being intelligent and speaking one's mind is uppity. It is against her being just such a woman, one who leaves ranching and the world of her father for an intellectual's life, that her father finally rages, saying, "[Mary] *somehow got the idea in her head she knows something, but by God she don't know a goddamned thing*" (36).

As is so often the case in western literature, the site of "high culture"— which is supposed to be a "northeastern" attribute—is where the gendered battle takes place. Mary's father has raised her and her younger sister as sons, that is, as legitimate heirs to a western legacy. They're as good as "cowboys," as easy on a horse as any boys around; they know something about running stock, haying, breaking horses, getting by. Blew's father loves his girls, wants them close to him, does not want young Mary to leave ranching and, by extension, him. For many years she and her sister are schooled by their mother at home. The father even sells one good ranch and buys another of lesser quality closer to town so that the family can stay together and also stay on a ranch while the girls go to the local high school. In his mind, Mary and her sister will inherit the ranch, will keep going a family tradition of cowboying that is dying out. He despairs to see it go.

And yet, that which he loves—cowboy culture and mythology—is that which Blew despises. As a growing adolescent, she senses both the economic and cultural changes that will render the cowboy increasingly irrelevant to modern ranch life and to modern Montana as an economic marketplace. She sees cowboys around her growing "bewildered," as they give up ranch work for waged work in town. By her early twenties, Blew is a young woman who wants nothing more than to be "free of the cowboy," free of a tradition she sees as "illusory." She is furious at the "romantic and despairing mythology which has racked and scarred so many lives" (45). She is furious too at the notion of "a mythic Montana of the past, of inarticulate strength and honor and courage irrevocably lost" (45). Her own experience of western self-reliance, the silent stoicism, the unending harshness of the workday, the strain upon strain of barely scraping by, of exhausted women and tight-lipped men, all of these realities add up to something less than myth, though Blew is honest enough to acknowledge too that "the myth has its grip on us all" (55).

Reminiscent of Louise Erdrich's comment on romantic and traditional notions of "Indianness," in Blew's Montana, cowboy mythology kills. One day her father inexplicably detours from a lifelong pattern of behavior and drives north into parts he's never before visited. This is a man who never left Montana. He gets out of his pickup, lies down on the side of a hill, and lets a Montana storm overtake him. Blew believes that it was the old western nostalgia—a sense that the better days are in the past and that all that makes up the present is lackluster and compromised—that motivated him to choose to die.

Indeed the myth *does* have its grip on Blew, for as much as she refuses seduction by cowboy mythology, she nonetheless makes a second marriage to a man who is as much a cowboy as her father. At forty-five, Blew is pregnant, ecstatically, with the first wanted child of her life (she has two other sons). She is happily married, too, for the first time. And then this oil-rigging, Marlboro-smoking, crazily charming western man is suddenly diagnosed with pulmonary fibrosis. Ever the self-reliant, stalwart cowboy figure, he will not consent to proper medical treatment. And this is a story that does not get better. He is wildly willful, won't admit he is sick, tries to the last to invent one or another money-making scheme, smokes all the way, and spends more time away from home to escape Blew's worrying. This is not a man who takes up with another woman, who drinks away the night, who is indifferent to his infant daughter. This is a man who is too proud—nursed on cowboy machismo—to do what it takes to secure the family and provide for his little girl and wife when he knows that he is dying. Blew divorces him, finally, raises the young daughter alone, and files a restraining order to keep the father from kidnapping her. The book's last scene is of the mother and seven-year-old child at graveside. They have not seen him for three years, and he has lived his final years alone, met death alone. Like her father, her husband has been fatally proud, a masculine man to the end, and it has cost him his family and his life.

The saddest story is that he is not the only one who pays. What little girl can understand that that kind of pride overrides even the deep, sacrificing love of parent for child? Blew's special message, in this memoir, is to demonstrate the visionless legacy that all of these fallen cowboys hand on to the women in their lives. Women inherit a world where, even if fathers and husbands give up, the women carry on. They wash another load of laundry, grade another student's exam, put another meal on the table, tuck another child into bed. They walk home from the funeral, one foot in front of the other, mother and daughter holding hands, as Blew does in the final sentence. They keep going. There is no martyrdom here, no bid for the cultural sanctification of white motherhood. But there is a grim and familiar kind of western female stoicism in operation, formed out of a history wherein men's dreams and foibles structure the problems that women inherit and where women, at the day's end, try to put together the pieces in order to give to their children at bedtime something other than a cynical story, a joyless kiss good night.

Thus we return at this memoir's end to the questions of the opening epigraph: what kind of new stories can white women tell that will narrativize their own values and desires? Part of Blew's answer is first to break with the cowboy myth insofar as it is a national mythology always nostalgic about a better past, individualistic to the point of suicide. In its place she implicitly forwards an alternative narrative of the nation, an alternative form of western knowledge, secured far less by western landscape than is that of cowboy mythology and culture. In Blew's family, this alternative program is associated with "women's values," which means both community but also education. It is her mother and grandmother who bestow the legacies of education upon the young Mary. From them she learns to read, to love books, to protect her independence. "Amo, amas, amat. In the story of how [my grandmother] scraped and labored and shouldered on," Blew notes, "and of the awful price she paid, this remains. She survived, and she handed on the tools for survival to those she could reach" (201). Blew herself, having paid a similar price, hands on this female legacy of culture, education, female self-respect.

When Blew claims that the sow's story is her own, she intervenes upon the heart of the dominant imaginary's picture of the nation. Her intervention shows how vulnerable women (and their children) are within that nationalist imaginary, how subject they are to abandonment. Further, she shows the kind of resistance and derision to which women's own claims upon alternative forms of knowledge are subjected. This text's final distance from ranching and cowboy culture suggests that it knows well the pitfalls of tying hopes for feminist national subjectivity to western landscape discourse. That discourse will inevitably emplot "American moments" in masculinist ways. The text's hesitancy to conceive alternative narratives of the nation in territorial terms breaks with western convention, and this break, I believe, permits the final embrace of Blew's program of female education and empowerment (including the power to name western knowledge). That program is more suggestive finally of northeastern spatial fields and the activist (versus self-reliant) State that northeastern geographical imaginations embody. Although certain core western female values remain in this tale, especially female stoicism in the face of all kinds of adversity, they are tempered by a self-conscious advocacy of interdependence, community, and finally, implicitly, an activist State. For as Blew's own story shows, a good deal of grimness remains in western women's lives. There is no way to put the starkness aside, but there is a way, Blew suggests, for women to hold hands and stick together, in the face of it.

Deterritorializing the Nation

The new regionalists, not just those three highlighted in this chapter, demonstrate a complex engagement with both the dominant narrative of nation found in the landscapes of literary and critical renderings of western space and with the various other alternative nationalist traditions they work in and through. In Jeanne Wakatsuki Houston's case, an emerging Asian American cultural nationalism is the broader context from which she rewrites the desert landscape of Manzanar into a landscape that, for her, ultimately symbolizes defiance. A quieter but equally influential complementary discourse is 1970s feminism—for otherwise she would not speak so deliberately as "woman," nor would she figure her own birth as subject upon the metaphoric site of the death of patriarchal authority (her father).

Like Houston, Blew is enabled but also disabled by the racialized nationalist tradition to which she is heir. For Blew, however, a final embrace of feminist spatial fields is overt, not ambivalent. Such an embrace isn't surprising, given the later date of Blew's memoir (1991) and the fully fleshed-out (not early-1970s emergent) character of feminist thought in these later years. Moreover, the implicit whiteness of feminism's dominant female subject presents Blew fewer racialized obstacles to overcome. But if feminism is a fairly "friendly" discourse for Blew, she nonetheless needs western imaginaries to stave off the "pinch" she feels about feminism's regional bias. To stay true to the western parts of her feminist tale, she works through images of female stoicism.

Interestingly and importantly, Blew, like Jeanne Wakatsuki Houston, is less overt about sexual subjectivity and its relationship to national discourse than is, say, Anzaldúa. Each of them, in the rare moments when sexuality comes to the fore as a topic, locates female sexual self-consciousness either in "American moments" or in moments that signal antiwestern or northeastern spatial identity. In Blew's case, we get a 1990s woman retelling the story of the late 1950s. In an otherwise nonsexual book, Blew breaks voice to note that everybody was "sick of making out" and wanted to have, implicitly, orgasmic release. The tone she uses to adopt this momentary casual attitude, an attitude that is not present in the general narrative, is connected to a memory of college life. The conclusions to be drawn from this are sketchy but, I think, still suggestive. First, Blew locates female sexual subjectivity in a moment that also signals antiwestern subjectivity—the moment of higher education, which in western discourse is usually associated with eastern or female symbols. Recall that for Jeanne Wakatsuki Houston, sexual awareness also emerges in educational contexts, though for her it is high school culture, not college, that alerts her not only to herself as sexual subject but equally to herself as Other, as orientalist object.

Relative to Anzaldúa's, Blew's and Houston's imaginative scales may seem comparatively quieter, for an overtly eroticized State is beyond the scope of what either Blew or Houston explicitly imagine. And yet even if Blew and Houston don't speak to a "third country" of mongrels or misfits or of same-sex lovers, it is clear that heterosexual as well as homosexual satisfaction will be possible for all these writers only when narratives of nation have been "queered"—identified more with an activist State and female solidarity than with a knee-jerk, western, "hands off," antigovernment, hyperindividualist sensibility. An activist State promises formal guarantee (or at least sponsorship in principle) of female, gay, and nonwhite civil rights. This kind of State is more likely to lead Americans away from patriotic landscapes and toward an embrace of multiracial love, same-sex love, and the production of a miscegenated, transgendered, twenty-first-century citizenry.

In order for western feminism not to end up reproducing a heterosexist and masculinist narrative of nation, these writers suggest, feminists must detach their own nationalist visions from firm territorial referents. The various counternationalist impulses visible in the three texts studied here loosen the seemingly necessary link between territorial specificity and narratives of nation. By disassociating or loosening the knot tying together specific locations (i.e., the physical land mass commonly called the United States) and the imagined political or cultural or ethnic communities figured under the sign of "nation," these writers make room for new kinds of nationalist affiliations. In so doing, they open up nationalist imaginaries to those whose claims upon national subjectivity would otherwise be tenuous, those who could not, under the preceding terms, lay functional claim to national belonging.

In most respects, then, these narratives work within what is increasingly called "postnational" discourse.[27] They reject the idea of a single symbolic order of nation under which American citizenship can be named or contained. One major feature of new regionalist discourse—the notion of political or national subjectivity figured along the lines of an interdependent, *not* an autonomous, subject—is dramatically illustrated by the role that children play in the western stories studied here. For Houston and Blew, motherhood forces many issues that directly affect the kinds of nations they ultimately value. Anzaldúa, too, closes her text via a moment of generational torch-passing to her niece, one that reminds younger women and/or girls to keep the faith but also keep up the fight.

The kinds of desires present here go well beyond those of the classic bourgeois, autonomous subject. There is no talk, as there is by contrast in David Wyatt's *Fall Into Eden*, of finding "others" less susceptible to monologic projection, because the cultural logic underlying postnational, feminist, western subjectivity has to do less with models of aggressive individualism than with models of relationality, nonmilitarism, and human interconnection. The national political subject is in process of being fundamentally redefined, in terms that ultimately correspond (for better and worse) with many of the characteristic features of global capitalism today.

Which is to say that the new female regionalists' postnational agendas dovetail with those of that vague but still extant entity called "transnational Capital." The politics guiding each project are vastly dissimilar, but the seeming overlap between the two may generate complicated potential confusions. It is my hope that by calling attention to both their similar but finally divergent political visions and commitments, critics and intellectuals will be better able to combat the inevitable effort to appropriate and discipline what is new and progressive within the new female regionalism.

In a post–Cold War world, global cooperation and interdependence are no longer utopic or pacifistic hopes but rather constitute foreign policy imperatives upon which rest world peace and continued capitalist accumulation. The last point about the consolidation of capitalism as *the* dominant global economic philosophy is critical, for it alerts us to the contradictory politics of current efforts to maintain world peace. Unlike during much of twentieth-century First World history, these days, peace is more profitable than war. Peace secures consumers and foreign markets for corporations' products at the same time that peaceable participation in global capitalism means that foreign governments are not wholeheartedly investigating alternative methods of economic organization. As long as there is no other way to get by but the capitalist way, capitalism will further entrench its control of the world's economic options, and economic justice will continue to be pitifully defined by one's "right" to consume.

A related contradiction of postmodern times can be seen in the behavior of capitalist enterprises toward their "home" nations. Never has it been truer that the logic of *trans*national capital circulation operates quite independently of, and often in opposition to, the particular social policies or social good of specific nation-states. The traditional ability of the state to police corporate dealings has been accordingly diminished. Transnational capital today operates by way of a postnational logic. It invokes the rhetorics of national belonging when it serves the bottom line, but if a break with the national good is more profitable, it goes global—invoking the rhetorics of the new economic order and the need for global interdependence and heralding the great democratizing potential of the new information age.

Even if the recent embrace of models of interdependence in global foreign policy, environmental policy, and much social theory owes less to feminist interventions of the kinds illustrated by the new female regionalism than it owes to globalization and the pressures that digitalization has exerted on every aspect of contemporary culture,[28] critics should still support more interdependent visions of the state and planet. The real challenge is to distinguish any less militaristic program for the twenty-first century from that proposed by the new transnational order. I believe the landscapes of new westernness available in feminist regionalism offer a viable and distinct alternative, for in those landscapes feminist desire cannot be ignored. In the "queered" New West, I want to suggest in conclusion, transnational capitalists are not likely to find western landscapes that support their balder ventures—at least not for a while. If co-optation is ultimately inevitable, as I believe it is, it falls to critics to stay ahead of the game and, above all, to avoid becoming unwitting spokespeople for the opposition.

Epilogue

At the close of this writing, the new female regionalism stood at a crossroads. The popularly conceived "center" of the movement—the Rocky Mountain regionalists like Mary Clearman Blew, Teresa Jordan, Cyra McFadden, and Annick Smith, as well as southwesterners like Barbara Kingsolver, Terry Tempest Williams, and Leslie Silko—were continuing to produce western female tales that often worked to relandscape western spaces so that feminist values and western subjectivity did not cancel one another out. At the same time, some of the California writers who have written in high-culture genres, and whom I have taken pains to place also at the "center" of the new female regionalism, increasingly were turning their creative attentions toward popular genres like detective novels, science fiction, magical realism, and even Disney adaptations of high literature. Interestingly, this change was most observable in works by nonwhite writers, such as Cynthia Kadohata, Lucha Corpi, Lisa See, Maxine Hong Kingston, and Karen Tei Yamashita (although Joan Didion's latest book, *The Last Thing He Wanted*, also radically experiments with form). Finally, a new generation of young female writers was in the making, performing poetry in venues like "Taco Shops" and often expressing female subjectivity through the new, sometimes postfeminist philosophies of "grrrl power," as the battle growl of the girl power movement goes.[1]

How will western and feminist criticism make sense of these cultural developments? Several books could easily be written about female literary culture or individual writers in any of the western subregions. The most obvious studies to be done are those of the Rocky Mountain regionalists, whose collective sensibilities are best represented in anthologies like *Circle of Women* or Teresa Jordan and James Hepworth's *The Stories That Shape Us*. Such studies necessarily would be more concerned with realism as a genre than am I, and they would work differently from (though not, I don't think, outside of) postmodern discourse. Any critical work should be cautious, in my estimation, about reinscribing upon any western subregion the status of "authentic" twenty-first-century landscape.

And then, of course, critics could go the cultural studies route, forgo literary textuality as a criterion of study, and pursue, quite constructively and ingeniously it seems to me, studies of western culture more broadly defined. That methodology would enable scholars to investigate and theorize far more elegant links to political economy, in particular, than I have known how to accomplish here. Given that symbols of westernness have weathered downsizing, restructuring, plant relocations, and the like, and continue to be profitable as ever in the fast and furious world of contemporary transnational capitalism, a careful and very specific rendering of any part of the political economy of western cultural production would be well worth the while. In Chapter 3, I have made some elementary attempts at an analysis that links environmental discourse to what I have named, deliberately generally, the "realm of commodity aesthetics." But given the vast participation of symbols of westernness in unabashedly commercial enterprises, the potential topics one might investigate are limitless. In this kind of materialist undertaking, scholars would be challenged to not compromise feminist analysis or politics and to foreground the ways that gender issues permeate political economy itself.

If we as critics could gather together a quantity of studies about any number of topics inflected through western spaces, we could reflect with greater precision upon some of the more complicated issues I have tried to raise about western women's relationship to modernity; the formation of nationalist, counternationalist, and postnationalist discourses; and the production of alternative economies of desire. With other case studies in mind, we could test the claim I've made about the importance of urban imaginaries to feminist western literature. For I am well aware that although the city, in this study, would seem to suggest the real or truly representative west, it remains just as true that both the imagined and actual landscapes westerners inhabit everyday evidence enormous variety. They aren't simply rural or urban or wild.

On the topic of nationalism, I would like to make a final point about the suitability of this notion of a "deterritorialized" nation to studies of Asian

American and (western) African American cultural production in particular. One of the reasons that notions of nationhood and counternationhood seem inevitably suggestive of specific land areas for American Indians, whites, and Mexican Americans is because those same groups historically have laid claim, both practically and imaginatively, to those same (if contested) topographies. Anglo and Mexican American national imaginaries especially took "territorial" or spatial forms because they were linked to broader colonial projects in the New World. That case cannot be made, en masse, however, for Asian Americans or African Americans. On the whole, I think this is less of a political problem for African Americans, because by invoking northern/southern spatial fields, African Americans confer upon themselves the status of citizen subjects. But for Asian Americans, who battle continual erasure of their status as citizens of the national body politic and for whom, generally, there exists no comparable historical memory or territorialized spatial field that instantly invokes national presence (Hawaii may be an exception for Japanese Americans),[2] tying contemporary notions of citizenship to particular western lands just doesn't make political sense. Western landscape discourse, that is, generally will not produce an empowered citizen subject who is also Asian American. This fact partly explains the relative absence of landscape representation in the works of Asian American writers and would suggest support for recent calls in Asian American studies to locate national belonging on the site of a nongeographically imagined or deterritorialized culture.[3]

In closing, I want to discuss briefly Judith Freeman's *The Chinchilla Farm* (1989), a novel that received uninspired reviews but which for me captures much of where I see new western landscapes heading in the years to come. It's a classic western tale insofar as it is about a white protagonist, down on her luck, who goes to California to turn things around. But, and this is what is interesting, the California she finds is no space of renewal or redemption, even though she manages by book's end (and to the uniform exasperation of feminist reviewers)[4] to find a rich husband, live on the beachfront with a new baby, and, as she discloses on the last page, to "writ[e] this book" (307) while sitting, as she puts it, "still on the [Pacific] rim" (308).

Now this "happily ever after" ending might bother me too, except for the fact that what it reveals about western spaces at the turn of the twenty-first century is the degree to which they are unstable, unfriendly, possibly even fatal to a woman like Freeman's protagonist, Verna—who is all working-class sensibility, with next to no upper-middle-class feminist panache and certainly no, repeat *no*, professional connections. It isn't self-awareness or hard work that finally adds up to Verna's happy ending but instead the profoundly troubling and capricious fact of simple dumb luck. Our protagonist Verna just lucks out, finds a decent guy who happens to be rich. And that's pretty much the moral of this story. Which is not to say that Verna is not a thoughtful woman, not a caring or deserving woman. She is all of those things. She acts in her own best interests (is not, that is, either self-destructive or a victim), but in the final analysis, none of these Jeffersonian efforts at American self-improvement secures her economic, physical, creative, or emotional future so much as does her serendipitous relationship with a rich and respectful man. So much for new feminist landscapes of westernness, right?

What I would call attention to are the ways in which this novel illustrates the changing languages through which critics might understand western regionalism at century's turn. If Freeman charts Verna's history through some of the more familiar genealogical tropes of western regional studies—that of the Mormon homesteader, the settler, descendent of pioneer or frontier family, the New World religious freedom fighter, willing to forge virtuous communities in hostile territories, etc.—Freeman also, by the time Verna gets to Los Angeles, makes use of the new language and conceptual grammar of cultural geography that is remaking regionalism today. Verna negotiates the overlapping borderlands or cultural contact zones[5] of MacArthur Park, El Segundo, East L.A., Beverly Hills, and points further south, finally ending up at Bahia de los Angeles, on the Baja peninsula in Mexico. This is every bit as much of a "new world" as was the last, but it is governed now by a new world order, meaning transnational (not mercantilist) capital. In this new transnational world, the *maquiladora* is the representative worker, a woman who works in a transnational sweatshop operated by corporations that do business everywhere except within their own First World nations, where labor is costly. If the *maquiladora*'s paid labor is cheap, her reproductive labor—that small matter of carrying, bearing, nursing, and then raising children—is free. Most of *Chinchilla Farm*'s female characters (including Verna) implicitly fit the bill, even if to differing degrees.

Even as they put in motion classic western plots, the landscapes of this text simultaneously disemplot the familiar "western moment" by registering the radically embattled social spaces in which women carry out their lives. Thus, if Verna goes out west to the lovely land of orange trees and sparkling water to make some better life for herself, if she travels that imaginative landscape of westernness that allows the autonomous national subject some form of mobility, some relief from social and personal problems, she hits a whole series of class- and gender-related bumps in the road, which detour her and force her, if she is not going to write against herself, onto another imaginative path.

It is on this alternative path—a landscape of postmodern, transnational, feminist solidarity—that Verna finds a new life, a renovated self. So the competing "western road trip" I would like to close with is the one in which Mormon Verna drives her Mexican American, Catholic, former sister-in-law and the woman's adult daughter (Verna's niece) across the border deep into Baja, Mexico, to escape a battering husband. When the man follows, the daughter Christobel, a retarded woman, "accidentally" murders this abusive man, who has also molested her. Included in the cast of characters making the transnational trek is homeless and malnourished Duluth, a man who perhaps has a new chance at life if he can manage to stay sober, eat regularly, and remain connected to some people—like these women—who recognize his humanity and are willing to put themselves out to help him get on his feet again.

The point about "putting themselves out" is crucial, because it separates Verna's brand of feminist practice from that of the other character more likely to be named "feminist" in this text—Jolene. Jolene is the identified "artist" of this text, a woman who talks about "my studio" and is very good, the reader can almost hear her say, at "taking care of herself." Indeed, it is to Jolene's posh, Beverly Hills house that Verna initially flees from Utah, so Jolene, quite explicitly, serves the role of "safety net" for Verna—but only if it doesn't inconvenience her too much or distract her. In the different kinds of personal politics each woman lives out we get Freeman's comment on the difference between a feminism of female networking versus a feminism of female solidarity. This latter brand, with its implicit critique of the class privilege and radical pretense of the self-absorbed feminist professional, is finally the one Freeman's chooses.

Such a definition returns contemporary feminist practice to its earlier more activist roots, but with a matured appreciation for the various contexts out of which radical politics grow. For, at least in my reading, Freeman ultimately invites the reader to locate Verna's feminist politics not within some commitment to women or "equality" per se, but rather—and I find this gesture movingly provocative—within the deep, caring ethic of community-oriented Mormonism. Verna, even if she drinks, smokes, and doesn't wear her Mormon undergarments, is less of a "fallen" Mormon than she thinks, for at heart she still takes it upon herself to get involved with people in need, even when, as community service always is, it's a serious hassle.

I hope, by the above discussion, to have quieted readerly qualms that I might end with some spin on the "sisterhood is global" thesis. Freeman doesn't cheat at the end of her tale, and neither will I. By implying above that the most politically effective way to relandscape the West of today is via an ethic of transnational, postmodern, feminist solidarity, I'm not saying that justice, thereafter, will prevail. Speaking only for myself, I've given up that hope. After all, the white woman is the luckiest one at the end of *Chinchilla Farm*. So even dumb luck isn't random.

But a refusal to flatten out differences between these women should not blind intellectuals to the fact that in the marketplace of the new global economy, these women *are* more or less the same, Jolene's "room of her own" notwithstanding. Without her benevolent benefactor, Verna, like most First World women across race and class, would be working in some limited-wage, service industry job. Pink-collar labor does not begin to be as bad as labor conditions for women get, given the backbreaking labor most women of Third World economies perform: staffing female sweatshops, hauling water, or tending crops and small livestock.

In the deepwater revolution days of the 1960s and early 1970s, idealism wasn't hard to come by, and nobody would've laid money on luck, when justice seemed obvious and "ours." But those days are a long time gone and the solutions, so easy to come by then, seem incredible now, foreign. Meanwhile, even if I can't imagine disavowing political engagement, I confess that lottery tickets hold more appeal than they used to. Although for many years I've turned up my nose at the religiosity of big skies, preferring instead to go swimming, perhaps it's time to pray.

Notes

Introduction

1. Regionalist leanings in literary criticism are most often associated with the Southern Agrarians, especially as expressed by critics Warren or Brooks, or by texts like *I'll Take My Stand* by Twelve Southerners (1930). For a look at the Texas regionalist movement in both history and literature see Dugger, *Three Men in Texas* (1967); in western history, see DeVoto, *Across the Wide Missouri* (1948); for the midwestern strain, see Jensen, *Regionalism in America* (1951). A number of significant literary studies that have become known as "national" rather than "regional" studies include Matthiessen's *American Renaissance* (1941) and Perry Miller's *The New England Mind* (1939).

2. The recent resurgence of regionalism has occasioned several reflections on earlier regionalist activities. For a lengthy discussion of the breadth of the regionalist project in the 1930s, see Brown, "The New Regionalism in America, 1970–81." See also Dorman, *Revolt of the Provinces*; Lamar, "Keeping the Faith: The Forgotten Generation of Literary Turnerians, 1920–60"; and Jordan, *Regionalism Reconsidered*. Although I am aware of the flurry of feminist critical activities focused on nineteenth-century "local color" writing by Sarah Orne Jewett, Mary Wilkins Freeman, Harriet Beecher Stowe, and others, in the main I do not link my own project to that one. Given its historical distance, the different racial composition of those regions, the sketch and short story forms of regionalism during most of the nineteenth century, and the already large task of reconsidering regionalism within postmodern western contexts, I ultimately chose to take indirect inspiration, if not direct instruction, from that commendable feminist project.

3. Some of the texts classified as belonging to the "American mind" school, such as Smith's *Virgin Land* (1950) or Matthiessen's *American Renaissance* (1941), could also be identified as regional texts.

4. Brown makes this point in relation to Pacific Northwestern regionalism, but it is one I would extend to the West (including California) at large. For a study of the shifting regional base of the national political machinery that sheds light on this change in leadership, see Sale, *Power Shift*.

5. This claim may surprise both critics and historians. For fuller discussion of the origins of the new western history in western literary discourse, see Comer, "Literature, Gender Studies, and the New Western History."

6. Exceptions to this statement exist, especially in the examples of Jack London, Frank Norris, Bret Harte, and the turn-of-the-century literary culture of San Francisco. Willa Cather is also a conspicuous exception. I should acknowledge, too, that I refer here to academic, not popular, reception of western literature, for western literature has long had widespread popular readership. Qualifications aside, I believe it remains true that even popular readers don't conceive of, say, Willa Cather as

part of a *"western* literary tradition,"because the academy is generally disinvested in conferring high-culture status on western cultural production. It is mainly in select western colleges and universities that there exists anything called "western literature."

7. The conspicuous exception is Patricia Limerick, an avid promoter of the new literary regionalism who also tries to understand its origins. See Limerick, "The Realization of the American West." For Limerick's further thoughts on western literature, refer to a plenary on western history and literature held at the 1996 joint meeting of the Western Historical Association and the Western Literature Association in Lincoln, Nebraska. For a more writerly view, see Stegner, "Coming of Age: The End of the Beginning." For a critic's comments, see Kowalewski, "Introduction," in *Reading the West;* for an earlier perspective focused on women's writing, see Norwood and Monk, *The Desert Is No Lady.*

8. See especially Love, *New Americans.* Also see Stegner, "History, Myth and the Western Writer" and "Born a Square."

9. Milton, *The Novel of the American West.* Milton does not include any female writers among those he studies. If he had, he might have come to more complex conclusions, for Kolodny's *The Land Before Her* demonstrates that western female literary traditions develop also from nineteenth-century domestic fiction.

10. Bevis, "Region, Power, Place," 22.

11. Periodization is by no means a settled matter in postmodern theoretical debates. Waugh sees postmodernist form and pathos as early as the British Romanticism of the early 1800s (see *Practising Postmodernism, Reading Modernism*). My own inclination is to begin from 1972, the moment of economic/political and cultural metamorphosis that geographer Harvey claims in *The Condition of Postmodernity,* and which is the more agreed-upon periodization. Also see Mercer, " '1968': Periodizing Postmodern Politics and Identity."

12. In one of the only essays to date to ponder the role of postmodernism in contemporary western cultural production, Bevis characterizes regionalism as "subversive" of what he calls postmodernist culture's bottomless "liquidity," wherein all human needs and desires are commodified and negotiable. Native American writers and the Rocky Mountain regionalists, what Bevis calls the "dry land realists," refuse to barter identity and place in exchange for mobility and freedom. Although Bevis's formulation compels, I disagree finally with its general anti-postmodern bent and, as will become clear, regard some of those same writers through different conceptual and historical frames. See Bevis, "Region, Power, Place."

13. On the notion of postmodernist subjectivity as akin to the fractured subjectivities of many an oppressed person, see Harper's *Framing the Margins.* Also see Hogue, *Race, Modernity, Postmodernity;* and hooks, *Yearning.*

14. Commentators and theorists regularly note the slipperiness of definitions of postmodernism. For a concise statement of the problematic, see Hutcheon's entry on postmodernism in *Encyclopedia of Contemporary Literary Theory.* For more developed discussions, see Lyotard, "Answering the Question: What Is Postmodernism"; Huyssen, "Mapping the Postmodern"; and J. Butler, "Contingent Foundations."

15. F. Jameson, *Postmodernism,* 6.

16. I refer here to some of the major arguments in the "big books" on postmod-

ernism: Jameson's *Postmodernism*, Harvey's *The Condition of Postmodernity*, and Soja's *Postmodern Geographies*.

17. Selected materials that have influenced my own understanding of the relationships between modernity, feminism, and debates about postmodernism include Harstock, "Rethinking Modernism: Minority vs. Majority Theories"; Fraser and Nicholson, "Social Criticism Without Philosophy: An Encounter Between Feminism and Postmodernism"; Hutcheon, *A Poetics of Postmodernism* and *The Politics of Postmodernism*; Nicholson, *Feminism/Postmodernism*; Haraway, *Simians, Cyborgs, and Women*; and J. Butler, "Contingent Foundations: Feminism and the Question of Postmodernism." I also have been influenced by postcolonial theory, and its inflection of conversations about postmodernity and advanced capitalism with postcolonial thematics like "location" and "mobile subjectivities." See especially Bhabha, *The Location of Culture*; and Blunt and Rose, *Writing Women and Space*.

18. The political impetus and logic for contemporary American and western European feminisms owe unacknowledged debts to anticolonial ideologies and movements worldwide—hence my choice of the word "overlooked." Though scholars frequently locate the roots of second-wave American feminism in domestic civil rights movements, the larger, post–World War II, anti-imperial milieu that fueled the political aspirations of American blacks in particular has not been adequately investigated. Thus the involved task of attributing more complex and transnational origins to contemporary feminism awaits doing. For some indication of what such an investigation might look like, but one that is focused on nineteenth- and early-twentieth-century feminist agitation, see Rupp, *Worlds of Women*.

19. I wish to thank Stephen Tatum for suggestions that aided me in developing this section more elaborately than I originally intended.

20. Dainotto, " 'All the Regions Do Smilingly Revolt.' "

21. I refer here to *The West as America: Reinterpreting Images of the Frontier*, a spring 1991 exhibition of western art at the National Museum of American Art of the Smithsonian Institution, Washington, D.C.

22. See "Coda: A Wilderness Letter," 147. The actual quote is "[wilderness] is the challenge against which our character as a people was formed." Stegner did not qualify his remark with the adjective "dominant," as have I.

23. Berlant's work, though focused mainly on the nineteenth century, nonetheless pertains. She defines the National Symbolic as "the order of discursive practices whose reign within a national space . . . transforms individuals into subjects of a collectively held history. Its traditional icons, its metaphors, its heroes, its rituals, and its narratives provide an alphabet for a collective consciousness or national subjectivity; through the National Symbolic, the historical nation aspires to achieve the inevitability of the status of natural law, a birthright" (*Anatomy of National Fantasy*, 20).

24. This argument does not implicitly suggest that previous generations of western writers (i.e., midcentury writers like Frank Waters, A. B. Guthrie, Walter Van Tilburg Clark, or Wallace Stegner) were uncritical consumers or producers of mainstream American masculinist nationalism. Such a claim vastly oversimplifies a far more complex production of masculine subjectivity and gendered national affiliation. Thus, I would be inclined to argue something more in keeping with the work of

Carton, cited more fully in note 30 below. Nonetheless, comparatively, the new regionalists thoroughly part company with their predecessors, and the reasons for this owe to the vastly more racially diverse composition of new regionalist discourse as well as to the impact of feminism upon social policy and the ways that people understand and perform gender relations.

25. For a history of this moment, see Limerick, Milner, and Rankin, *Trails*.

26. Again I owe thanks to Stephen Tatum, who urged more analytic pressure on Reaganism and the new regionalism.

27. For a discussion of "cowboy diplomacy," see Sale, *Power Shift*.

28. In the language of a "remasculinized America," I borrow from Jeffords's fine work on the political effect of literature of the Vietnam War, *The Remasculinization of America*. Jeffords argues that narratives about the discovery of male-centered community in "the Vietnam experience" (as represented in film, criticism, and literature) ultimately served the purposes of a larger, anti–affirmative action and antifeminist cultural project at home. Such an argument translates aptly to the ways that Reagan deployed alleged tenets of "the authentic western experience" to justify administrative philosophies that ultimately attacked some of the most important policy gains made by feminists and civil rights activists during the 1970s.

29. See Faludi, *Backlash: The Undeclared War against American Women*.

30. I have located the new regionalism here in opposition to Reaganism, whereas earlier I have implied that some antifeminist impulses also motivate early male new regionalist discourse. Readers may therefore wonder what kinds of *different* masculinist projects these contending western enterprises produce. Although I do not attempt in this book a fully elaborated answer to this question, I do offer some beginning thoughts in Chapter 1. For now, I would say that Jeffords's reading of the cultural work of Vietnam literatures seems ripe for application to many tales of masculinity that take western topographies as their starting point. Vietnam veterans' searches for new modes of masculine self-identification while in the midst of war, one of the most indelibly masculinist of contexts, reminds me of the efforts western male writers make to rearticulate masculine self-hood from the heart of the nation's most masculinist landscape, that of the West. I would suggest, however, as does Carton in "Vietnam and the Limits of Masculinity," that a far more equivocal and complex masculinism than that of Reaganism or veteran war narratives is at work in western literary projects that forward male bonding (whether Chicano, Asian American, or white) as an implicit base for social change, renewal, or justice. These masculine projects may, indeed, destabilize the antifeminism of the Reagan era.

31. I draw here from the research of Brown University graduate student Laura Santigian. See her dissertation in progress, "Revision and Resistance: Gender, Race and Memory in Public History of the American West."

32. The Steamboat event, held in September 1993, was called "Literary Sojourn: Steamboat Springs Festival of Women Authors." An annual "Writers and Readers Rendezvous" in McCall, Idaho, was established in 1992, and its 1993 meeting featured a special segment on women writers.

33. A MacArthur was awarded to Silko in 1980 and to Cisneros in 1995. For *Love Medicine*, Erdrich won both the Book Critics Circle Award for fiction and the *Los*

Angeles Times award for the best novel of 1985. *The Woman Warrior: Memoirs of a Girlhood Among Ghosts* won Kingston the 1976 National Book Critics Circle Award for nonfiction.

34. There is a quite developed literature on the problematic politics of "multiculturalism." For one recent discussion, see Aparicio, "On Multiculturalism and Privilege." For a differently focused but quite relevant perspective, see duCille, "The Occult of True Black Womanhood." On 1980s and 90s politics and white supremacy, see Omi and Winant, *Racial Formation in the United States*. See also Gordon and Newfield, *Mapping Multiculturalism*.

35. See Johnson, " 'A Memory Sweet to Soldiers.' "

36. Consider the titles of many major twentieth-century literary Westerns, poetry, and prose: Mary Austin's *The Land of Little Rain* (1903), Ole Rolvaag's *Giants in the Earth* (1927), Vardis Fisher's *Toilers in the Hills* (1928), Conrad Richter's *The Sea of Grass* (1936), Walter Van Tilburg Clark's *The Ox-Bow Incident* (1940), Wallace Stegner's *The Big Rock Candy Mountain* (1943), Mildred Walker's *Winter Wheat* (1944), A. B. Guthrie's *The Big Sky* (1947) and *The Way West* (1949), Jean Stafford's *The Mountain Lion* (1947), Wallace Stegner's *Wolf Willow* (1962), Joan Didion's *Run River* (1963), N. Scott Momaday's *House Made of Dawn* (1968), Edward Abbey's *Desert Solitaire* (1968), Jeanne Wakatsuki Houston's *Farewell to Manzanar* (1973), James Welch's *Winter in the Blood* (1974), Ivan Doig's *This House of Sky* (1978), Gretel Ehrlich's *The Solace of Open Spaces* (1985), Mitsuye Yamada's *Desert Run* (1986), Gloria Anzaldúa's *Borderlands/La Frontera: The New Mestiza* (1987), Barbara Kingsolver's *The Bean Trees* (1988), Terry Tempest Williams's *Refuge* (1991), Jane Candia Coleman's *No Roof But Sky* (1991), Him Mark Lai, Ginny Lim, and Judy Yung's *Island* (1991), Sandra Cisneros's *Woman Hollering Creek* (1991), William Kittredge's *A Hole in the Sky* (1992), Lisa See's *On Gold Mountain* (1995).

37. Western landscape is very important to critics, too; see Quantic, *The Nature of the Place*; Engel, *The Big Empty*; Nelson, *Place and Vision*; Thacker, *The Great Prairie Fact and Literary Imagination*; Wyatt, *Fall Into Eden*. Feminist studies of the literary west—for example, Kolodny's *The Lay of the Land* and *The Land Before Her* and Norwood and Monk's *The Desert Is No Lady*—also participate in this tradition.

38. Daniels, "Introduction," *Fields of Vision*, 8.

39. See, for example, Pugh, *Reading Landscape*; Daniels, *Fields of Vision*; W. G. T. Mitchell, *Landscape and Power*; or treatments of landscape in the works of any of the most prominent of feminist geographers, such as Rose or Massey.

40. Most of the western studies critics that I have thus far listed ascribe to the notion of a redemptive nature. A few are to some extent self-critiquing. Critics of Native American women's and Chicana literature also hold out this belief.

41. The perceptual geographers most often cited by western critics and historians include Meinig, *Interpretation of Ordinary Landscapes*; Lowenthal and Bowden, *Geographies of the Mind*; and Tuan, *Topophilia*.

42. Bevis, *Ten Tough Trips*; Silko, "Landscape, History, and the Pueblo Imagination"; Nelson, *Place and Vision*; Papanikolas, *Trickster in the Land of Dreams*.

43. From W. G. T. Mitchell, "Introduction," *Landscape and Power*, 2.

44. The language of "cultural practice" I draw from Mitchell.

45. I gratefully acknowledge ecocritic and feminist Patrick Murphy, who initially pointed out to me this crucial point.

46. W. G. T. Mitchell, *Landscape and Power*, 6.

47. Massey, *Space, Place and Gender*, 4. Like most theoretical geographers, Massey credits Lefebvre (*The Production of Space*) for his groundbreaking emphasis on space as a social agent.

48. I draw very closely here, in my goals, from Gregory, *Geographical Imaginations*.

49. For comments on the political conservatism of "place," see Harvey, *The Condition of Postmodernity*, 302. Also see Massey, *Space, Place and Gender*, 6–13, for a concise political evaluation.

50. The feminist literature on southern and New England women's regional traditions is developed, and I am no expert in it. I have learned much from various introductions to selected regional literary texts, and also from Donovan, *New England Local Color*; Fetterley and Pryse, *American Women Regionalists 1850–1910*; Fetterley, "Theorizing Regionalism"; Pryse, "Origins of American Literary Regionalism"; and Kaplan, "Nation, Region, and Empire."

51. Quoted in Inness and Royer, "Introduction," 4. I hesitate to name Brodhead (*Cultures of Letters*) because the antifeminism of his other work would seem to discredit this observation.

Chapter One

1. Stegner and Etulain, *Conversations with Wallace Stegner*, 141. On Steinbeck's disbelief, see *Los Angeles Times*, Oct. 26, 1962, Calendar Section, page number illegible.

2. *Los Angeles Times*, Oct. 26, 1992, page number illegible. Also see Espmark, *Nobel Prize in Literature*. Espmark quotes Nobel panelist Lundkvist, who reasoned that "if attention had been focused on the *renewal* of narrative fiction, then Steinbeck would at once have been out of the picture in favor of authors like Durrell, Beckett, or Claude Simon, who from an artistic and psychological point of view are much more central" (82).

3. *New York Times*, Oct. 26, 1962, 30:2.

4. Mizener, "Does a Moral Vision," VII:4.

5. Ibid., VII:44.

6. Ibid.

7. Haase, "Steinbeck Detractors."

8. Ibid.

9. Ibid.

10. Mizener, "Does a Moral Vision," VII:45.

11. On the relationship between an Archimedean worldview, stable points of origin, modernity, and postmodernity, see Gregory, *Geographical Imaginations*, 9. Gregory draws, in part, from Clifford, "Introduction: Partial Truths," in Clifford and Marcus, *Writing Culture*, 1–26.

12. The gendered notion of "visual ideology" I want to forward is developed in Rose, *Feminism and Geography*.

13. The claim that social relations always assume spatialized forms, that spatial logics mirror American social values, can be illustrated in any number of ways. Think, for instance, of the historical links between emerging industrial capitalism and the slow segmentation of American society into public and private spheres. Or the links between racial segregation (in housing, education, public facilities, etc.) and ideologies of racial inferiority. Social logics underlie all cartographic operations and appearances, whether they distinguish the rural from the urban, the workaday world from that of leisure, the racialized from deracialized spaces, the sexualized from "family" spaces, or the national heartland from the borderlands. The above spaces not only suggest different social worlds but also, usually, unequal worlds— some highly regarded, some deeply denigrated. We speak today of "women's culture," "mall culture," "gay culture," "youth culture," "ghetto culture," "country club culture," or "cyberculture." Each of these cultures implies spatial dimensions, social geometry. Country club culture is linked to explicit topographies—golf courses, tennis courts, swimming pools, expansive greenbelts. Upon them, club members live out who they are, prohibit entry to those they are not. Ghetto culture, likewise, is linked to explicit topographies—high-rise urban projects, high-density demographics, poverty. Through them, members also express who they are, albeit with absolutely compromised abilities to prohibit entry to those whom they are not.

14. Most theoreticians credit the development of theories of space and their implication in social relations to Lefebvre, *The Production of Space*. Space-based analyses play a defining role in the restructuring of much modern critical social theory (i.e., the works of "giants" like Jameson, Foucault, Berger). Feminist theory also locates itself in this tradition, though with considerable critique. For an example, see "Flexible Sexism," Massey's review of Soja's *Postmodern Geographies* and Harvey's *Condition of Postmodernity*.

15. Massey, *Space, Place and Gender*, 2.

16. The new western history has taken up these questions with increasing vigor. For studies that offer changing approaches to western regionalism, see Udall's *Contested Terrain* (1996) and Morrissey's *Mental Territories* (1998). Also see Ostler and Johnston, "Politics and Antipolitics of Western History."

17. Quoted as epigraph in McClure, "Late Imperial Romance," 111.

18. The term "contingency" I draw from contexts developed by Judith Butler in "Contingent Foundations," though the notion of contingency is a political conclusion drawn by many theorists, in quite different terms. See Lefebvre's notion of "differential space," Gregory's notion of "traveling," Rose's notion of "paradoxical space," Bhabha's notion of "third space," and so on.

19. For specific works devoted to different approaches to these issues, see Kirby, "Thinking through the Boundary"; Gutiérrez-Jones, "Desiring B/Orders"; Haraway, "Situated Knowledges"; Higonnet and Templeton, *Reconfigured Spheres*.

20. Rose, *Feminism and Geography*, 2.

21. Ibid., 143.

22. This point is the starting point for most British landscape studies and is ripe

for development in western studies. One recent book that addresses the colonialist narrative inherent in much nineteenth-century, American women's writing is Georgi-Findlay's *Frontiers of Women's Writing*.

23. The most recent example is Baym, *American Women Writers and the Work of History, 1790–1860* (1995), in which Baym distinguishes between "official history" and "public history." However, also see Tompkins, *Sensational Designs* (1985); Kelley, *Private Woman, Public Stage* (1984); Gilbert and Gubar, *The Madwoman in the Attic* (1974); Carby, *Reconstructing Womanhood* (1987); and Ammons, *Conflicting Stories* (1992). Less explicitly focused on this issue but still relevant is Showalter, *New Feminist Criticism*.

24. These are complicated claims, for many exceptions to my generalizations exist. "Major" works would include the type listed in note 23 just above, Ammons being a conspicuous exception. Certainly the notion of "location" has been around a while, as, for example, in Adrienne Rich's "Notes Toward a Politics of Location" (1986). But the real impetus to reconsider the role of space in the production of power has commenced more recently, as feminists have engaged postmodernity and postcolonial theory. For examples of the reconsideration, see responses to Rich, including Probyn, "Travels in the Postmodern: Making Sense of the Local"; and Kirby, "Thinking Through the Boundary."

25. For an example that inspired my own intents, see Kaplan, "Romancing the Empire."

26. The exceptions are Norwood and Monk, *The Desert Is No Lady*; and Graulich, "O Beautiful for Spacious Guys."

27. One writer, Mary Austin, is sometimes mentioned. But in all, studies of western literature are 90 percent devoted to male literature and literary history; they are conceived without attention to feminist concerns or gendered analysis (of men or women) or to influences upon men by women writers or female literary traditions. As examples, see Wyatt, *Fall Into Eden*; Bredahl, *New Ground*; Milton, *Novel of the American West*; Pilkington, *Critical Essays on the Western American Novel*; Siegel, "Contemporary Trends in Western American Fiction."

28. On economic and social change, see Limerick, "Realization of the American West"; and Brown, "The New Regionalism in America, 1970–1981."

29. On alternative publishing, see Haslam, "Unknown Diversity: Small Presses and Little Magazines in the West"; and Bodian, "Influence of the Small Press on American Book Publishing."

30. The running dates of these publications are *Revista Chicano-Riquena* (1973–85), *El Grito* (1967–74), *Dacotah Territory* (1971–80), *Greenfield Review Press* (1970–87). Lorna Dee Cervantes's "Beneath the Shadow of the Freeway" first comes out in a slightly more highbrow, but still similar, magazine, *Latin American Literary Review*.

31. For some examples of Black Arts cultural production, see Harper and Stepto, *Chant of Saints*. On the undervalued nature of the movement, see D. L. Smith, "Black Arts Movement and Its Critics."

32. The writers and movements associated with the following literary trajectories invoke primarily northern/southern spatial fields: writers of the colonial period (especially Phyllis Wheatley), abolitionist slave narratives, the post–Civil War lib-

eral elite of Philadelphia, modernism and the Harlem Renaissance, contemporary southerners, and so on.

33. On the California link, see K. K. Miller, "Black Studies in California Higher Education, 1965–1980," excerpted as "Black Studies and Higher Education," in Chan, Daniels, García, and Wilson, *Peoples of Color in the American West*, 533–39.

34. A developed literature exists on Aztlán and its meaning for early 1960s Chicano community building and cultural nationalism. For a highly regarded introduction to some of these issues, see Anaya and Lomeli, *Aztlán*.

35. The phrase "topospatial analysis" appears in Saldívar's *Border Matters*, 72–91. Also see Gutiérrez-Jones, *Rethinking the Borderlands*; Anzaldúa, *Borderlands/La Frontera*; and Calderon and Saldívar, *Criticism in the Borderlands*, to name only the best known.

36. This impression is created by both fictional and historical narratives. Most of Asian American literature, especially in the early twentieth century, locates itself in western states. Asian American historiography is also weighted heavily in favor of western labor patterns, western Chinatowns and Japantowns, and western gender relations, because so much of immigration-related legal history is centered in California. To rectify this western-weighted influence, the annual conference "East of California" was established, sponsored by a New York–based group of Asian Americanists.

37. For an excellent example of criticism on interethnic difference, see Cheung, *Interethnic Companion to Asian American Literature*; on the differences between immigration trends of the late 1800s to early 1900s versus those of the 1960s to 1980s, see Takaki, *Strangers from a Different Shore*.

38. For comment on the West Coast phenomenon, see Wong, *Reading Asian American Literature*, 3. For a comparative perspective about what indeed constitutes "multiculturalism," one that shows that Asian American academic strongholds remain in California, consider Gordon and Newfield, *Mapping Multiculturalism*.

39. See, for example, Berkhofer, *The White Man's Indian*; Fiedler, *Return of the Vanishing American*.

40. For example, in *The Novel of the American West*, Milton speaks often of the "mysticism" of western literature.

41. On the history of Arte Público Press, see Rivera, "Rules of Chicano Cultural Production."

42. I indicate in what follows only a sampling of the most frequently cited magazines, journals, and small presses. Hundreds were founded and published at least a few issues in this period. Two archives with particularly rich holdings are the Memorial Literary Special Collections on Little Magazines at Brown University's Hay Library and the University of Wisconsin at Madison's Special Collection on Literary Magazines. These are among the best national sources for future scholarly work in this area. Len Fulton, founder of Dustbooks Press in Paradise, California, a legendary small press and publisher of the annual *International Directory of Little Magazines and Small Presses* (in its thirty-second edition in 1997–98), is an excellent resource on this topic; he also possesses a treasure trove of a personal library. Gerald Haslam is the informal overseer of another promising collection now forming at California State University at Sonoma.

43. For instance, several poems by Garrett Hongo appear in *Mango* 2 (1979–80): n.p.

44. These examples are drawn from the acknowledgments sections in Bruchac, *Songs from This Earth on Turtle's Back*; Fisher, *The Third Woman*; and Asian Women United of California, *Making Waves*. For attention to the publishing history of Chicana literary production, see Rebolledo and Rivero, *Infinite Divisions*. For some sense of early Asian American male literary history, see Chan, Chin, Fusao, and Wong, *The Big Aiiieeeee!*

45. See note 27 above for some of the field's founding critical books. The major male writers include Frank Waters, A. B. Guthrie, Walter Van Tilburg Clark, and Wallace Stegner.

46. These critical writings include Stegner, "History, Myth and the Western Writer" (1967) and "Born a Square" (1964); Stegner and Etulain, *Conversations with Wallace Stegner on Western Literature and History*, esp. "The Literary West" (1979) and "Ten Years Later" (1989); Stegner, *The American West as Living Space* (1987); and Stegner, *Where the Bluebird Sings to the Lemonade Springs* (1992).

47. Stegner's biography is well-known, at least among western critics. On Stegner as "dean" of western literature, see Stegner and Etulain, *Conversations with Wallace Stegner*, 94–98. For tributes honoring Stegner's life and work, see "A Tribute to Wallace Stegner," a collection of essays originally published in 1993 in the journal *Montana* and later expanded and reissued in Rankin, *Wallace Stegner: Man and Writer*. For a very critical rendering, see Cook-Lynn, *Why I Can't Read Wallace Stegner*.

48. Critics like Robinson and Tatum have taken up popular genres with much more sophistication than this statement allows. See Robinson, *Having It Both Ways*; and Tatum, "The Problem of the 'Popular' in the New Western History."

49. This anxiety is visible in both "Born a Square" and "History, Myth and the Western Writer."

50. Stegner, "History, Myth and the Western Writer," 189. Stegner imports into his own reading of western culture the racist assumptions of Frederick Jackson Turner. See Turner, "Significance of the Frontier in American History" (1986 [1893]).

51. Stegner, "Born a Square," 178. .

52. If one doubts the degree to which white, Anglo men look up to Stegner as a man, consider Rankin, *Wallace Stegner: Man and Writer*, or any of the Stegner biographies.

53. Stegner with Etulain, *Conversations with Wallace Stegner*, 138.

54. Ibid.

55. The lecture series was published as *The American West as Living Space* (1987).

56. Stegner, "Introduction," in *Where the Bluebird Sings*, xv. See also "Born a Square."

57. Stegner, "Coda," 153.

58. Stegner, "Born a Square" and *Where the Bluebird Sings*.

59. Stegner, "Introduction," in *Where the Bluebird Sings*.

60. I would refer the reader to Limerick's "Realization of the American West," as well as Morrissey's excellent "Commentary," on Limerick's speech.

61. Martin Bucco, "Epilogue: The Development of Western Literary Criticism,"

in Western Literature Association, *Literary History of the American West*, 1283–1316.

62. Bredahl, *New Ground*, 48.

63. See Stegner and Stegner, *Geography of Hope* (1996); and Benson's biography, *Wallace Stegner* (1996).

64. Stegner, "Introduction," in *Where the Bluebird Sings*, xv ("cautious"); "Ten Years Later," in *Conversations with Wallace Stegner*, xxii ("pessimistic"); "Striking the Rock," in *American West as Living Space*, 60 ("no more the Eden").

65. From Stegner, "Coming of Age, The End of the Beginning," in *Where the Bluebird Sings*.

66. See Comer, "Wallace Stegner and the Problem of the 'Authentic West,'" unpublished manuscript.

67. Graulich in particular finds a usable past in Stegner's emphasis on "the legitimate inclination of the sexes." See Graulich, "O Beautiful for Spacious Guys," "Gettin' Hitched," and "The Guides to Conduct that a Tradition Offers."

68. Stegner to author, personal correspondence, Oct. 27 and Sept. 22, 1992.

69. Stegner to author, personal correspondence, Sept. 25, 1992.

70. Ibid.

71. See, for example, *One Nation* (1945), which shows Stegner's sophisticated understanding of the economic, cultural, and social factors that make for racist discrimination.

72. I am grateful to historian Ruth Feldstein for first suggesting this possibility to me.

73. See Allen, *Sacred Hoop* (1986), and Allen's reading of Silko in "The Psychological Landscape of *Ceremony*." See also Fisher, *Third Woman*, 18–23.

74. See Chambram-Dernersesian, "I Throw Punches for My Race." For a survey of early 1970s writings that critiqued the masculinism of Aztlán, see Fernandez, "*Abriendo caminos* in the Brotherland"; also see Gutiérrez, "Community, Patriarchy, and Individualism."

75. See Bow, "'For Every Gesture of Loyalty, There Doesn't Have to Be a Betrayal': Asian American Criticism and the Politics of Locality"; and Ling, *Between Worlds*.

76. See, for example, Schneir, *Feminism in Our Time*; Echols, *Daring to Be Bad*; and Evans, *Personal Politics*.

77. Echols, *Daring to Be Bad*, 387–90.

78. The Schneir text circulates widely as a textbook in introductions to women's studies, evidence of its perceived accuracy. A promotional blurb on the front jacket cover touts it as "a landmark collection . . . that provides the most powerful portrait to date" of contemporary feminism. What I would draw attention to is use of the word "powerful," and my claim is that that claim is empowered because 90 percent of the women featured herein, and the kinds of political documents they write, are associated with what is already the most intellectually and politically powerful region in the nation, the Northeast. A similar sensibility operates in Echols's and Evans's books.

79. I use the example of the Asian American movement because it is conceived not so much through civil rights rhetorics as through anti-Vietnam protest. See Chan, "Asian American Movement, 1960s–1980s."

80. See Armitage and Jameson, *The Women's West*; Schlissel, Ruíz, and Monk, *Western Women*; or the conceptual framework of a book like Deutsch, *No Separate Refuge*.

81. For an elegant elaboration of this problem as it relates to feminist environmentalism, see Sturgeon, *Ecofeminist Natures*.

82. Lipsitz, *Time Passages*; Radway, *Reading the Romance*.

83. Franzen, "Differences and Identities"; K. Jay, *Tales of the Lavender Menace*.

84. Lipsitz makes this point about Joplin in *Time Passages*, 129.

85. See Harjo and Bird, et al., *Reinventing the Enemy's Language*.

86. I'm thinking here of the boost that the women's movement got from President Kennedy's Commission on the Status of Women, from Title VII of the Civil Rights Act of 1964, and the Hearings on Women's Rights sponsored by the New York City Commission on Human Rights in 1970. In terms of literary gatekeepers, I refer to the general tolerance of the northeastern reviewing staff, the majority of whom during these years were men. If one compares the receptiveness of the *New York Times* or the *Nation* to the boldest of feminist texts—like *Woman Warrior*—to that of other papers, the northeastern press is leagues ahead in feminist conscience.

87. *The Nation*, June 5, 1989, 768–72.

88. Lefebvre deals with this extensively in "From the Contradictions of Space to Differential Space," in *Production of Space*, 352–400; also see note 18 for elaborations of "contingent" spatialities.

89. The term "place" has wide theoretical play. I am drawing here from the historiographic genealogy set up by Rose in *Feminism and Geography*, 86–112.

90. The language of "all spatial scales" belongs to Massey, *Space, Place, and Gender*, 5.

Chapter Two

1. Also see Findlay, *Magic Lands*; Abbott, *Metropolitan Frontier*; Nash and Etulain, *Twentieth-Century West*, esp. 14–51.

2. For a discussion of contemporary regional identity and its incorporation of urbanism, see particularly Findlay, *Magic Lands*; also Wetherby and Witt, *Urban West*.

3. To make this claim is to negotiate complex theoretical terrain. Feminist theorists like Judith Butler, Joan Scott, Linda J. Nicholson, and Donna Haraway have demonstrated the compromised pitfalls and complications of such an urge or hope, locating female oppression within the formation of the very idea of the bourgeois, autonomous political subject, that is, within the political ideals of the Enlightenment and humanist modernism. For a recent discussion, see J. W. Scott, *Only Paradoxes to Offer*. Recent feminist theorists have thus often placed their own political hopes in poststructural and also postmodernist theories of political subjectivity due to their conviction that the terms of "the political" need thorough recasting if the hope of liberation in other than male terms is to be realized. See Nicholson, *Feminism/Postmodernism*; J. Butler, "Contingent Foundations."

4. Graulich, "O Beautiful for Spacious Guys"; also see Rudnick, "Re-Naming the Land."

5. As regards nineteenth-century Mexican American literary history, I am refer-

ring to the vast amounts of material emerging from "Recovering the Hispanic Literary Past," a project sponsored by Arte Público Press in Houston, Texas. For an overview of what the Recovery Project may ultimately accomplish, see Gutiérrez and Padilla, *Recovering the U.S. Hispanic Literary Heritage*, esp. "Introduction," 17–25. On recent findings in Asian American literary history, see Matsumoto, "Desperately Seeking 'Dierdre' "; and Ling, "Chinese American Women Writers." For selected essays that speak to early-twentieth-century developments in Asian American cultural production, see Cheung, *Interethnic Companion to Asian American Literature*.

6. One notable example coming out of the Recovery Project cited above is that of María Amparo Ruiz de Burton, a relatively unknown writer who is sure to become a pivotal figure in nineteenth-century American literary studies. It is by no means clear that Ruiz de Burton was in any sense an antimodernist. She certainly did not partake of primitivist discourse and did not look to Native American culture for Mexican or American salvation. She fully invested herself, her money, influence, political energies, and literary talents in what she saw as the only hope for the Californio elite: modern European American nation-building. See Aranda, "Contradictory Impulses." Also see Ruiz de Burton, *Who Would Have Thought It?*

7. The longer quote from which I select appears in Sizemore, "Masculine and Feminine Cities," 91. It is drawn from de Lauretis's *Alice Doesn't*.

8. This claim holds for Soja's survey of European radical theories of space in *Postmodern Geographies*. Harvey's theoretical histories in *Condition of Postmodernity* are similarly male. For a useful critique of the male-gendered genealogy through which contemporary urban planning theory is charted, see Hooper, " 'Split at the Roots.' " For very thoughtful and extended responses to both Harvey and Soja, see Gregory, *Geographical Imaginations*.

9. Squier, *Women Writers and the City*.

10. Mike Davis alludes to this fact as it relates to Central European intellectuals who arrived in L.A. fleeing fascism in "The Exiles," *City of Quartz*, 46–54.

11. Soja, *Postmodern Geographies*, 221.

12. Feminists in urban history, planning, and geography have criticized Soja and Harvey, in particular. See Hayden, *Power of Place*; Massey, "Flexible Sexism." For a critique of Soja, see Hooper, "Split at the Roots."

13. For example, Cynthia Kadohata, Lisa See, Kate Braverman, Lucha Corpi, Carolyn See, Lucille Clifton, the "Taco Shop" Poets, etc.

14. Quoted in epigraph, DeLeon, *Left Coast City*, 1.

15. The subheading of this section takes off from Carey McWilliams's paradigm-setting book, *California: The Great Exception*.

16. Walter Nugent's survey of historians and writers, "Where Is the American West," finds that it is Californians, usually, who see themselves as westerners, whereas non-Californians see Californians as nonwesterners.

17. A groundbreaking book that evidences a similar sense for California as part of the West is Haslam's recent anthology *Many Californias*.

18. See Loris's *Innocence, Loss, and Recovery in the Art of Joan Didion*, which addresses this topic in "*Run River*: Paradise Lost," 11–29.

19. See the introduction to the book's reissue in 1864, "Twenty-Four Years After."

The introduction looks back upon the "original" California with a fondness that is absent in the original text. The interim nostalgia has been created by the end of the Gold Rush and the creation of an emerging, broader western mythology.

20. Wyatt, *Fall Into Eden*.

21. By "others," I offer as examples the writers showcased in the anthology *Many Californias*, edited by Gerald Haslam.

22. My largest debt on Los Angeles culture is to Davis's *City of Quartz*. Other critics who take up the negative image that Los Angelenos hold of their city include Reid, *Sex, Death, and God in L.A.*; and Fine, *Los Angeles in Fiction*, esp. Lehan, "The Los Angeles Novel and the Idea of the West."

23. For a sample of Didion criticism, see Friedman, *Joan Didion*; Brady, "Points West, Then and Now"; and Felton, *Critical Response to Joan Didion*. Interestingly, one of Didion's most able reviewers is Guy Davenport at *National Review*. Similarly conservative, Davenport understands and empathizes with what he sees as Didion's portrayal of the "running out of tradition"; see Davenport, "Midas' Grandchildren" and "On the Edge of Being."

24. Didion, *The White Album*. See especially part 3, "Women," 109–32.

25. In an earlier essay, I argued against locating a feminist legacy in Didion; see Comer, "Joan Didion's California."

26. This claim that Didion does not find a "home" is a very big one, and I can take it up only briefly here. After *Run River* and *Play It as It Lays*, Didion never again writes what feels like a "western" book, though western themes remain central to her essays and though some of the later books also remain centered upon westernlike regional studies (for example, Miami, Salvador, and the fictional Central American country featured in *Book of Common Prayer*). I think Didion cannot resolve the issue of form and its relationship to gendered subjectivity, and her reliance on postmodernist formal strategies alone does not adequately incorporate for her her own western but female sensibilities. She is forced between two categories, woman and western, and she opts out of both. I think the move is finally detrimental to the strange kind of heart visible in her early work.

27. Davis, *City of Quartz*, 20.

28. Many reviewers objected vigorously to *Run River*. The *New Yorker* called it a "depiction of human leftovers" (May 11, 1963, 39:178). Similar sentiments were expressed in the *London Times Literary Supplement*, Jan. 30, 1964, 92; *Los Angeles Times*, May 19, 1963, Calendar section, 18. For an interesting exception, see *National Review*, May 7, 1963, 14:371.

29. Plimpton, *Paris Review Interviews*, 347.

30. Didion's belief that Sacramento is the "real California" is drawn from "Notes from a Native Daughter," in *Slouching Towards Bethlehem*.

31. Ibid., 187.

32. It should thus come as no surprise that, of all of her reviewers, the *National Review* (conservative William Buckley's publication) is usually Didion's most comprehending one, for it too, like Didion, generally enacts an anti–civil rights, white racialist social philosophy. See Davenport sources cited in note 23.

33. See Comer, "Joan Didion's California."

34. Subsequent references to this book are noted parenthetically in the text.

35. For Didion's existentialism, see Fine's *Los Angeles in Fiction* (esp. the introduction, 1–29) and Peters's "The Los Angeles Anti-Myth."

36. Fine, *Los Angeles in Fiction*, 2, 7.

37. Davis provides these examples: the novels of Didion herself, John Gregory Dunne (Didion's husband), and Evelyn Wambaugh; the movies *Chinatown* and *Blade Runner*; and the Chandler and Cain remakes (Davis, *City of Quartz*, 21). For the politics of this evolution, see ibid., 30–45.

38. Both Fine's and Davis's histories of noir are gleaned from an all-male cast of characters, Didion being the sole female exception. Davis discusses the racial politics of the noir tradition in the 1930s in order to account for studio attacks on black male writers like Chester Himes but does not extend his notion of "difference" or studio power plays to account for gender oppression.

39. See Gosselin, *Multicultural Detective Fiction*.

40. Much has been written about the riots. I draw from Gooding-Williams, *Reading Rodney King, Reading Urban Uprisings* (1993); also see "Epilogue" in Omi and Winant, *Racial Formation in the United States*, 145–59.

41. Hayden, *Power of Place*, 6.

42. Coleman, *Hand Dance*.

43. See Magistrale and Ferreira, "Sweet Mama Wanda Tells Fortunes," 502. I am grateful to Michelle Taylor, a graduate student currently at Rice University, for showing me this citation.

44. Carby, *Reconstructing Womanhood*.

45. Recounted in "A Career in Brief," in Coleman, *Native in a Strange Land*, 1–5.

46. Coleman's poetry volumes include *Mad Dog, Black Lady* (1979), *Imagoes* (1983), *Heavy Daughter Blues* (1987), *A War of Eyes and Other Stories* (1988), *The Dicksboro Hotel* (1989), *African Sleeping Sickness* (1990), and *Hand Dance* (1993). Also see "A Career in Brief," in Coleman's *Native in a Strange Land*.

47. Recent developments that show the trend is changing are Coleman's inclusion in the *Norton Anthology of African American Literature* (1996), edited by Henry Louis Gates Jr. and Nellie Y. McKay. Another exception to critical neglect, though it is geared toward blues as established African American art form, is Jeffries, "Toward a Redefinition of the Urban." Again thanks go to Michelle Taylor for showing me these materials.

48. Magistrale and Ferreira, "Sweet Mama Wanda," 499.

49. Ibid., 502.

50. Harvey, *Condition of Postmodernity*.

51. hooks, *Yearning*, 25.

52. Jeffries, "Toward a Redefinition of the Urban," 160.

53. James Baldwin, "A Talk for Teachers" (1963), quoted in Hayden, *Power of Place*, 2.

54. C. Mitchell, " 'A Laying On of Hands.' "

55. For a related discussion, see Hayden, *Power of Place*, 22–34.

56. Magistrale and Ferreira, "Sweet Mama Wanda," 499.

57. Literary histories that survey Northern California literature do not have the regional angst one sees in work about L.A. See Davidson, *San Francisco Renaissance*; Ferlinghetti and Peters, *Literary San Francisco*; Charters, *Portable Beat Reader*. For a

work that does not tie Northern California literature exclusively to the Bay Area, see Haslam, *Many Californias*.

58. "Homegrown intelligentsia" is a phrase from Davis, *City of Quartz*, 17.

59. Kevin Starr, who comes in for criticism from Mike Davis and others, is the most prominent promoter of this argument, in his *Americans and the California Dream, 1850–1915* (1973). David Fine's introduction to *Los Angeles in Fiction* (1–29) also addresses the issue. Certainly there are other pictures—Nathanael West in particular comes to mind. By and large, however, this generalization, I would argue, holds.

60. See Wang, "Maxine Hong Kingston's Reclaiming of America"; Cliff, "The Making of Americans." Also see Robert Lee, "*The Woman Warrior* as an Intervention in Asian American Historiography." Because I worked with Lee when I was a graduate student, his approach to Kingston (sans the regionalist bent) sometimes informs my own, and I acknowledge gratefully his influence.

61. Exceptions include Nomura, Endo, and Sumida, *Frontiers of Asian American Studies*; Berson, "Fighting the Religion of the Present"; and Wong, *Reading Asian American Literature*.

62. In their representations of Gold Mountain, *Woman Warrior* and *China Men* signify western themes. Although Gold Mountain can mean any place of opportunity on the North American continent (or the Caribbean too), California, especially as it is represented in *China Men*, is "home base" for immigrants during their stay on Gold Mountain, a kind of clearinghouse for Chinese American experience.

63. For a discussion of the relationship between music, acid, the counterculture, and San Francisco, see Whiteley, *The Space Between Notes*, esp. 1–5, 61–81.

64. Quotes are from the Vintage edition, 1990; all subsequent page references are cited parenthetically in the text.

65. Here I am most directly indebted to Robert Lee.

66. Josephine Lee, *Performing Asian America*, 1.

67. Both of these quotes are drawn from DeLeon, *Left Coast City*, 2. The first quote belongs to California congresswoman Nancy Pelosi, the second to historian Kenneth Starr.

68. I rely very heavily here on DeLeon's reading of San Francisco politics in this period.

Chapter Three

1. Bowden, "Dead Minds, Live Places," 16.

2. For a history of the genre of desert writing, particularly the change from nineteenth-century landscapes of desolation to twentieth-century landscapes of the sublime, see Wild, "Sentimentalism in the American Southwest."

3. If the downwind impact of nuclear testing during the 1950s on local southwestern residents were a regular feature of public discussion, the consequences for the Southwest's regional image might destroy not just the defense dollars coming into the region but also the retirement industries in Scottsdale, Phoenix, Tucson, Santa Fe, and Taos. The prospect of a nuke-infested region obviously wouldn't help

sell tract homes to young families or attract tourists who travel to the Southwest precisely to consume clean, not carcinogenic, air. The mystification of southwestern identity also disables public discussion about the environmental impact of huge cities on waterless terrain. The investment of various profit-driven industries in the cultural production of a mystified Southwest is understandable enough; without it, the region doesn't pay.

4. Plumwood, *Feminism and the Mastery of Nature*, 17.

5. For a very cogent discussion of these issues, see Di Chiro, "Nature as Community."

6. To be sure, some of the focus on nature by ecocritics is self-consciously human-centered. See, for example, Slovic, *Seeking Awareness in American Nature Writing*. For a very explicit discussion of nature as "fantasy topography," see Kolodny, *The Land Before Her*.

7. Lyon, "The Nature Essay in the West," 221. It should be noted here that Thomas Lyon is not only a founding member of ecocriticism but a dedicated revisionist. He is general editor of the massive project that produced *Updating the Literary West*, compiled by the Western Literature Association.

8. Bergon, "Wilderness Aesthetics."

9. Buell, *The Environmental Imagination*.

10. R. Nash, *Wilderness and the American Mind*. See also Oelschlaeger, *The Idea of Wilderness*.

11. Stegner, "Coda: A Wilderness Letter" (1969), 146–47. This letter was to become, like Aldo Leopold's *Sand County Almanac* (1966), something of a bible to the environmental movement.

12. Stegner with Etulain, *Conversations with Wallace Stegner*, xiv.

13. Guha, "Radical American Environmentalism." Richard White has made a similar point about the classed dimensions of environmental ethics in an American context in "Are You an Environmentalist or Do You Work for a Living?"

14. Martin, "New with Added Ecology?" 6.

15. For a brief history of the emergence of this field, see Cheryll Glotfelty's introduction to Glotfelty and Fromm, *Ecocriticism Reader*. The *Ecocriticism Reader* also provides a wide-ranging sample of current ecocritical perspectives. For an early example of an ecocritical agenda, see Reuckert, "Literature and Ecology: An Experiment in Ecocriticism" (1978). For a later but similar piece, see Love, "Revaluing Nature: Toward an Ecological Criticism" (1990). Also see Finch and Elder, *Norton Book of Nature Writing*.

16. Cronon, "The Trouble with Wilderness."

17. See responses to Cronon featured in *Environmental History* 1.1 (1996); see especially Cohen, "Resistance to Wilderness," 29–46.

18. Cronon, "The Trouble with Wilderness," 72.

19. Ibid., 79–80.

20. Dan Flores used this language at an NEH-sponsored Summer Institute for Southwestern Studies in San Marcos, Texas, in 1996. I adopt Cronon's own language of "home" here, using quotes to denote the tricky ground the word "home" negotiates.

21. Cronon, "The Trouble with Wilderness," 78.

22. Revisionists include M. W. Lewis, *Green Delusions*; Evernden, *Social Creation of Nature*; and Biehl, *Rethinking Ecofeminist Politics*. For a very insightful essay about the relationship of western historical narrative to environmentalism, see Merchant, "Reinventing Eden."

23. Specifically, see McAllister, "Homeward Bound." By citing this essay, I do not single it out for special negative attention, for all of the essays noted later, unless specifically exempted, make a "resistance to the traditional" argument.

24. This insightful possibility was suggested to me by Noël Sturgeon.

25. Appropriation need not inevitably or absolutely result in the oppression of American Indian peoples, even if usually it does just this. Sturgeon's *Ecofeminist Natures* makes an articulate defense of strategic appropriations and essentialisms.

26. See Silko, "Landscape, History, and the Pueblo Imagination"; also Silko, "Language and Literature from a Pueblo Indian Perspective." For a related argument, see Allen, "The Sacred Hoop."

27. Allen, "The Psychological Landscape of *Ceremony*." For a more complex argument that still proves the point, see Swan, "Laguna Symbolic Geography and Silko's *Ceremony*." Also see Smith with Allen, "Earthly Relations, Carnal Knowledge."

28. Stegner made this claim often, as early as the 1960s and as late as the 1990s. For a late version, see "Introduction," *Where the Bluebird Sings*, xv–xxiii.

29. For more on the narrative as sacred, see Shaddock, "Mixed Blood Women."

30. R. White makes a similar point about the status of Native Americans in American discourse in "Discovering Nature in North America."

31. Castillo, "Postmodernism, Native American Literature and the Real."

32. Theorists take different positions regarding the relationship between history and postmodern cultural forms. Frederic Jameson contends that postmodernist practice at base is antihistoricist.

33. Aside from *Animal Dreams*, Kingsolver's novels include *The Bean Trees* (1988), *Homeland and Other Stories* (1989), and *Pigs in Heaven* (1993). Other major works are the poetry collection *Another America* and the nonfiction work *Holding the Line* (1989).

34. The exception is Swartz, " 'Saving Grace.' " Because this essay is of such a celebratory bent, and thus overlaps with reviewers' praise for *Animal Dreams*, I do not take it up individually in my own argument.

35. See, for example, review by George Johnson, *New York Times Book Review*, July 28, 1991, 28; Joseph A. Cincotti, "Intimate Revelations," *New York Times Book Review*, Sept. 2, 1990, 2; Keith Graham, " 'Ecofeminist' Author Relishes Political Role," *Atlanta Constitution*, Sept. 21, 1990, 1; Margaret Randall, "Time, Space and Heartbeats," *Los Angeles Times Book Review*, Sept. 9, 1990, 1; Ursula K. Le Guin, "The Fabric of Grace," *Washington Post Book Review*, Sept. 2, 1990, 1; Melissa Pritchard, "Saving the Planet," *Chicago Tribune*, Aug. 26, 1990, 14:1; Jane Smiley, "In One Small Town, the Weight of the World," *New York Times Book Review*, Sept. 2, 1990, 7:2.

36. Plumwood begins *Feminism and the Mastery of Nature* by way of this specific discussion. On the ecofeminist tendency to romanticize American Indian cultures, see Gaard, "Ecofeminism and Native American Cultures." For a sophisticated in-

quiry into this terrain, but one focused more on literature, see Murphy, *Literature, Nature and Other.*

37. See Plumwood, *Feminism and the Mastery of Nature,* esp. "Feminism and Ecofeminism," 19–40. For the standard reference on the masculinization of science, see Merchant, *The Death of Nature.*

38. Plumwood, *Feminism and the Mastery of Nature,* 19–40, esp. 27.

39. In "Reinventing Eden," Merchant considers with provocative implications the links between what I call western optimism and environmentalists' positivism.

40. For a history of ecofeminist activism, see Spretnak, "Ecofeminism," in Diamond and Orenstein's collection *Reweaving the World.* Note that the majority of contributors to this book live and work in California. Also consider the fact that the most prominent witches, like Starhawk and Z. Susanna Budapest, have long lived, worked, and practiced in Oakland, and that scholars like Carolyn Merchant, Donna Haraway, Annette Kolodny, Val Plumwood, Noël Sturgeon, and others make their scholarly "homes" in western spaces.

41. Ben Linder was an American agronomist ambushed by contras. He had been assisting farmers in their attempts to reorient the economy away from one based on export and cash crops, like cattle, toward one that would feed Nicaragua's people and establish its self-sufficiency.

42. Graham, " 'Ecofeminist' Author Relishes Political Role," *Atlanta Constitution,* Sept. 21, 1990, 1.

43. A case in point is a lecture Kingsolver delivered to promote *Pigs in Heaven* in Iowa City, Iowa, during the summer of 1994.

44. *NewsHour,* Nov. 24, 1995. The interview coincided with the release of an essay collection by Kingsolver, *High Tide in Tucson* (1995).

45. See Matthew Gilber, "The Moral Passion of Barbara Kingsolver," *Boston Globe,* July 23, 1993, 25. Also see interview with Kingsolver in Perry, *Backtalk,* 143–71.

46. For a brief discussion of "postmodernism as green politics," see Pepper, *Ecosocialism,* esp. 55–59; and Oelschlaeger, "Cosmos and Wilderness," in *Idea of Wilderness,* 320–53. For a related discussion, see Campbell, "The Land and Language of Desire."

47. For discussions of community in Kingsolver's recent *Pigs in Heaven,* see Dierdre Donahue, "Books about Human Bonds and Barriers," *USA Today,* July 15, 1993, D:1; Megan Rosenfeld, "Novelist in Hog Heaven," *Washington Post,* July 14, 1993, D:1.

48. For a study of the Mescalero, which locates tribal history not removed from but rather at the center of contemporary American nuclear policy, see Hanson, "From Environmental Goods to Economic Bads: Marketing Nuclear Waste to American Indians."

49. Temple makes a similar case in the introduction to *Open Spaces, City Places.*

50. For a sense of the emerging rhetoric of difference, see Hull, Scott, and Smith, *All the Women Are White;* or Anzaldúa, *Making Faces, Making Soul.*

51. On "wilderness" as a consumer phenomenon, see Price, "Looking for Nature at the Mall."

52. I draw directly from Cronon's argument in "The Trouble with Wilderness."

53. For a concise revisionist agenda, see Martin, "New with Added Ecology?"

54. Oelschlaeger, *Idea of Wilderness,* 10.

55. See Crosby, *Ecological Imperialism;* Harcourt, *Feminist Perspectives on Sustainable Development.*

Chapter Four

1. This section's heading recalls the title of Irigaray's foundational text on female sexuality within masculinist discourse, *The Sex Which Is Not One* (1985 [1977]).

2. Conspicuous exceptions include Papanikolas's *Trickster in a Land of Dreams,* Gutiérrez's *When Jesus Came, the Corn Mothers Went Away,* and Allmendinger's *The Cowboy.*

3. Cross-racial heterosexual relations are a matter of historical consensus. Less conceded, but increasingly documented, is the incidence of homosexual relations. See Katz, *Gay American History,* esp. 35–36, 508–12, but also 50, 281–332. Also see Duberman, Vicinius, and Chauncey, *Hidden from History.* On tolerance for homosexuality among American Indians, see Dynes and Donaldson, *Ethnographic Studies of Homosexuality.* On the problems of subsuming the American Indian berdache figure into Euro-Anglo, gay history recovery projects, see Whitehead, "The Bow and the Burden Strap." On western male homosociality, see Kimmel, *Manhood in America,* 58–70; also, for the most developed discussion to date, Allmendinger, *The Cowboy.*

4. Johnson makes this case in " 'A Memory Sweet to Soldiers.' " Tompkins makes a related case in *West of Everything,* esp. 23–45.

5. I take these examples from Johnson, " 'A Memory Sweet to Soldiers,' " 498, although the interconnections between these figures are well known. For a related argument, see Robinson, "The Roosevelt-Wister Connection." Also see Vorpahl, "Roosevelt, Wister, Turner and Remington," 276–302; and Vorpahl, *My Dear Wister* (1972). For an early study of masculinity, see E. G. White, *The Eastern Establishment and the Western Experience* (1968).

6. Bederman, *Manliness and Civilization* (1995), esp. chap. 4. Also see "Conclusion," for a discussion of Robert Bly and the contemporary men's movement that has tantalizing implications for western studies.

7. Though western discourse is not her primary focus, Bederman's general conclusion suggests a link between it and male sexuality.

8. Kolodny, *The Land Before Her.*

9. Graulich, "O Beautiful for Spacious Guys," 192. Foote limited these subjects to her private correspondence, from a sense that western literary subject matter, as well as western writers, should be male. But it was her need to speak, as a woman, about the "wild West" that drove this genteel writer to reveal, even if only privately, such unlikely subjects.

10. Luhan's love of women is drawn from Katz, *Gay American History.* Also see Mabel Dodge Luhan, *Intimate Memories.* Rudnick's biography, *Mabel Dodge Luhan,* also addresses some of these issues.

11. See especially Kaye, *Isolation and Masquerade;* O'Brien, *Willa Cather;* and Loeffelholz, *Experimental Lives.* Also Fryer, "Desert, Rock, Shelter, Legend."

12. On the landscape as sexual partner for Austin and Luhan, see Rudnick, "Re-Naming the Land."

13. I give a more extended reading of this text in Comer, "Literature, Gender Studies, and the New Western History."

14. For a "sampler" of some of these writers, see Egli, *No Rooms of Their Own.*

15. See Rebolledo, "Tradition and Mythology," 96–124; and Smith with Allen, "Earthly Relations, Carnal Knowledge." Also see Allen, *The Sacred Hoop*; and Harjo and Bird, et al., *Reinventing the Enemy's Language.*

16. Belsey, *Desire,* 7.

17. See Comer, "Literature, Gender Studies, and the New Western History."

18. Canonical sensibility—that of Hamlin Garland, Frank Waters, Walter Van Tilburg Clark, A. B. Guthrie, Wallace Stegner—retains a significant investment in what historian Bederman calls "Victorian moral manliness." It is brutally ironic. The price of "progress" in the West, so literary westerns of the 1920s–1960s argue, turns out to have been high indeed. Literary westerns bring sustained critique to a masculine identity based on frontier aggression, white arrogance, and masculine narcissism. On the topic of sex, male writers of literary westerns align themselves with the restraint and respectability associated with nineteenth-century "manly men" more so than they do with the implied virility or prowess of, say, *The Virginian.* Sex is a pleasurable but *private* matter for western writers, Wallace Stegner said in a representative remark made in the early 1960s.

19. See Tatum, "The Problem of the 'Popular' in the New Western History."

20. This topic is taken up at length by Robinson in *Having It Both Ways.*

21. Certainly counter-readings of this classic should be made more regularly. In *West of Everything,* Tompkins offers one: that *The Virginian* shows the conflicts of a masculine ideal premised on emotional stoicism, upward mobility, compulsory heterosexuality, social responsibility, and marriage to disempowered women. Robinson, in an equally compelling argument, calls Wister's dual narrative "having it both ways" (*Having It Both Ways,* 41–54). Both critics revise an earlier critical tradition, which saw the Virginian as a character who transcends rather than evades conflict. See in particular Scharnhorst, "The Virginian as a Founding Father."

22. The classic images of Nebraska and Kansas women on sod farms prove the point.

23. By now, the "white female drudge/good-hearted prostitute" dichotomy and the sensual Mexican or Indian woman are well-established in western women's history. See especially Armitage and Jameson, *The Women's West*; and Schlissel, Ruíz, and Monk, *Western Women.* For a wonderful visual rebuttal to these hackneyed mental images, see Luchetti and Olwell's photo collection *Women of the West,* esp. 11, 12, 108, 110, 113, 234.

24. See Bederman, *Manliness and Civilization.*

25. For a discussion of satire and Jean Stafford, see Graulich's "O Beautiful for Spacious Guys." Also see Rosowski, "Jean Stafford Rewrites the Western." Jean Stafford's *The Mountain Lion* (1947) is one of the more chilling demonstrations of the masculinism of the western sexual imaginary. Its protagonist, the precocious and artistic Molly, is killed off by her brother at precisely the moment when she is

about to come of sexual age: puberty. This is Stafford's grim take on wilderness spaces or the Old West as a feminist imaginative arena for women.

26. Sexuality is a significant topic for all the writers featured in this book as well as for Ella Leffland, Dorothy Bryant, Lorna Dee Cervantes, Amy Tan, Carolyn See, Cherríe Moraga, Mary Helen Ponce, Janice Mirikitani, Cynthia Kadohata, Sallie Tisdale, Kate Braverman, Terry McMillan, Melanie Rae Thon, Teresa Jordan, Terry Tempest Williams, Ana Castillo, Denise Chavez, Helena Maria Viramontes, Kim Barnes, Joy Harjo, Wendy Rose, and this list could be extended.

27. Hartmann, *From Margin to Mainstream*, offers a useful survey of 1970s legislations.

28. Houston's magazine articles include "A Sexual Woman," *Elle*, Jan. 1995, 70+; "Whatever Happened to Your Sense of Adventure?" *Redbook*, Sept. 1994, 56+; "The Call of the Wild," *Working Woman*, Aug. 1993, 52+; "Defining Moments," *Women's Sports and Fitness*, Mar. 1994, 78; "Running Snaggletooth," *Ski*, May 1994, 56+; "Biking in Burgundy," *Food and Wine*, Apr. 1995, 76+.

29. She has published one scholarly essay, "A Hopeful Sign" (1992).

30. The book of essays is *Women on Hunting* (1994). The novel's working title is *Wilder than Rain*. The screenplay is an adaptation of a British novel. Source: "The Writer's Voice," Press Release for Mar. 17, 1994, Reading at Billings, Montana, Family YMCA. Contact Corby Skinner, (406) 248-1685.

31. R. Norwood, *Women Who Love Too Much*. For lukewarm reviews of Houston's work, see Sandra Scofield, "Men and Other Wild Animals," *New York Times Book Review*, Jan. 12, 1992, 10; Gail Pool, *Women's Review of Books* 9.6 (Mar. 1992), 20; review of *Cowboys Are My Weakness*, *New Yorker*, Feb. 24, 1992, 101–2; Bill Oliver, review of *Cowboys Are My Weakness*, in *New England Review*, Summer 1993, 208–12; and Grace Lichenstein, "Just Plain Crazy for Cowboys," *Washington Post*, Mar. 30, 1992, B2. For an exception, see Judith Freeman, "Where a Range Is Not a Stove," *Los Angeles Times Book Review*, Feb. 23, 1992, 3.

32. Cheryll Burgess Glotfelty, "I'm Game, But Please Don't Shoot: Women on the Hunt in Pam Houston's *Cowboys Are My Weakness*," paper presented at annual meeting of Western Literature Association, Wichita, Kansas, 1993, 11–12. Although my reading of this text departs from Glotfelty's, I wish to acknowledge her exemplary generosity in providing me with not only her paper but also various primary source materials, including some of those mentioned above, gathered by herself and Janet Kolsky and Robin Briscoe, graduate students at the University of Nevada at Reno.

33. Ibid., 12.

34. "The Writer's Voice," press release for Mar. 17, 1994, reading.

35. Schrager, "Questioning the Promise of Self-Help."

36. A similar observation is made briefly in H. R. Miller, "America the Big Lie, the Quintessential."

37. Cisneros's works include *The House on Mango Street* (1984); *My Wicked Wicked Ways* (1987); *Woman Hollering Creek and Other Stories* (1991); and *Loose Woman* (1994).

38. Gloria Anzaldúa's *Borderlands/La Frontera* (1987) paved the way for this current reputation of South Texas, for it was that text that articulated the notion of

Texas Chicanas as "borderlands" subjects and which for many Chicanos and Chicanas galvanized the ethnic mythos emanating from this regional imaginary. Thereafter, with South Texas firmly etched on the Chicana literary map, Cisneros was able to write herself into a regional and racial literary tradition very much in keeping with her own frontline interests in feminist and sexual politics.

39. Surprisingly, critics have so far written little about this book and nothing about its relationship to the West. See L. M. Lewis, "Ethnic and Gender Identity"; also Thomson, " 'What Is Called Heaven.' " For a guide to some principles for criticism for Chicana texts, see Alarcón, "Cognitive Desires."

40. One could see Cisneros's two collections of poetry—*My Wicked Wicked Ways* (1987) and *Loose Woman* (1994)—in the same light.

41. The myth of La Llorona survives in various forms. For a discussion of several of them, see Anzaldúa, *Borderlands/La Frontera*, 25–39.

42. This language is borrowed from Anderson, *Imagined Communities*.

43. Dorris is quoted in an interview with Coltelli, *Winged Words*, 46. Erdrich's subsequent books include *The Beet Queen* (1986), *Tracks* (1987), *The Bingo Palace* (1994).

44. Dunn and Morris, *The Composite Novel*, 70.

45. For my purposes, the original of 1984 and the new version issued by Henry Holt in 1993 are similar enough to cause no disturbance to my arguments.

46. This topic of female desire recurs in this series as well as in *Baptism of Desire* (1989) and *The Blue Jay's Dance* (1995).

47. Dorris committed suicide in 1997 amidst reports that he had sexually abused at least one of his daughters. See Colin Covert, "The Anguished Life of Michael Dorris," *Minneapolis Star Tribune*, Aug. 3, 1997, A1+.

48. For an unusual reading of *Ceremony*, one that, if it were a standard reading, would overturn the book's status in western discourse, see Ronnow, "Tayo, Death, and Desire."

49. For an argument that sees more of the "personal" in Erdrich than do I, see Silberman, "Opening the Text."

50. I borrow the combined use of these three terms from Creekmur and Doty, *Out in Culture*, introduction.

Chapter Five

1. See, for example, Tuska and Piekarski, *Encyclopedia of Frontier and Western Fiction*; Hyde, *An American Vision*; Meldrum, *Under the Sun*; and Mogen, Busby, and Bryant, *The Frontier Experience and the American Dream*.

2. See Thacker, *The Great Prairie Fact and Literary Imagination*; Wyatt, *Fall Into Eden*; Milton, *Novel of the American West*. Also see Cronon, "The Trouble with Wilderness."

3. For a study not conceived through western studies paradigms, see Jehlen, *American Incarnation*.

4. Wyatt, *Fall Into Eden*, 206.

5. For a very interesting discussion of the absence of an "innocence" narrative in the tribal landscape discourse of the Shoshone, see Papanikolas, *Trickster in a Land of*

Dreams, who notes: "In all of the tales, there never was a longed-for Golden Age. . . . There was no nostalgia and there was no tragedy. The world the People had was the world they desired" (3).

6. Lowe, *Immigrant Acts.*

7. I am drawing closely from Robert David Sack, quoted in Massey and Allen, *Geography Matters!*, 10.

8. Stegner, "Coda," in *Sound of Mountain Water*, 146.

9. Here I draw explicitly from the basic premise of Parker, Russo, Sommer, and Yaeger, *Nationalisms and Sexualities.*

10. Melody Graulich makes a related point in "O Beautiful for Spacious Guys," 186–201.

11. See Saldívar, *Dialectics of Our America*, preface, xxii.

12. I draw here from a principal premise of Anderson's *Imagined Communities.*

13. See Bhabha's *Nation and Narration* and *Location of Culture.*

14. See Norwood and Monk, *The Desert Is No Lady*; Kolodny, *The Land Before Her.*

15. Rebolledo, "Tradition and Mythology," 96–124; Rebolledo, *Women Singing in the Snow.*

16. Anderson, *Imagined Communities*, 6.

17. Ibid.

18. For a discussion of nations without a state, see Whyte, *Gendering the Nation.* For transnationality, see Saldívar, *Dialectics* and *Border Matters*; for performative nationality, see Sedgwick, *Tendencies*; for nationalism as textuality, see the work of Bhabha, esp. *Nation and Narration.*

19. The Modern Language Association bibliography lists no critical work on this book for the last six years.

20. Bo Mason of Stegner's *Big Rock Candy Mountain* comes to mind as one example of an Anglo man of this type.

21. This observation was originally made by Shannon Leonard, a graduate student at Rice University.

22. Sandoval, "U.S. Third World Feminism," 1–4.

23. Rebolledo, *Women Singing in the Snow.*

24. See, for example, Aranda, "Recovering Our Alienated Selves"; and Aranda, *When We Arrive.* Also see Gutiérrez-Jones, "Desiring B/Orders," 99–112.

25. An exception is Adams, "Northamerican Silences," 130–55.

26. Barnes and Blew, *Circle of Women*, x.

27. One well-known rendering of the evolution of this term and sensibility can be found in Pease, *National Identities and Post-Americanist Narratives.*

28. This point about the overlap of postmodernity with feminist notions of interdependent subjectivity has been made in other theoretical contexts, which shed light on my argument. See, for example, Hoff, "Toward a Theory of Women's Legal History," 1–20.

Epilogue

1. I am grateful to Shannon Leonard, an ace graduate student and research assistant, for giving me the initial "scoop" on girl power. A number of studies about girl

power have appeared or are underway, and several anthologies of young feminist thought are currently available. Thus far, none acknowledges the East Coast bent to coverage of the movement. However, a space-sensitive analysis might shed light on the different feminisms (or postfeminisms) that young *western* "girls" currently exhibit. For example, when young, East Los Angeles Chicanas access this discourse about "girls," they do so with a very different sense of what "girl politics" means and will accomplish than do the young Manhattanites who get the most press. The same could be said for surfer girls, whose girl power politics dialogue with a long-standing regional discourse about "California girls." Another example is the Riot Girls, who, unlike other girl power bands like the Spice Girls or Sleater-Kinney, responds to and critiques an explicitly West Coast musical tradition, male grunge, which is anchored in Seattle. For a quick, if hypercritical, gloss on girl power, see the cover story of *Time*, June 29, 1998. Also see Carlip, *Girl Power*; Guerrilla Girls, *Confessions*; Pratt and Pryor, *For Real*; and Findlen, *Listen Up*.

2. I allude here to the claim upon American national identity that is sometimes negotiated by Japanese Americans through Hawaiian landscape discourse—that is, that this deployment is a colonialist gesture, since it displaces the indigenous land claims of Hawaiians.

3. Lowe, *Immigrant Acts*.

4. Diane Johnson, "The Lost World of the Mormons," *New York Review of Books*, Mar. 15, 1990, 28–31; Fern Kupfer, "Deserts and Desertions," *Washington Post*, Nov. 20, 1989, B:4; Carolyn See, "A Utah Farm Wife's Westward Drift," *Chicago Tribune*, Oct. 22, 1989, 14:6; untitled essay by Elizabeth Judd, *Village Voice Literary Supplement*, Nov. 1989; Pagan Kennedy, "On the Road," *The Nation*, Dec. 11, 1989, 723–24.

5. For an excellent review and critique of the notion of "culture zones," see P. Jay, "The Myth of 'America' and the Politics of Location." For a timely review essay about the status of literature in the new cultural geography, see Blair, "Cultural Geography."

Bibliography

Abbott, Carl. *The Metropolitan Frontier: Cities in the Modern American West*. Tucson: University of Arizona Press, 1992.

Adams, Kate. "Northamerican Silences: History, Identity, and Witness in the Poetry of Gloria Anzaldúa, Cherríe Moraga, and Leslie Marmon Silko." In *Listening to Silences: New Essays in Feminist Criticism*, edited by Elaine Hedges and Shelley Fisher Fishkin, 130–55. New York: Oxford University Press, 1994.

Aguilar-San Juan, Karin. *The State of Asian America: Activism and Resistance in the 1990s*. Boston: South End, 1994.

Aiken, Susan Hardy, Ann Brigham, Sallie A. Marston, and Penny Waterstone, eds. *Making Worlds: Gender, Metaphor, Materiality*. Tucson: University of Arizona Press, 1998.

Alarcón, Norma. "Cognitive Desires: An Allegory of/for Chicana Critics." In *Listening to Silences: New Essays in Feminist Criticism*, edited by Elaine Hedges and Shelley Fisher Fishkin, 260–74. New York: Oxford University Press, 1994.

Allen, Paula Gunn. "The Psychological Landscape of *Ceremony*." *American Indian Quarterly* 5 (1979): 7–12.

———. *The Sacred Hoop: Recovering the Feminine in American Indian Traditions*. Boston: Beacon, 1986; reissued 1992.

Allmendinger, Blake. *The Cowboy: Representations of Labor in an American Work Culture*. New York: Oxford University Press, 1995.

———. *Ten Most Wanted: The New Western Literature*. New York: Routledge, 1998.

Allmendinger, Blake, and Valerie J. Matsumoto, eds. *Over the Edge: Remapping the American West*. Los Angeles: University of California Press, 1998.

Ammons, Elizabeth. *Conflicting Stories: American Women Writers at the Turn into the Twentieth Century*. New York: Oxford University Press, 1992.

Anaya, Rudolfo A., and Francisco A. Lomeli, eds. *Aztlán: Essays on the Chicano Homeland*. Albuquerque, N.Mex.: Academia/El Norte Publications, 1989.

Anderson, Benedict. *Imagined Communities*. London: Verso, 1983; revised and reissued 1991.

Anthias, Floya, and Nira Yuval-Davis, eds. *Woman-Nation-State*. London: Macmillan, 1989.

Anzaldúa, Gloria. *Borderlands/La Frontera: The New Mestiza*. San Francisco, Calif.: Spinsters/Aunt Lute Press, 1987.

———. *Making Faces, Making Soul: Haciendo Caras*. San Francisco, Calif.: Spinsters/Aunt Lute Press, 1990.

Aparicio, Frances R. "On Multiculturalism and Privilege: A Latina Perspective." *American Quarterly* 46.4 (Dec. 1994): 575–88.

Aranda, José F., Jr. "Contradictory Impulses: María Amparo Ruiz de Burton, Resistance Theory, and the Politics of Chicano/a Studies." *American Literature* 70.3 (Sept. 1998): 551–81.

——. "Recovering Our Alienated Selves: Making the Case for the New Chicano/a Studies." Paper delivered at annual meeting of American Studies Association, Washington, D.C., 1997.

——. *When We Arrive: Literature, Colonial History, and the Politics of a Chicano Nation.* Forthcoming.

Armitage, Susan, Elizabeth Jameson, and Joan Jensen. "A Western Forum Response: The New Western History, Another Perspective." *Journal of Western History* 3.2 (July 1993): 5–6.

Armitage, Susan, Helen Bannan, Katherine G. Morrissey, and Vicki L. Ruiz, eds. *Women in the West: A Guide to Manuscript Sources.* New York: Garland, 1991.

Armitage, Susan, and Elizabeth Jameson, eds. *The Women's West.* Norman: University of Oklahoma Press, 1987.

——. *Writing the Range: Race, Class, and Culture in the Women's West.* Norman: University of Oklahoma Press, 1997.

Asian Women United of California, ed. *Making Waves.* Boston: Beacon Press, 1989.

Barnes, Kim, and Mary Clearman Blew, eds. *Circle of Women: An Anthology of Contemporary Western Women Writers.* New York: Penguin, 1994.

Bataille, Gretchen M., and Kathleen Mullen Sands. *American Indian Women: Telling Their Lives.* Lincoln: University of Nebraska Press, 1984.

Baym, Nina. *American Women Writers and the Work of History, 1790–1860.* New Brunswick, N.J.: Rutgers University Press, 1995.

Bederman, Gail. *Manliness and Civilization: A Cultural History of Gender and Race in the United States, 1880–1917.* Chicago: University of Chicago Press, 1995.

Belsey, Catherine. *Desire: Love Stories in Western Culture.* Oxford: Blackwell, 1994.

Benson, Jackson. *Wallace Stegner: His Life and Work.* New York: Viking, 1996.

Bergon, Frank. "Wilderness Aesthetics." *American Literary History* 9.1 (1997): 128–60.

Berkhofer, Robert F., Jr. *The White Man's Indian: Images of the American Indian from Columbus to the Present.* New York: Knopf, 1978.

Berlant, Lauren. *Anatomy of a National Fantasy.* Chicago: University of Chicago Press, 1991.

——. *The Queen of America Goes to Washington City: Essays on Sex and Citizenship.* Durham, N.C.: Duke University Press, 1997.

Berlant, Lauren, and Elizabeth Freeman. "Queer Nationality." In *National Identities and Post-Americanist Narratives,* edited by Donald E. Pease, 149–80. Durham, N.C.: Duke University Press, 1994.

Bernstein, Richard, "Unsettling the Old West." *New York Times Magazine,* Mar. 18, 1990, 34, 56–59.

Berson, Misha. "Fighting the Religion of the Present: Western Motifs in the First Wave of Asian American Plays." In *Reading the West: New Essays on the Literature of the American West,* edited by Michael Kowalewski, 251–72. New York: Cambridge University Press, 1996.

Berube, Allan, and Jeffrey Escoffier. "Queer/Nation." *Outlook* 11 (Winter 1991): 13–15.

Bevis, William M. "Region, Power, Place." In *Reading the West: New Essays on the Literature of the American West*, edited by Michael Kowalewski, 21–43. New York: Cambridge University Press, 1996.

——. *Ten Tough Trips: Montana Writers and the West*. Seattle: University of Washington Press, 1990.

Bhabha, Homi K. *The Location of Culture*. New York: Routledge, 1994.

——. *Nation and Narration*. New York: Routledge, 1990.

Biehl, Janet. *Rethinking Ecofeminist Politics*. Boston: South End, 1991.

Blair, Sara. "Cultural Geography and the Place of the Literary," *American Literary History* 10.3 (Fall 1998): 544–67.

Bodian, Nate. "The Influence of the Small Press on American Book Publishing." *COSMEP* 24.12 (1993): 9–10.

Bow, Leslie. " 'For Every Gesture of Loyalty, There Doesn't Have to Be a Betrayal': Asian American Criticism and the Politics of Locality." In *Who Can Speak?: Authority and Critical Identity*, edited by Judith Roof and Robyn Wiegman, 30–55. Urbana: University of Illinois Press, 1995.

Bowden, Charles. "Dead Minds, Live Places." In *Open Spaces, City Places: Contemporary Writers on the Changing Southwest*, edited by Judy Nolte Temple, 13–24. Tucson: University of Arizona Press, 1994.

Bradbury, John. *Renaissance in the South: A Critical History of the Literature, 1920–1960*. Chapel Hill: University of North Carolina Press, 1963.

Brady, Jennifer. "Points West, Then and Now: The Fiction of Joan Didion." *Contemporary Literature* 20.4 (1979): 452–70.

Bredahl, A. Carl, Jr. *New Ground: Western American Narrative and the Literary Canon*. Chapel Hill: University of North Carolina Press, 1989.

Brodhead, Richard H. *Cultures of Letters: Scenes of Reading and Writing in Nineteenth-Century America*. Chicago: University of Chicago Press, 1993.

Brown, Richard Maxwell. "The New Regionalism in America, 1970–81." In *Regionalism and the Pacific Northwest*, edited by William G. Robbins, Robert J. Frank, and Richard E. Ross, 37–96. Corvallis: Oregon State University Press, 1983.

Bruchac, Joseph. *Songs from This Earth on Turtle's Back*. New York: Greenfield Review Press, 1983.

Bucco, Martin. "Western American Literary Criticism." *Western Writers Series* 62. Boise, Idaho: Boise State University Press, 1984.

Buell, Lawrence. *The Environmental Imagination: Thoreau, Nature Writing and the Formation of American Culture*. Cambridge, Mass.: Harvard University Press, 1995.

Busby, Mark. "The Importance of the Frontier in Contemporary Fiction." In *The Frontier Experience and the American Dream: Essays on American Literature*, edited by David Mogen, Mark Busby, and Paul Bryant, 95–106. College Station: Texas A&M University Press, 1989.

Butler, Ann. *Daughters of Joy, Sisters of Misery: Prostitutes in the American West, 1865–1920*. Urbana: University of Illinois Press, 1985.

Butler, Judith. "Contingent Foundations: Feminism and the Question of Postmodernism." In *Feminists Theorize the Political*, edited by Judith Butler and Joan Scott, 3–21. New York: Routledge, 1992.

Calderon, Hector, and José David Saldívar, eds. *Criticism in the Borderlands: Studies in Chicano Literature, Culture, and Ideology*. Durham, N.C.: Duke University Press, 1991.

Campbell, SueEllen. "The Land and Language of Desire: Where Post-Structuralism and Deep Ecology Meet." *Western American Literature* 24.3 (1989): 199–211.

Carby, Hazel. *Reconstructing Womanhood: The Emergence of the Afro-American Woman Novelist*. New York: Oxford University Press, 1987.

Carlip, Hillary. *Girl Power: Young Women Speak Out!* New York: Warner, 1995.

Carton, Evan. "Vietnam and the Limits of Masculinity." *American Literary History* 3.2 (1991): 294–318.

Cash, W. J. *The Mind of the South*. New York: Knopf, 1941.

Castillo, Susan Perez. "Postmodernism, Native American Literature and the Real: The Silko-Erdrich Controversy." *Massachusetts Review* 32.2 (1991): 285–94.

Cervantes, Lorna Dee. "Beneath the Shadow of the Freeway." *Latin American Literary Review* 3.1 (1975).

"The Challenge of Writing Multicultural Women's History." Special issue, *Frontiers* 12.1 (1991).

Chambram-Dernersesian, Angie. "I Throw Punches for My Race, But I Don't Want to Be a Man: Writing Us—Chica-nos (Girl, Us)/Chicanas—into the Movement Script." In *Cultural Studies*, edited by Lawrence Grossberg, Cary Nelson, and Paula Treichler, 81–95. New York: Routledge, 1992.

Chan, Jeffrey Paul, Frank Chin, Lawson Fusao, and Shawn Wong, eds. *The Big Aiiieeeee!: An Anthology of Chinese American and Japanese American Literature*. New York: Penguin, 1991.

Chan, Sucheng. "The Asian-American Movement, 1960s–1980s." In *Peoples of Color in the American West*, edited by Sucheng Chan, Douglas Henry Daniels, Mario T. García, and Terry P. Wilson, 525–32. Lexington, Mass.: D. C. Heath, 1994.

Chan, Sucheng, Douglas Henry Daniels, Mario T. García, and Terry P. Wilson, eds. *Peoples of Color in the American West*. Lexington, Mass.: D. C. Heath, 1994.

Charters, Ann, ed. *The Portable Beat Reader*. New York: Viking, 1992.

Chase, Richard. *The American Novel and Its Tradition*. New York: Doubleday, 1957.

Cheung, King-Kok, ed. *An Interethnic Companion to Asian American Literature*. New York: Cambridge University Press, 1997.

Cisneros, Sandra. "Cactus Flowers: In Search of Tejana Feminist Poetry." *Third Woman* 3.1–2 (1986): 73–80.

——. *The House on Mango Street*. Houston, Tex.: Arte Público Press, 1984.

——. *Loose Woman*. New York: Knopf, 1994.

——. *My Wicked Wicked Ways*. Berkeley, Calif.: Third Woman Press, 1987.

——. *Woman Hollering Creek and Other Stories*. New York: Random House, 1991.

Cliff, Michelle. "The Making of Americans: Maxine Hong Kingston's Crossover Dreams." *Village Voice Literary Supplement* 74 (May 1989): 11–14.

Clifford, James, and George Marcus, eds. *Writing Culture: The Politics and Poetics of Ethnography*. Berkeley: University of California Press, 1986.

Cohen, Michael. "Resistance to Wilderness." *Environmental History* 1.1 (1996): 29–46.

Coleman, Wanda. *African Sleeping Sickness*. Santa Barbara, Calif.: Black Sparrow, 1990.

——. *Bathwater Wine*. Santa Barbara, Calif.: Black Sparrow, 1998.

——. *The Dicksboro Hotel*. Santa Barbara, Calif.: Black Sparrow, 1989.

——. *Hand Dance*. Santa Barbara, Calif.: Black Sparrow, 1993.

——. *Heavy Daughter Blues*. Santa Barbara, Calif.: Black Sparrow, 1987.

——. *Imagoes*. Santa Barbara, Calif.: Black Sparrow, 1983.

——. *Mad Dog, Black Lady*. Santa Barbara, Calif.: Black Sparrow, 1979.

——. *Native in a Strange Land: Trials and Tremors*. Santa Barbara, Calif.: Black Sparrow, 1996.

——. *A War of Eyes and Other Stories*. Santa Barbara, Calif.: Black Sparrow, 1988.

Colomina, Beatriz. *Sexuality and Space*. New York: Princeton Architectural Press, 1992.

Coltelli, Laura. *Winged Words: American Indian Writers Speak*. Lincoln: University of Nebraska Press, 1990.

Comer, Krista. "Feminism and the New Western Regionalism: Revising Critical Paradigms." In *Updating the Literary West*, compiled by WLA, 17–34. Fort Worth: Texas Christian University Press, 1997.

——. "Joan Didion's California." In *Updating the Literary West*, compiled by WLA, 346–51. Fort Worth: Texas Christian University Press, 1997.

——. "Literature, Gender Studies, and the New Western History." *Arizona Quarterly* 53.2 (1997): 99–134.

——. "Sidestepping Environmental Justice: 'Natural' Landscapes and the Wilderness Plot." In "Intersections of Feminisms and Environmentalists," special issue edited by Noël Sturgeon. *Frontiers* 28.2 (1997): 73–101.

——. "Wallace Stegner and the Problem of the 'Authentic West,'" unpublished manuscript.

Cook-Lynn, Elizabeth. *Why I Can't Read Wallace Stegner, and Other Essays: A Tribal Voice*. Madison: University of Wisconsin Press, 1996.

Cracroft, Richard. " 'Meliorism, Optimism, and the Stiff Upper Lip': Wallace Stegner's Western Naif and Judith Freeman's *Set for Life*." Paper presented at Western Literature Association conference, Reno, Nev., Oct. 7, 1992.

Creekmur, Corey K., and Alexander Doty, eds. *Out in Culture: Gay, Lesbian and Queer Essays on Popular Culture*. Durham, N.C.: Duke University Press, 1995.

Cronon, William. "A Place for Stories: Nature, History, and Narrative." *Journal of American History* 78.4 (1992): 1347–76.

——. "The Trouble with Wilderness, Or Getting Back to the Wrong Kind of Nature." In *Uncommon Ground: Toward Reinventing Nature*, edited by William Cronon, 69–90. New York: Norton, 1995.

——, ed. *Uncommon Ground: Toward Reinventing Nature*. New York: Norton, 1995.

Crosby, Alfred. *Ecological Imperialism*. New York: Cambridge University Press, 1986.

Crow, Charles L., ed. *Essays on California Writers*. Introduction by Kevin Starr. Bowling Green, Ohio: Bowling Green State University Press, 1978.

Dainotto, Roberto Maria. " 'All the Regions Do Smilingly Revolt': The Literature of Place and Region." *Critical Inquiry* 22 (Spring 1996): 486–505.

Dana, Richard Henry. *Two Years Before the Mast and Twenty-Four Years After*. The

Harvard Classics, edited by Charles W. Eliot. New York: P. F. Collier and Son, 1909 [1840].

Daniels, Stephen. *Fields of Vision: Landscape Imagery and National Identity in England and the United States.* London: Polity, 1993.

——. *The Iconography of Landscape: Essays on the Symbolic Representation, Design and Use of Past Environments.* New York: Cambridge University Press, 1988.

Davenport, Guy. "Midas' Grandchildren." *National Review,* May 7, 1963, 14:371.

——. "On the Edge of Being." *National Review,* Aug. 25, 1970, 903.

Davidson, Michael. *The San Francisco Renaissance: Poetics and Community at Mid-Century.* New York: Cambridge University Press, 1989.

Davis, Mike. *City of Quartz: Excavating the Future in L.A.* New York: Verso, 1990.

de Graef, Lawrence B. "Race, Sex, and Region: Black Women in the American West, 1850–1920." *Pacific Historical Review* 49.2 (May 1980): 285–314.

de Lauretis, Teresa. *Alice Doesn't: Feminism, Semiotics, Cinema.* Bloomington: Indiana University Press, 1984.

DeLeon, Richard Edward. *Left Coast City: Progressive Politics in San Francisco, 1975–1991.* Lawrence: University Press of Kansas, 1992.

Deutsch, Sarah. *No Separate Refuge: Culture, Class and Gender on an Anglo-Hispanic Frontier in the American Southwest, 1880–1940.* New York: Oxford University Press, 1987.

Devall, Bill. *Simple in Means, Rich in Ends: Practicing Deep Ecology.* London: Green Spring, 1990.

DeVoto, Bernard. *Across the Wide Missouri.* Boston: Little, Brown, 1947.

Di Chiro, Giovanna. "Nature as Community: The Convergence of Environment and Social Justice." In *Uncommon Ground: Toward Reinventing Nature,* edited by William Cronon, 298–320. New York: Norton, 1995.

Didion, Joan. Interview with Linda Kuehl. In *The Paris Review Interviews: Writers at Work,* 5th ser., edited by George Plimpton, 339–58. New York: Penguin, 1981.

——. *Play It as It Lays.* New York: Bantam, 1970.

——. *Run River.* New York: Pocket, 1963.

——. *Slouching Towards Bethlehem.* New York: Pocket, 1968.

——. *The White Album.* New York: Simon and Schuster, 1979.

Donovan, Josephine. *New England Local Color Literature: A Women's Tradition.* New York: Ungar, 1983.

Dorman, Robert. *Revolt of the Provinces: The Regionalist Movement in America, 1920–1945.* Chapel Hill: University of North Carolina Press, 1993.

Duberman, Martin, Martha Vicinius, and George Chauncey Jr., eds. *Hidden from History: Reclaiming the Gay and Lesbian Past.* New York: Meridian, 1989.

duCille, Ann. "The Occult of True Black Womanhood: Critical Demeanor and Black Feminist Studies." *Signs* 19.3 (1994): 70–108.

Dugger, Ronnie, ed. *Three Men in Texas: Bedichek, Webb, and Dobie, Essays by Their Friends in the Texas Observer.* Austin: University of Texas Press, 1967.

Dunn, Maggie, and Ann Morris. *The Composite Novel: The Short Story Cycle in Transition.* New York: Twayne, 1995.

DuPlessis, Rachel Blau. *Writing Beyond the Ending: Narrative Strategies of Twentieth-Century Women Writers.* Bloomington: Indiana University Press, 1984.

Dynes, Wayne R., and Stephen Donaldson, eds. *Ethnographic Studies of Homosexuality*. New York: Garland, 1992.

Echols, Alice. *Daring to Be Bad: Radical Feminism in America 1967–1975*. Minneapolis: University of Minnesota Press, 1989.

Egli, Ida Rae. *No Rooms of Their Own: Women Writers of Early California*. Berkeley: Heydey, 1992.

Ehrlich, Gretel. *Heart Mountain*. New York: Viking Penguin, 1988.

——. *The Solace of Open Spaces*. New York: Viking Penguin, 1985.

——. *Wyoming Stories*. Santa Barbara, Calif.: Capra, 1986.

Engle, Leonard, ed. *The Big Empty: Essays on Western Landscape as Narrative*. Albuquerque: University of New Mexico Press, 1994.

Erdrich, Louise. *Baptism of Desire: Poems*. New York: HarperCollins, 1989.

——. *The Beet Queen*. New York: Henry Holt, 1986.

——. *The Bingo Palace*. New York: HarperCollins, 1994.

——. *The Blue Jay's Dance: A Birth Year*. New York: HarperCollins, 1995.

——. *Love Medicine*. New York: Henry Holt, 1984; revised and reissued 1993.

——. *Tracks*. New York: HarperCollins, 1987.

Espmark, Kjell. *The Nobel Prize in Literature: A Study of the Criteria Behind the Choices*. Boston: G. K. Hall, 1991.

Etulain, Richard W. "The American Literary West and Its Interpreters: The Rise of a New Historiography." In *The Western: A Collection of Critical Essays*, edited by James K. Folsom, 137–73. Englewood Cliffs, N.J.: Prentice Hall, 1979.

Evans, Sara. *Personal Politics: The Roots of Women's Liberation in the Civil Rights Movement and the New Left*. New York: Vintage, 1979.

Evernden, Neil. *The Social Creation of Nature*. Baltimore, Md.: Johns Hopkins University Press, 1992.

Faludi, Susan. *Backlash: The Undeclared War against American Women*. New York: Crown, 1991.

Faragher, John Mack. *Women and Men on the Overland Trail*. New Haven, Conn.: Yale University Press, 1979.

Felton, Sharon, ed. *The Critical Response to Joan Didion*. Westport, Conn.: Greenwood, 1994.

Ferlinghetti, Lawrence, and Nancy Peters. *Literary San Francisco*. New York: Harper and Row, 1980.

Fernandez, Roberta. "*Abriendo caminos* in the Brotherland: Chicana Writers Respond to the Ideology of Literary Nationalism." *Frontiers* 14.2 (1994): 23–50.

Fetterley, Judith, and Marjorie Pryse, eds. *American Women Regionalists 1850–1910*. New York: Norton, 1992.

——. "Theorizing Regionalism: Celia Thaxter's *Among the Isles of Shoals*." In *Breaking Boundaries: New Perspectives on Women's Regional Writing*, edited by Sherrie A. Inness and Diana Royer, 38–53. Iowa City: University of Iowa Press, 1997.

Fiedler, Leslie A. *The Return of the Vanishing American*. New York: Stein and Day, 1968.

Finch, Robert, and John Elder, eds. *The Norton Book of Nature Writing*. New York: Norton, 1990.

Findlay, John M. *Magic Lands: Western Cityscapes and American Culture After 1940.* Berkeley: University of California Press, 1992.

Findlen, Barbara, ed. *Listen Up: Voices from the Next Feminist Generation.* Seattle, Wash.: Seal, 1995.

Fine, David, ed. *Los Angeles in Fiction.* Albuquerque: University of New Mexico Press, 1984.

Fisher, Dexter, ed. *The Third Woman: Minority Women Writers of the United States.* Boston: Houghton Mifflin, 1980.

Foerster, Norman, ed. *The Reinterpretation of American Literature: Some Contributions Toward the Understanding of Its Historical Development.* New York: Harcourt, Brace, 1928.

Folsom, James K., ed. *The Western: A Collection of Critical Essays.* Englewood Cliffs, N.J.: Prentice Hall, 1979.

Foote, Kenneth E., Peter J. Hugill, Kent Mathewson, and Jonathan M. Smith, eds. *Rereading Cultural Geography.* Austin: University of Texas Press, 1994.

Foreman, Dave. *Confessions of an Eco-Warrior.* New York: Harmony, 1991.

Franzen, Tricia. "Differences and Identities: Feminism and the Albuquerque Lesbian Community." *Signs* 18.4 (1993): 297–312.

Fraser, N., and Linda Nicholson. "Social Criticism Without Philosophy: An Encounter Between Feminism and Postmodernism." *Theory, Culture and Society* 5 (1988): 373–94.

Freeman, Judith. *The Chinchilla Farm.* New York: Vintage, 1990.

Friedan, Betty. *The Feminine Mystique.* New York: Norton, 1963.

Friedman, Ellen G., ed. *Joan Didion: Essays and Conversations.* Princeton: Ontario Review Press, 1984.

Fryer, Judith. "Desert, Rock, Shelter, Legend." In *The Desert Is No Lady: Southwestern Landscapes in Women's Writing and Art,* edited by Vera Norwood and Janice Monk, 27–46. New Haven, Conn.: Yale University Press, 1986.

Fussell, Edwin. *Frontier: American Literature and the American West.* Princeton, N.J.: Princeton University Press, 1965.

Gaard, Greta. "Ecofeminism and Native American Cultures: Pushing the Limits of Cultural Imperialism." In *Ecofeminism: Women, Animals, Nature,* edited by Greta Gaard, 295–314. Philadelphia, Pa.: Temple University Press, 1993.

García, Mario T. "The Chicana in American History: The Mexican Women of El Paso, 1880–1920, A Case Study." *Pacific Historical Review* 49.2 (May 1980): 315–37.

Gates, Henry Louis, Jr., and Nellie Y. McKay, eds. *Norton Anthology of African American Literature.* New York: W. W. Norton, 1996.

Georgi-Findlay, Brigitte. *The Frontiers of Women's Writing: Women's Writing and the Rhetoric of Westward Expansion.* Tucson: University of Arizona Press, 1996.

Gilbert, Sandra M., and Susan Gubar. *The Madwoman in the Attic: The Woman Writer and the Nineteenth-Century Literary Imagination.* New Haven, Conn.: Yale University Press, 1974.

Glotfelty, Cheryll, and Harold Fromm, eds. *The Ecocriticism Reader.* Athens: University of Georgia Press, 1996.

Gooding-Williams, Robert, ed. *Reading Rodney King, Reading Urban Uprising.* New York: Routledge, 1993.

Gordon, Avery F., and Christopher Newfield. *Mapping Multiculturalism*. Minneapolis: University of Minnesota Press, 1996.

Gosselin, Adrienne Johnson, ed. *Multicultural Detective Fiction: Murder from the "Other" Side*. New York: Garland, 1998.

Graulich, Melody. "Gettin' Hitched in the West." Paper presented at "Western Literature: A Symposium," University of Wyoming, 1992.

———. "The Guides to Conduct That a Tradition Offers: Wallace Stegner's *Angle of Repose*." *South Dakota Review* 23.4 (Winter 1985): 87–106.

———. "O Beautiful for Spacious Guys: On the Legitimate Inclination of the Sexes." In *The Frontier Experience and the American Dream: Essays on American Literature*, edited by David Mogen, Mark Busby, and Paul Bryant, 186–201. College Station: Texas A&M University Press, 1989.

Gray, Richard. *Writing the South: Ideas of an American Region*. Cambridge, Mass.: Cambridge University Press, 1986.

Gregory, Derek. *Geographical Imaginations*. Cambridge, Mass.: Blackwell, 1994.

Guerrilla Girls. *Confessions of the Guerrilla Girls*. New York: HarperCollins, 1995.

Guha, Ramachandra. "Radical American Environmentalism and Wilderness Preservation: A Third World Critique." *Environmental Ethics* 11.1 (1989): 71–84.

Gurian, Jay. *Western American Writing: Tradition and Promise*. Deland, Fla.: Everett/Edwards, 1975.

Gutiérrez, Ramón. "Community, Patriarchy, and Individualism: The Politics of Chicano History and the Dream of Equality." *American Quarterly* 45.1 (Mar. 1993): 44–72.

———. *When Jesus Came, the Corn Mothers Went Away: Marriage, Sexuality, and Power in New Mexico, 1500–1846*. Palo Alto, Calif.: Stanford University Press, 1991.

Gutiérrez, Ramón, and Genaro Padilla, eds. *Recovering the U.S. Hispanic Literary Heritage*. Vol. 1. Houston, Tex.: Arte Público Press, 1993.

Gutiérrez-Jones, Carl. "Desiring B/Orders." *diacritics* 25.1 (Spring 1995): 99–112.

———. *Rethinking the Borderlands: Between Chicano Discourse and Legal Discourse*. Berkeley: University of California Press, 1995.

Haase, John. "Steinbeck Detractors Sow an Unfruitful Crop of Wrath." *Los Angeles Times*, Dec. 23, 1962, Calendar section, 18.

Hanson, Randel D. "From Environmental Bads to Economic Goods: Marketing Nuclear Waste to American Indians." Ph.D. dissertation, University of Minnesota, 1998.

Haraway, Donna. *Simians, Cyborgs, and Women: The Reinvention of Nature*. New York: Routledge, 1991.

———. "Situated Knowledges: The Science Question in Feminism and the Privilege of Partial Perspective." *Feminist Studies* 14 (Fall 1988): 575–99.

Harcourt, Wendy, ed. *Feminist Perspectives on Sustainable Development*. London: Zed, 1994.

Harjo, Joy, Gloria Bird, with Patricia Blanco, Beth Cuthand, and Valerie Martínez, eds. *Reinventing the Enemy's Language: Contemporary Native Women's Writing of North America*. New York: Norton, 1997.

Harper, Michael S., and Robert B. Stepto, eds. *Chant of Saints: A Gathering of Afro-*

American Literature, Art, and Scholarship. Introduction by John H. Franklin. Champaign: University of Illinois Press, 1975.

Harper, Philip Brian. *Framing the Margins: The Social Logic of Postmodern Culture.* New York: Oxford University Press, 1994.

Harstock, Nancy. "Rethinking Modernism: Minority vs. Majority Theories." *Cultural Critique* 7 (1987): 187–206.

Hartmann, Susan M. *From Margin to Mainstream: American Women and Politics Since 1960.* New York: Knopf, 1981.

Harvey, David. *The Condition of Postmodernity: An Enquiry into the Origins of Cultural Change.* Cambridge, Mass.: Blackwell, 1990.

Haslam, Gerald W. "Unknown Diversity: Small Presses and Little Magazines in the West, 1960–1980." In *A Literary History of the American West,* compiled by WLA, 1167–77. Fort Worth: Texas Christian University Press, 1987.

———, ed. *Many Californias: Literature from the Golden State.* Reno: University of Nevada Press, 1992.

Hayden, Dolores. *The Power of Place: Urban Landscapes as Public History.* Cambridge, Mass.: MIT Press, 1995.

Hazard, Lucy. *The Frontier in American Literature.* New York: Frederick Ungar, 1961 [1927].

Hedges, Elaine, and Shelley Fisher Fishkin, eds. *Listening to Silences: New Essays in Feminist Criticism.* New York: Oxford University Press, 1994.

Higonnet, Margaret R., and Joan Templeton, eds. *Reconfigured Spheres: Feminist Explorations of Literary Spaces.* Amherst: University of Massachusetts Press, 1994.

Hirata, Lucie Cheng. "Chinese Immigrant Women in Nineteenth-Century California." In *Women of America: A History,* edited by Carol Berkin and Mary Beth Norton, 223–44. Boston: Houghton Mifflin, 1979.

Hoff, Joan. "Toward a Theory of Women's Legal History." In *Law, Gender and Injustice: A Legal History of U.S. Women,* 1–20. New York: New York University Press, 1991.

Hoffman, Michael J., and Patrick D. Murphy, eds. *Critical Essays on American Modernism.* New York: G. K. Hall, 1992.

Hogue, W. Lawrence. *Race, Modernity, Postmodernity: A Look at the History and the Literatures of People of Color Since the 1960s.* Albany: State University Press of New York, 1996.

hooks, bell. *Yearning: Race, Gender, and Cultural Politics.* Boston: South End, 1990.

Hooper, Barbara. " 'Split at the Roots': A Critique of Philosophical and Political Sources of Modern Planning Doctrine." *Frontiers* 13.1 (1992): 45–80.

Horsman, Reginald. *Race and Manifest Destiny: The Origins of Racial Anglo-Saxonism.* Cambridge, Mass.: Harvard University Press, 1981.

Houston, Pam. *Cowboys Are My Weakness.* New York: Norton, 1992.

———. "A Hopeful Sign: The Making of Metonymic Meaning in Munro's *Menesetueng.*" *Kenyon Review* 14.4 (Fall 1992): 79+.

———. *Wilder Than Rain: A Seduction in Letters.* Forthcoming.

———. *Women on Hunting: Essays, Fiction, and Poetry.* New York: Ecco, 1994.

Hull, Gloria, Patricia Bell Scott, and Barbara Smith, eds. *All Women Are White, All*

the Men Are Black, but Some of Us Are Brave: Black Women's Studies. Old West-
bury, N.Y.: Feminist Press, 1982.

Hutcheon, Linda. *A Poetics of Postmodernism: History, Theory, Fiction.* New York:
Routledge, 1988.

———. *The Politics of Postmodernism.* New York: Routledge, 1989.

———. "Postmodernism." In *Encyclopedia of Contemporary Literary Theory: Approaches, Scholars, Terms,* edited by Irena R. Makaryk, 612–13. Toronto: University of Toronto Press, 1993.

Hutchinson, John. *Nationalism.* New York: Oxford University Press, 1994.

Hutchinson, John, and Anthony D. Smith, eds. *The Dynamics of Cultural Nationalism.* London: Allen and Unwin, 1987.

Hutchinson, W. H. "The Cowboy in Short Fiction." In *A Literary History of the
American West,* compiled by WLA, 515–22. Fort Worth: Texas Christian University Press, 1987.

Huyssen, Andreas. *After the Great Divide: Modernism, Mass Culture, Postmodernism.* Bloomington: Indiana University Press, 1986.

———. "Mapping the Postmodern." In *Feminism/Postmodernism,* edited by Linda J.
Nicholson, 234–77. New York: Routledge, 1990.

Hyde, Anna Farrar. *An American Vision: Far Western Landscape and National Culture, 1820–1920.* New York: New York University Press, 1990.

Inness, Sherrie A., and Diana Royer, eds. *Breaking Boundaries: New Perspectives on
Women's Regional Writing.* Iowa City: University of Iowa Press, 1997.

Irigaray, Luce. *The Sex Which Is Not One.* Translated by Catherine Porter. Ithaca,
N.Y.: Cornell University Press, 1985 [1977].

Jackson, Peter. *An Introduction to Cultural Geography.* London: Unwin Hyman,
1989.

Jameson, Elizabeth. "Toward a Multicultural History of Women in the Western
United States." *Signs* 13.4 (1988): 761–91.

Jameson, Fredric. *Postmodernism, or the Cultural Logic of Late Capitalism.* Durham,
N.C.: Duke University Press, 1991.

Jay, Karla. *Tales of the Lavender Menace: A Memoir of Liberation.* Boulder, Colo.:
Basic, 1998.

Jay, Paul. "The Myth of 'America' and the Politics of Location: Border Studies, and
the Literature of the Americas." *Arizona Quarterly* 54.2 (Summer 1998): 165–
92.

Jeffords, Susan. *The Remasculinization of America: Gender and the Vietnam War.*
Bloomington: Indiana University Press, 1989.

Jeffrey, Julie Roy. *Frontier Women: The Trans-Mississippi West, 1840–1880.* New
York: Hill and Wang, 1979.

Jeffries, John. "Toward a Redefinition of the Urban: The Collision of Culture." In
Black Popular Culture, a project of Michelle Wallace, edited by Gina Dent, 153–
63. Seattle, Wash.: Bay Area Press, 1992.

Jehlen, Myra. *American Incarnation: The Individual, the Nation, the Continent.*
Cambridge, Mass.: Harvard University Press, 1986.

Jensen, Joan, and Darliss Miller, eds. *New Mexican Women: Intercultural Perspectives.* Albuquerque: University of New Mexico Press, 1986.

Jensen, Merrill. *Regionalism in America*. Madison: University of Wisconsin Press, 1951.

Johnson, Susan Lee. " 'The Gold She Gathered': Difference and Domination in the California Gold Rush, 1848–1853." Ph.D. dissertation, Yale University, 1993.

——. " 'A Memory Sweet to Soldiers': The Significance of Gender in the History of the 'American West.' " *Western Historical Quarterly* 24.4 (Nov. 1993): 465–518.

Jones, Jacqueline. *Labor of Love, Labor of Sorrow*. New York: Random House, 1986.

Jones-Eddy, Julie. *Homesteading Women: An Oral History of Colorado 1890–1950*. New York: Twayne, 1992.

Jordan, David, ed. *Regionalism Reconsidered: New Approaches to the Field*. New York: Garland, 1994.

Jordan, Teresa, and James Hepworth, eds. *The Stories That Shape Us: Contemporary Women Write about the West*. New York: W. W. Norton, 1995.

Kaplan, Amy. "Nation, Region, and Empire." In *Columbia History of the American Novel*, edited by Emory Elliott, 240–66. New York: Columbia University Press, 1991.

——. "Romancing the Empire: The Embodiment of American Masculinity in the Popular Historical Novel of the 1890s." *American Literary History* 2.4 (Dec. 1990): 659–90.

Katz, Jonathan. *Gay American History: Lesbians and Gay Men in the USA*. New York: Harper and Row, 1985 [1976].

Kaye, Frances W. *Isolation and Masquerade: Willa Cather's Women*. New York: Peter Lang, 1993.

Kelley, Mary. *Private Woman, Public Stage: Literary Domesticity in Nineteenth-Century America*. New York: Oxford University Press, 1984.

Kimmel, Michael. *Manhood in America*. New York: Simon and Schuster, 1996.

Kingsolver, Barbara. *Animal Dreams: A Novel*. New York: HarperCollins, 1990.

——. *Another America: Otra America*. Emeryville, Calif.: Seal, 1992.

——. *Bean Trees: A Novel*. New York: Harper and Row, 1988.

——. *High Tide in Tucson: Essays from Now or Never*. New York: HarperCollins, 1995.

——. *Holding the Line: Women in the Great Arizona Mine Strike of 1983*. IRL Book Series. Ithaca, N.Y.: Cornell University Press, 1989; republished 1996.

——. *Homeland and Other Stories*. New York: Perennial Library, 1989.

Kingston, Maxine Hong. *China Men*. New York: Knopf, 1980.

——. *Tripmaster Monkey: His Fake Book*. New York: Knopf, 1989; reprint, New York: Vintage, 1990.

——. *The Woman Warrior: Memoirs of a Girlhood among Ghosts*. New York: Knopf, 1976.

Kirby, Kathleen M. "Thinking Through the Boundary: The Politics of Location, Subjects, and Space." *boundary 2* 20.2 (1993): 174–89.

Kocks, Dorothee. *The Geographic Embrace: Land and Social Justice in the Twentieth Century*. Berkeley: University of California Press, forthcoming.

Kolodny, Annette. *The Land Before Her: Fantasy and Experience of the American Frontiers: 1630–1860*. Chapel Hill: University of North Carolina Press, 1984.

Kowalewski, Michael, ed. *Reading the West: New Essays on the Literature of the American West*. New York: Cambridge University Press, 1996.

Lamar, Howard R. "Keeping the Faith: The Forgotten Generation of Literary Turn-erians, 1920–60." In *Frontier and Regions*, edited by Robert C. Ritchie and Paul Andrew Hutton, 231–50. Albuquerque: University of New Mexico Press, 1997.

Lee, Josephine. *Performing Asian America: Race and Ethnicity on the Contemporary Stage*. Philadelphia: Temple University Press, 1997.

Lee, L., and Merrill Lewis, eds. *Women, Women Writers, and the West*. New York: Troy Publishing, 1979.

Lee, Robert. "*The Woman Warrior* as an Intervention in Asian American Histo-riography." In *Approaches to Teaching Kingston's The Woman Warrior*, edited by Shirley Geok-lin Lim, 52–63. New York: Modern Language Association of America, 1991.

Lefebvre, Henri. *The Production of Space*. Translated by Donald Nicholson-Smith. Malden, Mass.: Blackwell, 1991.

Lehan, Richard. "The Los Angeles Novel and the Idea of the West." In *Los Angeles in Fiction*, edited by David Fine, 29–42. Albuquerque: University of New Mexico Press, 1984.

Lensink, Judy Nolte. *Old Southwest/New Southwest*. Tucson, Ariz.: Tucson Public Library, 1988.

Leopold, Aldo. *Sand County Almanac: With Other Essays on Conservation from Round River*. Illustrated by Charles W. Schwartz. New York: Oxford University Press, 1966.

Lewis, L. M. "Ethnic and Gender Identity: Parallel Growth in Sandra Cisneros's *Woman Hollering Creek*." *Short Story* 2.2 (Fall 1991): 69–78.

Lewis, Martin W. *Green Delusions: An Environmentalist's Critique of Radical En-vironmentalism*. Durham, N.C.: Duke University Press, 1992.

Lewis, R. W. B. *The American Adam*. Chicago: University of Chicago Press, 1955.

Lim, Shirley Geok-lin, ed. *Approaches to Teaching Kingston's The Woman Warrior*. New York: Modern Language Association of America, 1991.

Limerick, Patricia Nelson. "Disorientation and Reorientation: The American Land-scape Discovered from the West." *Journal of American History* 79.3 (Dec. 1992): 1021–49.

——. *Legacy of Conquest*. New York: Norton, 1987.

——. "The Realization of the American West." In *The New Regionalism*, edited by Charles Reagan Wilson, 71–98. Jackson: University of Mississippi Press, 1998.

——. "Turnerians All: The Dream of a Helpful History in an Intelligible World." *American Historical Review* (June 1995): 697–716.

Limerick, Patricia Nelson, Clyde A. Milner II, and Charles E. Rankin, eds. *Trails: Toward a New Western History*. Lawrence: University Press of Kansas, 1991.

Ling, Amy. *Between Worlds: Women Writers of Chinese Ancestry*. New York: Per-gamon, 1990.

——. "Chinese American Women Writers: The Tradition Behind Maxine Hong Kingston." In *Redefining American Literary History*, edited by A. LaVonne Brown Ruoff and Jerry W. Ward Jr., 219–36. New York: Modern Language As-sociation of America, 1990.

Lipsitz, George. *Time Passages: Collective Memory and American Popular Culture*. Minneapolis: University of Minnesota Press, 1990.

Loeffelholz, Mary. *Experimental Lives: Women and Literature, 1900–1945*. New York: Twayne, 1995.

Loris, Michelle Carbone. *Innocence, Loss and Recovery in the Art of Joan Didion*. New York: Peter Lang, 1989.

Love, Glen A. *New Americans: The Westerner and the Modern Experience in the American Novel*. London: Association of University Presses, 1982.

——. "Revaluing Nature: Toward an Ecological Criticism." *Western American Literature* 27.3 (1990): 201–15.

Lowe, Lisa. *Immigrant Acts: On Asian American Cultural Politics*. Durham, N.C.: Duke University Press, 1996.

Lowenthal, D., and M. J. Bowden, eds. *Geographies of the Mind*. New York: Oxford University Press, 1976.

Luchetti, Cathy, and Carol Olwell. *Women of the West*. New York: Orion, 1982.

Luhan, Mabel Dodge. *Intimate Memories*. 4 vols. New York: Harcourt, Brace, 1933–37.

Lyon, Thomas J. "The Nature Essay in the West." In *A Literary History of the American West*, compiled by WLA, 221–65. Fort Worth: Texas Christian University Press, 1987.

——. "Revisionist Western Classics." In *Reading the West: New Essays on the Literature of the American West*, edited by Michael Kowalewski, 144–56. New York: Cambridge University Press, 1996.

Lyotard, J. F. "Answering the Question: What Is Postmodernism." In *The Post-Modern Condition*, 71–82. Minneapolis: University of Minnesota Press, 1984.

McAllister, Mick. "Homeward Bound: Wilderness and Frontier in American Indian Literature." In *The Frontier Experience and the American Dream: Essays on American Literature*, edited by David Mogen, Mark Busby, and Paul Bryant, 149–58. College Station: Texas A&M University Press, 1989.

McClure, John A. "Late Imperial Romance." *Raritan* 10.4 (Spring 1991): 111–30.

McKibben, Bill. *The End of Nature*. New York: Random House, 1989.

McMurtry, Larry. "How the West Was Won or Lost." *New Republic*, Oct. 22, 1990, 32.

McWilliams, Carey. *California: The Great Exception*. Santa Barbara, Calif.: Peregrine Smith, 1979.

Magistrale, Tony, and Patricia Ferreira. "Sweet Mama Wanda Tells Fortunes." *Black American Literature Forum* 24.3 (1990): 491–507.

Martin, Julia. "New with Added Ecology?: Hippos, Forests and Environmental Literacy." *ISLE: Interdisciplinary Studies in Literature and Environment* 2.1 (1994): 1–11.

Marx, Leo. *The Machine in the Garden*. New York: Oxford University Press, 1964.

Massey, Doreen. "Flexible Sexism." *Environment and Planning D: Society and Space* 9 (1991): 31–57.

——. *Space, Place, and Gender*. Cambridge, U.K.: Polity, 1994.

Massey, Doreen, and John Allen, eds. *Geography Matters!: A Reader*. New York: Cambridge University Press, 1984.

Matsumoto, Valerie. "Desperately Seeking 'Dierdre': Gender Roles, Multicultural Relations, and Nisei Women Writers of the 1930s." In *Writing the Range: Race,*

Class, and Culture in the Women's West, edited by Elizabeth Jameson and Susan Armitage, 461–74. Norman: University of Oklahoma Press, 1997.

——. *Farming the Home Place: A Japanese American Community in California, 1919–1982.* Ithaca: Cornell University Press, 1993.

Matthiessen, F. O. *American Renaissance: Art and Expression in the Age of Emerson and Whitman.* New York: Oxford University Press, 1941.

Meinig, D. W., ed. *The Interpretation of Ordinary Landscapes.* New York: Oxford University Press, 1979.

Meldrum, Barbara Howard, ed. *Under the Sun: Myth and Realism in Western American Literature.* Troy, N.Y.: Whitson Publishing, 1985.

Mercer, Kobena. " '1968': Periodizing Postmodern Politics and Identity." In *Cultural Studies,* edited by Lawrence Grossberg, Cary Nelson, and Paula Treichler, 424–49. New York: Routledge, 1992.

Merchant, Carolyn, ed. *The Death of Nature: Women, Ecology, and the Scientific Revolution.* San Francisco: Harper and Row, 1980.

——. *Major Problems in Environmental History.* Lexington, Mass.: D. C. Heath, 1993.

——. "Reinventing Eden: Western Culture as a Recovery Narrative." In *Uncommon Ground: Toward Reinventing Nature,* edited by William Cronon, 132–70. New York: Norton, 1995.

Michaels, Leonard, David Reid, and Raquel Scherr, eds. *West of the West: Imagining California.* San Francisco: North Point, 1989.

Miller, Heather Ross. "America the Big Lie, the Quintessential." *Southern Review* 29.2 (Spring 1993): 420–30.

Miller, Karen K. "Black Studies in California Higher Education, 1965–1980." Ph.D. dissertation, University of California Santa Barbara, 1986.

Miller, Perry. *The New England Mind.* Cambridge, Mass.: Harvard University Press, 1939.

Milner, Clyde A., II, ed. *Major Problems in the History of the American West.* Lexington, Mass.: D. C. Heath, 1989.

Milton, John R. *The Novel of the American West.* Lincoln: University Press of Nebraska, 1980.

Mitchell, Carolyn. " 'A Laying On of Hands': Transcending the City in Ntozake Shange's *for colored girls who have considered suicide/when the rainbow is enuf.*" In *Women Writers and the City: Essays in Feminist Literary Criticism,* edited by Susan Merrill Squier, 230–48. Knoxville: University of Tennessee Press, 1984.

Mitchell, W. G. T. *Landscape and Power.* Chicago: University of Chicago Press, 1994.

Mizener, Arthur. "Does a Moral Vision of the Thirties Deserve a Nobel Prize?" *New York Times Book Review,* Dec. 9, 1962, VII:4+.

Mogen, David. "The Frontier Archetype and the Myth of America: Patterns That Shape the American Dream." In *The Frontier Experience and the American Dream: Essays on American Literature,* edited by David Mogen, Mark Busby, and Paul Bryant, 15–30. College Station: Texas A&M University Press, 1989.

Mogen, David, Mark Busby, and Paul Bryant, eds. *The Frontier Experience and the American Dream: Essays on American Literature.* College Station: Texas A&M University Press, 1989.

Moon, Michael, and Cathy N. Davidson, eds. *Subjects and Citizens: Nation, Race and Gender from Oroonoko to Anita Hill*. Durham, N.C.: Duke University Press, 1995.

Morin, Karin. "The Gender of Geography" (review of Gillian Rose's *Feminism and Geography*). *Postmodern Culture* 5.2 (Jan. 1995).

Morrissey, Katherine G. "Commentary on Patricia Limerick's 'Realization of the American West.'" In *The New Regionalism*, edited by Charles Reagan Wilson, 98–103. Jackson: University of Mississippi Press, 1998.

———. *Mental Territories: Mapping the Inland Empire*. Ithaca, N.Y.: Cornell University Press, 1997.

Murphy, Patrick D. *Literature, Nature and Other: Ecofeminist Critiques*. Albany: State University of New York, 1995.

Myers, Sandra L. *Westering Women and the Frontier Experience, 1880–1915*. Albuquerque: University of New Mexico Press, 1982.

Naremore, James, and Patrick Brantlinger. *Modernity and Mass Culture*. Bloomington: Indiana University Press, 1991.

Nash, Gerald. "Point of View: One Hundred Years of Western History." *Journal of the West* 32.1 (Jan. 1993): 3–4.

Nash, Gerald D., and Richard W. Etulain, eds. *The Twentieth-Century West: Historical Interpretations*. Albuquerque: University of New Mexico Press, 1989.

Nash, Roderick. *Wilderness and the American Mind*. New Haven, Conn.: Yale University Press, 1982.

Nelson, Robert M. *Place and Vision: The Function of the Landscape in Native American Fiction*. New York: Peter Lang, 1993.

Newey, Vincent, and Ann Thompson, eds. *Literature and Nationalism*. Liverpool, U.K.: Liverpool University Press, 1991.

Nicholson, Linda, ed. *Feminism/Postmodernism*. New York: Routledge, 1990.

Nomura, Gail M., Russell Endo, and Stephen Sumida, eds. *Frontiers of Asian American Studies*. Pullman: Washington State University Press, 1989.

Norwood, Robin. *Women Who Love Too Much: When You Keep Wishing and Hoping He'll Change*. New York: St. Martin's, 1985.

Norwood, Vera. *Made from this Earth: American Women and Nature*. Chapel Hill: University of North Carolina Press, 1993.

Norwood, Vera, and Janice Monk, eds. *The Desert Is No Lady: Southwestern Landscapes in Women's Writing and Art*. New Haven, Conn.: Yale University Press, 1987.

Nugent, Walter. "Where Is the American West: Report on a Survey." *Montana: The Magazine of Western History* 42.3 (1992): 1–24.

O'Brien, Sharon. *Willa Cather: The Emerging Voice*. New York: Oxford University Press, 1987.

Oelschlaeger, Max. *The Idea of Wilderness: From Prehistory to the Age of Ecology*. New Haven, Conn.: Yale University Press, 1991.

Omi, Michael, and Howard Winant. *Racial Formation in the United States: From the 1960s to the 1990s*. 2d ed. New York: Routledge, 1994 [1986].

Ong, Paul, Edna Bonachich, and Lucie Cheng, eds. *The New Asian Immigration to Los Angeles and the Globalization of World Economy*. Philadelphia, Pa.: Temple University Press, 1994.

Ostler, Jeffrey, and Robert Johnston. "The Politics and Antipolitics of Western History." Paper delivered at the Western History Association Conference, Denver, Colo., 1995.

Papanikolas, Zeese. *Trickster in a Land of Dreams*. Lincoln: University of Nebraska Press, 1995.

Parker, Andrew, Mary Russo, Doris Sommer, and Patricia Yaeger, eds. *Nationalisms and Sexualities*. New York: Routledge, 1992.

Pease, Donald E., ed. *National Identities and Post-Americanist Narratives*. Durham, N.C.: Duke University Press, 1994.

Pepper, David. *Eco-Socialism: From Deep Ecology to Social Justice*. New York: Routledge, 1993.

Perry, Donna. *Backtalk: Women Writers Speak Out*. New Brunswick, N.J.: Rutgers University Press, 1993.

Peters, J. U. "The Los Angeles Anti-Myth." In *Essays on California Writers*, edited by Charles L. Crow, 21–32. Bowling Green, Ohio: Bowling Green State University Press, 1978.

Petrik, Paula. *No Step Backward: Women and Family on the Rocky Mountain Mining Frontier, Helena, Montana: 1865–1900*. Helena: Montana Historical Society Press, 1987.

Pilkington, William T. *Critical Essays on the Western American Novel*. Boston: G. K. Hall, 1980.

Plimpton, George, ed. *The Paris Review Interviews: Writers at Work*. 5th ser. New York: Penguin, 1981.

Plumwood, Val. *Feminism and the Mastery of Nature*. New York: Routledge, 1993.

Pratt, Jane, and Kelli Pryor. *For Real: The Uncensored Truth About America's Teenagers*. New York: Hyperion, 1995.

Price, Jennifer. "Looking for Nature at the Mall: A Field Guide to the Nature Company." In *Uncommon Ground: Toward Reinventing Nature*, edited by William Cronon, 186–204. New York: Norton, 1995.

Probyn, Elspeth. "Travels in the Postmodern: Making Sense of the Local." In *Feminism/Postmodernism*, edited by Linda J. Nicholson, 176–89. New York: Routledge, 1990.

Pryse, Marjorie. "Origins of American Literary Regionalism: Gender in Irving, Stowe, and Longstreet." In *Breaking Boundaries: New Perspectives on Women's Regional Writing*, edited by Sherrie A. Inness and Diana Royer, 17–37. Iowa City: University of Iowa Press, 1997.

Pugh, Simon, ed. *Reading Landscape: Country, City, Capital*. New York: St. Martin's, 1990.

Quantic, Diane Dufva. *The Nature of the Place: A Study of Great Plains Fiction*. Lincoln: University of Nebraska Press, 1995.

Radway, Janice A. *Reading the Romance: Women, Patriarchy, and Popular Literature*. Chapel Hill: University of North Carolina Press, 1984.

Rankin, Charles E., ed. *Wallace Stegner: Man and Writer*. Foreword by Stewart L. Udall. Albuquerque: University of New Mexico Press, 1996.

Rebolledo, Tey Diana. "Tradition and Mythology: Chicana Literature." In *The Desert Is No Lady: Southwestern Landscape in Women's Writing and Art*, edited by

Vera Norwood and Janice Monk, 96–124. New Haven, Conn.: Yale University Press, 1987.

———. *Women Singing in the Snow: A Cultural Analysis of Chicana Literature*. Tucson: University of Arizona Press, 1995.

Rebolledo, Tey Diana, and Eliana S. Rivero. *Infinite Divisions: An Anthology of Chicana Literature*. Tucson: University of Arizona Press, 1993.

Reid, David, ed. *Sex, Death, and God in L.A.* Berkeley: University of California Press, 1994.

Reuckert, William. "Literature and Ecology: An Experiment in Ecocriticism." *Iowa Review* 9.1 (1978): 71–87.

Rich, Adrienne. "Notes Toward a Politics of Location." In *Blood, Bread, and Poetry: Selected Prose 1979–1985*. New York: W. W. Norton, 1986.

Riley, Glenda. *Women and Indians on the Frontier, 1825–1915*. Albuquerque: University of New Mexico Press, 1984.

Rivera, John-Michael. "The Rules of Chicano Cultural Production: Arte Público and the Dialectics of the Chicano 'Field.' " Unpublished manuscript, University of Texas, Austin.

Robbins, Jim. "Righting History: Exposing the Myth of the American West." *Boston Sunday Globe*, July 15, 1990.

Robinson, Forrest. *Having It Both Ways: Self-Subversion in Western Popular Classics*. Albuquerque: University of New Mexico Press, 1993.

———. "The Roosevelt-Wister Connection: Some Notes on the West and the Uses of History." *Western American Literature* 14 (1979): 95–114.

Ronnow, Gretchen. "Tayo, Death, and Desire: A Lacanian Reading of *Ceremony*." In *Narrative Chance: Postmodern Discourse on Native American Literatures*, edited by Gerald Vizenor, 69–90. Norman: University of Oklahoma Press, 1993.

Rose, Gillian. *Feminism and Geography: The Limits of Geographical Knowledge*. Minneapolis: University of Minnesota Press, 1993.

Rosowski, Susan J. "Jean Stafford Rewrites the Western." In *Reading the West: New Essays on the Literature of the American West*, edited by Michael Kowalewski, 157–76. New York: Cambridge University Press, 1996.

Rouse, Richard. "Mexican Migration and the Social Space of Postmodernism." *Diaspora* 1.1 (1991): 8–23.

Rudnick, Lois Palken. *Mabel Dodge Luhan: New Woman, New Worlds*. Albuquerque: University of New Mexico Press, 1984.

———. "Re-Naming the Land: Anglo Expatriate Women in the Southwest." In *The Desert Is No Lady: Southwestern Landscapes in Women's Writing and Art*, edited by Vera Norwood and Janice Monk, 10–26. New Haven, Conn.: Yale University Press, 1986.

Ruiz de Burton, María Amparo. *Who Would Have Thought It?* Edited and introduction by Rosaura Sanchez and Beatrice Pita. Houston: Arte Público Press, 1995 [1872].

Rupp, Leila J. *Worlds of Women: The Making of an International Women's Movement*. Princeton, N.J.: Princeton University Press, 1998.

Rusk, Ralph Leslie. *The Literature of the Middle Western Frontier*. New York: Columbia University Press, 1925.

Said, Edward. *Orientalism*. New York: Random House, 1979.

Saldívar, José David. *Border Matters: Remapping American Cultural Studies*. Berkeley: University of California Press, 1997.

———. *The Dialectics of Our America: Genealogy, Cultural Critique, and Literary History*. Durham, N.C.: Duke University Press, 1991.

Sale, Kirkpatrick. *Power Shift: The Rise of the Southern Rim and Its Challenge to the Eastern Establishment*. New York: Random House, 1975.

Sandoval, Chela. "U.S. Third World Feminism: Theory and Method of Oppositional Consciousness in the Postmodern World." *Genders* 10 (Spring 1991): 1–24.

Santigian, Laura. "Revision and Resistance: Gender, Race, and Memory in Public History of the American West." Ph.D. dissertation, Brown University, in progress.

Scharnhorst, Gary. "The Virginian as a Founding Father." *Arizona Quarterly* 40 (1984): 227–41.

Schlissel, Lillian, Susan Armitage, and Byrd Gibbons. *Far from Home: Families of the Westward Journey*. New York: Schocken, 1989.

Schlissel, Lillian, Vicki L. Ruíz, and Janice Monk, eds. *Western Women: Their Land, Their Lives*. Albuquerque: University of New Mexico Press, 1988.

Schneir, Miriam, ed. *Feminism in Our Time: The Essential Writings, World War II to the Present*. New York: Vintage, 1994.

Schrager, Cynthia D. "Questioning the Promise of Self-Help: A Reading of *Women Who Love Too Much*." *Feminist Studies* 19.1 (Spring 1993): 177–92.

Scott, Bonnie Kime, ed. *The Gender of Modernism*. Bloomington: Indiana University Press, 1990.

Scott, Joan Wallach. *Only Paradoxes to Offer: French Feminists and the Rights of Man*. Cambridge, Mass.: Harvard University Press, 1996.

Sedgwick, Eve Kosofsky. *Tendencies*. London: Routledge, 1994.

Shaddock, Jennifer. "Mixed Blood Women: The Dynamic of Women's Relations in the Novels of Louise Erdrich and Leslie Silko." In *Feminist Nightmares: Feminism and the Problem of Sisterhood*, edited by Susan Ostrov and Jennifer Fleischner, 106–21. New York: New York University Press, 1994.

Showalter, Elaine, ed. *The New Feminist Criticism: Essays on Women, Literature and Theory*. New York: Pantheon, 1985.

Siegel, Mark. "Contemporary Trends in Western American Fiction." In *A Literary History of the American West*, compiled by WLA, 1182–1201. Fort Worth: Texas Christian University Press, 1987.

Silberman, Robert. "Opening the Text: *Love Medicine* and the Return of the Native American Woman." In *Narrative Chance: Postmodern Discourse on Native American Literatures*, edited by Gerald Vizenor, 101–20. Norman: University of Oklahoma Press, 1993.

Silko, Leslie Marmon. *Almanac of the Dead*. New York: Simon and Schuster, 1991.

———. *Ceremony*. New York: Penguin, 1977.

———. "Landscape, History, and the Pueblo Imagination." *Antaeus* 57 (Autumn 1986): 83–94.

———. "Language and Literature from a Pueblo Indian Perspective." In *English Literature: Opening Up the Canon*, edited by Leslie Fiedler and Houston A. Baker, 54–72. Baltimore, Md.: Johns Hopkins University Press, 1981.

Simonson, Harold Peter. *Beyond the Frontier: Writers, Western Regionalism and a Sense of Place*. Fort Worth: Texas Christian University Press, 1989.

Sizemore, Christine W. "Masculine and Feminine Cities: Marge Piercy's *Going Down Fast* and *Fly Away Home*." *Frontiers* 13.1 (1992): 90–110.

Slotkin, Richard. *Regeneration Through Violence: The Mythology of the American Frontier, 1600–1860*. Middletown, Conn.: Wesleyan University Press, 1973.

Slovic, Scott. *Seeking Awareness in American Nature Writing*. Salt Lake City: University of Utah Press, 1992.

Smith, David Lionel. "The Black Arts Movement and Its Critics." In *The American Literary History Reader*, edited by Gordon Hutner, 204–21. New York: Oxford University Press, 1995.

Smith, Henry Nash. *Virgin Land: The American West as Symbol and Myth*. Cambridge, Mass.: Harvard University Press, 1950.

Smith, Patricia Clark, with Paula Gunn Allen. "Earthly Relations, Carnal Knowledge: Southwestern American Indian Women Writers and Landscape." In *The Desert Is No Lady: Southwestern Landscapes in Women's Writing and Art*, edited by Vera Norwood and Janice Monk, 174–96. New Haven, Conn.: Yale University Press, 1987.

Snyder, Gary. *The Real Work: Interviews and Talks, 1964–1979*. Edited by Scott McLean. New York: New Directions, 1980.

———. *Turtle Island*. New York: New Directions, 1974.

Soja, Edward W. *Postmodern Geographies: The Reassertion of Space in Critical Social Theory*. London: Verso, 1989.

"The Southwest by Women." Special issue, *Southwestern American Literature* (Summer 1995).

Spretnak, Charlene. "Ecofeminism: Our Roots and Flowering." In *Reweaving the World: The Emergence of Ecofeminism*, edited by Irene Diamond and Gloria Feman Orenstein, 3–14. San Francisco, Calif.: Sierra Club Books, 1990.

Squier, Susan Merrill, ed. *Women Writers and the City: Essays in Feminist Literary Criticism*. Knoxville: University of Tennessee Press, 1984.

Stafford, Jean. *The Mountain Lion*. New York: Harcourt, Brace, 1947.

Starr, Kevin. *Americans and the California Dream, 1850–1915*. New York: Oxford University Press, 1973.

Stauffer, Helen Winter, and Susan J. Rosowski, eds. *Women and Western American Literature*. Troy, N.Y.: Whitson, 1982.

Stegner, Page, and Mary Stegner. *The Geography of Hope: A Tribute to Wallace Stegner*. San Francisco, Calif.: Sierra Club Books, 1996.

Stegner, Wallace. *The American West as Living Space*. Ann Arbor: University of Michigan Press, 1987.

———. "Born a Square." In *The Sound of Mountain Water*, 170–86.

———. "Coda: A Wilderness Letter." In *The Sound of Mountain Water*, 145–53.

———. "History, Myth and the Western Writer." In *The Sound of Mountain Water*, 186–201.

———. *One Nation*. Boston: Houghton Mifflin, 1945.

———. "Out Where the Sense of Place Is a Sense of Motion." *Los Angeles Times Book Review*, June 13, 1990, 15.

———. *The Sound of Mountain Water*. New York: Doubleday, 1969; reprint, Lincoln: University of Nebraska Press, 1985.

———. "Variations on a Theme by Conrad." *Yale Review* 49 (Mar. 1950).

———. *Where the Bluebird Sings to the Lemonade Springs: Living and Writing in the West*. New York: Random House, 1992.

Stegner, Wallace, with Richard W. Etulain. *Conversations with Wallace Stegner on Western History and Literature*. Salt Lake City: University of Utah Press, 1983; revised 1990.

Sturgeon, Noël. *Ecofeminist Natures: Race, Gender, Feminist Theory, and Political Action*. New York: Routledge, 1997.

———, ed. "Intersections of Feminisms and Environmentalists," Special issue, *Frontiers* 28.2 (1997).

Swan, Edith E. "Laguna Symbolic Geography and Silko's *Ceremony*." *American Indian Quarterly* 12.3 (Summer 1988): 229–49.

Swartz, Patti Capel. " 'Saving Grace': Political and Environmental Issues and the Role of Connections in Barbara Kingsolver's *Animal Dreams*." *ISLE: Interdisciplinary Studies in Literature and Environment* 1.1 (Spring 1993): 65–79.

Takaki, Ronald T. *Strangers from a Different Shore: A History of Asian Americans*. Boston: Little, Brown, 1989.

Tatum, Stephen. "The Problem of the 'Popular' in the New Western History." *Arizona Quarterly* 53.2 (1997): 153–90.

Temple, Judy Nolte, ed. *Open Spaces, City Places: Contemporary Writers on the Changing Southwest*. Tucson: University of Arizona Press, 1994.

Thacker, Robert. *The Great Prairie Fact and Literary Imagination*. Albuquerque: University of New Mexico Press, 1989.

Thomson, Jeff. " 'What Is Called Heaven': Identity in Sandra Cisneros's *Woman Hollering Creek*." *Studies in Short Fiction* 31.3 (Summer 1994): 415–24.

Tompkins, Jane. *Sensational Designs: The Cultural Work of American Fiction, 1790–1860*. New York: Oxford University Press, 1985.

———. *West of Everything: The Inner Life of Westerns*. New York: Oxford University Press, 1992.

"A Tribute to Wallace Stegner." Special issue, *Montana: The Magazine of Western History* 41.4 (1993).

Truettner, William H., ed. *The West as America: Reinterpreting Images of the Frontier, 1820–1920*. Washington, D.C.: Smithsonian Institution Press, 1991.

Tuan, Yi-Fu. *Space and Place: The Perspective of Experience*. Minneapolis: University of Minnesota Press, 1977.

———. *Topophilia: A Study of Environment Perception, Attitudes and Values*. Englewood Cliffs, N.J.: Prentice Hall, 1974.

Turner, Frederick Jackson. "The Significance of the Frontier in American History." Originally published 1893; republished in *The Frontier in American History*, foreword by Wilbur R. Jacobs, 1–38. Tucson: University of Arizona Press, 1986.

Tuska, John, and Vicki Piekarski. *Encyclopedia of Frontier and Western Fiction*. New York: McGraw-Hill, 1983.

Twelve Southerners. *I'll Take My Stand: The South and the Agrarian Tradition*. New York: Harper, 1930.

Udall, Sharyn Rohlfsen. *Contested Terrain: Myth and Meanings in Southwest Art*. Albuquerque: University of New Mexico Press, 1996.

Vizenor, Gerald. *Narrative Chance: Postmodern Discourse on Native American Literatures*. Norman: University of Oklahoma Press, 1993.

Vorpahl, Ben Merchant. *My Dear Wister: The Frederic Remington–Owen Wister Letters*. Palo Alto, Calif.: American West, 1972.

———. "Roosevelt, Wister, Turner and Remington." In *A Literary History of the American West*, edited by J. Golden Taylor et al., 276–302. Fort Worth: Texas Christian University Press, 1987.

Walker, Martin. "How the West Was Won, or Was It?" *The Guardian*, June 13, 1991.

Wang, Alfred S. "Maxine Hong Kingston's Reclaiming of America: The Birthright of the Chinese American Male." *South Dakota Review* 26.1 (Spring 1988): 18–29.

Waugh, Patricia. *Practising Postmodernism, Reading Modernism*. London: Edward Arnold, 1992.

Western Literature Association (WLA), comp. *A Literary History of the American West*. Sponsored by the Western Literature Association. Fort Worth: Texas Christian University Press, 1987.

———. *Updating the Literary West*. Fort Worth: Texas Christian University Press, 1997.

"Western Women's History Revisited." Special issue, *Pacific Historical Review* 61.4 (1992).

Wetherby, James B., and Stephanie L. Witt. *The Urban West: Managing Growth and Decline*. Westport, Conn.: Greenwood, 1994.

White, Edward G. *The Eastern Establishment and the Western Experience: The West of Frederic Remington, Theodore Roosevelt and Owen Wister*. New Haven, Conn.: Yale University Press, 1968.

White, Richard. "Are You an Environmentalist or Do You Work for a Living?: Work and Nature." In *Uncommon Ground: Toward Reinventing Nature*, edited by William Cronon, 171–85. New York: Norton, 1995.

———. "Discovering Nature in North America." *Journal of American History* 79.3 (Dec. 1992): 874–91.

———. *It's Your Misfortune and None of My Own: A New History of the American West*. Norman: University of Oklahoma Press, 1991.

———. "The Made and Unmade Worlds: Labor and Western Spaces." Paper presented at annual meeting of the Western Historical Association, Albuquerque, N.Mex., 1994.

Whitehead, Harriet. "The Bow and the Burden Strap: A New Look at Institutionalized Homosexuality in Native North America." In *The Gay and Lesbian Studies Reader*, edited by Henry Abelove, Michele Aina Barale, and David Halperin, 498–527. New York: Routledge, 1993.

Whiteley, Sheila. *The Space Between Notes: Rock and the Counter-Culture*. New York: Routledge, 1992.

Whyte, Christopher. *Gendering the Nation: Studies in Modern Scottish Literature*. New York: Columbia University Press, 1995.

Wild, Peter. "Sentimentalism in the American Southwest: John C. Van Dyke, Mary Austin, and Edward Abbey." In *Reading the West: New Essays on the Literature of* the *American West*, edited by Michael Kowalewski, 127–43. New York: Cambridge University Press, 1996.

Williams, Raymond. *The Country and the City*. London: Chatto and Windus, 1973.

——. *Culture and Society*. London: Chatto and Windus, 1958.

Williams, Terry Tempest. *Desert Quartet: An Erotic Landscape*. New York: Pantheon, 1995.

——. *Pieces of White Shell; A Journey to Navajoland*. New York: Scribner, 1984.

——. *Refuge: An Unnatural History of Family and Place*. New York: Pantheon, 1991.

Willis, Meredith Sue. "Barbara Kingsolver, Moving On." *Appalachian Journal* 22.1 (Fall 1994): 78–86.

Winchell, Mark Royden. *Joan Didion*. New York: Twayne, 1980.

Wong, Sau-Ling Cynthia. *Reading Asian American Literature: From Necessity to Extravagance*. Princeton, N.J.: Princeton University Press, 1993.

Worster, Donald. *Rivers of Empire: Water, Aridity, and the Growth of the American West*. New York: Pantheon, 1985.

Wyatt, David. *The Fall Into Eden: Landscape and Imagination in California*. New York: Cambridge University Press, 1986.

Yalom, Marilyn. *West Coast Women Writers*. Palo Alto, Calif.: Stanford University Press, 1984.

Zimmerman, Michael E., ed. *Environmental Philosophy from Animal Rights to Radical Ecology*. Englewood Cliffs, N.J.: Prentice Hall, 1993.

Index

Abbey, Edward, 3, 6, 39, 42, 125
Abortion, 75–76, 79, 100
Acosta, Oscar Zeta, 37, 108, 112
Adventure genre, 170–71, 193
African American writers: spatial terrain of, 34–35, 90, 248–49 (n. 32); Coleman's poetry, 87, 88–103; and "deterritorialization," 237. *See also* specific writers
Allen, Paula Gunn, 102, 159
American Indian writers. *See* Native American writers
"American mind" school, 1, 241 (n. 3)
Anaya, Rudolfo, 6, 37, 43, 86, 101, 139
Anderson, Benedict, 207
Anzaldúa, Gloria, 9–11, 159, 173, 210, 215–23, 233, 262–63 (n. 38)
Asian American writers: and literary magazines, 33, 38; western literature by, 36, 38, 105, 109–10, 249 (n. 36); spatial terrain of, 36, 249 (n. 36); and feminist questions, 48–49; early materials on, 63–64; and new female regionalism, 102; Kingston's works, 104–17; Wakatsuki Houston's *Farewell to Manzanar*, 209–16, 231; and "deterritorialization," 236–37. *See also* specific writers
Association for Study of Literature and the Environment (ASLE), 129
Atherton, Gertrude, 108, 109, 158
Austin, Mary, 40, 46, 63, 125, 157–59, 206, 207, 248 (n. 27)
Autobiographies: Wakatsuki Houston's *Farewell to Manzanar*, 209–16; Anzaldúa's *La Frontera/The Borderlands*, 216–23; Blew's *All But the Waltz*, 224–30

Baker, Alison, 139
Baldwin, James, 95
Barnes, Kim, 8, 126, 139, 262 (n. 26)
Battered women, 175–76, 239
Baywatch, 82–83, 87
Beaches, 80–85, 87–88, 95–99, 117
Bederman, Gail, 47, 156, 261 (n. 18)
Belsey, Catherine, 159
Bergon, Frank, 127
Berlant, Lauren, 6, 243 (n. 23)
Berry, Wendell, 39
Bevis, William, 3, 242 (n. 12)
Bhabha, Homi, 206
Bierce, Ambrose, 108, 109
Black Arts Movement, 34
Black Elk, 43
Blew, Mary Clearman, 8, 33, 126, 139–40, 223–33, 235
Bly, Robert, 193, 260 (n. 6)
"Borderlands," 27, 36, 177–78, 216–17, 221–22, 238, 263 (n. 38)
Bower, B. M., 158
Brand, Max, 39
Braverman, Kate, 139, 262 (n. 26)
Bredahl, A. Carl, 44–45
Brodhead, Richard, 15
Brownmiller, Susan, 49
Bryant, Dorothy, 262 (n. 26)
Bucco, Martin, 44
Buell, Lawrence, 127
Bukowski, Charles, 102
Bulosan, Carlos, 43, 108, 109
Butler, Judith, 196, 247 (n. 18), 252 (n. 3)

Cabeza de Baca, Fabiola, 31, 206, 207
California: as western continuum, 68–69, 117–19, 253 (n. 16); landscapes of generally, 69; Didion's Los

Angeles, 70, 77–88, 91, 101, 117; Didion's Sacramento, 72–74, 254 (n. 30); sexuality in, 80–85; beaches in, 80–85, 87–88, 95–99, 117; Coleman's Los Angeles, 87, 88–103, 117, 119; Kingston's San Francisco, 104–18; "canon" of California literature, 108–9; Wyatt on, 201–2; Japanese American family's internment during World War II, 209–16; in Freeman's *Chinchilla Farm*, 237–40

Campbell, Janet. *See* Hale, Janet Campbell

Carey, Alice, 157

Carton, Evan, 244 (nn. 24, 30)

Castillo, Ana, 102, 139, 262 (n. 26)

Cather, Willa, 40, 46, 158, 241–42 (n. 6)

Cervantes, Lorna Dee, 33, 38, 102, 262 (n. 26)

Charros, 173, 174, 178–79

Chavez, Denise, 159, 262 (n. 26)

Chicano/a writers: and literary magazines, 33, 37; spatial terrain of, 35–36, 159; and feminism, 48–49, 54; and mystery and detective novels, 86; and new female regionalism, 102; Cisneros's *Woman Hollering Creek*, 172–83, 194–95; and South Texas landscape, 173–74, 180–83, 194–95, 217–23, 262–63 (n. 38); and nationalism, 206–7; Anzaldúa's *La Frontera/The Borderlands*, 216–23. *See also* Hispaña writers; Mexican American writers; and specific writers

Chin, Frank, 6, 36, 43, 54, 101, 105, 112

Circle of Women (Barnes and Blew), 126, 139–40, 165, 224–25, 235

Cisneros, Sandra: success of, 7, 33, 37, 139, 244 (n. 33); as "western" writer, 8–9; female desire in, 164–65, 172–83; compared with Houston, 172–73, 179; *charros* in, 173, 174, 179; Texas landscape of, 173–74, 180–83, 194–95, 262–63 (n. 38); Mexico and Mexicans in, 175, 177–78, 181–82, 195; battered women in, 175–76; *telenovelas* (Mexican soap operas) in, 175–76, 183; *jouissance* (joy) in, 177, 183, 195; female gaze in, 178–79; gender in, 178–83, 195; compared with Coleman, 183; writings by, 262 (n. 37); poetry collections by, 263 (n. 40)

—works: *House on Mango Street*, 37; "Bien Pretty," 172, 178, 180–83; *Woman Hollering Creek*, 172–83, 194–95; "My Lucy Friend Who Smells Like Corn," 174; "Never Marry a Mexican," 174–78; "Woman Hollering Creek," 175; "Eyes of Zapata," 178–80

Cities. *See* Urbanscapes; and specific cities

Civil rights literatures: geographical imaginations of, 34–38; and white western spatialities, 43; and feminist questions, 48–49. *See also* African American writers; Asian American writers; Chicano/a writers; Native American writers; Race

Clark, Walter Van Tilburg, 40, 41, 243 (n. 24), 250 (n. 45), 261 (n. 18)

Cohen, Michael, 129

Coleman, Wanda: critical reception of, 9, 35, 90, 255 (n. 47); as "western" writer, 68, 90–91; Los Angeles in poetry of, 87, 88–103, 117, 119; sexuality in, 89; as soap opera screenwriter, 89; as *Los Angeles Times* columnist, 89, 90; writing career of, 90; poetry volumes by, 90, 255 (n. 46); compared with Didion, 91, 94, 95, 100–101, 117; gender in, 93–95, 100–101; beach poems by, 95–99, 117; and postmodernism, 96, 103; restricted mobility in, 100; female bodies in, 100–101; literary influences on, 102; and new female regionalism, 102–3; and "politics of difference," 103; and simultaneity, 103; and noir tradition, 117; compared with Kingston, 119; compared with Cisneros, 183; cross-racial relations in, 195

—works: "Malice in Movieland," 89; *Mad Dog, Black Lady*, 91–99; "Where I Live," 92–95; "His Old Flame, Lady Venice," 96–97; "Beaches. Why I Don't Care for Them," 97–99; *Native in a Strange Land*, 195

Colomina, Beatriz, 155, 165
Contact II, 33, 248 (n. 30)
Contingency, 26, 247 (n. 18)
Cook-Lynn, Elizabeth, 39
Coolbrith, Ina, 46, 158
Cooper, James Fenimore, 41
Corpi, Lucha, 86, 235, 253 (n. 13)
Counterculture, 51–53, 54, 105–7, 112–13, 115, 116
Cowboys, 165–66, 173, 179, 192–93, 228–30
Cronon, William, 127, 129–30
Cultural contact zones, 238
Cummins, Maria Susanna, 157
Curandero/a, 174, 180

Dacotah Territory, 33, 248 (n. 30)
Dainotto, Roberto, 5
Dana, Richard Henry, 68, 253–54 (n. 19)
Daniels, Stephen, 11, 199, 208, 209
Davidson, Cathy, 205
Davis, Mike, 69, 70, 78–79, 255 (nn. 37–38), 256 (n. 59)
Deep ecology, 125, 127–31, 133–34, 137, 141. *See also* Environmentalism; "Natural" landscapes
De Hojos, Angela, 102, 173
De Lauretis, Teresa, 64
DeLeon, Richard, 116
The Desert Is No Lady, 159

Desire. *See* Sexuality
Detective novels, 86–87
"Deterritorialization," 217, 223, 231–34, 236–37
Didion, Joan: critical reception of, 9; on women writers, 19, 30; Stegner on, 46; as "western" writer, 68; "lost west" theme in, 68, 69, 85; and noir tradition, 69, 70, 77–88, 117; anti-feminism of, 69–70, 76, 77; white racialist pathos of, 70, 73–74, 87–88; and postmodernism, 70, 85–86, 254 (n. 26); inability to find spatial "home," 70, 254 (n. 26); suicide in, 71, 75, 82; reviewers' responses to, 71, 254 (n. 32); on Sacramento and Sacramento River, 72–74, 254 (n. 30); on pioneer past, 74–75; abortion in, 75–76, 79; sexuality in, 75–76, 79, 80–85; gender in, 75–77, 79–85, 100–101; existentialism of, 78; "nothingness" in, 78, 79, 84; beaches in, 80–85, 87–88, 117; "crossroads" desire in, 83–84; mother-daughter relations in, 83–85; compared with Coleman, 91, 94, 95, 100–101, 117; female bodies in, 100–101

—works: "Slouching Towards Bethlehem," 52; *Play It as It Lays*, 53, 70, 76, 77–88, 254 (n. 26); *White Album*, 69; *Run River*, 70, 71–77, 163, 254 (nn. 26, 28); *Last Thing He Wanted*, 235; *Book of Common Prayer*, 254 (n. 26)

Doerr, Harriet, 39, 46
Doig, Ivan, 3, 6, 10, 39, 42, 102
Dorris, Michael, 184–85, 263 (n. 47)
Dustbooks Press, 249 (n. 42)

East: West versus, 20–31; feminism in northeast, 49–51, 54, 252 (n. 86); Coleman on, 90
Eaton, Edith (Sui Sin Far), 43, 158
Ecocriticism, 126–27, 129, 131, 152
Ecofeminism, 52, 53, 125, 138, 140–41,

151, 259 (n. 40). *See also* Environmentalism

Ehrlich, Gretel, 8, 33, 46, 139

Environmentalism, 13, 41–42, 52, 53, 125–31, 135, 136, 151–52, 164, 236, 256–57 (n. 3). *See also* "Natural" landscapes

Erdrich, Louise: awards, 7, 244–45 (n. 33); visibility of, 33; Stegner on, 46; Silko on, 137; female desire in, 164–65, 183–94, 263 (n. 46); narrative technique of, 184–85; reservation life in, 185–87, 193–94; nature in, 185–88, 193–94; compared with Silko, 186, 187–88, 193; community survival in, 191–92; compared with Blew, 228; novels by, 263 (n. 46)

—work: *Love Medicine*, 183–92

Existentialism, 78

Fante, John, 64, 108, 109

Farnham, Eliza, 157

Father-daughter relationship, 210–15, 227–28

Female gaze, 82, 178–79

Feminism: and public versus private space, 27–28, 54–55, 65–66; and civil rights literatures, 48–49; and postmodernism, 49, 55, 58–59, 63, 252 (n. 3); northeastern feminism, 49–51, 54, 252 (n. 86); spatialities of, 49–55; and race generally, 50; cultural féminism, 51, 53–54; western feminism, 51–55; ecofeminism, 52, 53, 125, 138, 140–41, 151; and ethics of place/space-time, 58–59; and western cities, 65–66; Didion's anti-feminism, 69–70, 76, 77; and Kingston, 110–12, 114; and Kingsolver, 150, 160; and nationalism, 204–9, 214, 230, 232; and Wakatsuki Houston, 214, 231; and Blew, 231; and Freeman, 239–40; roots of second-wave American feminism, 243 (n. 18)

Ferber, Edna, 31

Fergusson, Harvey, 41

Fetterley, Judith, 205

Fine, David, 78, 255 (n. 38), 256 (n. 59)

Firestone, Shulamith, 49

Fisher, Vardis, 40, 41

Fitzgerald, F. Scott, 20–21

Flores, Dan, 130, 257 (n. 20)

Foote, Mary Hallock, 158, 260 (n. 9)

Fowler, Earlene, 87

Freeman, Jo, 49

Freeman, Judith, 33, 139, 237–40

Freeman, Mary Wilkins, 241 (n. 2)

Friedan, Betty, 49, 71, 72

Friendship between women, 171, 174, 196

Fuller, Margaret, 157

Fulton, Len, 249 (n. 42)

Gaines, Ernest, 35, 39

Garland, Hamlin, 261 (n. 18)

Gellner, Ernest, 207

Gender: Stegner on, 40, 45–48; in Didion's works, 75–77, 79–85, 100–101; in noir, 85; in Coleman's poetry, 93–95, 100–101; in Kingston's *Tripmaster Monkey*, 110–12; in Kingsolver's *Animal Dreams*, 145–46; and female sexuality, 164; in Cisneros's *Woman Hollering Creek*, 178–83, 195; nationalisms and multiracial female West, 205–9; in Anzaldúa's *La Frontera/The Borderlands*, 219–21; in Blew's *All But the Waltz*, 226–28. *See also* Masculinity; Sexuality

Girl power, 235, 264–65 (n. 1)

Globalization, 66–67, 91–92, 103, 233–34, 238

Gonzalez, Rebecca, 159, 173

Greenberg, Joanne, 31

"Green fascism," 152

Guha, Ramachandra, 123, 128

Guthrie, A. B., 40, 41, 243 (n. 24), 250 (n. 45), 261 (n. 18)

Haase, John, 20–23
Hagedorn, Jessica, 102
Hale, Janet Campbell, 33, 102
Hall, Sharlot, 158
Haraway, Donna, 5, 252 (n. 3)
Harjo, Joy, 102, 158, 262 (n. 26)
Harte, Bret, 41, 108, 109, 241 (n. 6)
Harvey, David, 4, 58, 64, 67, 92, 242
    (n. 11)
Haslam, Gerald, 42, 101, 249 (n. 42)
Hawaii, 237, 265 (n. 2)
Hayden, Dolores, 88, 95
Henderson, Mary Corbin, 158
Hendrix, Jimi, 52
Hepworth, James, 236
Hinojosa, Oscar, 37
Hispaña writers, 206–7. *See also*
    Chicano/a writers
Hogan, Linda, 46
Holley, Mary Austin, 157
Homosocial community among
    women, 171, 174, 196
Hongo, Garrett, 250 (n. 43)
hooks, bell, 92, 96, 103
"Hope trope," 44–45, 48, 55–56, 118,
    134
Hopkins, Sarah Winnemucca, 158
Houston, Jeanne Wakatsuki. *See*
    Wakatsuki Houston, Jeanne
Houston, Pam: popularity of, 7, 139,
    166; critical response to, 8, 262
    (n. 31); female desire in, 164–72,
    192–93; writings of, 166, 262
    (nn. 29–30); heroines who "love too
    much," 166–69; independence nar-
    rative of, 170–71; and adventure
    genre, 170–71, 193; compared with
    Kingsolver, 171; female friendship
    in, 171; compared with Cisneros,
    172–73, 179
—works: *Cowboys Are My Weakness*,
    165–73, 192–93; "Dall," 167; "You
    Talk About Idaho," 167, 168; "How
    to Talk to a Hunter," 169
Hudson, Lois Phillips, 31

Hugo, Richard, 42
Hybrid and hybridity, 5

Indian writers. *See* Native American
    writers
"Innocence" narrative, 263–64 (n. 5)
Irigaray, Luce, 260 (n. 1)

Jackson, Helen Hunt, 108, 109, 158
Jameson, Frederic, 4, 64, 258 (n. 32)
Jeffords, Susan, 244 (n. 30)
Jeffries, John, 95
Jewett, Sarah Orne, 241 (n. 2)
Johnson, Dorothy, 31, 46
Johnson, Susan, 10–11
Joplin, Janis, 52–53
Jordan, Teresa, 33, 139, 235, 236, 262
    (n. 26)

Kadohata, Cynthia, 139, 235, 253
    (n. 13), 262 (n. 26)
Kanellos, Nicolás, 37
Kelly, Edith Summers, 158
Kesey, Ken, 39, 42
Kingsolver, Barbara: critical response
    to, 8, 33, 138, 142; as "western"
    writer, 119, 235; writings by, 138,
    235, 258 (n. 33); and ecofeminism,
    140–41, 151; and wilderness plot,
    141–51, 195, 207; gender in, 145–46;
    as "progressive artiste," 146, 150–
    51; and postmodernism, 146–47;
    race in, 149–50; and feminism, 150,
    160; compared with Houston, 171
—work: *Animal Dreams*, 53, 125,
    130–31, 137–38, 141–51, 160
Kingston, Maxine Hong: success of,
    7, 33, 245 (n. 33); as "western"
    writer, 8–9, 36, 68, 105, 109–10; and
    Stegner, 39, 46; in 1970s, 102; criti-
    cal reception of, 104–5; San Fran-
    cisco in, 104–18; counterculture in,
    105–6, 107, 112–13, 115, 116; Chi-
    nese immigrant family in, 106–7; on
    Chinese American identity, 106–10,

114, 117–18; suicide in, 108; and play-within-the-novel, 109, 112, 114, 115, 116; gender in, 110–12; and feminism, 110–12, 114; and noir, 113–14; "crossover" identities in, 114–15; and performativity, 114–15; compared with Coleman, 119
—works: *Woman Warrior*, 48, 54, 104, 252 (n. 86); *Tripmaster Monkey*, 53, 85, 103–17, 256 (n. 62); *China Men*, 104, 256 (n. 62)
Kirkland, Caroline, 157
Kittredge, William, 10, 102
Kolodny, Annette, 46, 157, 162, 163, 203, 206, 242 (n. 9)

Landscape: Stegner on the West, 5–6, 40, 55–56, 96, 203; as "wild card," 11, 14–16, 29, 57; as social discourse, 11–12, 13; in western literature generally, 11–16, 62; redemptive nature of, 12, 245 (n. 40); and perceptual geography, 12–13; activity of landscape discourse, 13; and Native American literary traditions, 13; as "spatial history," 14; types of, 14; place and space in, 15–16, 57; "western" as sociocultural landscape, 21–22; of mountains, 22, 24, 25, 27, 28; of panorama, 24, 27; social relations in spatial contexts, 26–27, 57, 247 (nn. 13–14); of "borderlands," 27, 36, 177–78, 216–17, 221–22, 238, 263 (n. 38); female writers' engagements with generally, 28–29; functions of, in western discourse, 29; "hope trope" and West, 44–45, 48, 55–56, 118, 134; California landscapes generally, 69; in Didion's works, 72–74; beaches of Southern California, 80–85, 87–88, 95–99, 117; and white women's "promotional" literature of 1830s–1860s, 157–58; and sexuality, 157–65, 203;

of South Texas, 173–74, 180–83, 194–95, 217–23, 262–63 (n. 38); of Native American reservation, 185–86; nationalist rhetoric of patriotic western landscape, 200–205; in Wakatsuki Houston's *Farewell to Manzanar*, 210–15; in Anzaldúa's *La Frontera/The Borderlands*, 216–23; of Montana, 224–30; Hawaiian landscape discourse, 237, 265 (n. 2); of Freeman's *Chinchilla Farm*, 237–40. *See also* Nationalism; "Natural" landscapes; Sexuality; Space; Urbanscapes
Lee, Josephine, 114
Lee, Robert, 256 (n. 60)
Leffland, Ella, 262 (n. 26)
Le Guin, Ursula, 138
Leonard, John, 54
Leopold, Aldo, 125, 257 (n. 11)
Lesbianism, 33, 196, 216
Levine, Philip, 39
Limerick, Patricia, 242 (n. 7)
Linder, Ben, 142, 259 (n. 41)
Literary magazines, 33, 37, 38, 249 (n. 42)
La Llorona, 177
London, Jack, 64, 108, 109, 241 (n. 6)
Lopez, Barry, 125
Los Angeles: and postmodernism, 62, 66–67, 113, 118; as window onto global marketplace, 66–67, 91–92, 118; landscape of generally, 69; Didion's Los Angeles, 70, 77–88, 101, 117; Coleman's Los Angeles, 87, 88–103, 117, 119; segregation in, 88; African Americans in, 88, 89; riots in, 88, 89–90, 95; Kingston on, 113, 114; and noir tradition, 113, 116; compared with San Francisco, 113–14, 116, 118; Hollywood movie industry in, 114; in Freeman's *Chinchilla Farm*, 238–40
"Lost west" theme, 68, 69, 85
Lucero-Trujillo, Marcela Christine, 102

Luhan, Mabel Dodge, 63, 158, 159, 206
Lyon, Thomas, 257 (n. 7)

McFadden, Cyra, 235
McGuane, Tom, 39
Maclean, Norman, 3, 6, 10, 102
McMillan, Terry, 262 (n. 26)
McMurtry, Larry, 39, 42
McNickle, D'Arcy, 43
Malcolm X, 112
Marriage plot, 168–69, 195
Martin, Julia, 128–29
Masculinity: and Reaganism, 6–7;
    of Northeast, 21, 24–25; western
    men, 22–24, 25, 56–57; of western
    space and wilderness, 22–25, 27,
    28, 56–58, 129–30, 153, 159, 160,
    162–63, 193, 203–4; working-class
    men, 23; and discourses about "city,"
    64; and postmodern Los Angeles,
    66–67; in Kingston, 110–12; "crisis
    of masculinity" at turn of twentieth
    century, 156–57, 160, 261 (n. 18);
    cowboys as symbol of, 165–66, 173,
    179, 192–93, 228–30; *charros* as
    symbol of, 173, 174, 178–79; and
    defense of West as "imperiled
    female," 204
Massey, Doreen, 14, 261
Mexican American writers, 63–64,
    252–53 (nn. 5–6). *See also* Chi-
    cano/a writers
Mexican Indians, 181–82, 195, 223
Mexico, 175, 177–78, 181–82, 194,
    195, 239
Milton, John R., 242 (n. 9)
Mirikitani, Janice, 262 (n. 26)
Mitchell, Carolyn, 95
Mitchell, W. J. T., 13–14
Mizener, Arthur, 20, 22–23
Modernism, 2, 3, 5, 24–25, 33, 41, 63,
    252 (n. 3)
Momaday, N. Scott, 6, 36, 39, 43–44,
    101, 112
Monk, Janice, 159, 206

Montana, 224–30
Montoya, José, 37
Moon, Michael, 205
Mora, Pat, 159, 173, 174
Moraga, Cherríe, 262 (n. 26)
Morgan, Robin, 49
Mosley, Walter, 91
Motherhood, 83–85, 215, 232–33
Mourning Dove, 43
Muir, John, 108, 109, 203
Multiculturalism, 9
Mystery novels, 86–87
Myth and Symbol School, 1

Nance, J. J., 87
Nationalism: and regionalism, 5–6,
    12, 22–23, 200–209, 243 (n. 24); and
    patriotic western landscape, 200–
    205; western literary criticism on,
    200–205; defense of West as "imper-
    iled female," 204; and feminism,
    204–9, 214, 230, 232; as conserva-
    tive or imperial politics, 205–6;
    multiracial female West and nation-
    alisms, 205–9; and nineteenth-
    century women writers, 206, 207;
    Anderson on, 207; definition of
    nationalisms, 207–8; and Wakatsuki
    Houston's *Farewell to Manzanar*,
    209–16; and Anzaldúa's *La Fron-
    tera/The Borderlands*, 216–23; and
    "deterritorialization," 217, 223,
    231–34, 236–37; and Blew's *All But
    the Waltz*, 224–30; postnational dis-
    course, 232–34
National Symbolic, 6, 7, 23, 243 (n. 23)
Native American literature: landscape
    in, 13; female-centered origins tales
    and oral traditions of, 48; lack of
    "innocence" narrative in, 263–64
    (n. 5). *See also* Native American
    writers
Native American writers: and literary
    magazines, 33, 38; spatial terrain of,
    36–37, 159, 185–86; and feminism,

48–49, 53–54; Silko's *Ceremony*, 130–37; Erdrich's *Love Medicine*, 183–92, 193–94. *See also* specific writers

"Natural" landscapes: and reasons for wilderness plot, 124–25; and western stereotypes, 126, 161; and ecocriticism, 126–27; and characteristics of wilderness plot, 127; wilderness ideal and wilderness plot, 127–31; Cronon on, 129–30; in Kingsolver's *Animal Dreams*, 130–31, 137–38, 141–51, 171; in Silko's *Ceremony*, 130–37, 186; and Native American cosmology, 132–35, 159; and healing nature, 133–34; and sacred nature, 134; and de-idealizing wilderness, 151–53; nineteenth-century women's counterdiscourse on, 157–58, 162–63, 206, 207; of Houston, 170–71; in Erdrich's *Love Medicine*, 185–88, 193–94

Nava, Michael, 86

New Criticism, 1, 40

Ng, Fae, 139

Nichols, John, 3, 42, 102

Nicholson, Linda J., 252 (n. 3)

Niggli, Josephina, 31, 43

Noir tradition, 69, 70, 77–88, 113–14, 116, 117, 255 (nn. 37–38)

Norris, Frank, 108, 109, 241 (n. 6)

Northeast. *See* East

Norton, Eleanor Holmes, 49

Norwood, Vera, 159, 206

Nuclear testing, 256–57 (n. 3)

Nugent, Walter, 235 (n. 16)

Oelschlaeger, Max, 152

O'Keeffe, Georgia, 124, 193

Olsen, Tillie, 31, 39

Olson, Charles, 102

Otero-Warren, Nina, 31

Padgett, Abigail, 87

Pelosi, Nancy, 256 (n. 67)

Perceptual geography, 12–13

Pioneer woman, 161–62

Place, 15–16, 55–59. *See also* Landscape; Space

Plumwood, Val, 125, 140–41

Ponce, Mary Helen, 262 (n. 26)

Porter, Katherine Anne, 31

Postmodernism: and regionalism, 2–4, 15, 55–59, 242 (n. 12); definition of, 4–5; historical roots of, 4–5; compared with modernism, 5; and new female regionalism, 33–34; and feminism, 49, 55, 58–59, 63, 252 (n. 3); place, space-time, and postmodern West, 55–59; and space, 55–59, 103; and time-space compression, 58, 85–86; and Los Angeles, 62, 66–67, 113, 118; and Didion, 70, 85–86, 254 (n. 26); and hooks, 92; and Coleman, 96, 103; and simultaneity, 103; and history, 137, 258 (n. 32); and Kingsolver, 146–47; and "deterritorialization," 217, 223, 231–34; and transnational capitalism, 233–34; periodization in, 242 (n. 11)

Postnational discourse, 232–34

Poststructuralism, 51, 136, 252 (n. 3)

Prostitutes, 161

Race: Stegner on, 42–44; and feminism, 50; Didion's white racialist pathos, 70, 73–74, 87–88; in Coleman's poetry, 87, 88–103; in Silko's *Ceremony*, 132, 137; in Kingsolver's *Animal Dreams*, 149–50; cross-racial relations, 195–96; nationalisms and multiracial female West, 205–9. *See also* African American writers; Asian American writers; Chicano/a writers

Randall, Margaret, 138

Reaganism, 6–7, 113, 116, 205, 244 (nn. 28, 30)

Realism, 2–3, 33, 41–42

Rebolledo, Tey Diana, 206, 216

Reed, Ishmael, 35, 38, 112

Regionalism: of 1920s–1940s, 1, 241 (nn. 1–2); new regionalism, 1–16, 101–2, 242 (n. 7), 244 (n. 24); and postmodernism, 2–4, 15, 55–59, 242 (n. 12); and modernism, 3; and nationalism, 5–6, 12, 22–23, 200–209, 243 (n. 24); as "white thing," 9; "female" and "feminist" regionalism, 10, 49–55; and landscape generally, 11–16; nineteenth-century regionalism, 15; and unknown and marginal, 15; East versus West, 20–31; western character, 22–23; new female regionalism, 31–34, 102–3, 138–40, 192–97, 231–37; Stegnerian spatial field and new western literary history, 38–49, 55–56, 65, 96; West as geography of hope, 44–45; place, space-time, and postmodern West, 55–59; California as western continuum, 68–69, 117–19, 253 (n. 16); Rocky Mountain regionalists, 126, 140, 224–30, 235; and stereotypes of the West, 126, 161; and ecocriticism, 126–27; and white women's "promotional" literature of 1830s–1860s, 157–58; nationalist rhetoric of patriotic western landscape, 200–205; nationalisms and multiracial female West, 205–9. See also Landscape; Western literature

Reid, David, 67

Remington, Frederic, 156

Rhodes, Eugene Manlove, 40

Rich, Adrienne, 196, 248 (n. 24)

Richter, Conrad, 40

Riot Girls, 265 (n. 1)

Rivera, Tomás, 37, 43

Robinson, Forrest, 261 (n. 21)

Rocky Mountain regionalists, 126, 140, 224–30, 235

Rodriguez, Luis, 10

Rodriguez, Richard, 6, 10, 43, 102

Rolvaag, O. E., 40

Roosevelt, Theodore, 156–57, 160, 162

Rose, Gillian, 28

Rose, Wendy, 102, 262 (n. 26)

Ruiz de Burton, María Amparo, 158, 253 (n. 6)

Sacramento, 69, 72–74, 254 (n. 30)

Said, Edward, 26

Sandoz, Mari, 46

San Francisco: as "sanctuary city," 67; landscape of, 69; history of, 104; culture of, 104, 107, 113, 117–18; in Kingston's works, 104–18; counterculture in, 105–6, 107, 112–13, 115, 116; Golden Gate Park in, 105–6, 107, 113–14; compared with Los Angeles, 113–14, 116, 118; progressivism of, 115–17, 118; and "hope trope," 118

Saroyan, William, 108, 109

Schneir, Miriam, 251 (n. 78)

Schraeger, Cynthia, 168

Scott, Joan, 252 (n. 3)

See, Carolyn, 253 (n. 13), 262 (n. 26)

See, Lisa, 86–87, 235, 253 (n. 13), 262 (n. 26)

Sexuality: in Didion's works, 75–76, 79, 80–85; male homoerotics in Didion's works, 81–82; in Coleman's poetry, 89, 93–95; silence on, in western studies, 156–57, 161–62; and western frontier, 156–57, 161–62; and nineteenth-century western women writers, 157–58, 162–63; landscape's connection with, 157–65, 203; in Silko's Ceremony, 159–60; and prostitutes, 161; of white pioneer woman, 161–62; of nonwhite women generally, 162; and twentieth-century women writers generally, 163–65, 262 (n. 26); in Cisneros's Woman Hollering Creek, 164–65, 172–83, 194–95; in Erdrich's Love Medicine, 164–65,

183–94; in Houston's *Cowboys Are My Weakness*, 164–72, 192–93; and new female regionalism, 192–97; and cross-racial relations, 195–96; and lesbianism, 196; in Wakatsuki Houston's *Farewell to Manzanar*, 214–15, 232; in Blew's *All But the Waltz*, 231–32; white male western writers on, 261 (n. 18). *See also* Gender; Masculinity

Shange, Ntozake, 95

Silko, Leslie Marmon: awards for, 7, 244 (n. 33); as "western" writer, 8–9, 36, 119, 235; critical reception of, 9; poetry of, in literary magazines, 33; "crossover" success of, 33, 119; Stegner on, 46; in 1970s, 102; landscapes of, 130–37, 159, 186; and wilderness plot, 130–37; and healing nature, 133–34; and "hope trope," 134; and sacred nature, 134; and storied landscapes, 134–37; sexuality in, 159–60; compared with Erdrich, 186, 187–88, 193

—works: *Ceremony*, 125, 130–37, 159–60, 186, 188, 263 (n. 48); *Almanac of the Dead*, 132, 148

Simonson, Howard P., 45

Simultaneity, 103

Small presses. *See* Literary magazines

Smiley, Jane, 138

Smith, Annick, 46, 235

Smith, Barbara, 49

Smith, Henry Nash, 46

Snyder, Gary, 42

Soap operas, Mexican (*telenovelas*), 175–76, 183

Social ecology, 125, 130, 131, 134, 141. *See also* Environmentalism; "Natural" landscapes

Socialism, 23

Social relations in spatial contexts, 26–27, 57, 247 (nn. 13–14)

Soja, Edward, 4, 26, 64, 66, 67, 101

Sorenson, Virginia, 46

Sorkin, Michael, 77

Soto, Gary, 139

Soule, Caroline, 157

Southern Agrarians, 1, 241 (n. 1)

Southwest, 35–36. *See also* California; Texas

Southworth, E.D.E.N., 157

Space: and place in landscape, 15–16, 55–59; masculinity of western space, 22–25, 27, 28, 56–58, 129–30, 153, 159, 160, 162–63, 193, 203–4; spatial resistance, 26–27; and social relations, 26–27, 57, 247 (nn. 13–14); materiality of, 27; female spatial orientation and private space, 27–28; home and hearth as "female space," 27–28; public versus private, 27–28, 54–55, 65–66; feminist criticism on, 29–30, 248 (n. 24); of African American writers, 34–35, 90, 248–49 (n. 32); of civil rights literatures, 34–38; of Chicano/a writers, 35–36, 159; of Asian American writers, 36, 249 (n. 36); of Native American writers, 36–37, 159, 185–86; Stegnerian spatial field and new western literary history, 38–49, 55–56, 65, 96; feminist spatialities, 49–55; definition of, 55; and postmodernism, 55–59, 103; Whitmanesque cultural space, 182–83, 195. *See also* Landscape

Stafford, Jean, 31, 163, 261–62 (n. 25)

Starr, Kevin, 256 (n. 59), 256 (n. 67)

Stegner, Wallace: and modernism, 3, 41; on the West and wilderness ideal, 5–6, 40, 55–56, 96, 203, 243 (n. 22); as critic and advocate of western literature, 19, 39–49, 55–56, 108, 109; on Steinbeck's Nobel Prize, 20; students of, 39; significance of, 39–40, 250 (n. 45); on gender relations, 40, 45–48; as environmentalist, 41–42; and realism, 41–42; Anglo-centered bias of, 42–43; on race, 42–44, 251

(n. 71); and "hope trope," 44–45, 48, 55–56, 258 (n. 28); as humanist, 45; urbanscapes, 64–65; papers of, 65; and nationalism, 243 (n. 24); on sexuality, 261 (n. 18)

Steinbeck, John, 20–24, 27, 32, 39, 108, 109, 246 (n. 2)

Stereotypes of the West, 126, 161

Stevenson, Robert Louis, 108, 109

Stone, Robert, 39

Stowe, Harriet Beecher, 241 (n. 2)

Straight Arrow Press, 37

Suicide, 71, 75, 82, 108, 113

Sui Sin Far. *See* Eaton, Edith

Sykes, Hope, 31

Tafolla, Carmen, 102, 173

Tan, Amy, 262 (n. 26)

Tapahanso, Luci, 159

Telenovelas (Mexican soap operas), 175–76, 183

Texas, 173–74, 180–83, 194–95, 262–63 (n. 38)

Thomas, Piri, 112

Thompson, Hunter S., 108

Thon, Melanie Rae, 262 (n. 26)

Tisdale, Sallie, 262 (n. 26)

Tompkins, Jane, 261 (n. 21)

"Topospatiality," 36

Trambley, Estela Portillo, 102

Transnational capitalism, 233–34, 236, 238

Turner, Frederick Jackson, 76, 118, 156, 250 (n. 50)

Twain, Mark, 41, 108, 109

Updating the Literary West, 257 (n. 7)

Urbanscapes: Los Angeles and postmodernism, 62, 66–67; as "authentic" to contemporary western narratives, 62–63; western cities, 62–67, 124, 148; and mistrust of the urban, 63; masculinism of "great city" tradition, 64, 66; and western literary men, 64–65; and new female regionalism and western cities, 65–66; decentralized spatial organization of western cities, 66; San Francisco as "sanctuary city," 67; California's urbanism, 68–69; in Didion's works, 69–88, 117; in Coleman's poetry, 87, 88–103, 117; African Americans in, 88–89, 95; in Kingston's works, 104–17; and flight from urban history, 151–52; of Freeman's *Chinchilla Farm,* 237–40

Vietnam War, 34, 208, 244 (nn. 28, 30)

Vigil-Piñon, Evangelina, 163

Viramontes, Helena Maria, 262 (n. 26)

Wakatsuki Houston, Jeanne, 195, 209–16, 231–33

Wakoski, Diane, 31

Walker, Mildred, 31

Wallace, Michele, 49

Warren, Nina Otero, 206, 207

Waters, Frank, 40, 243 (n. 24), 250 (n. 45), 261 (n. 18)

Waugh, Patricia, 242 (n. 11)

Webb, Walter Prescott, 40

Welch, James, 6, 10, 43–44, 101

West. *See* Landscape; Regionalism; "Wilderness aesthetics"; Wilderness ideal; Wilderness plot

West, Jessamyn, 31

West, Nathanael, 64, 102, 114, 256 (n. 59)

Western art, 5–6, 7

Western literature: and modernism, 2, 3; reputation of, 2, 241–42 (n. 6); and realism, 2–3; women writers of generally, 7–11, 30–34, 46, 59, 157–59, 244–45 (nn. 32–33); criticism of, as field, 8, 32–33; social and political topics in women's writings, 11; landscape in generally, 11–16, 29; and Steinbeck's Nobel Prize, 20–24, 27, 32, 246 (n. 2); eastern establishment versus, 20–31; and sociocultural landscape of West, 21–22; new female regionalism, 31–34, 102–3, 138–40, 192–97, 231–37; by Chicano/a writers, 35–36; by Asian American writers, 36, 38, 105, 109–10, 249 (n. 36); by Native American writers, 36–38; Stegnerian spatial field and new western literary history, 38–49, 55–56, 65, 96; as interventionary discourse into the mythic west, 39; characteristics of, 40; gender relations in, 40, 45–48; and white spatial prerogatives, 42–43; and "hope trope," 44–45, 55–56; feminist spatialities in, 49–55; urban life as "authentic" to contemporary works, 62–63; "canon" of California literature, 108–9; female desire in generally, 156–64; white women's "promotional" literature of 1830s–1860s, 157–58; and nationalism, 200–205; titles of, 245 (n. 36). *See also* Regionalism; and specific writers

Western Literature Association (WLA), 32–33, 129, 257 (n. 7)

Wheatley, Phyllis, 248 (n. 32)

Whipple, Maxine, 46

White, Richard, 61, 123, 129, 257 (n. 13)

Whitmanesque cultural space, 182–83, 195

"Wilderness aesthetics," 127

Wilderness ideal, 127–34, 147–48, 152–53

Wilderness plot: reasons for, 124–25; characteristics of, 127, 140, 161; and wilderness ideal, 127–34, 147–48, 152–53; Cronon on, 129–30; in Kingsolver's *Animal Dreams*, 130–31, 137–38, 141–51, 195; in Silko's *Ceremony*, 130–37; and western criticism, 136–37; and *Circle of Women*, 140; and de-idealizing wilderness, 151–53; and sexuality, 159

Williams, Sherley Anne, 35

Williams, Terry Tempest, 8, 33, 125, 139, 235, 262 (n. 26)

Willis, Ellen, 49

Wister, Owen, 41, 161, 261 (n. 21)

Wittig, Monique, 196

WLA. *See* Western Literature Association (WLA)

Worster, Donald, 129

Wyatt, David, 68, 201–3, 233

Yamamoto, Hisaye, 31, 43, 102

Yamashita, Karen Tei, 102, 235

Young, Al, 35

Zamora, Bernice, 33

Zapata, Emiliano, 173, 178–80, 181, 182

Zitkala-Sa, 43, 158